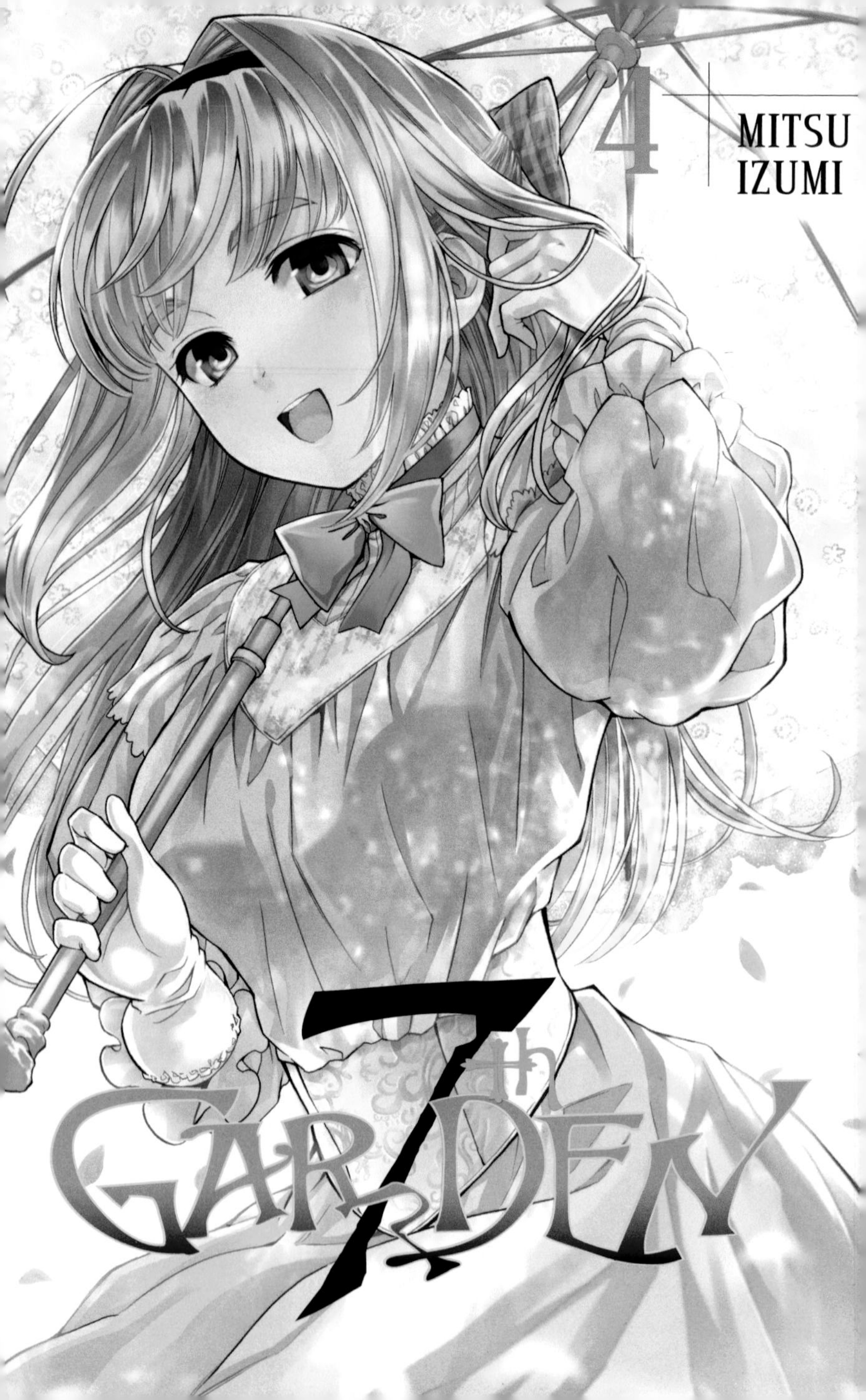
4
MITSU
IZUMI
7th GARDEN

The second angel...

...separated the day and the night...

...creating time.

7thGARDEN

CONTENTS

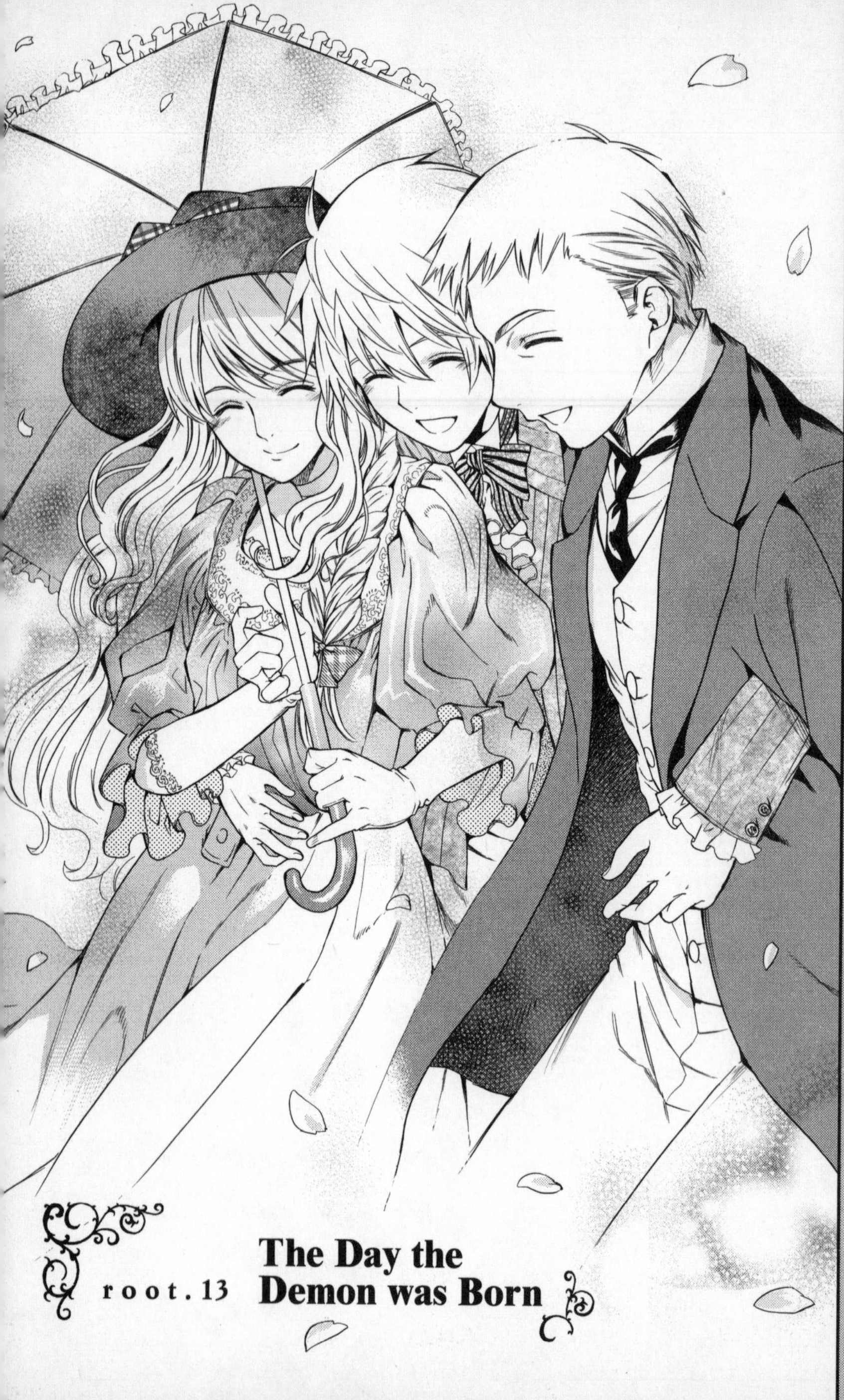
root.13
The Day the Demon was Born

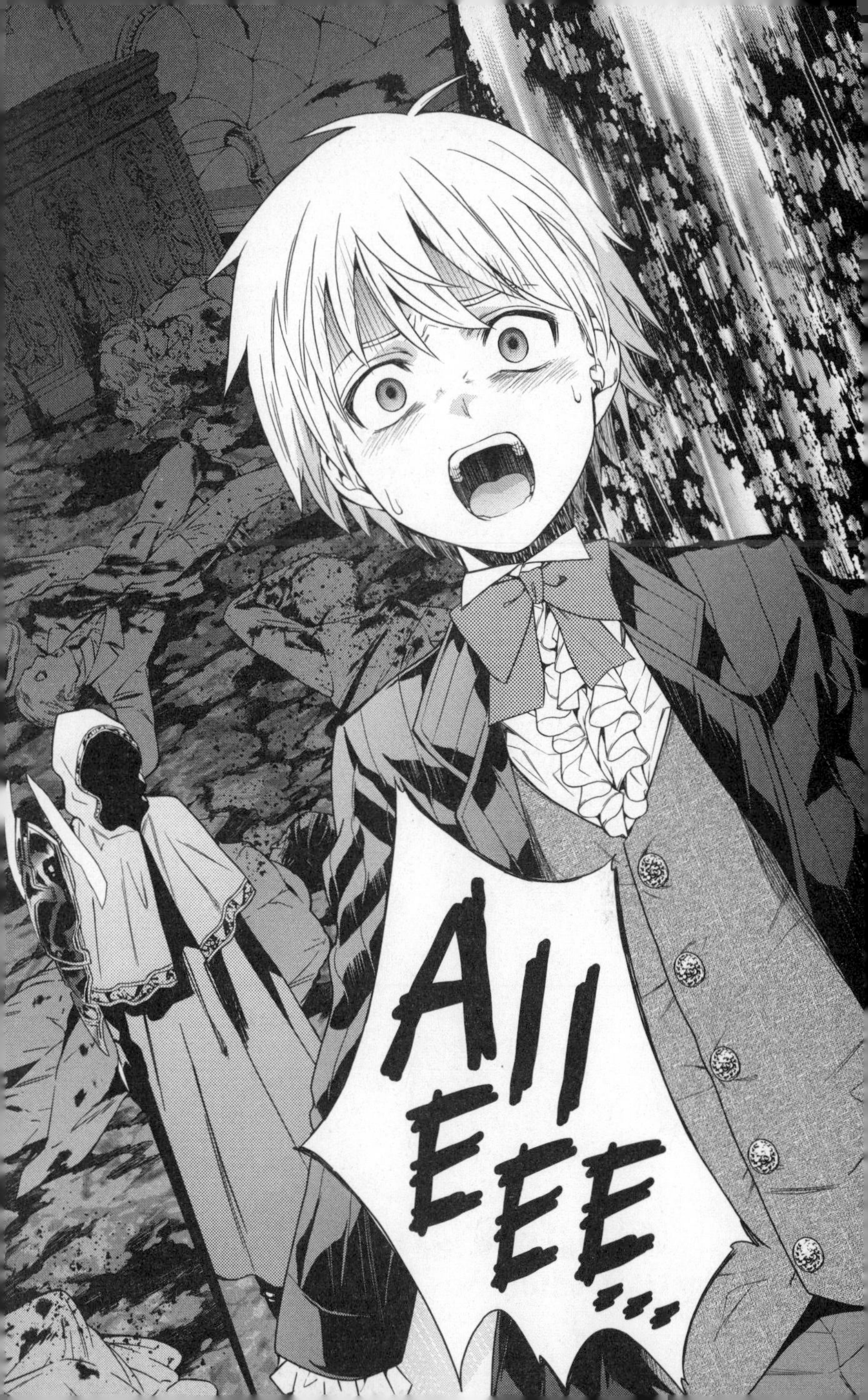
AIIEEE...

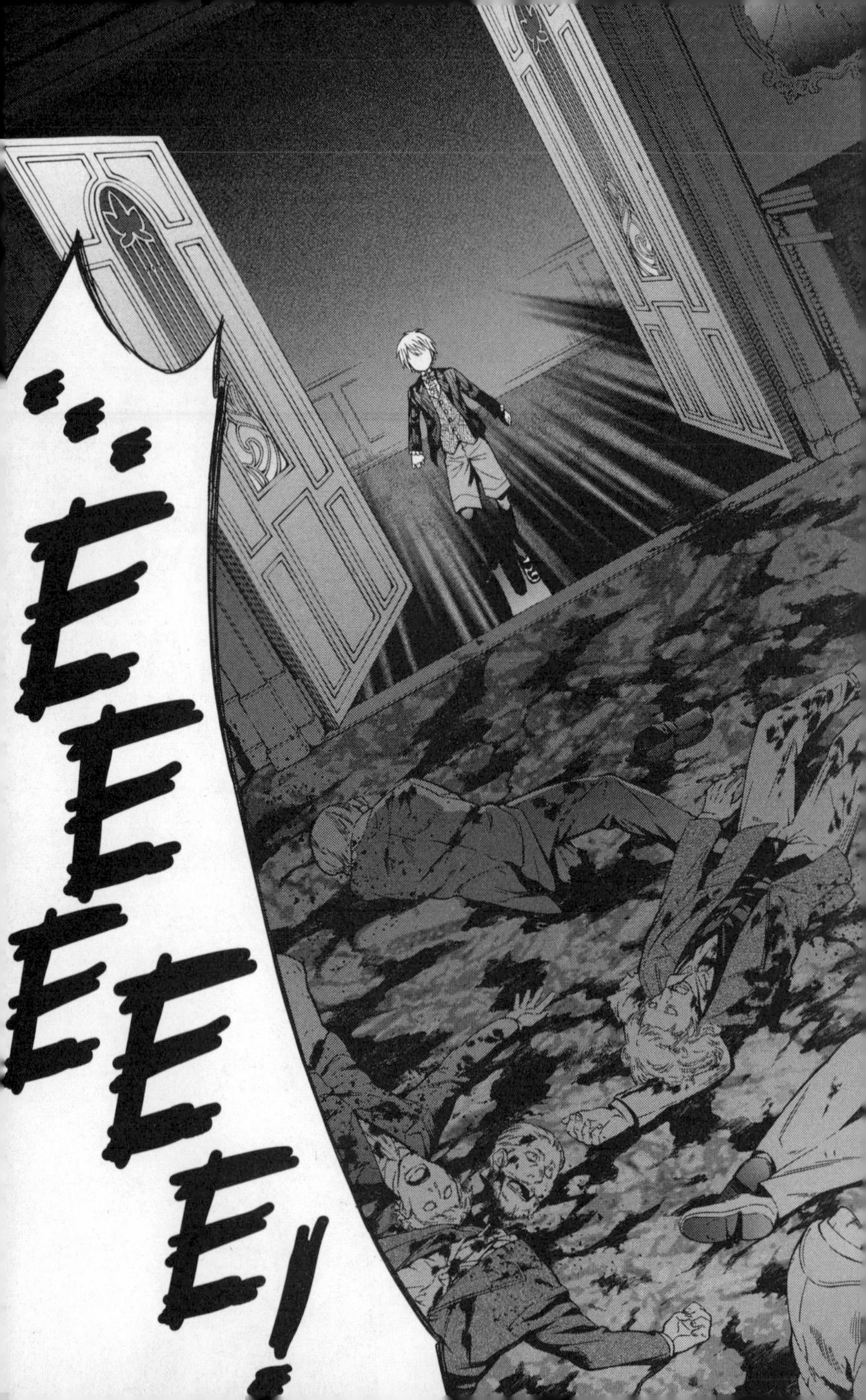
...EEEEE!

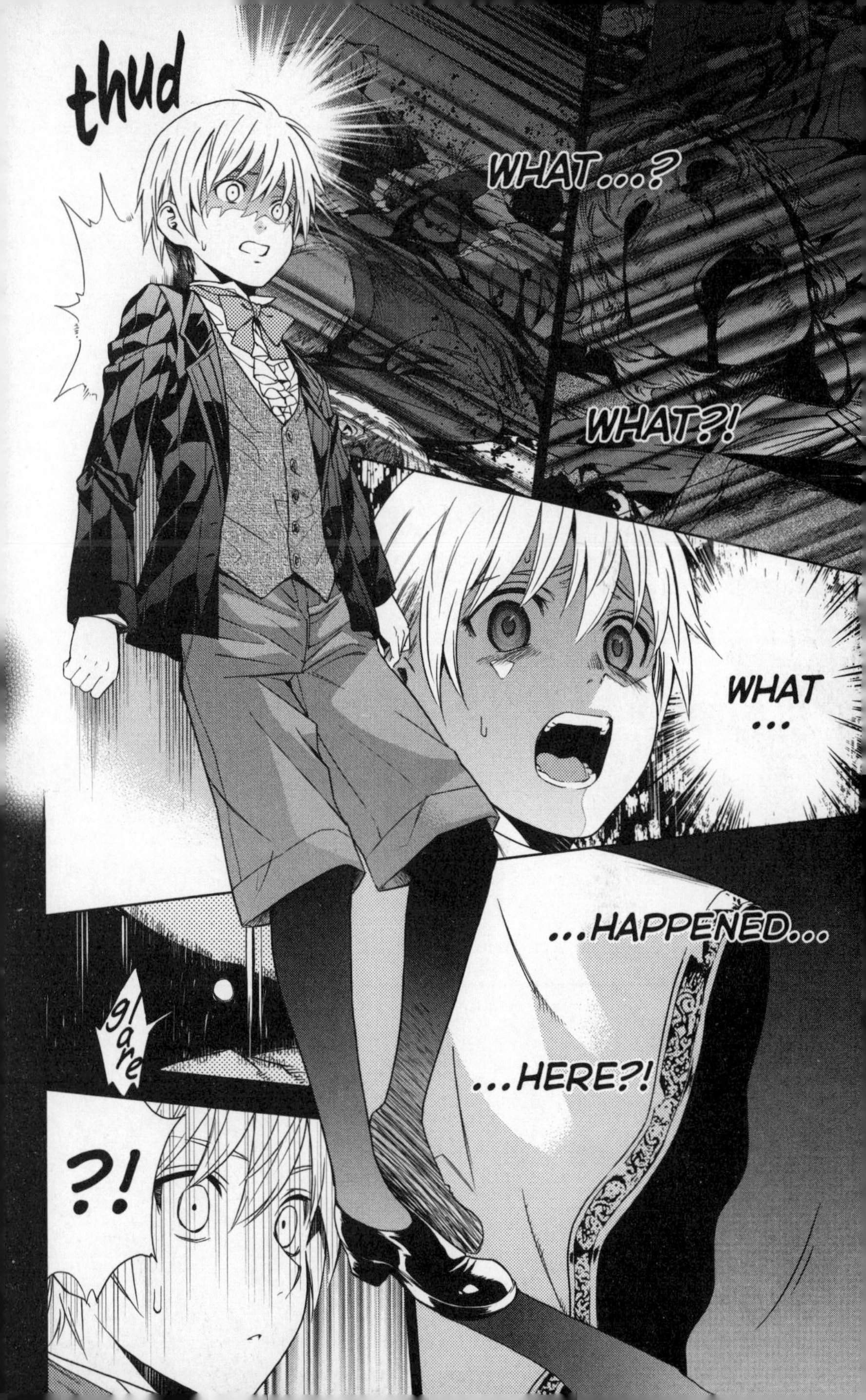
thud
WHAT...?
WHAT?!
WHAT...
...HAPPENED...
...HERE?!
glare
?!

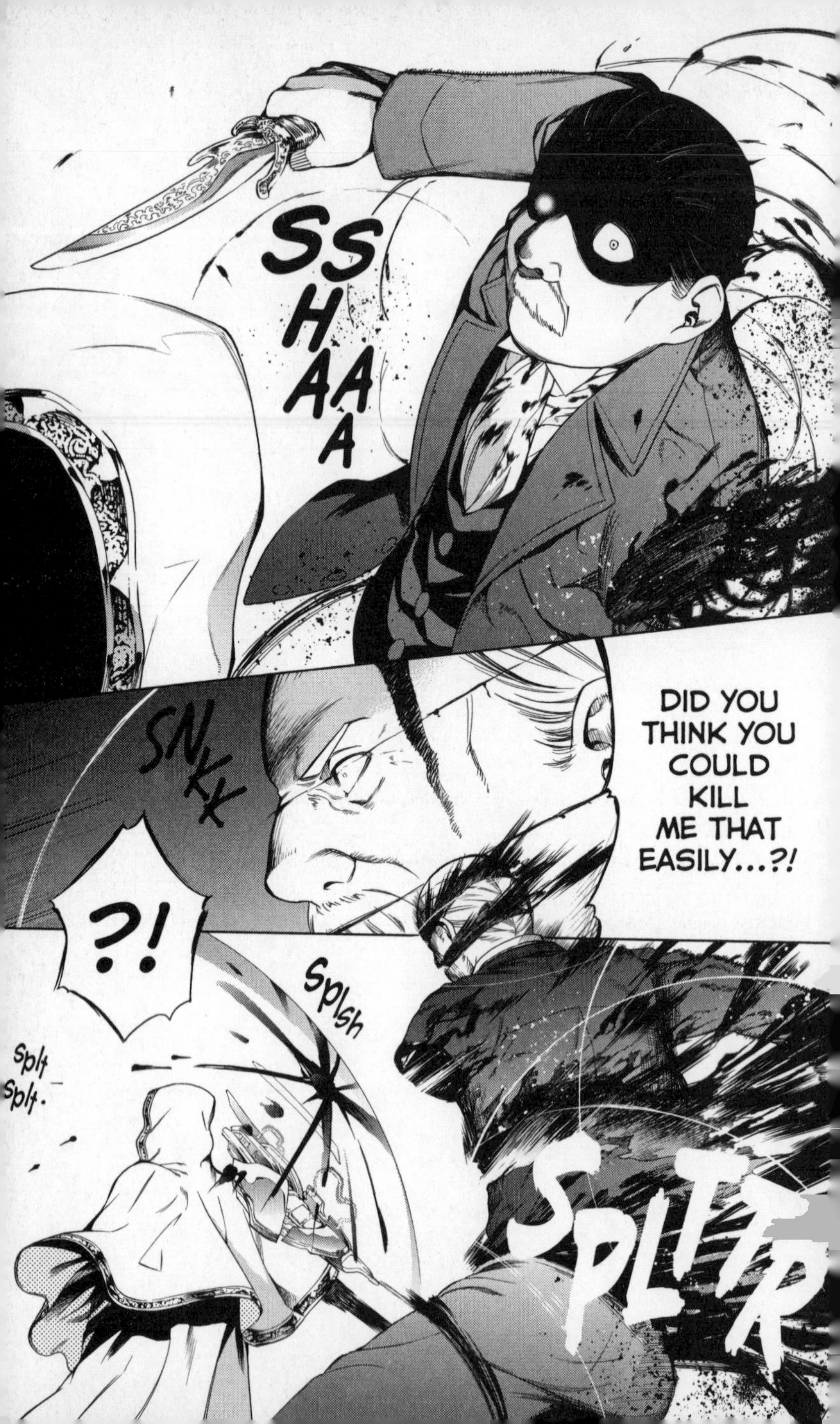
SSHAAAA
DID YOU THINK YOU COULD KILL ME THAT EASILY...?!
SNKK
?!
Splsh
Splt Splt.
SPLTTR

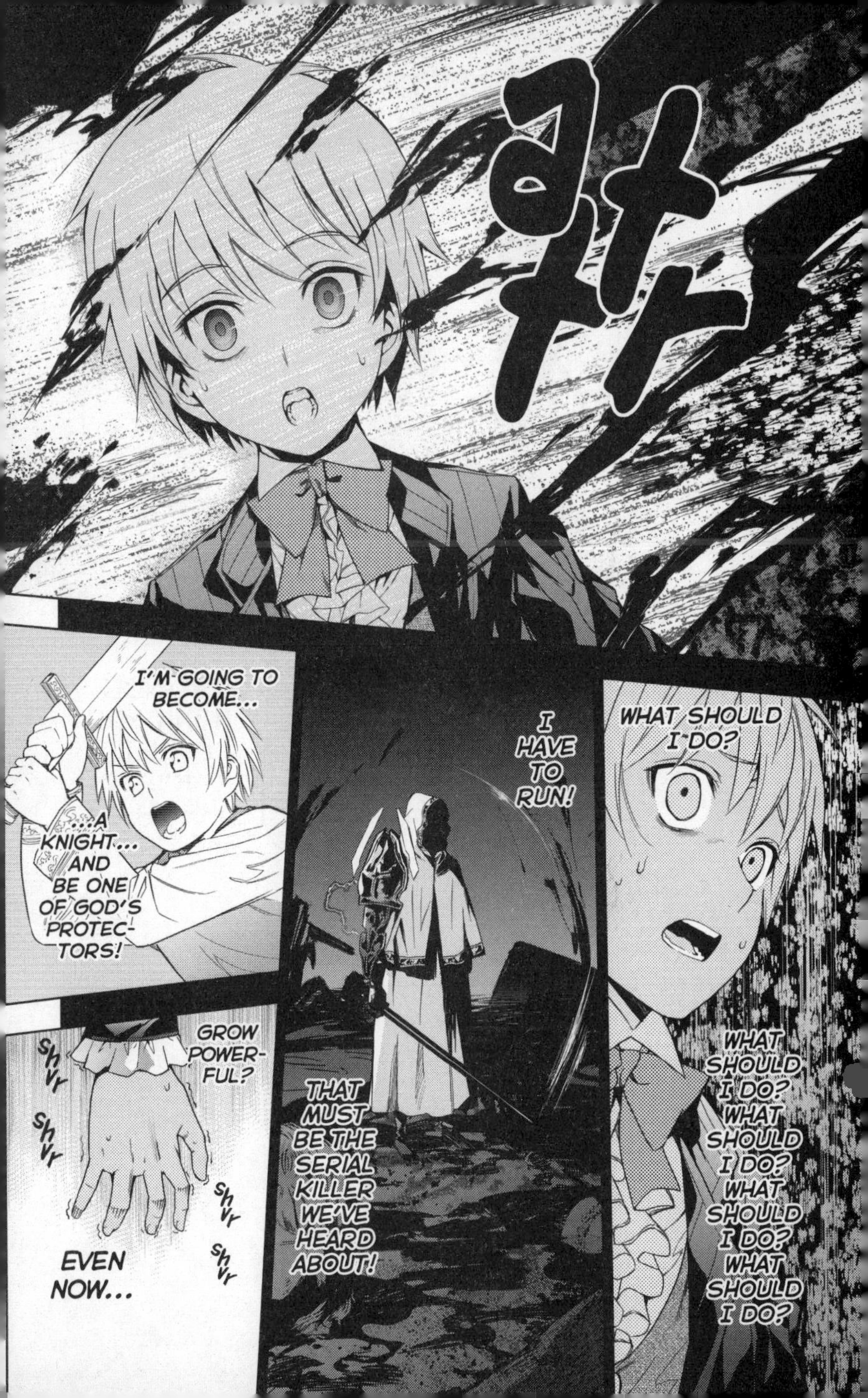
WHAT SHOULD I DO?
WHAT SHOULD I DO? WHAT SHOULD I DO? WHAT SHOULD I DO? WHAT SHOULD I DO?
I HAVE TO RUN!
THAT MUST BE THE SERIAL KILLER WE'VE HEARD ABOUT!
I'M GOING TO BECOME...
...A KNIGHT... AND BE ONE OF GOD'S PROTECTORS!
GROW POWERFUL?
shvr
shvr
shvr
shvr
EVEN NOW...

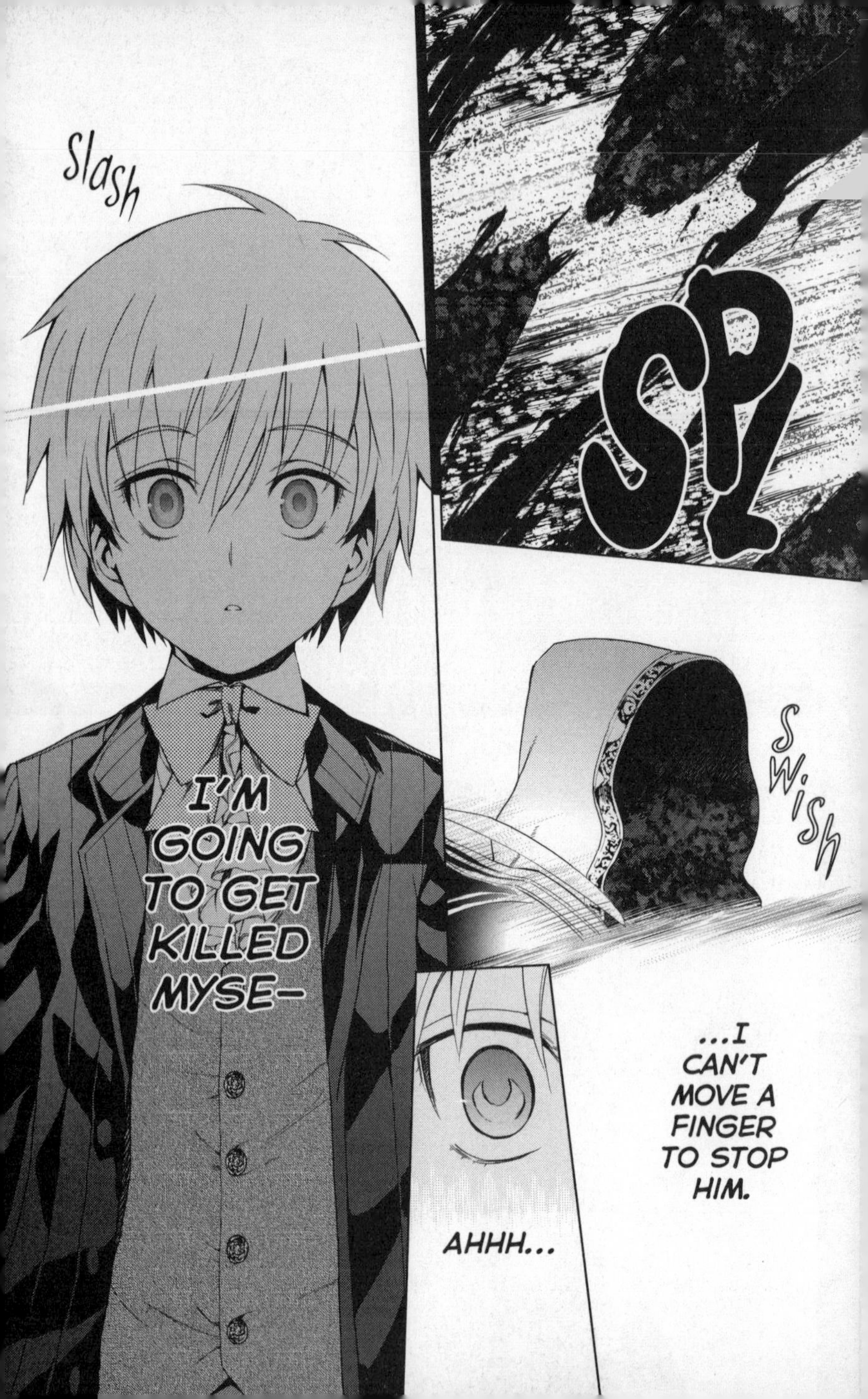
SPL
SWISH
...I CAN'T MOVE A FINGER TO STOP HIM.
AHHH...
Slash
I'M GOING TO GET KILLED MYSE-

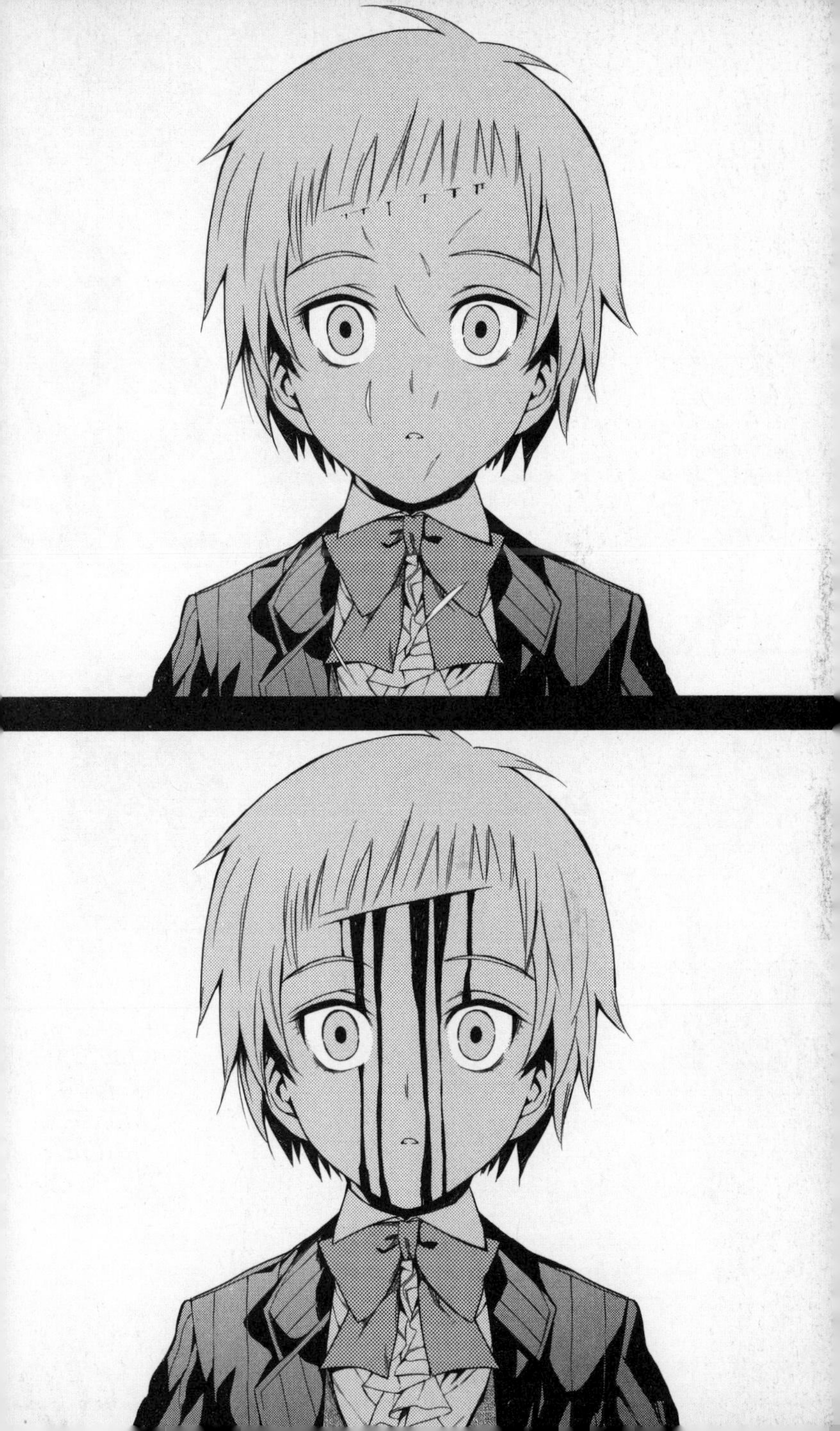

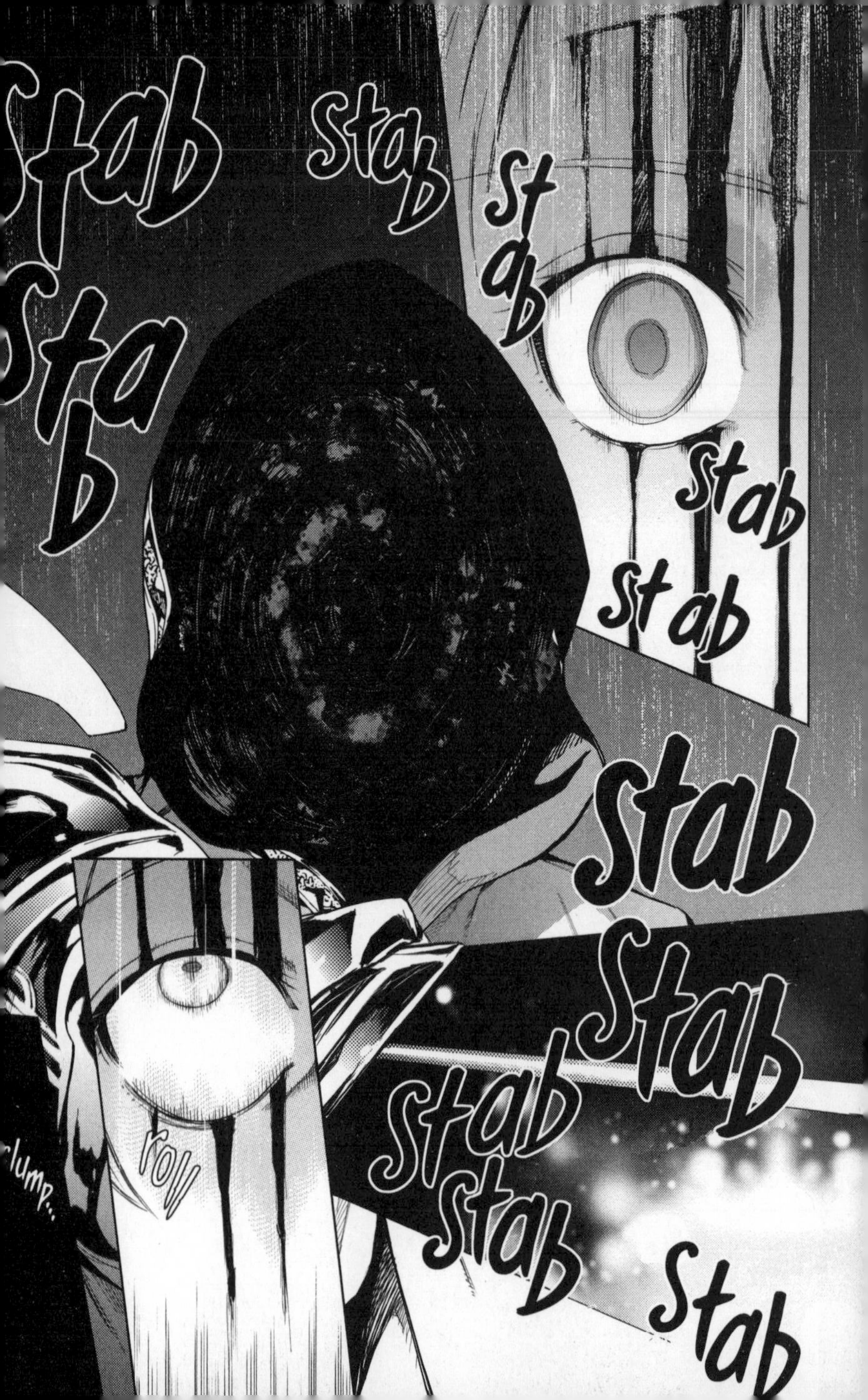

stab
stab
stab
stab
stab
stab
stab
stab
stab
stab
stab
roll
clump...

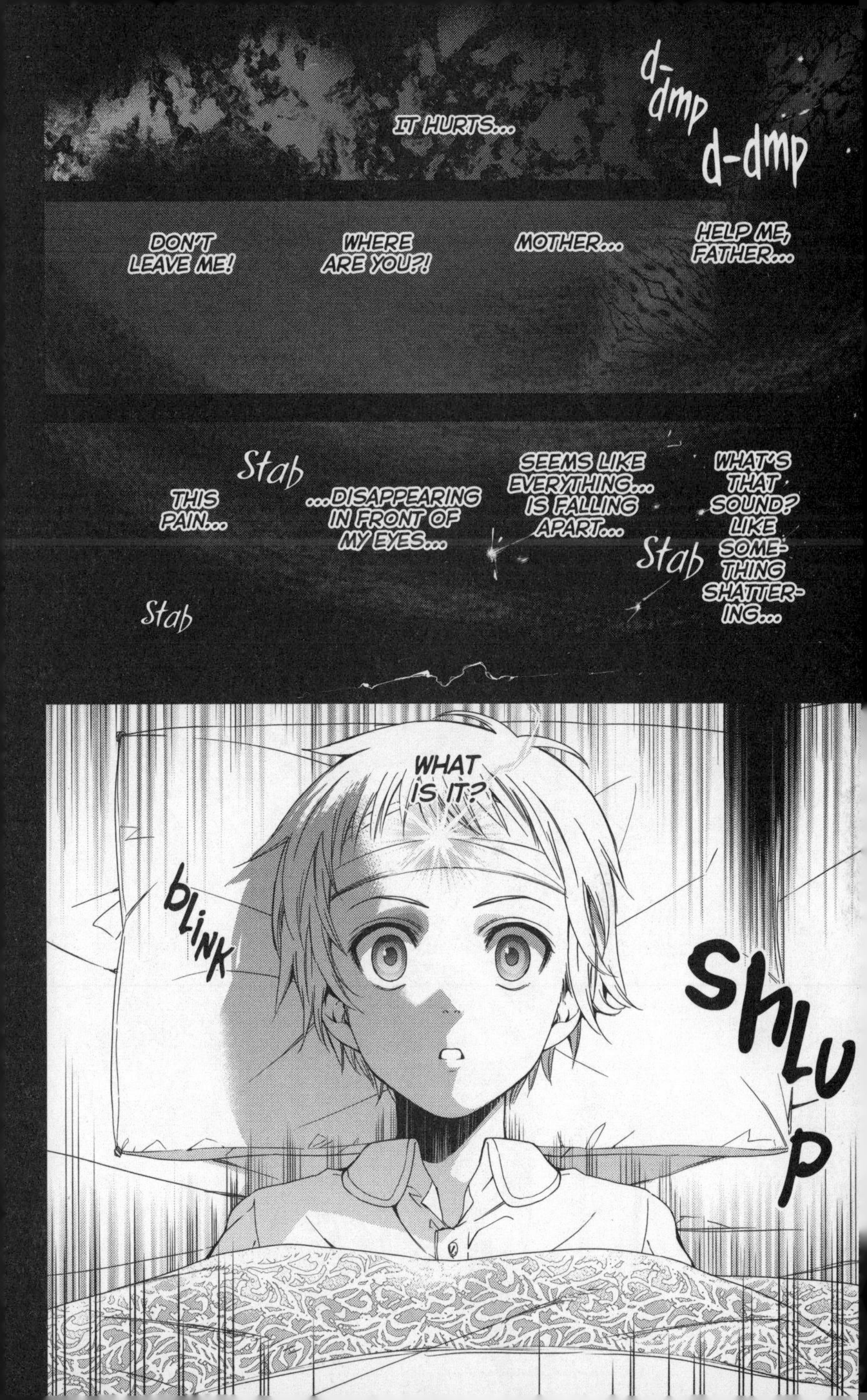
d-dmp d-dmp
IT HURTS...
HELP ME, FATHER...
MOTHER...
WHERE ARE YOU?!
DON'T LEAVE ME!
WHAT'S THAT SOUND? LIKE SOMETHING SHATTERING...
SEEMS LIKE EVERYTHING... IS FALLING APART...
Stab
...DISAPPEARING IN FRONT OF MY EYES...
Stab
THIS PAIN...
Stab
SHLUP
WHAT IS IT?
BLINK

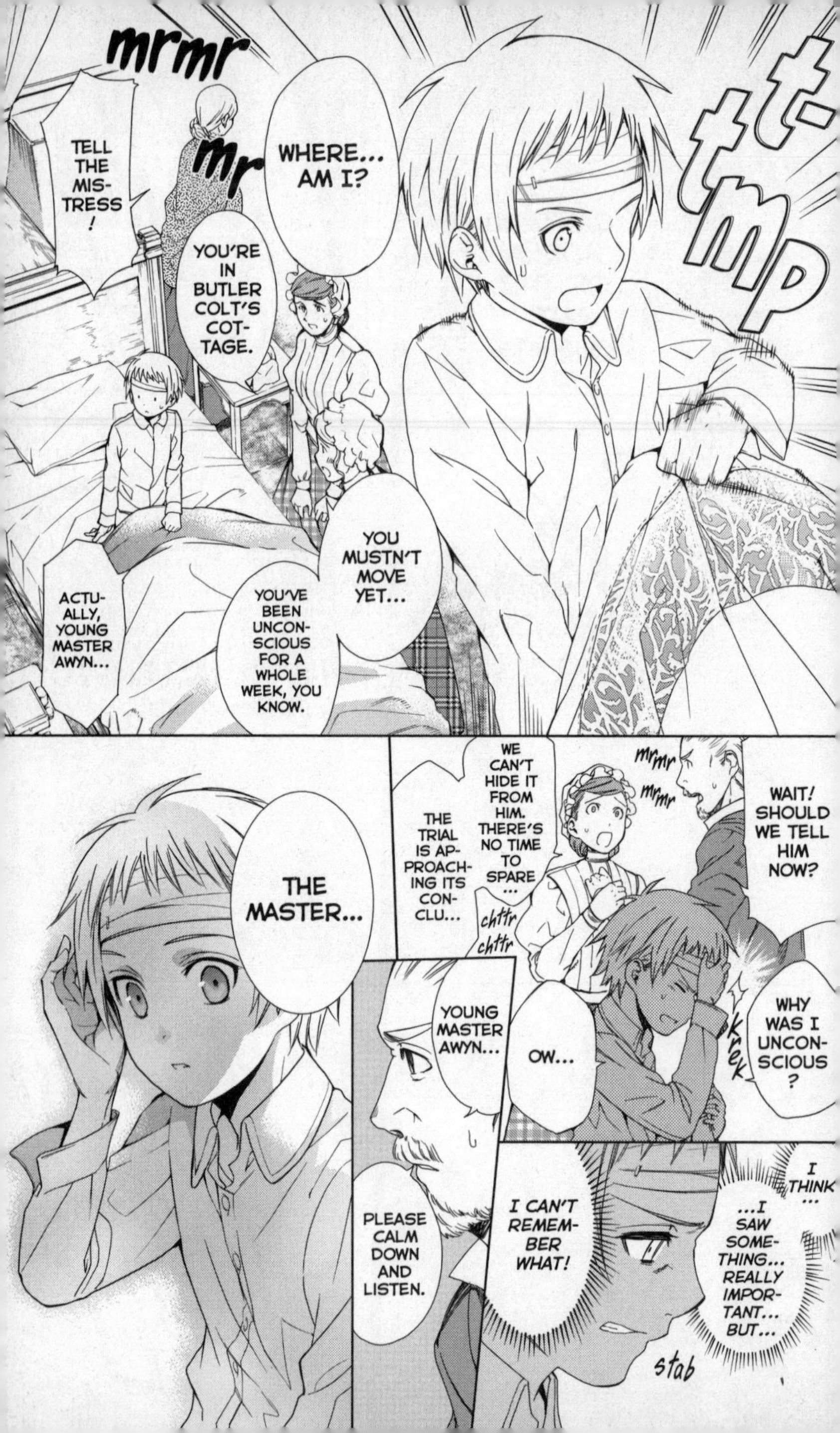
t-tmp
WHERE... AM I?
mrmr
mr
YOU'RE IN BUTLER COLT'S COTTAGE.
TELL THE MISTRESS!
YOU MUSTN'T MOVE YET...
YOU'VE BEEN UNCONSCIOUS FOR A WHOLE WEEK, YOU KNOW.
ACTUALLY, YOUNG MASTER AWYN...
WAIT! SHOULD WE TELL HIM NOW?
mrmr
mrmr
WE CAN'T HIDE IT FROM HIM. THERE'S NO TIME TO SPARE...
THE TRIAL IS APPROACHING ITS CONCLU...
chttr
chttr
WHY WAS I UNCONSCIOUS?
krek
OW...
YOUNG MASTER AWYN...
PLEASE CALM DOWN AND LISTEN.
I THINK...
...I SAW SOMETHING... REALLY IMPORTANT... BUT...
I CAN'T REMEMBER WHAT!
stab
THE MASTER...

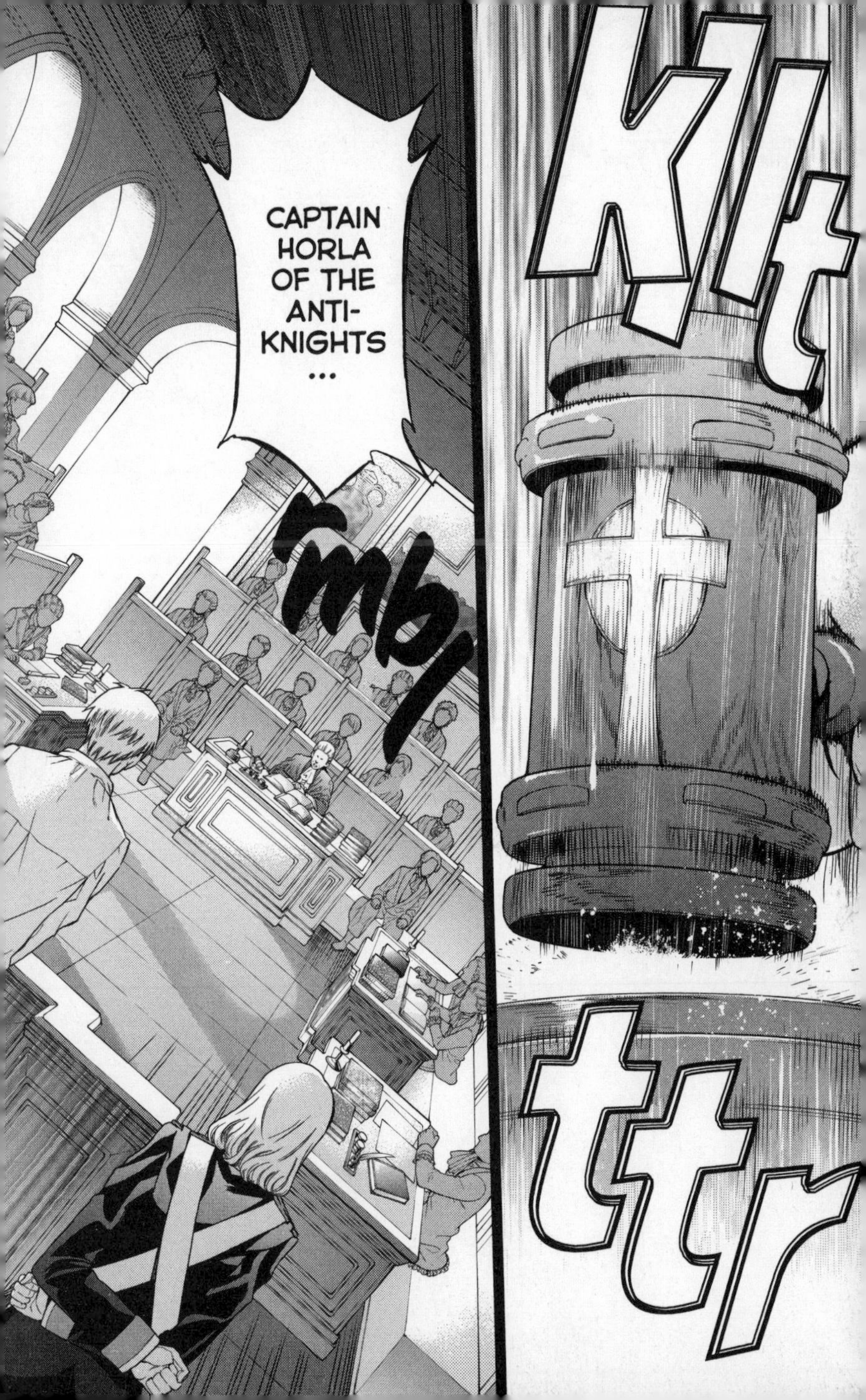
Klt
ttr
CAPTAIN HORLA OF THE ANTI-KNIGHTS...
rmbl

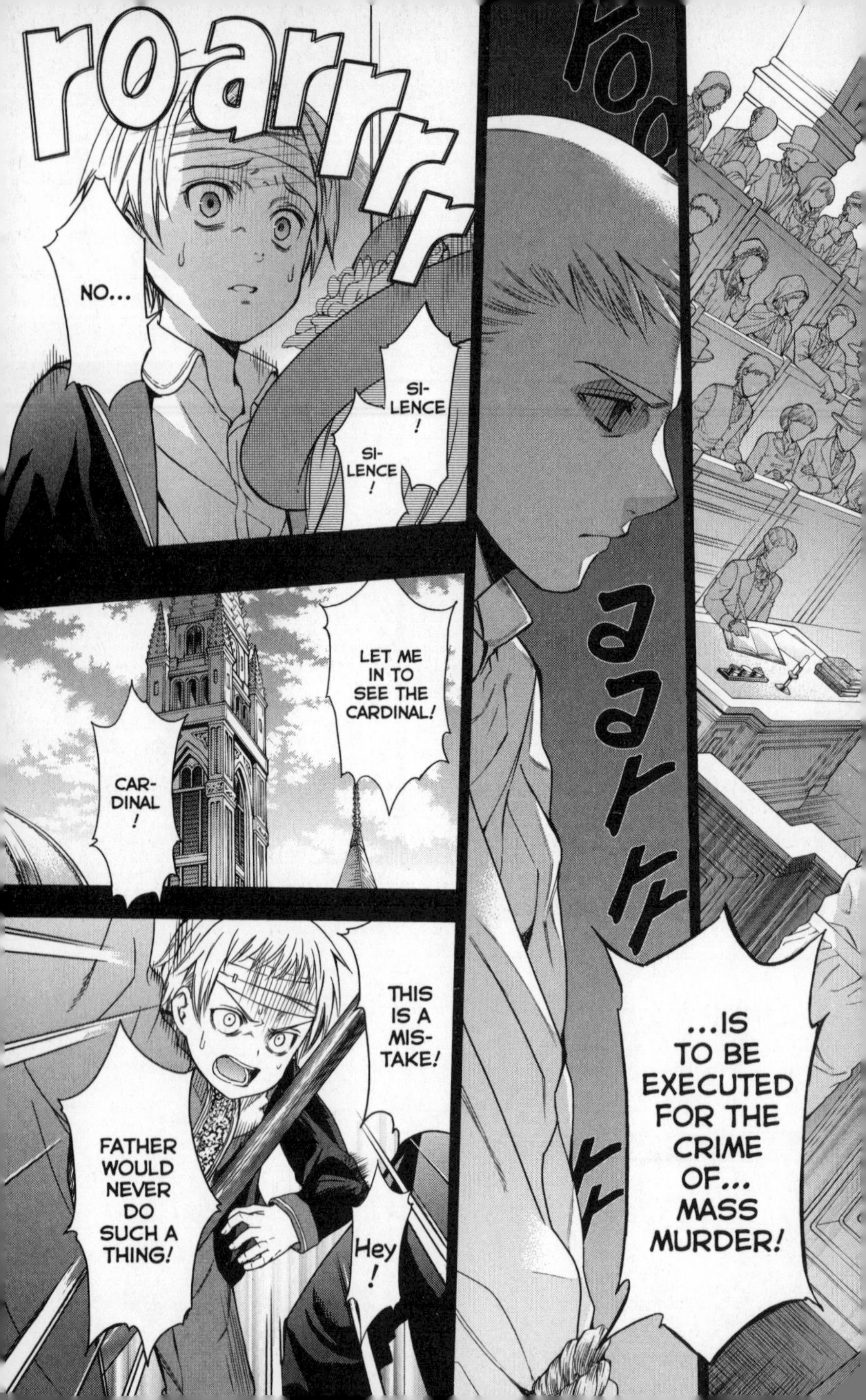
roo
aarrr
rr
...IS TO BE EXECUTED FOR THE CRIME OF... MASS MURDER!
roarrrr
SI-LENCE!
SI-LENCE!
NO...
LET ME IN TO SEE THE CARDINAL!
CAR-DINAL!
THIS IS A MIS-TAKE!
Hey!
FATHER WOULD NEVER DO SUCH A THING!

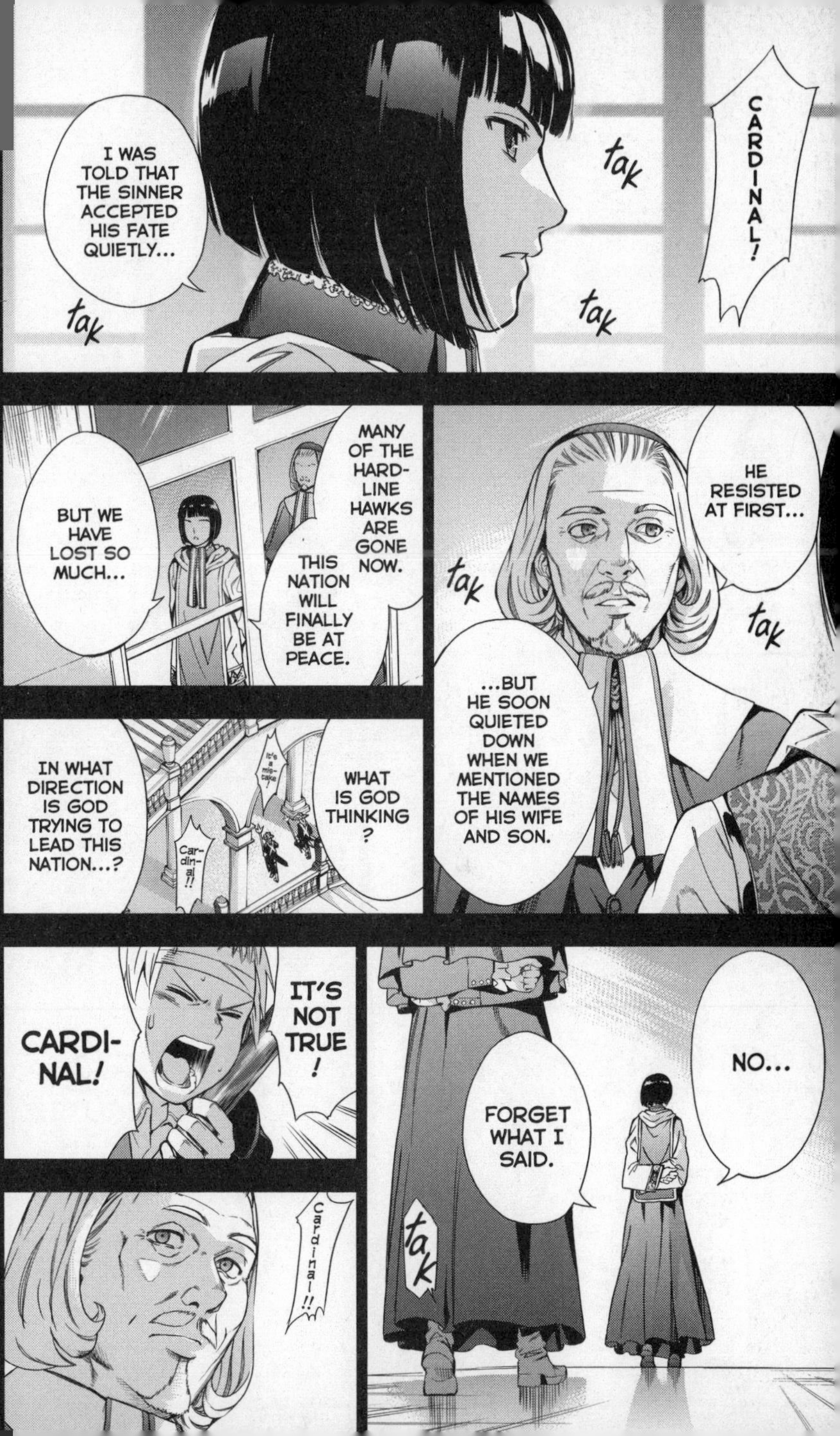
CARDINAL!
tak
I WAS TOLD THAT THE SINNER ACCEPTED HIS FATE QUIETLY...
tak
tak
HE RESISTED AT FIRST...
tak
tak
...BUT HE SOON QUIETED DOWN WHEN WE MENTIONED THE NAMES OF HIS WIFE AND SON.
MANY OF THE HARD-LINE HAWKS ARE GONE NOW.
THIS NATION WILL FINALLY BE AT PEACE.
BUT WE HAVE LOST SO MUCH...
WHAT IS GOD THINKING?
It's a mis-take!
Car-dina-al!!
IN WHAT DIRECTION IS GOD TRYING TO LEAD THIS NATION...?
NO...
FORGET WHAT I SAID.
tak
IT'S NOT TRUE!
CARDI-NAL!
Cardinal!!

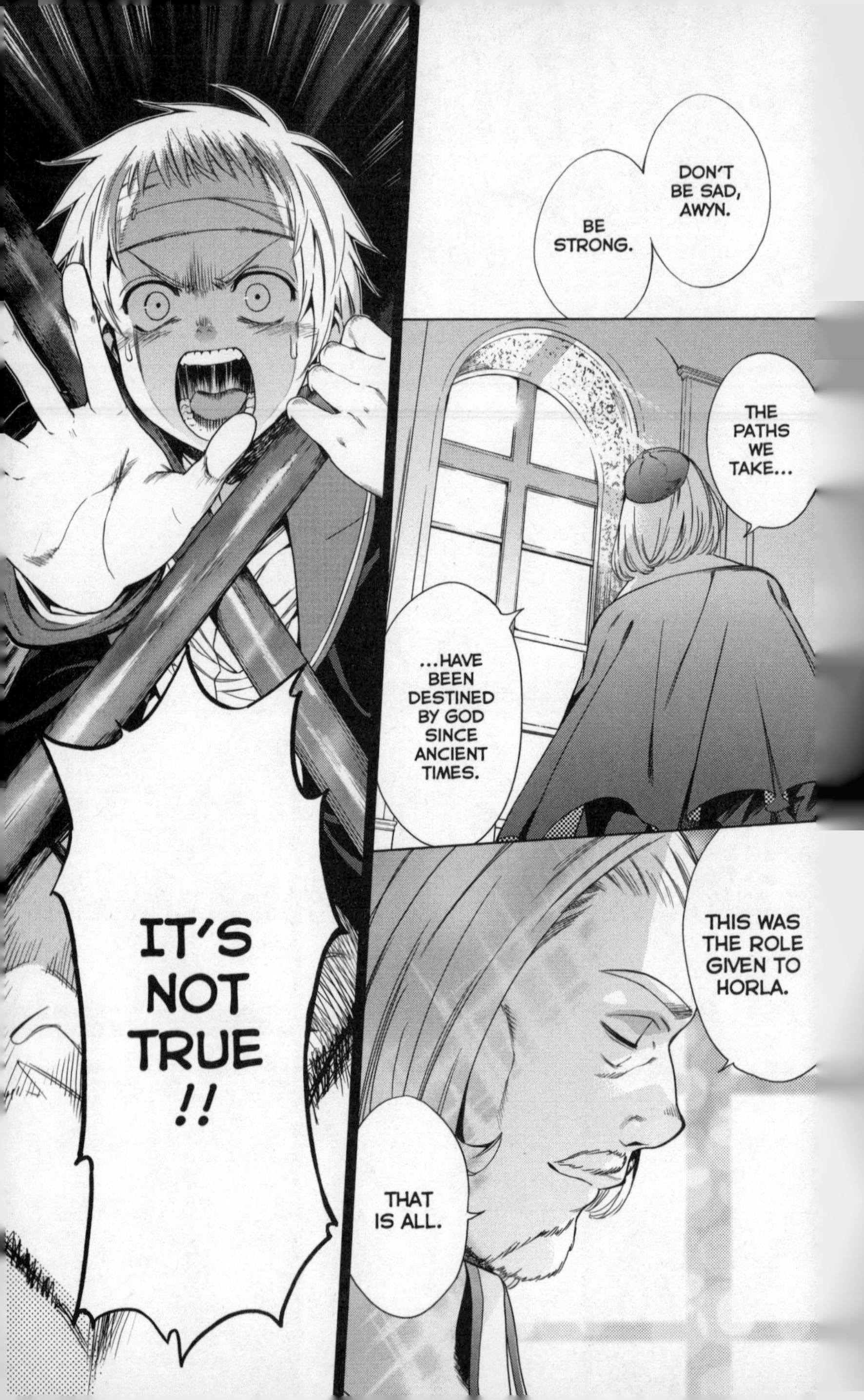
DON'T BE SAD, AWYN.
BE STRONG.
THE PATHS WE TAKE...
...HAVE BEEN DESTINED BY GOD SINCE ANCIENT TIMES.
THIS WAS THE ROLE GIVEN TO HORLA.
THAT IS ALL.
IT'S NOT TRUE!!

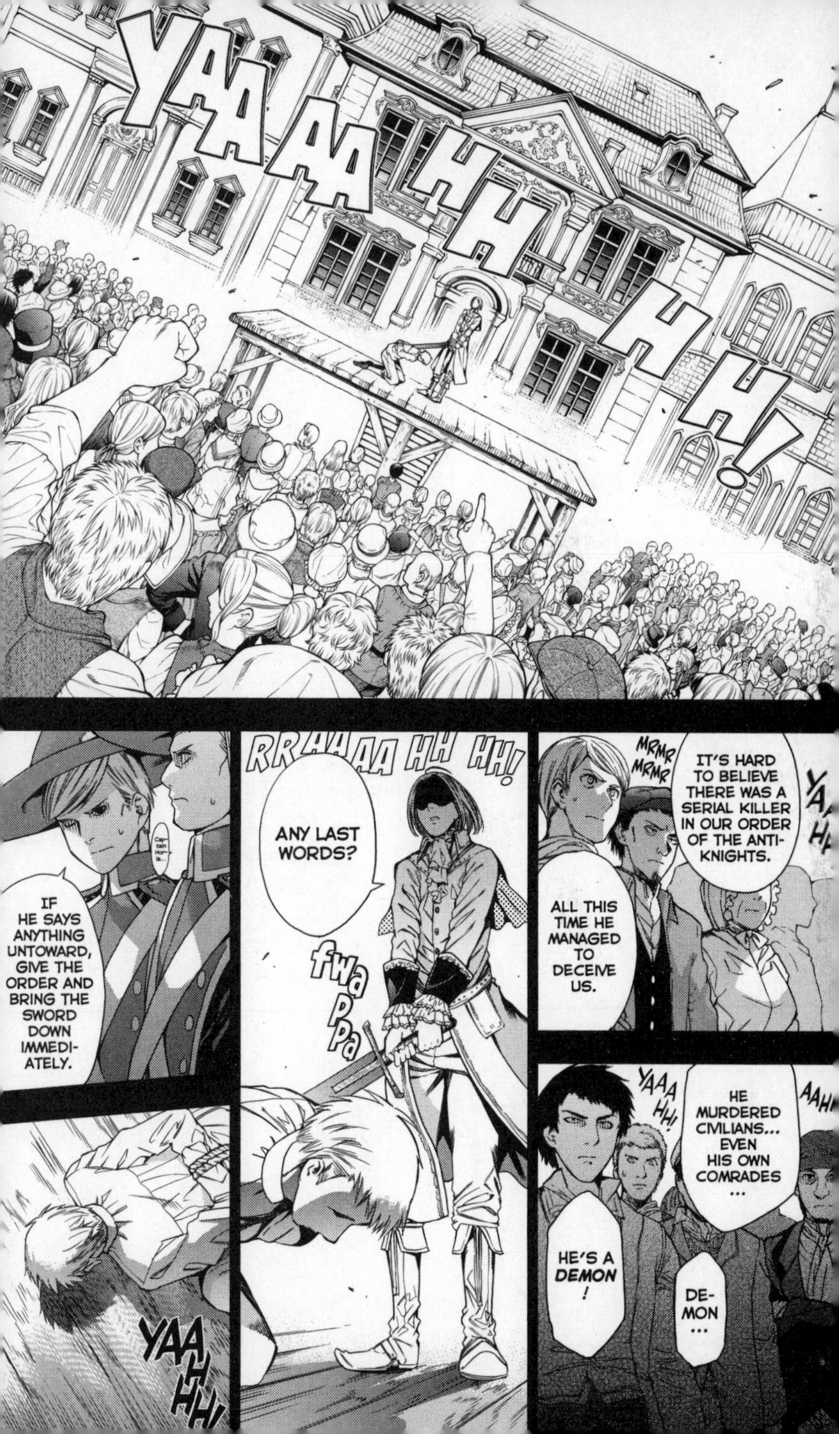
YAAAAHHHHH!
IT'S HARD TO BELIEVE THERE WAS A SERIAL KILLER IN OUR ORDER OF THE ANTI-KNIGHTS.
MRMR MRMR
ALL THIS TIME HE MANAGED TO DECEIVE US.
AAH
HE MURDERED CIVILIANS... EVEN HIS OWN COMRADES...
YAAAHH!
DE-MON...
HE'S A *DEMON*!
RRAAAAAHH HH!
ANY LAST WORDS?
fwapppa
IF HE SAYS ANYTHING UNTOWARD, GIVE THE ORDER AND BRING THE SWORD DOWN IMMEDI-ATELY.
YAAHHH!

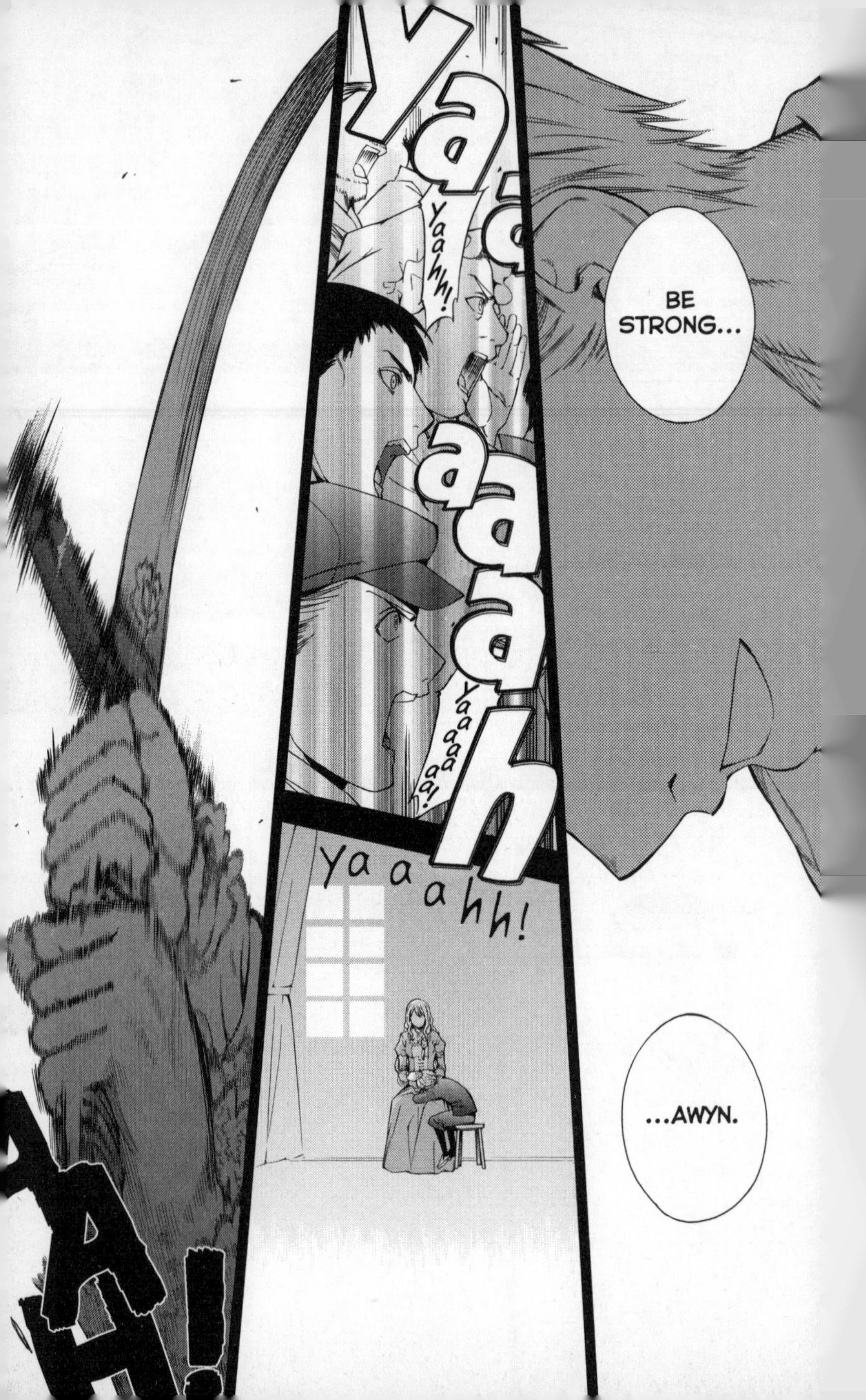
BE STRONG...
...AWYN.
Yaaaaah
Yaahh!
Yaaaaaa!
Yaaahh!
AAH!

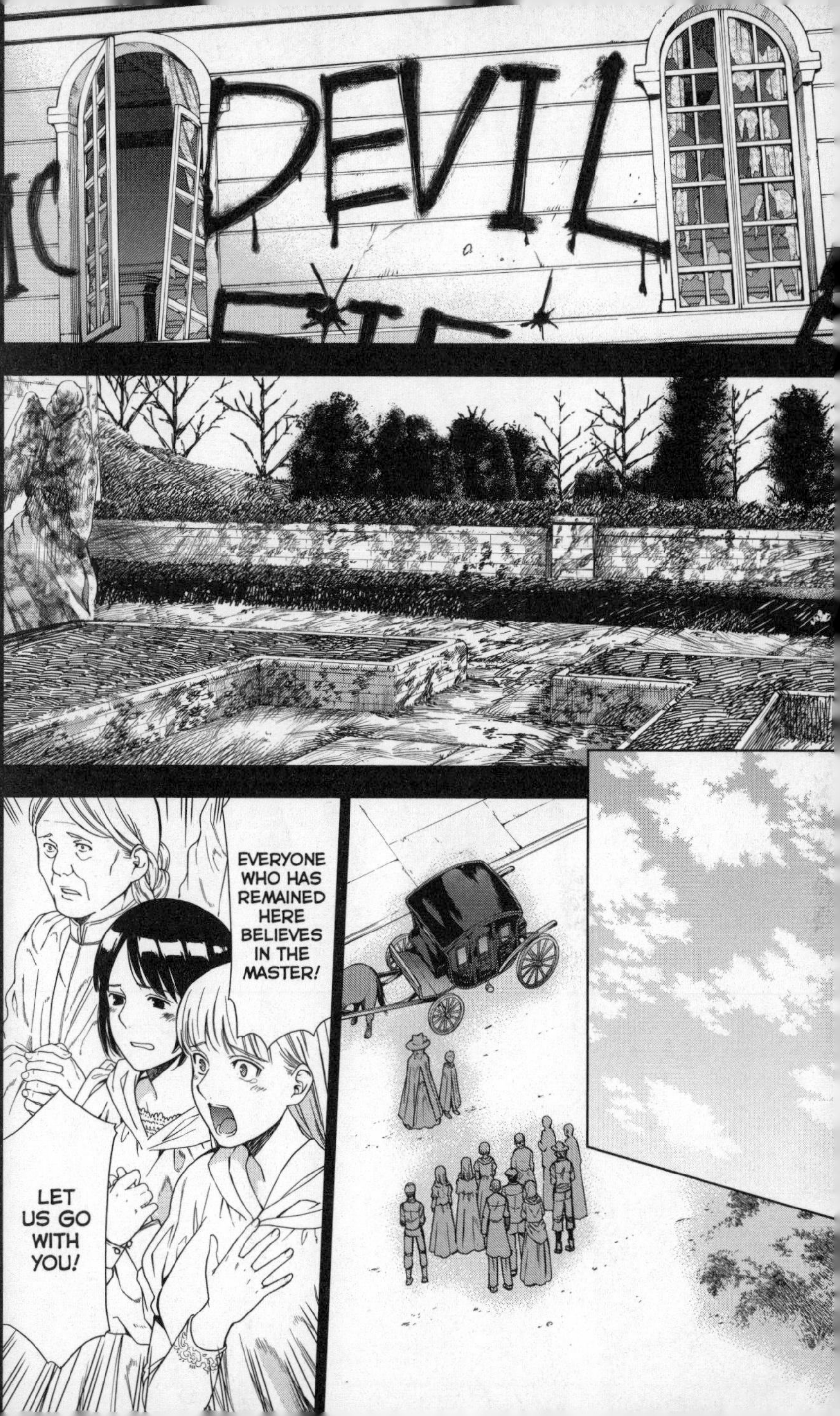
DEVIL
EVERYONE WHO HAS REMAINED HERE BELIEVES IN THE MASTER!
LET US GO WITH YOU!

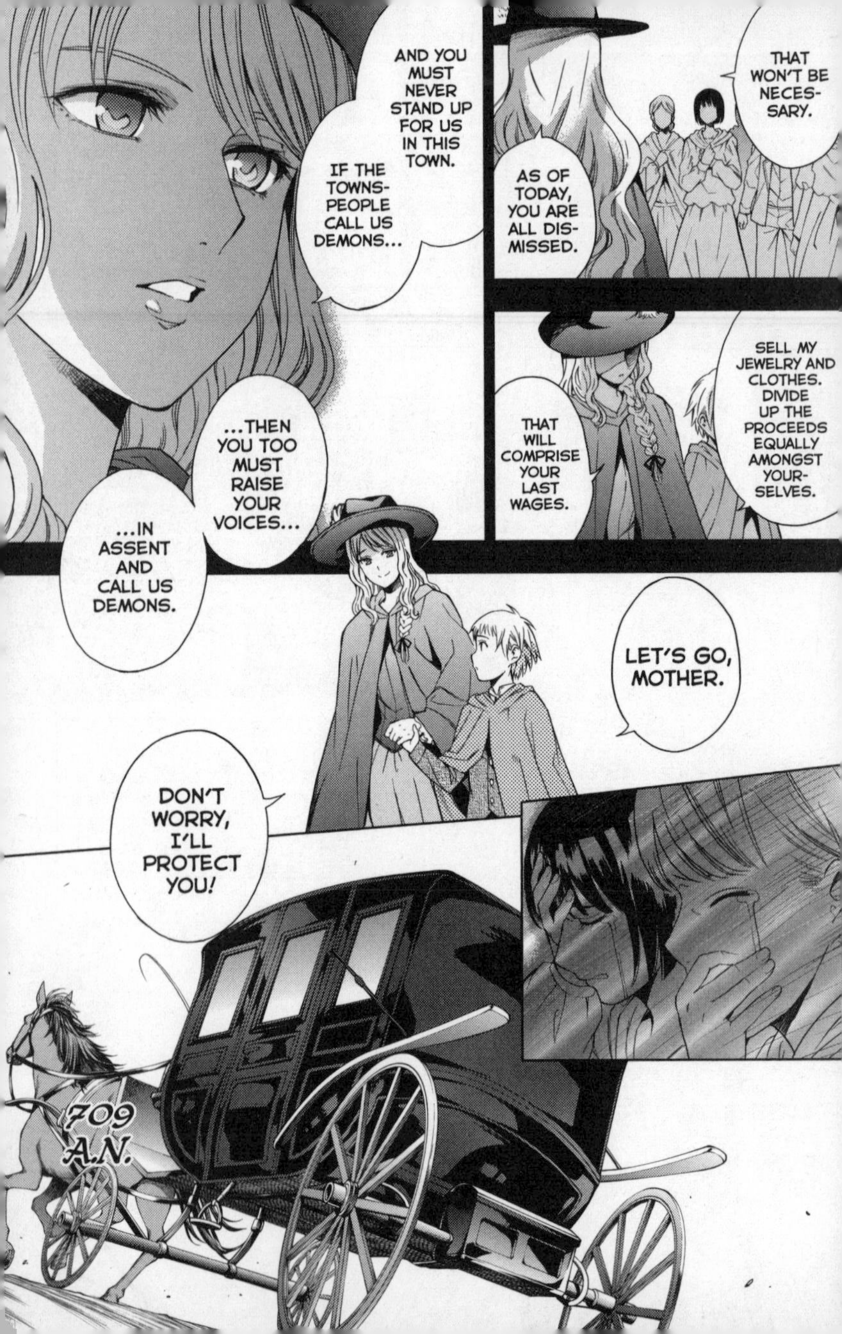
THAT WON'T BE NECESSARY.
AS OF TODAY, YOU ARE ALL DISMISSED.
SELL MY JEWELRY AND CLOTHES. DIVIDE UP THE PROCEEDS EQUALLY AMONGST YOURSELVES.
THAT WILL COMPRISE YOUR LAST WAGES.
AND YOU MUST NEVER STAND UP FOR US IN THIS TOWN.
IF THE TOWNSPEOPLE CALL US DEMONS...
...THEN YOU TOO MUST RAISE YOUR VOICES...
...IN ASSENT AND CALL US DEMONS.
LET'S GO, MOTHER.
DON'T WORRY, I'LL PROTECT YOU!
709 A.N.

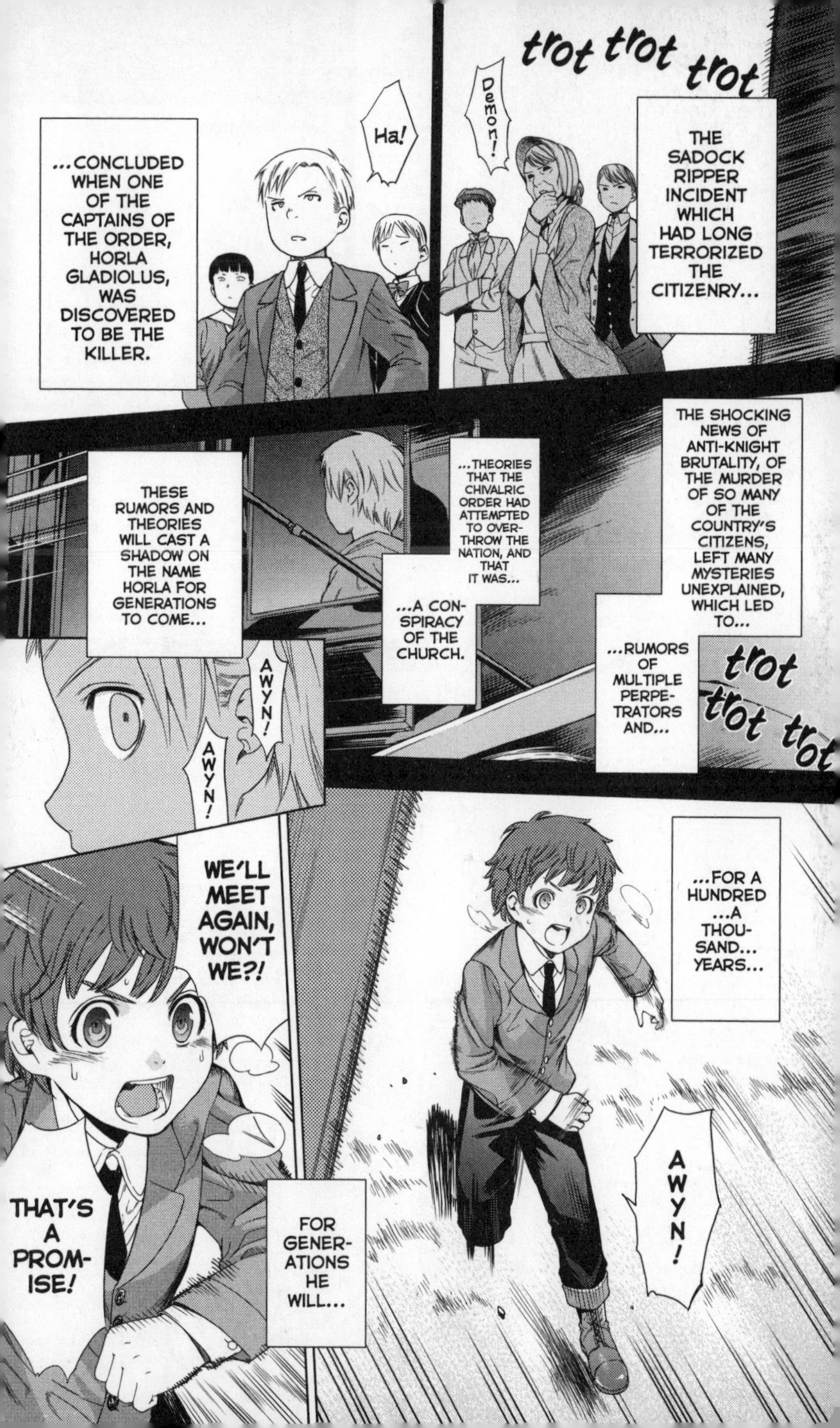
trot trot trot
THE SADOCK RIPPER INCIDENT WHICH HAD LONG TERRORIZED THE CITIZENRY...
Demon!
Ha!
...CONCLUDED WHEN ONE OF THE CAPTAINS OF THE ORDER, HORLA GLADIOLUS, WAS DISCOVERED TO BE THE KILLER.
THE SHOCKING NEWS OF ANTI-KNIGHT BRUTALITY, OF THE MURDER OF SO MANY OF THE COUNTRY'S CITIZENS, LEFT MANY MYSTERIES UNEXPLAINED, WHICH LED TO...
trot trot trot
...RUMORS OF MULTIPLE PERPETRATORS AND...
...THEORIES THAT THE CHIVALRIC ORDER HAD ATTEMPTED TO OVERTHROW THE NATION, AND THAT IT WAS...
...A CONSPIRACY OF THE CHURCH.
THESE RUMORS AND THEORIES WILL CAST A SHADOW ON THE NAME HORLA FOR GENERATIONS TO COME...
AWYN!
AWYN!
...FOR A HUNDRED ...A THOUSAND... YEARS...
AWYN!
FOR GENERATIONS HE WILL...
WE'LL MEET AGAIN, WON'T WE?!
THAT'S A PROMISE!

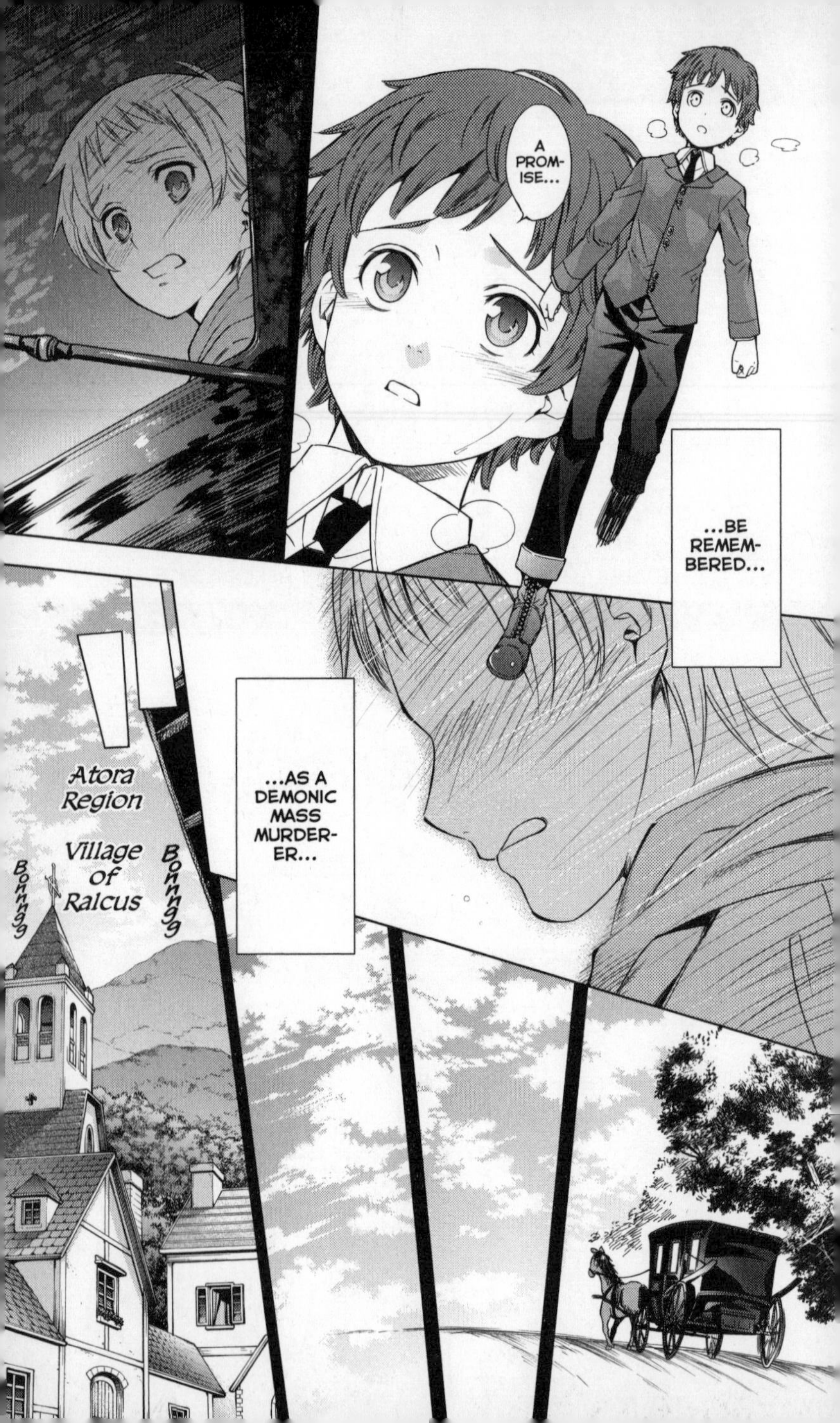
A PROMISE...
...BE REMEMBERED...
...AS A DEMONIC MASS MURDERER...
Atora Region
Village Of Ralcus
Bonnngg
Bonnngg

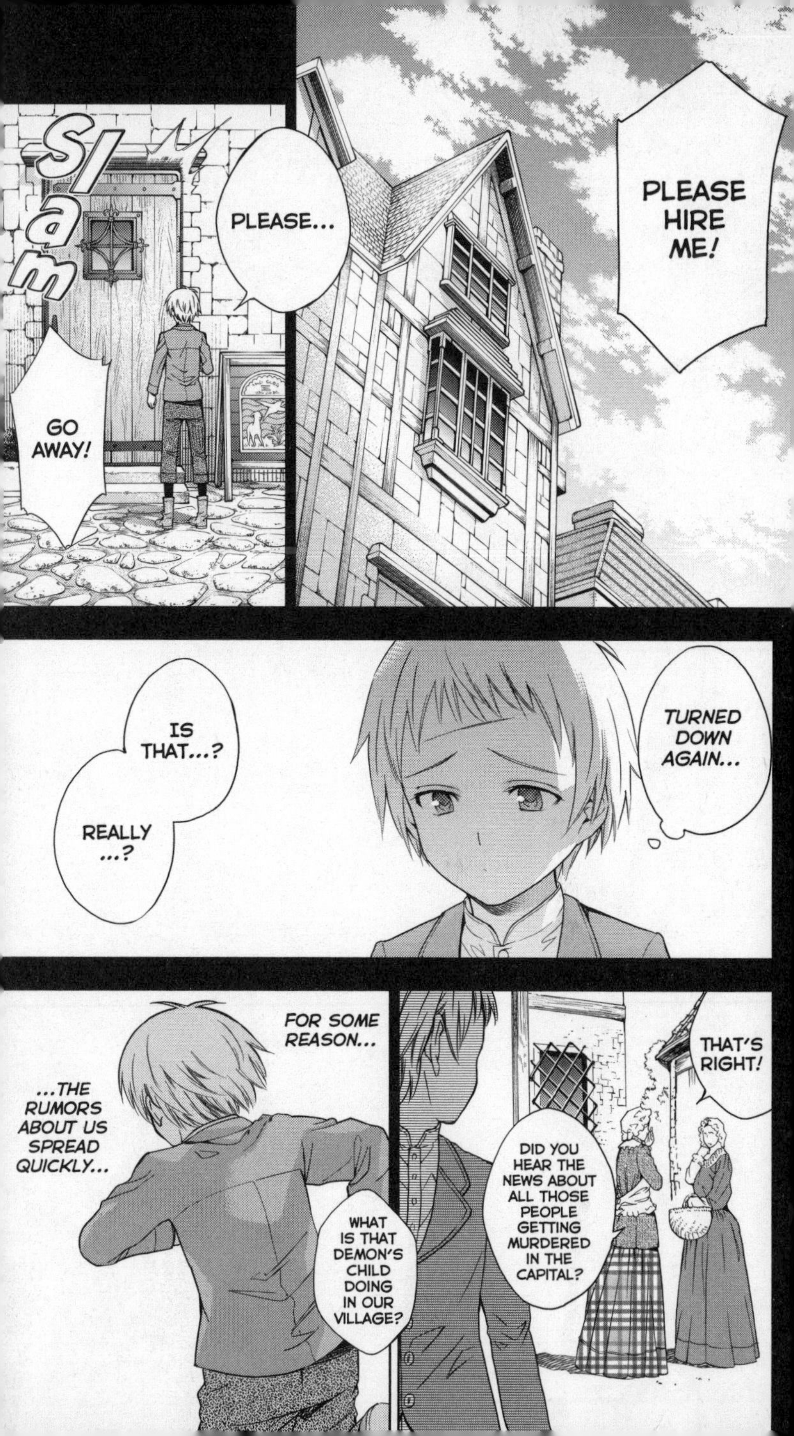
PLEASE HIRE ME!
PLEASE...
Slam
GO AWAY!
TURNED DOWN AGAIN...
IS THAT...?
REALLY ...?
THAT'S RIGHT!
DID YOU HEAR THE NEWS ABOUT ALL THOSE PEOPLE GETTING MURDERED IN THE CAPITAL?
WHAT IS THAT DEMON'S CHILD DOING IN OUR VILLAGE?
FOR SOME REASON...
...THE RUMORS ABOUT US SPREAD QUICKLY...

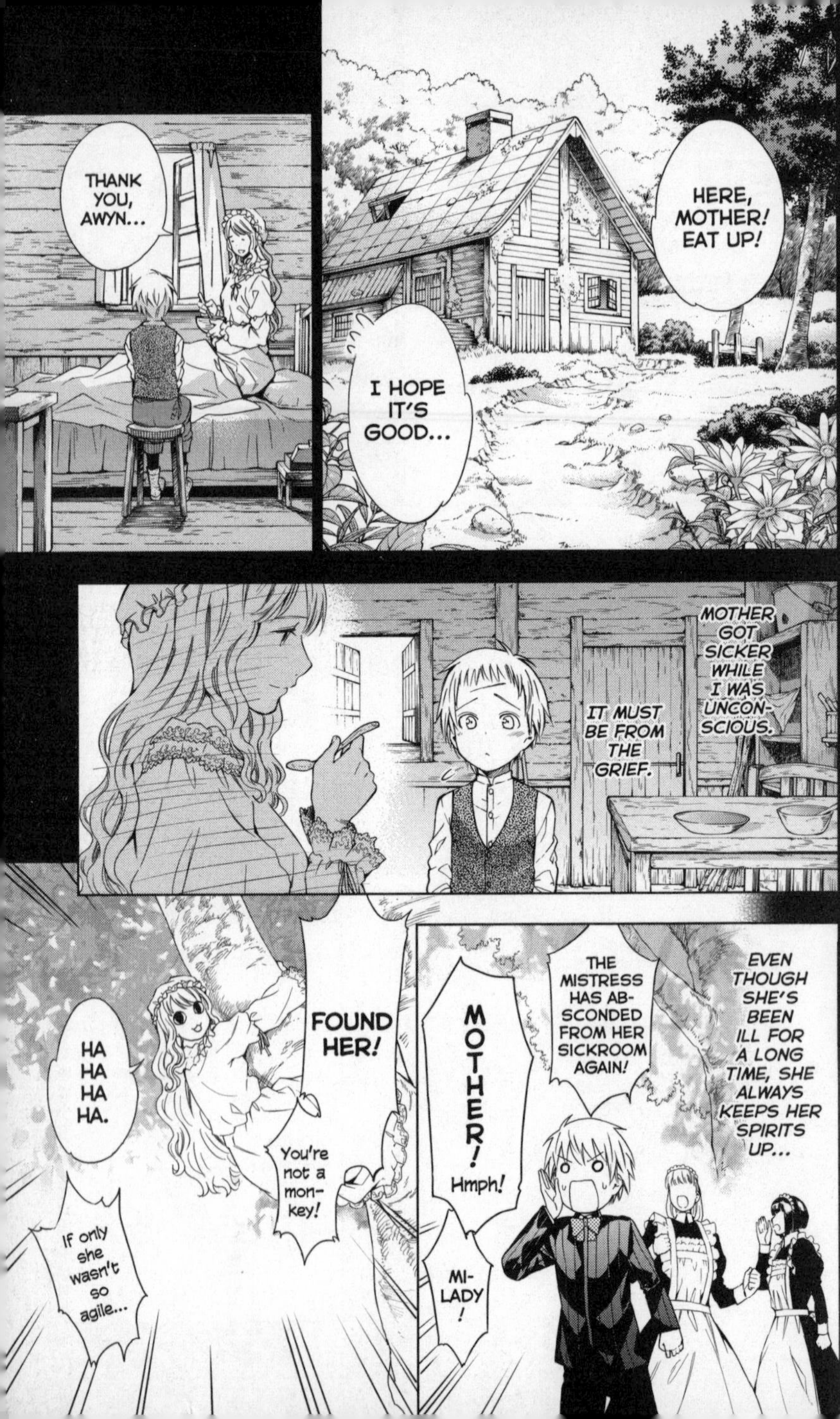
HERE, MOTHER! EAT UP!
I HOPE IT'S GOOD...
THANK YOU, AWYN...
MOTHER GOT SICKER WHILE I WAS UNCONSCIOUS.
IT MUST BE FROM THE GRIEF.
EVEN THOUGH SHE'S BEEN ILL FOR A LONG TIME, SHE ALWAYS KEEPS HER SPIRITS UP...
THE MISTRESS HAS ABSCONDED FROM HER SICKROOM AGAIN!
MOTHER!
Hmph!
MI-LADY!
FOUND HER!
You're not a monkey!
HA HA HA HA HA.
If only she wasn't so agile...

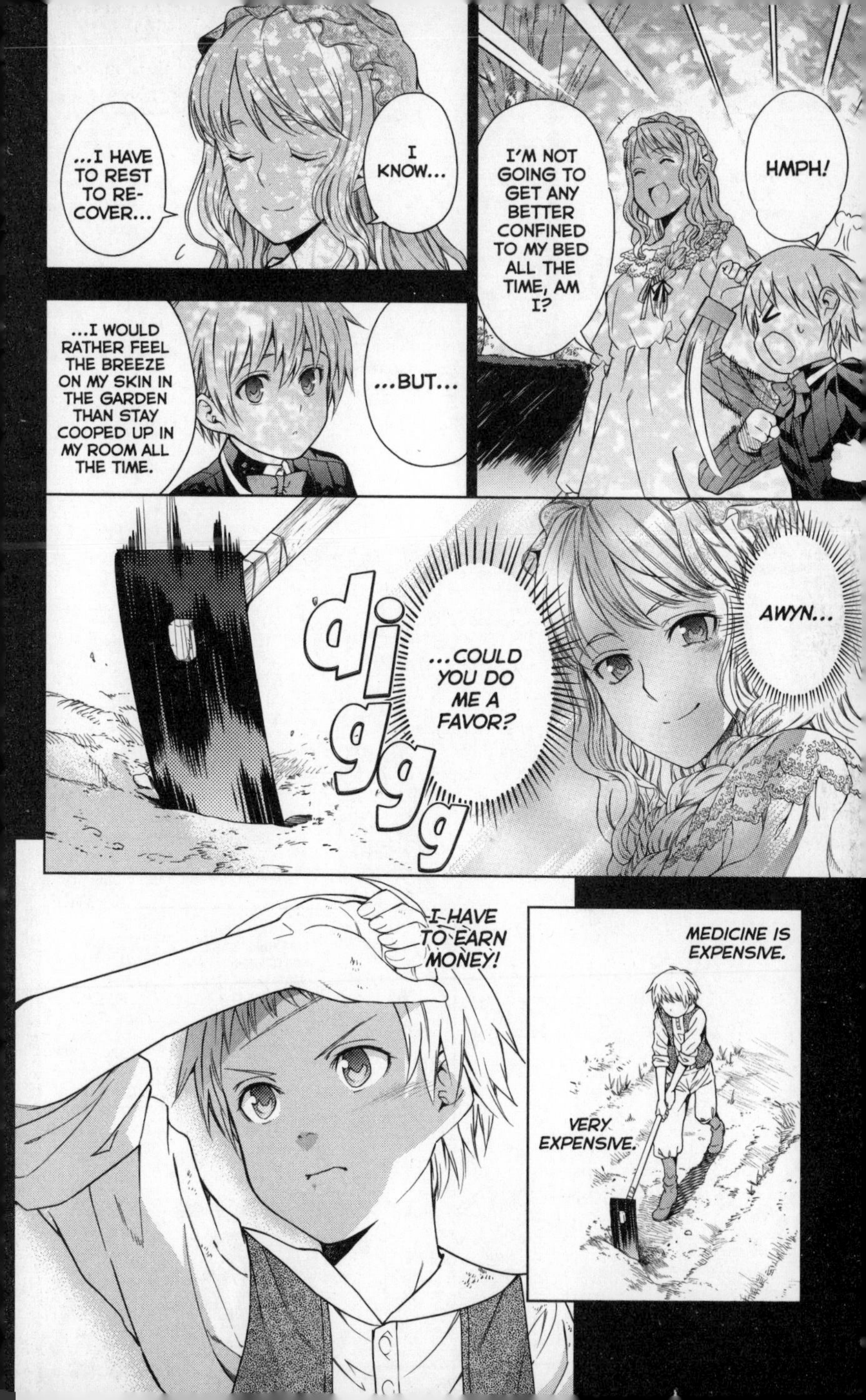
HMPH!
I'M NOT GOING TO GET ANY BETTER CONFINED TO MY BED ALL THE TIME, AM I?
I KNOW...
...I HAVE TO REST TO RE-COVER...
...BUT...
...I WOULD RATHER FEEL THE BREEZE ON MY SKIN IN THE GARDEN THAN STAY COOPED UP IN MY ROOM ALL THE TIME.
AWYN...
...COULD YOU DO ME A FAVOR?
diggg
MEDICINE IS EXPENSIVE.
VERY EXPENSIVE.
I-HAVE TO EARN MONEY!

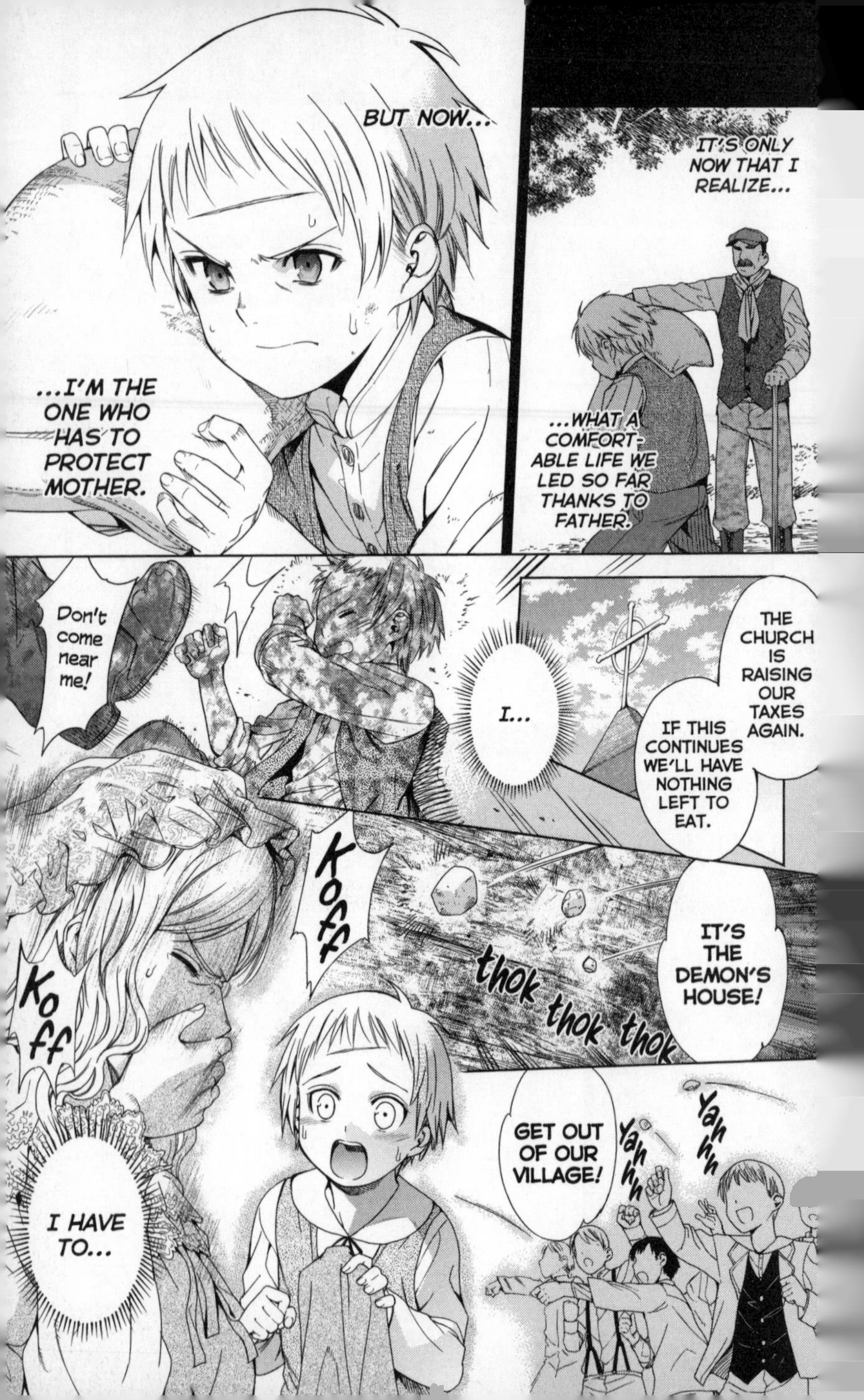
IT'S ONLY NOW THAT I REALIZE...
...WHAT A COMFORT-ABLE LIFE WE LED SO FAR THANKS TO FATHER.
BUT NOW...
...I'M THE ONE WHO HAS TO PROTECT MOTHER.
THE CHURCH IS RAISING OUR TAXES AGAIN.
IF THIS CONTINUES WE'LL HAVE NOTHING LEFT TO EAT.
I...
Don't come near me!
IT'S THE DEMON'S HOUSE!
thok thok thok
Koff
Koff
Yahhh
Yahhh
GET OUT OF OUR VILLAGE!
I HAVE TO...

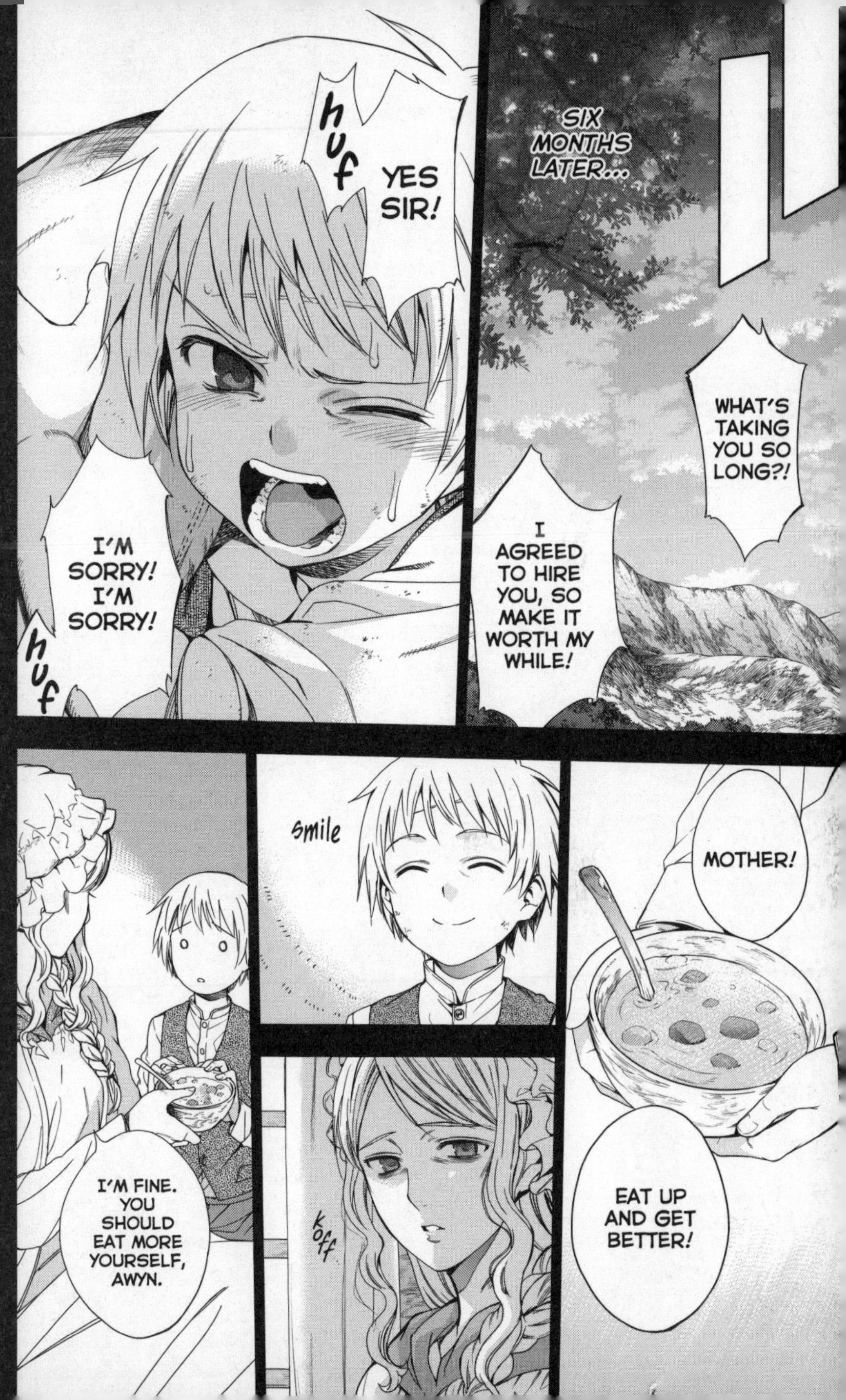
SIX MONTHS LATER...
WHAT'S TAKING YOU SO LONG?!
I AGREED TO HIRE YOU, SO MAKE IT WORTH MY WHILE!
huf
YES SIR!
I'M SORRY! I'M SORRY!
huf
MOTHER!
EAT UP AND GET BETTER!
smile
koff
I'M FINE. YOU SHOULD EAT MORE YOURSELF, AWYN.

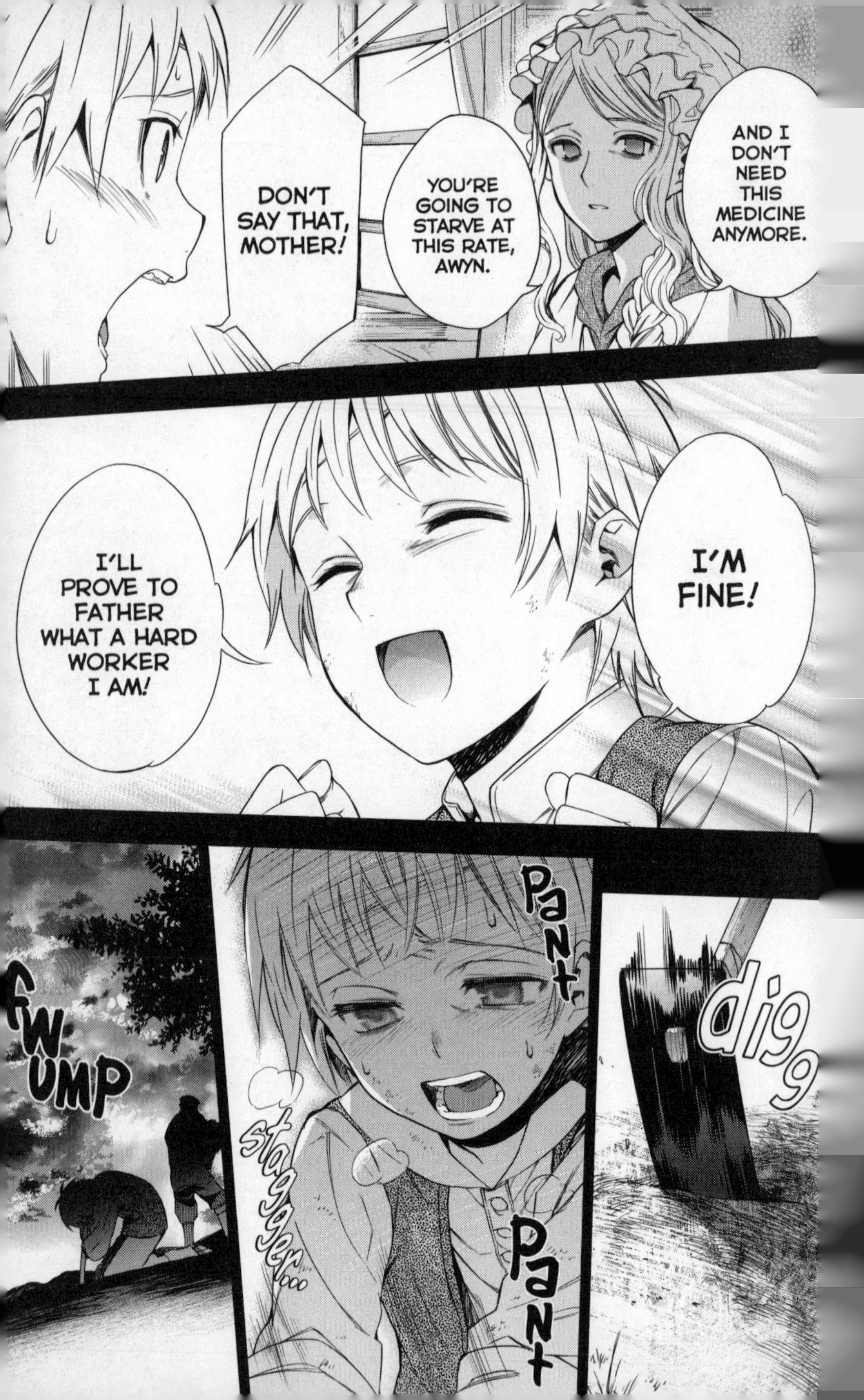
AND I DON'T NEED THIS MEDICINE ANYMORE.
YOU'RE GOING TO STARVE AT THIS RATE, AWYN.
DON'T SAY THAT, MOTHER!
I'M FINE!
I'LL PROVE TO FATHER WHAT A HARD WORKER I AM!
digg
Pant
Pant
stagger...
FWUMP

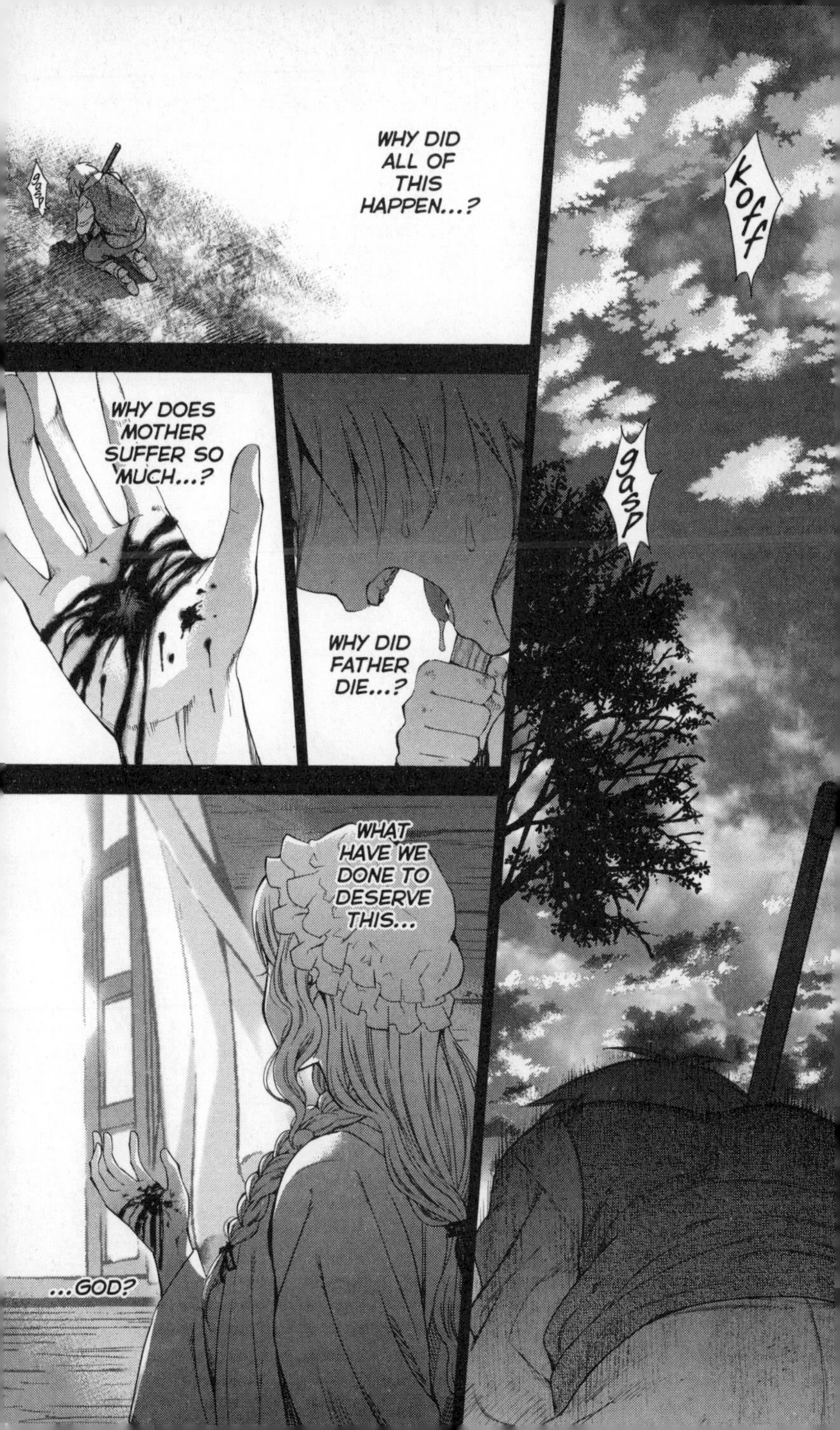
koff
gasp
WHY DID ALL OF THIS HAPPEN...?
gasp
WHY DID FATHER DIE...?
WHY DOES MOTHER SUFFER SO MUCH...?
WHAT HAVE WE DONE TO DESERVE THIS...
...GOD?

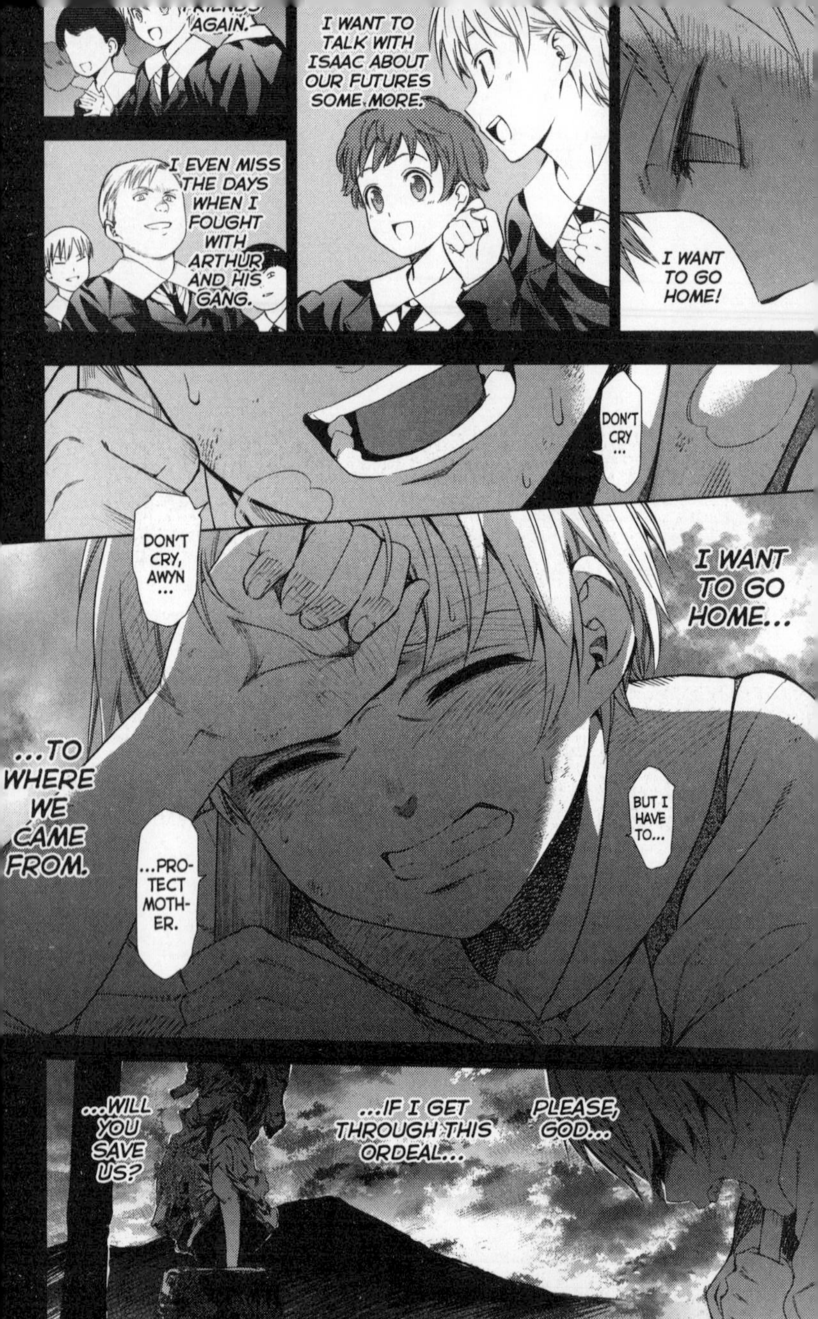
I WANT TO GO HOME!
I WANT TO TALK WITH ISAAC ABOUT OUR FUTURES SOME MORE.
AGAIN.
I EVEN MISS THE DAYS WHEN I FOUGHT WITH ARTHUR AND HIS GANG.
DON'T CRY...
I WANT TO GO HOME...
DON'T CRY, AWYN...
BUT I HAVE TO...
...TO WHERE WE CAME FROM.
...PRO-TECT MOTH-ER.
PLEASE, GOD...
...IF I GET THROUGH THIS ORDEAL...
...WILL YOU SAVE US?

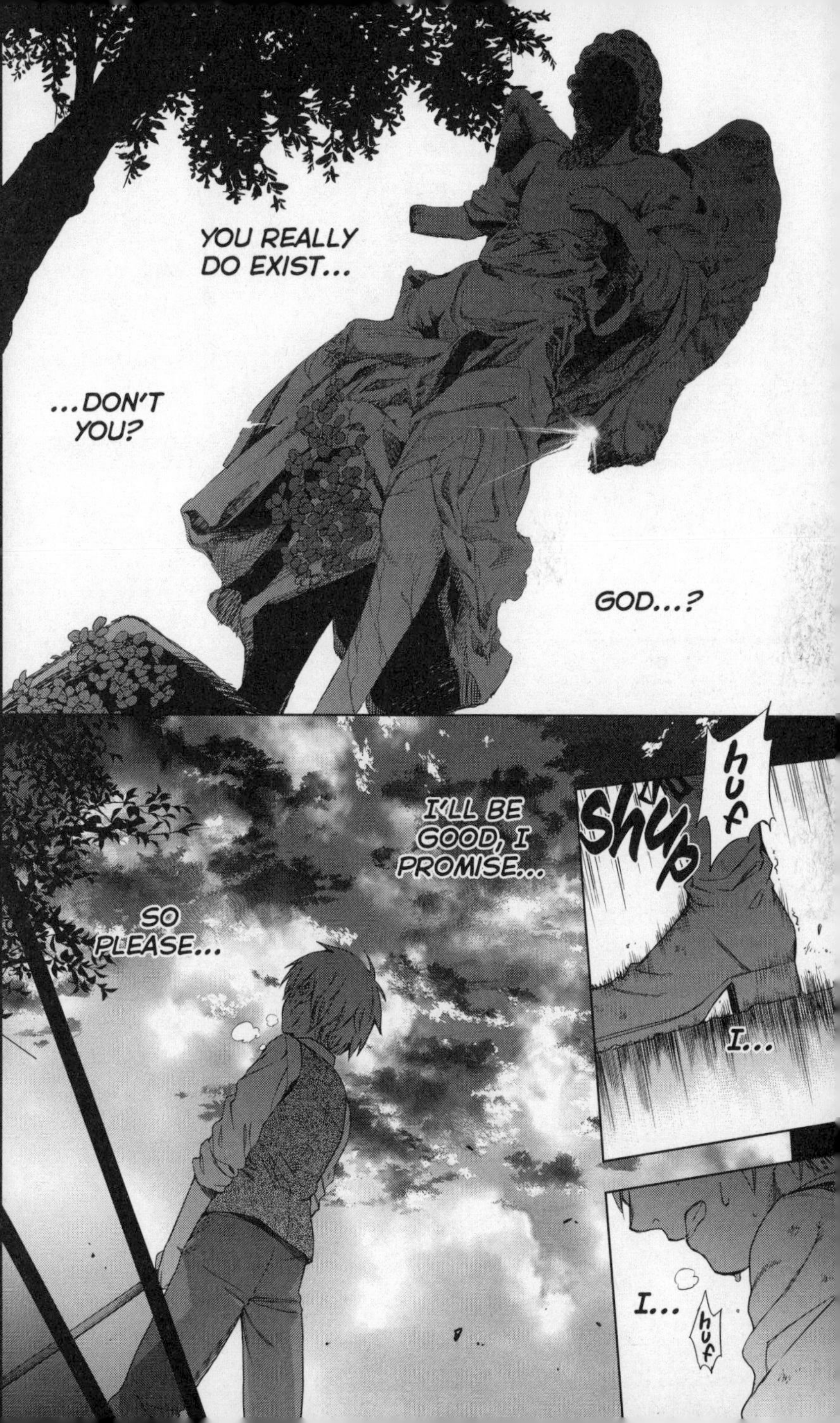
YOU REALLY DO EXIST...
...DON'T YOU?
GOD...?
huf
SHUP
I...
I...
huf
I'LL BE GOOD, I PROMISE...
SO PLEASE...

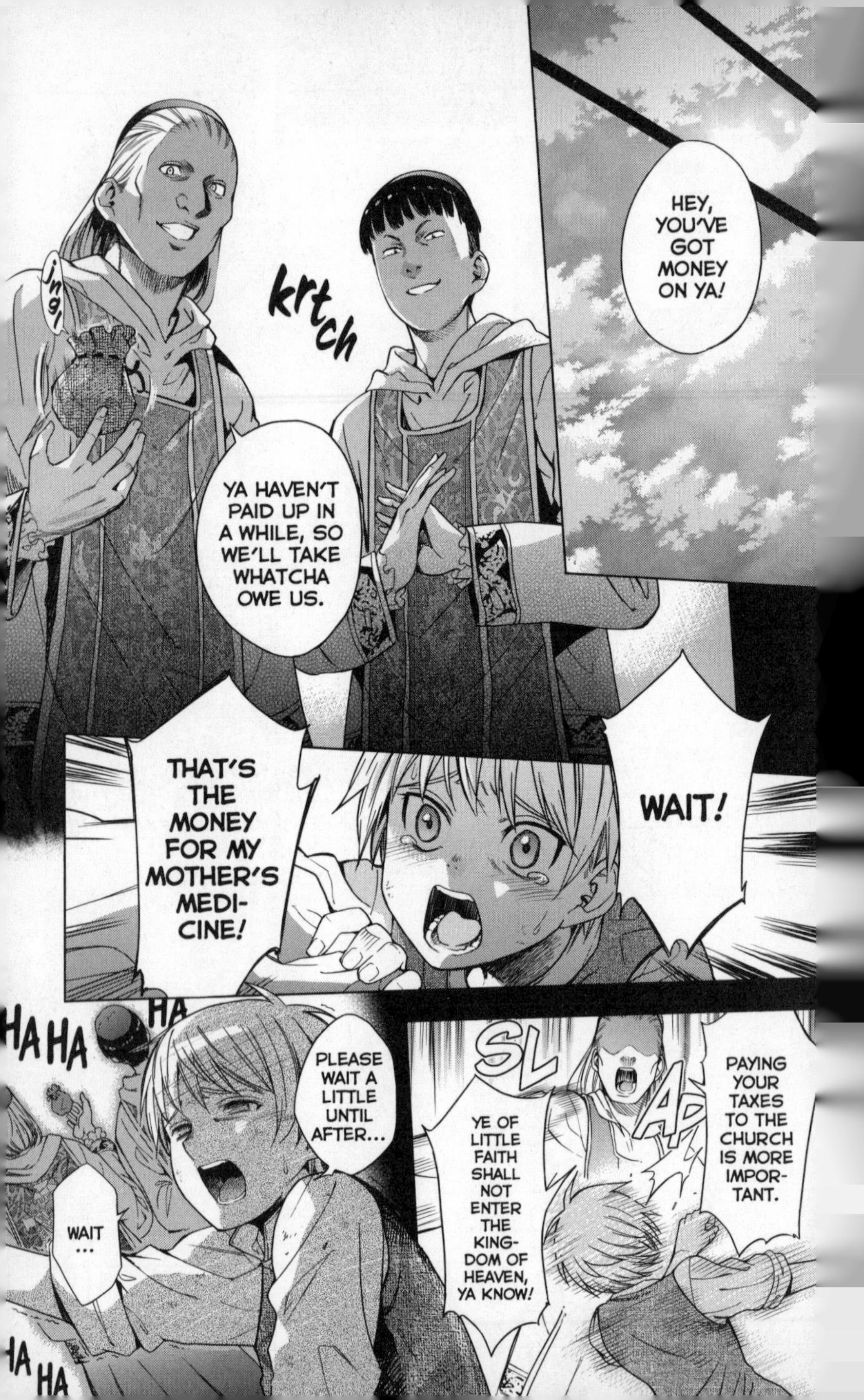

HEY, YOU'VE GOT MONEY ON YA!
krtch
jngl
YA HAVEN'T PAID UP IN A WHILE, SO WE'LL TAKE WHATCHA OWE US.
WAIT!
THAT'S THE MONEY FOR MY MOTHER'S MEDI-CINE!
SLAP
PAYING YOUR TAXES TO THE CHURCH IS MORE IMPOR-TANT.
YE OF LITTLE FAITH SHALL NOT ENTER THE KING-DOM OF HEAVEN, YA KNOW!
HA HA HA
PLEASE WAIT A LITTLE UNTIL AFTER...
WAIT ...
HA HA

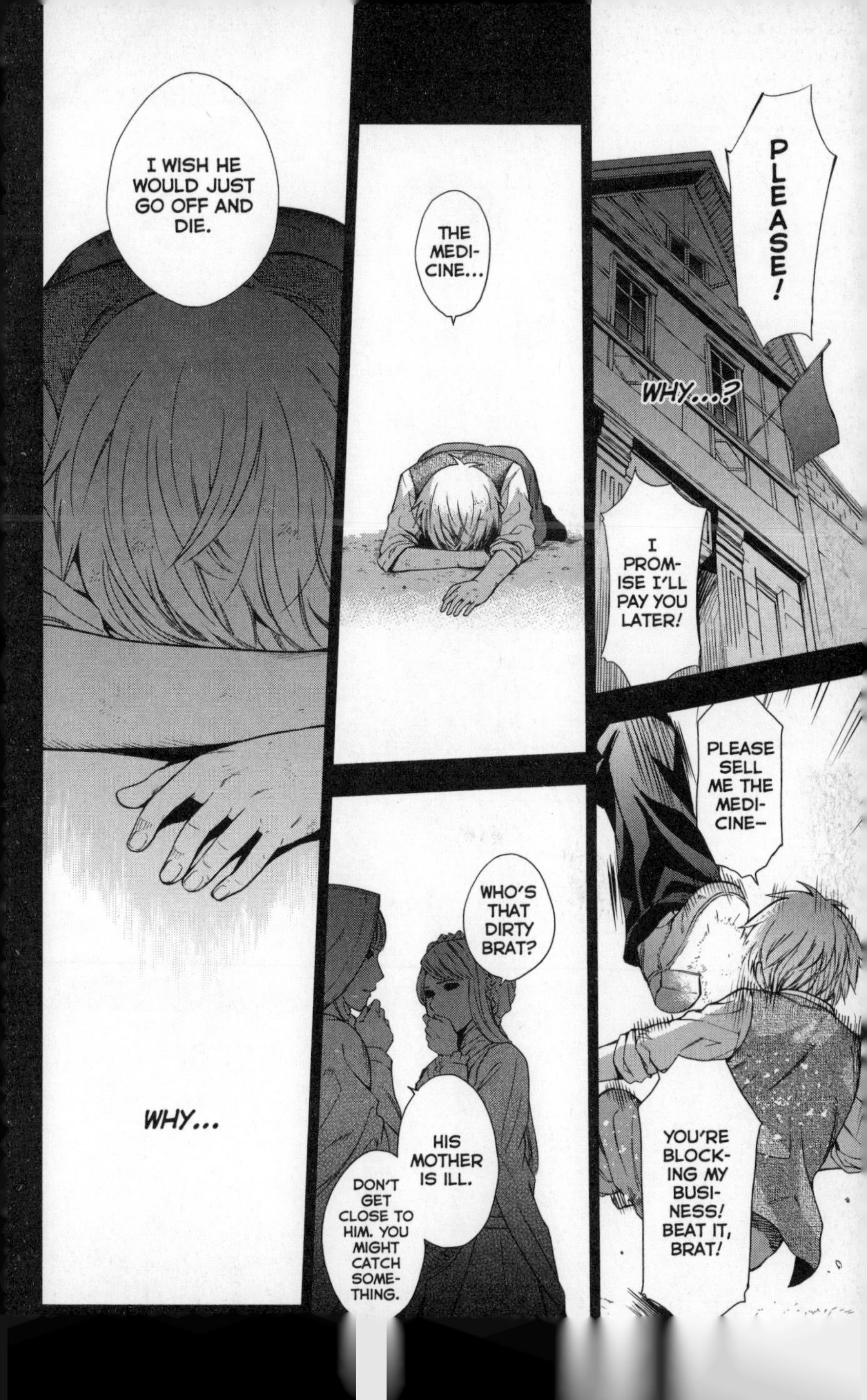
PLEASE!
WHY...?
I PROMISE I'LL PAY YOU LATER!
PLEASE SELL ME THE MEDICINE–
YOU'RE BLOCKING MY BUSINESS! BEAT IT, BRAT!
THE MEDICINE...
WHO'S THAT DIRTY BRAT?
HIS MOTHER IS ILL.
DON'T GET CLOSE TO HIM. YOU MIGHT CATCH SOMETHING.
I WISH HE WOULD JUST GO OFF AND DIE.
WHY...

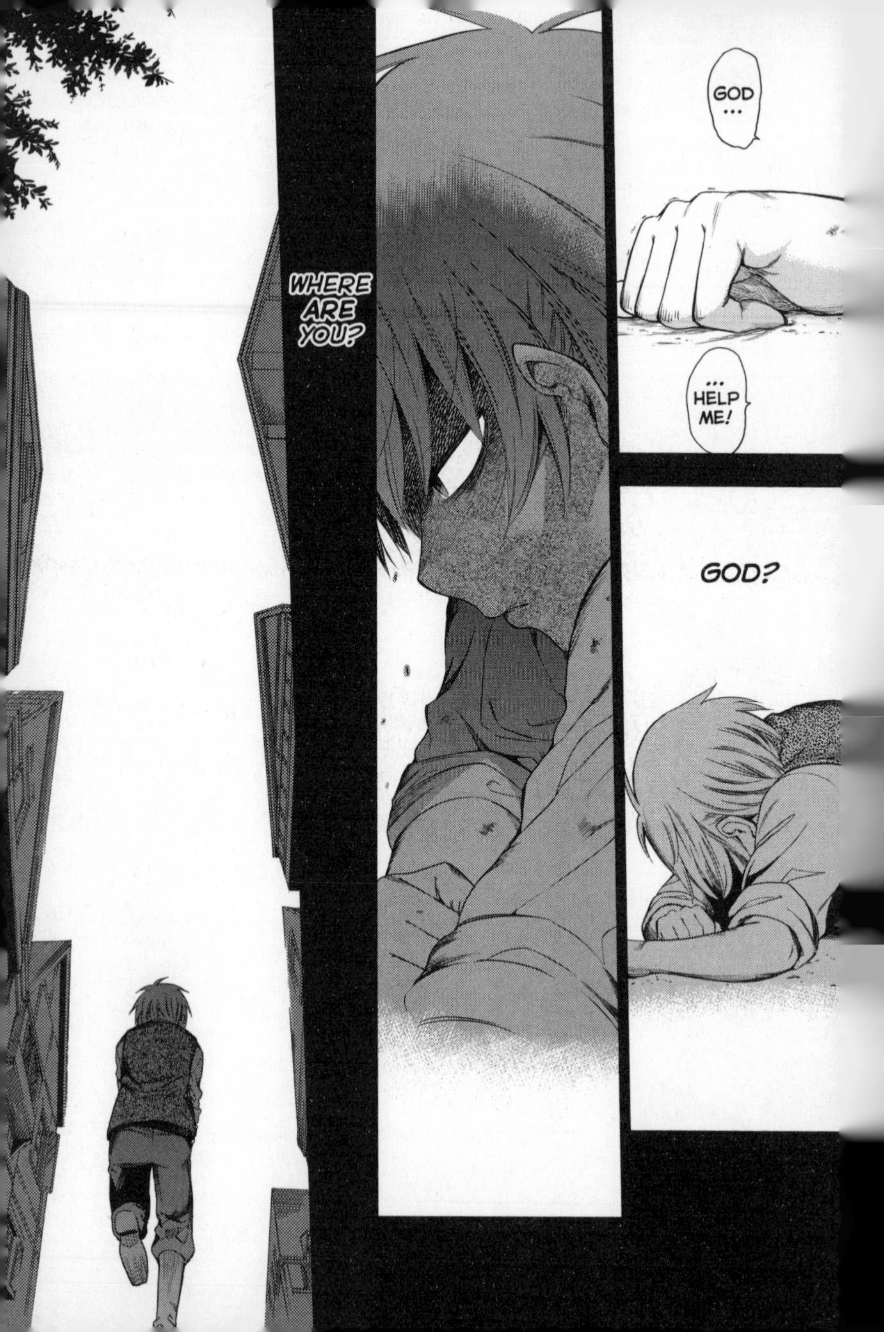
GOD ...
... HELP ME!
GOD?
WHERE ARE YOU?

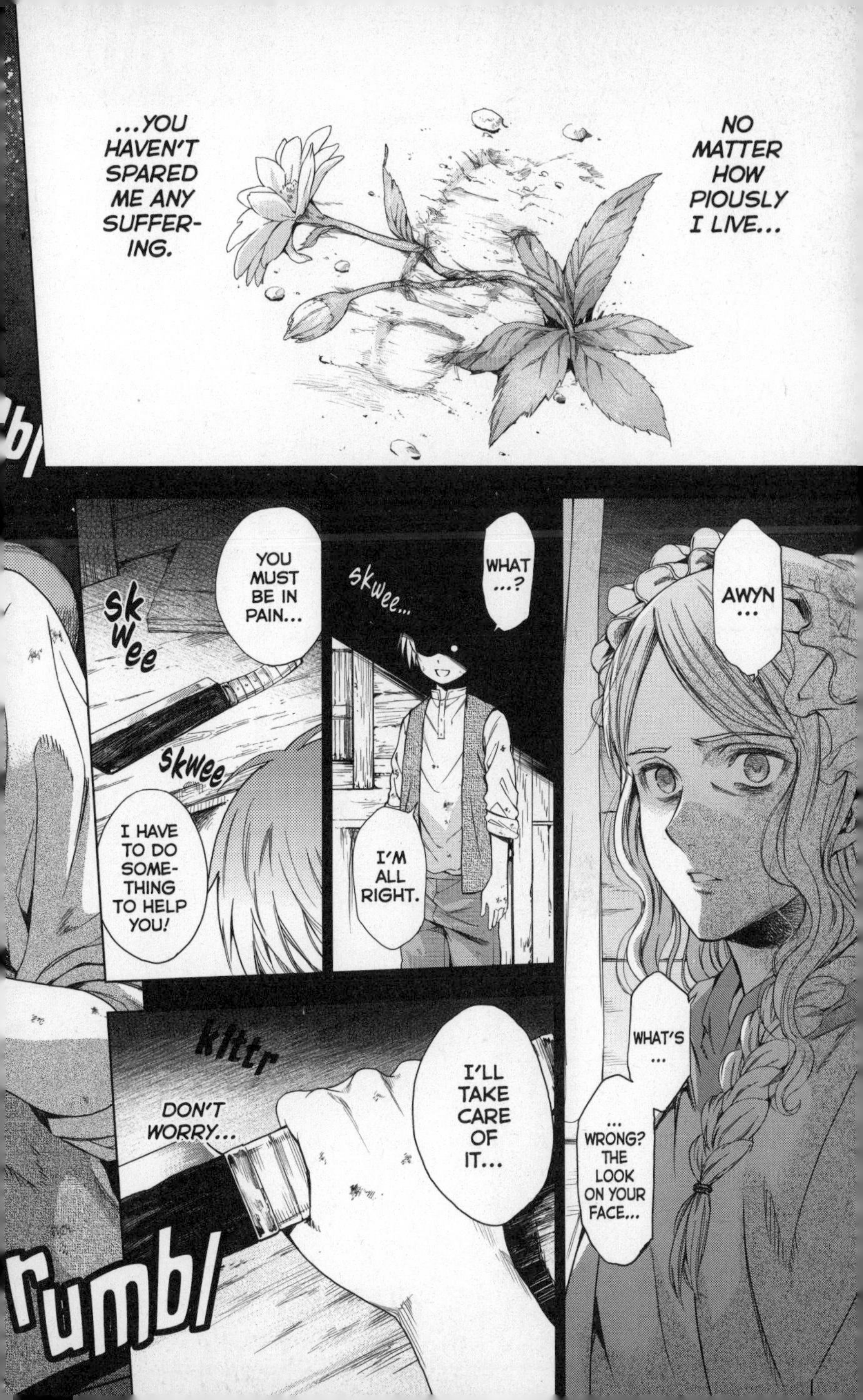
NO MATTER HOW PIOUSLY I LIVE...
...YOU HAVEN'T SPARED ME ANY SUFFER-ING.
AWYN...
WHAT'S...
...WRONG? THE LOOK ON YOUR FACE...
WHAT...?
skwee...
I'M ALL RIGHT.
YOU MUST BE IN PAIN...
skwee
skwee
I HAVE TO DO SOME-THING TO HELP YOU!
kittr
I'LL TAKE CARE OF IT...
DON'T WORRY...
rumbl

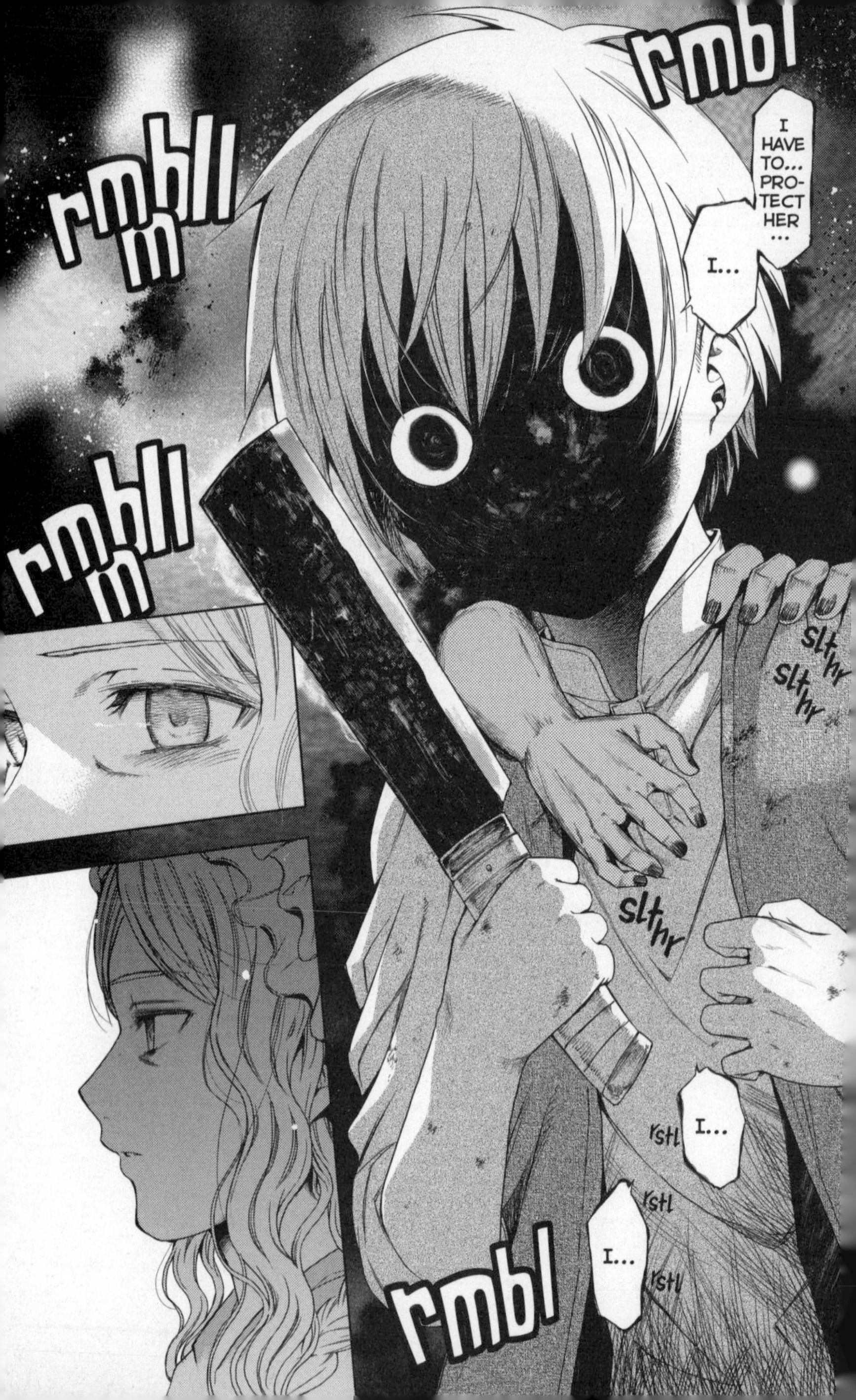
rmbl
I HAVE TO... PRO-TECT HER...
I...
rmbll m
rmbll m
sltpr
sltpr
sltpr
I...
rstl
rstl
I...
rstl
rmbl

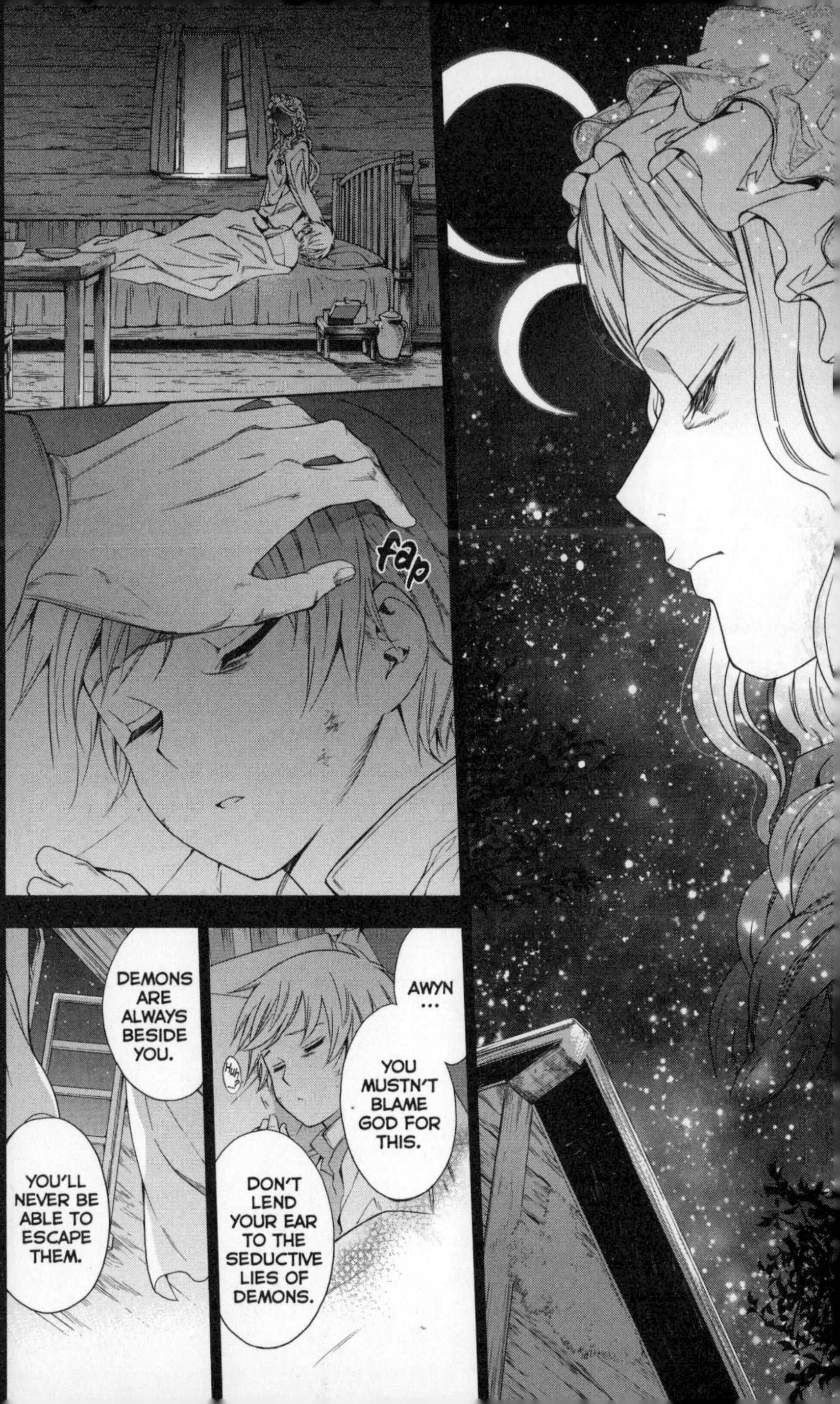
fap
AWYN...
YOU MUSTN'T BLAME GOD FOR THIS.
Huh...?
DON'T LEND YOUR EAR TO THE SEDUCTIVE LIES OF DEMONS.
DEMONS ARE ALWAYS BESIDE YOU.
YOU'LL NEVER BE ABLE TO ESCAPE THEM.

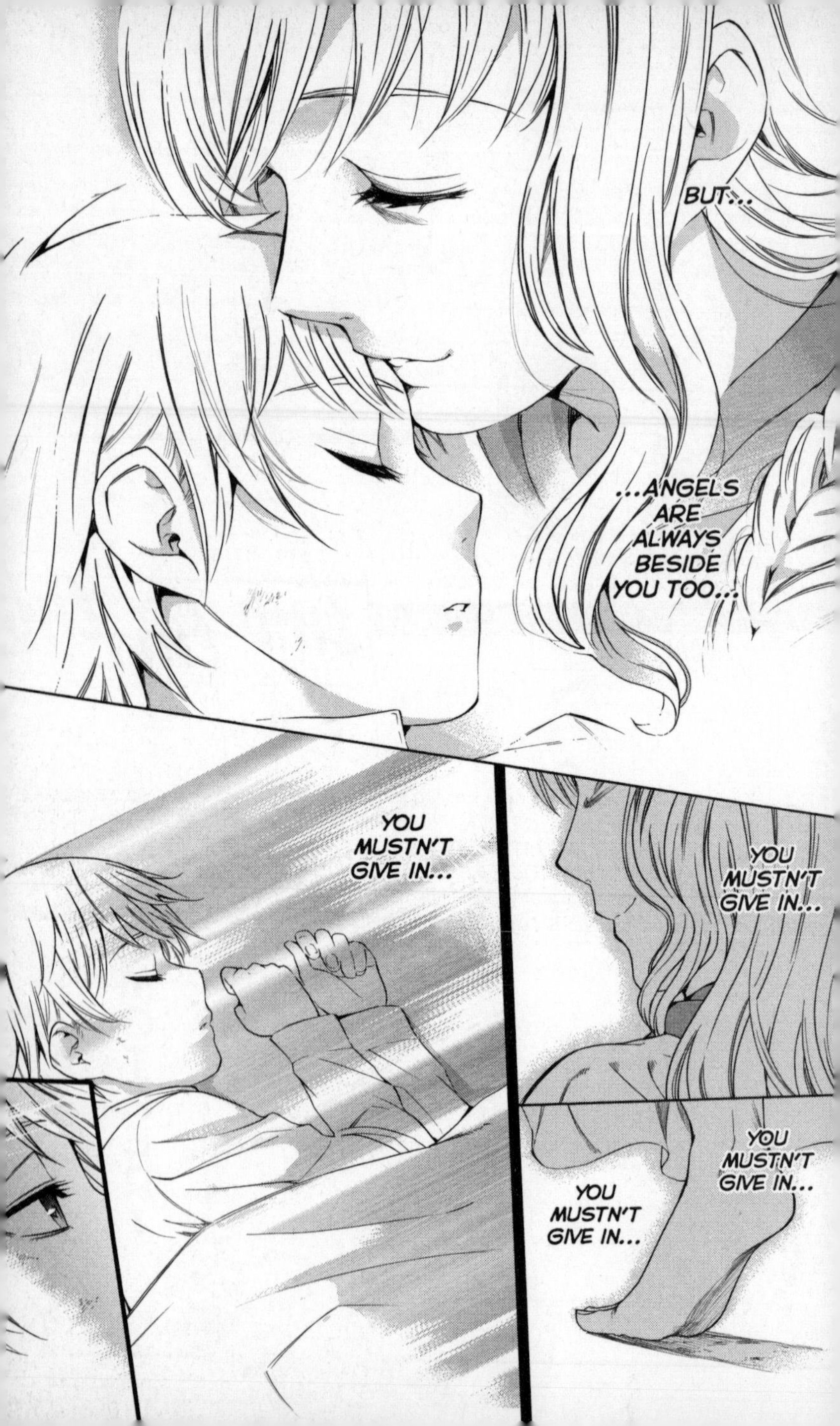
BUT...
...ANGELS ARE ALWAYS BESIDE YOU TOO...
YOU MUSTN'T GIVE IN...
YOU MUSTN'T GIVE IN...
YOU MUSTN'T GIVE IN...
YOU MUSTN'T GIVE IN...

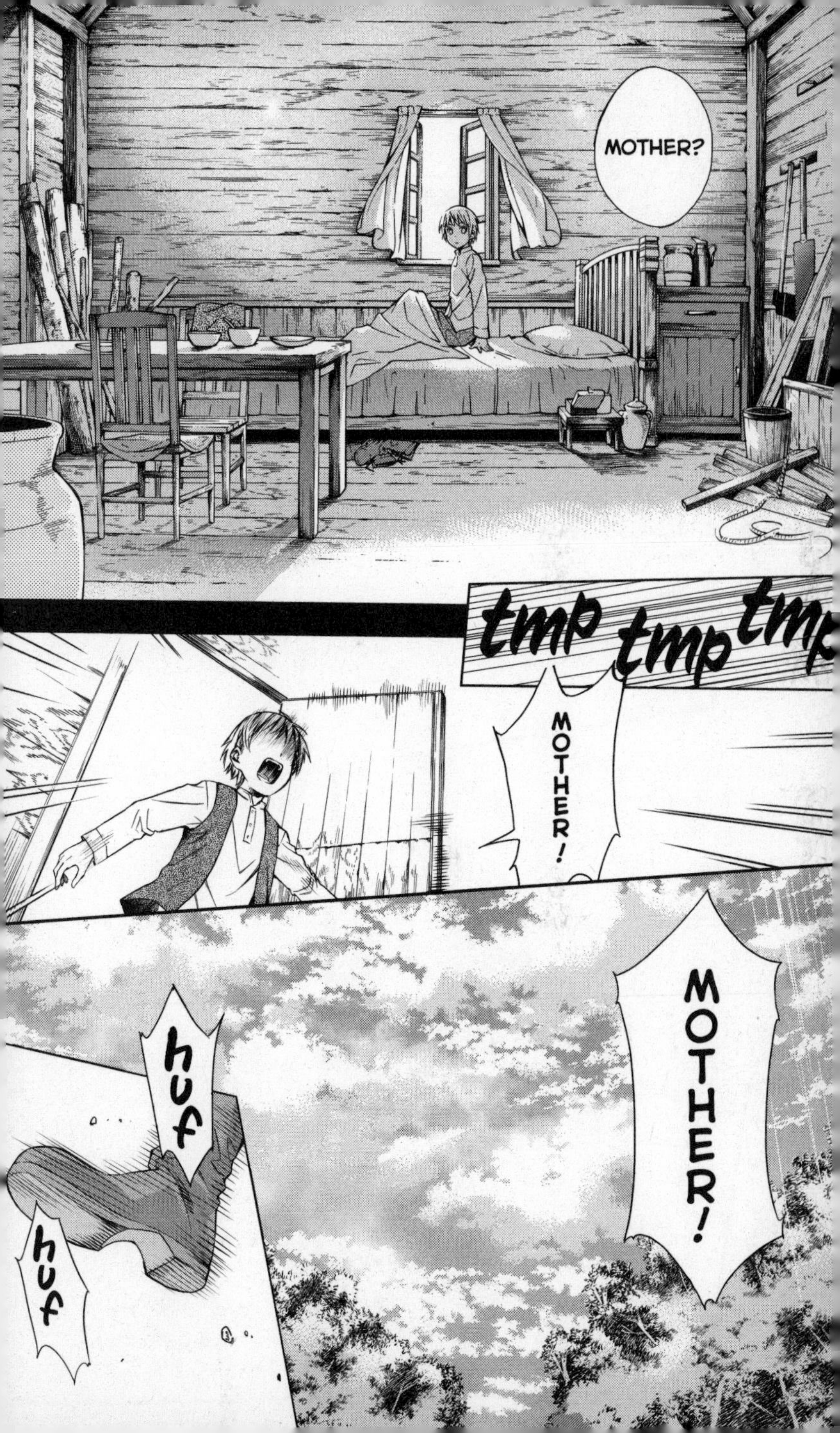
MOTHER?
tmp tmp tmp
MOTHER!
MOTHER!
huf
huf

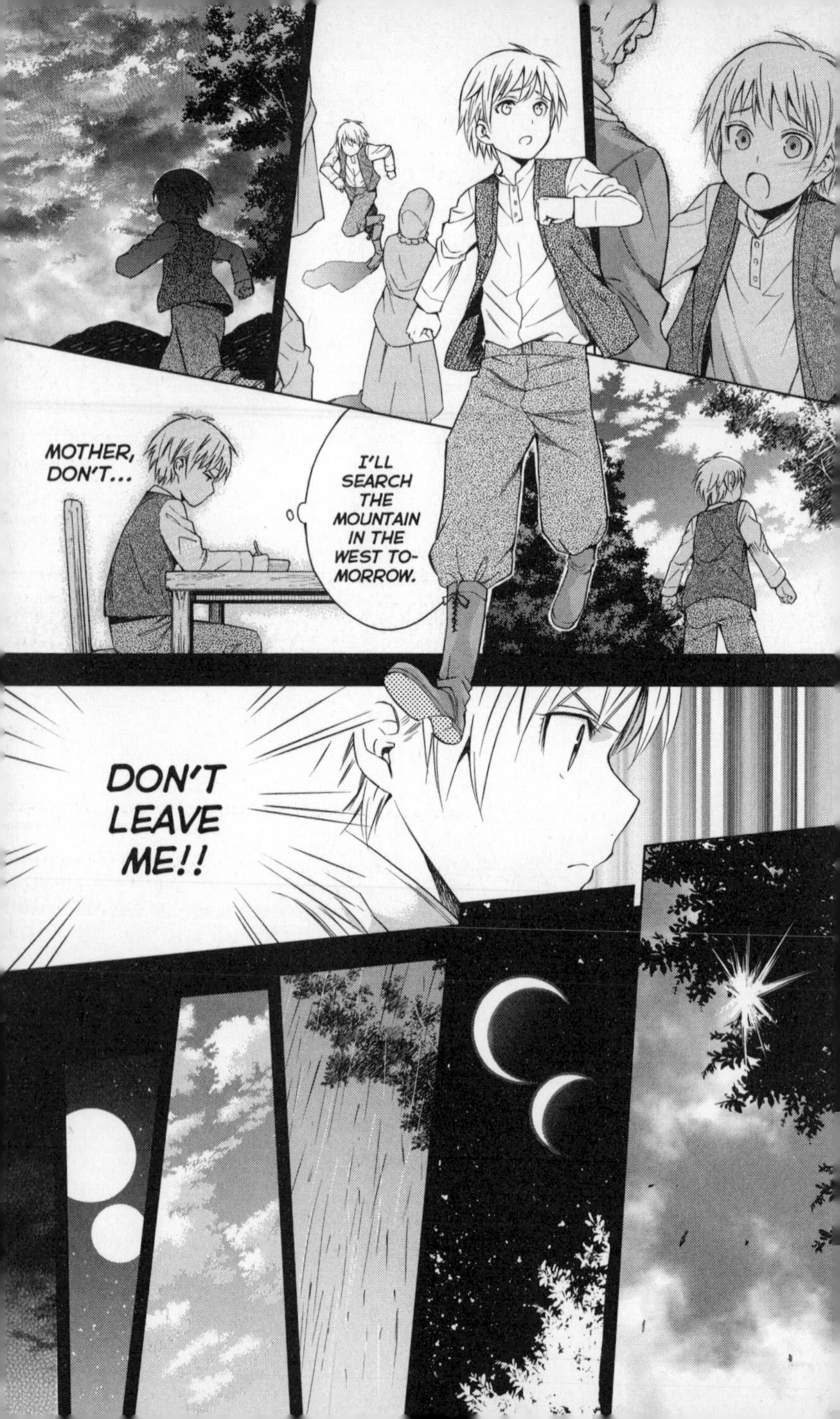
I'LL SEARCH THE MOUNTAIN IN THE WEST TO-MORROW.
MOTHER, DON'T...
DON'T LEAVE ME!!

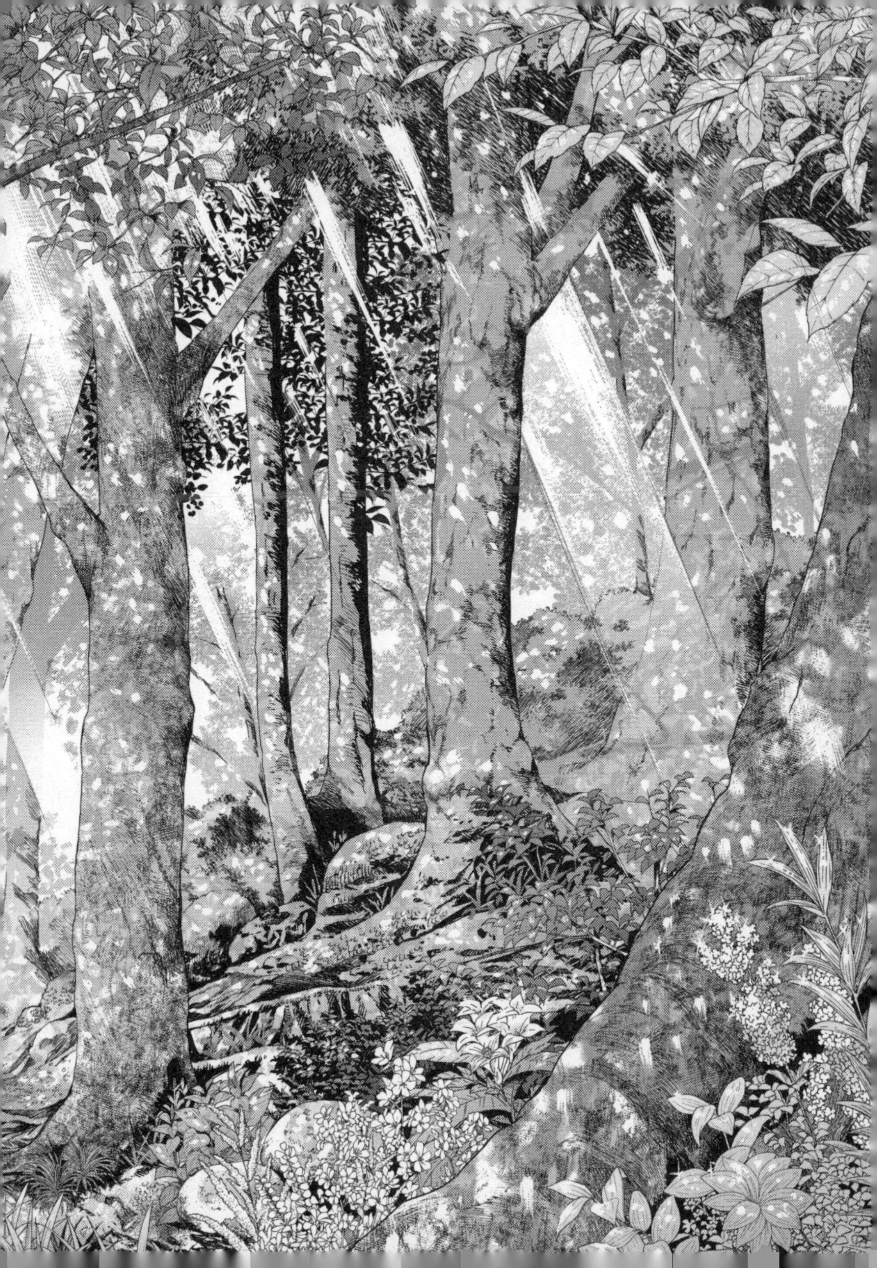

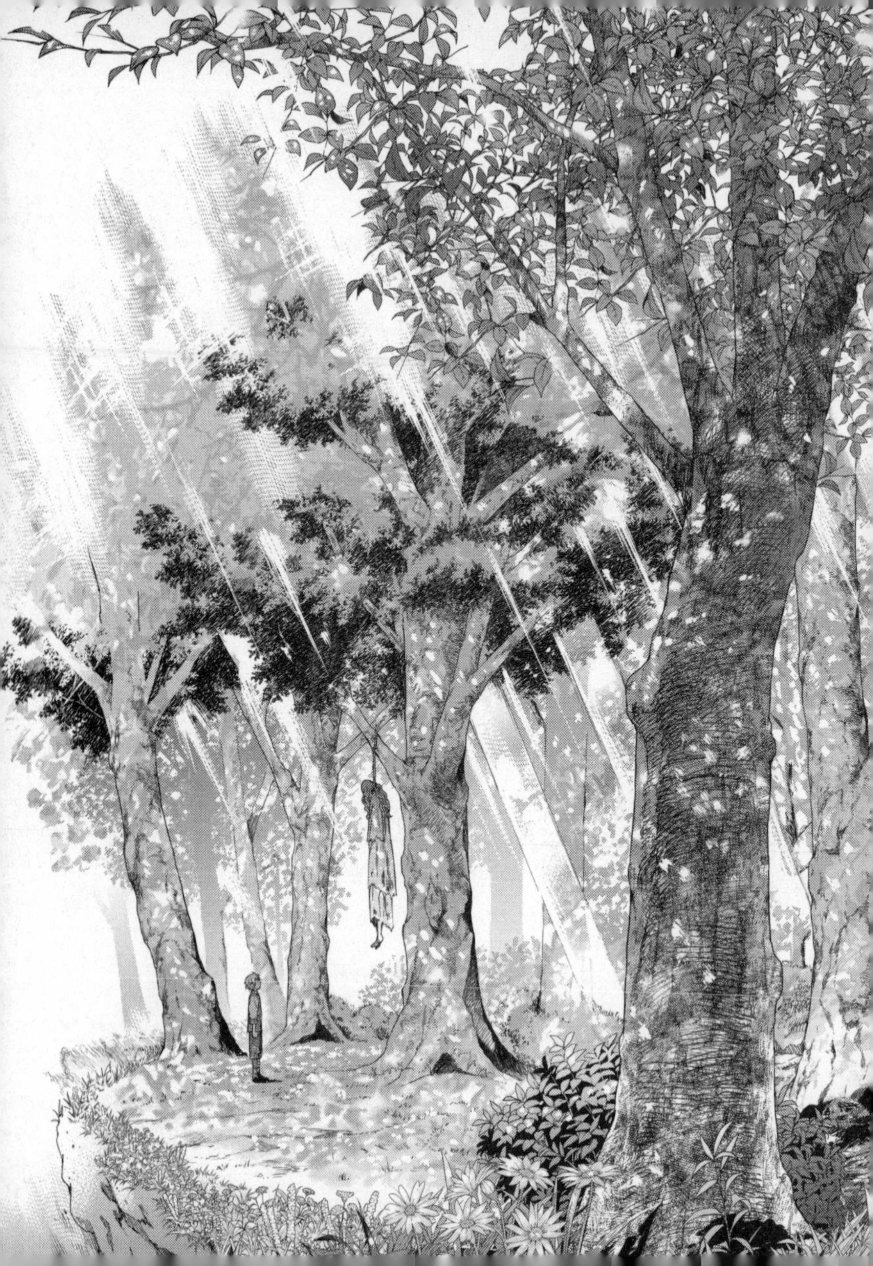

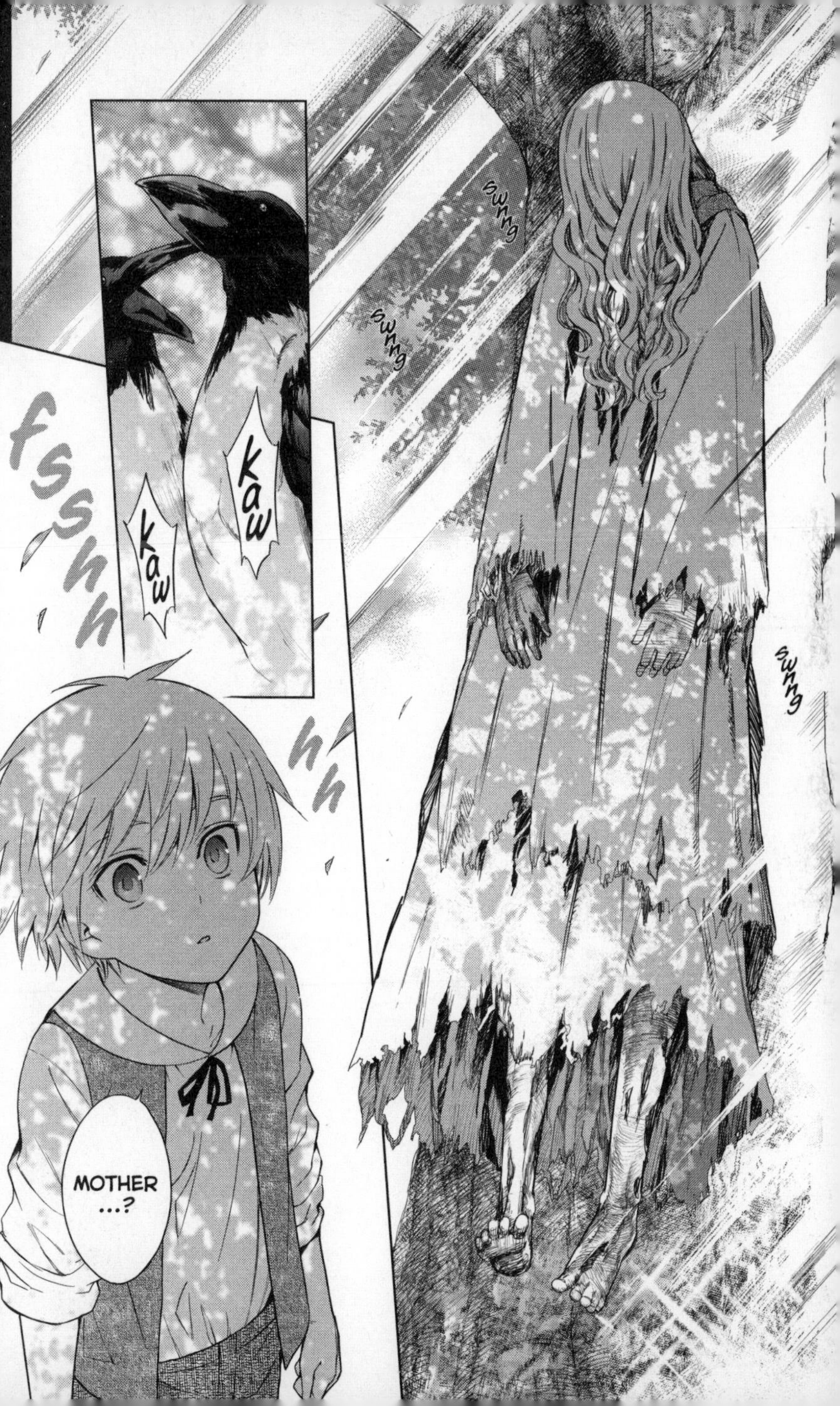
swnng
swnng
swnng
kaw
kaw
fsshhh
hhh
MOTHER ...?

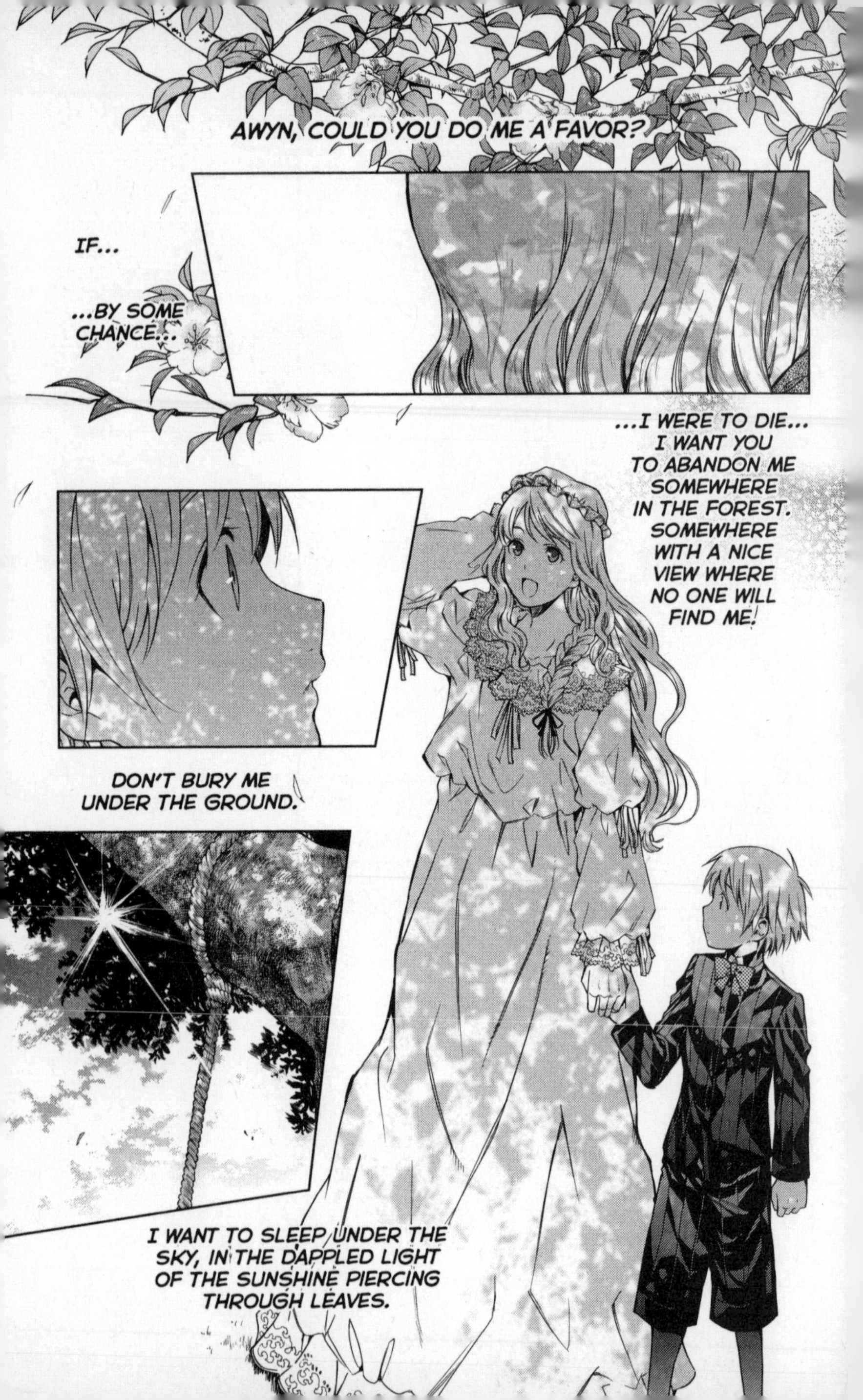
AWYN, COULD YOU DO ME A FAVOR?
IF...
...BY SOME CHANCE...
...I WERE TO DIE... I WANT YOU TO ABANDON ME SOMEWHERE IN THE FOREST. SOMEWHERE WITH A NICE VIEW WHERE NO ONE WILL FIND ME.
DON'T BURY ME UNDER THE GROUND.
I WANT TO SLEEP UNDER THE SKY, IN THE DAPPLED LIGHT OF THE SUNSHINE PIERCING THROUGH LEAVES.

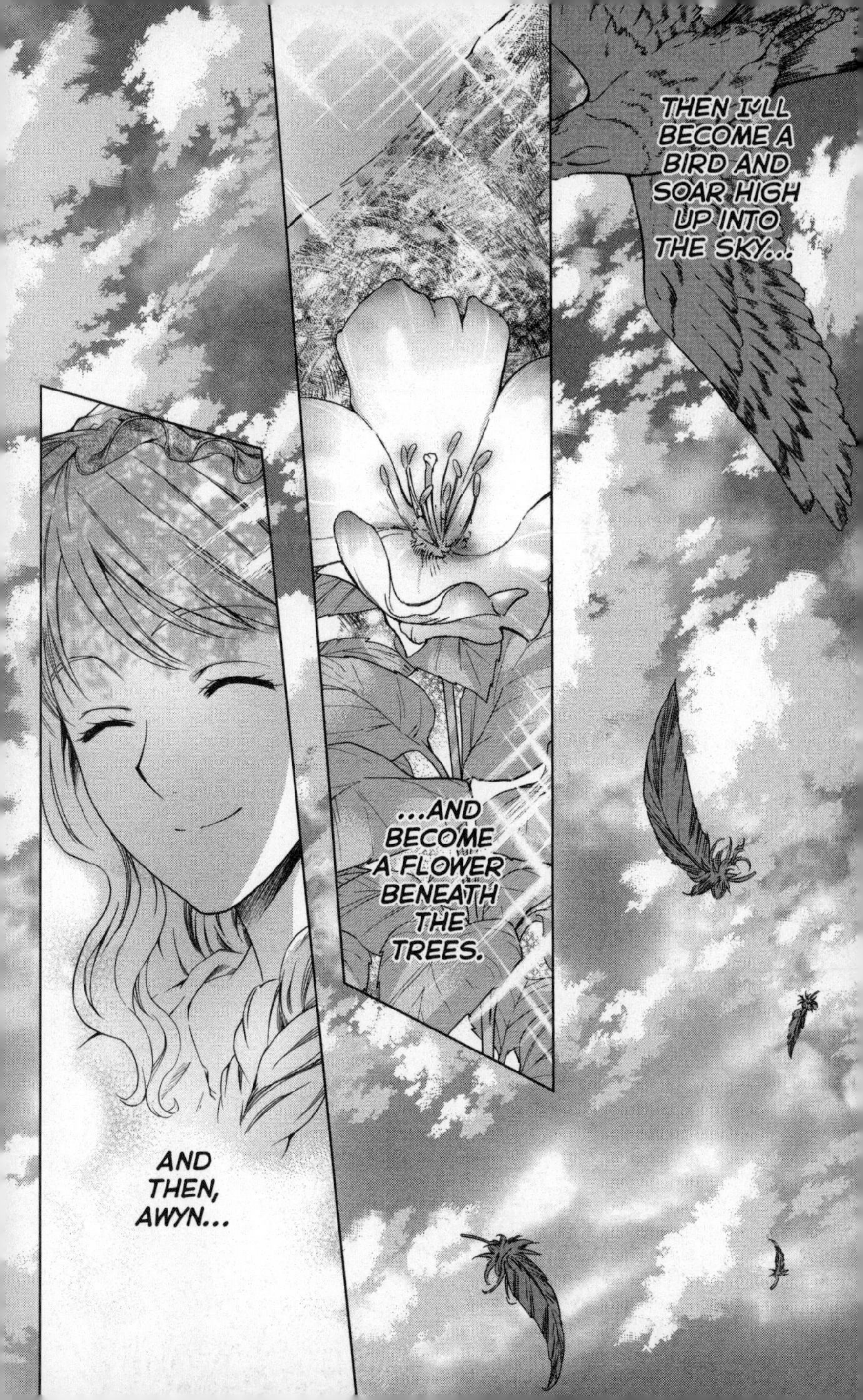
THEN I'LL BECOME A BIRD AND SOAR HIGH UP INTO THE SKY...
...AND BECOME A FLOWER BENEATH THE TREES.
AND THEN, AWYN...

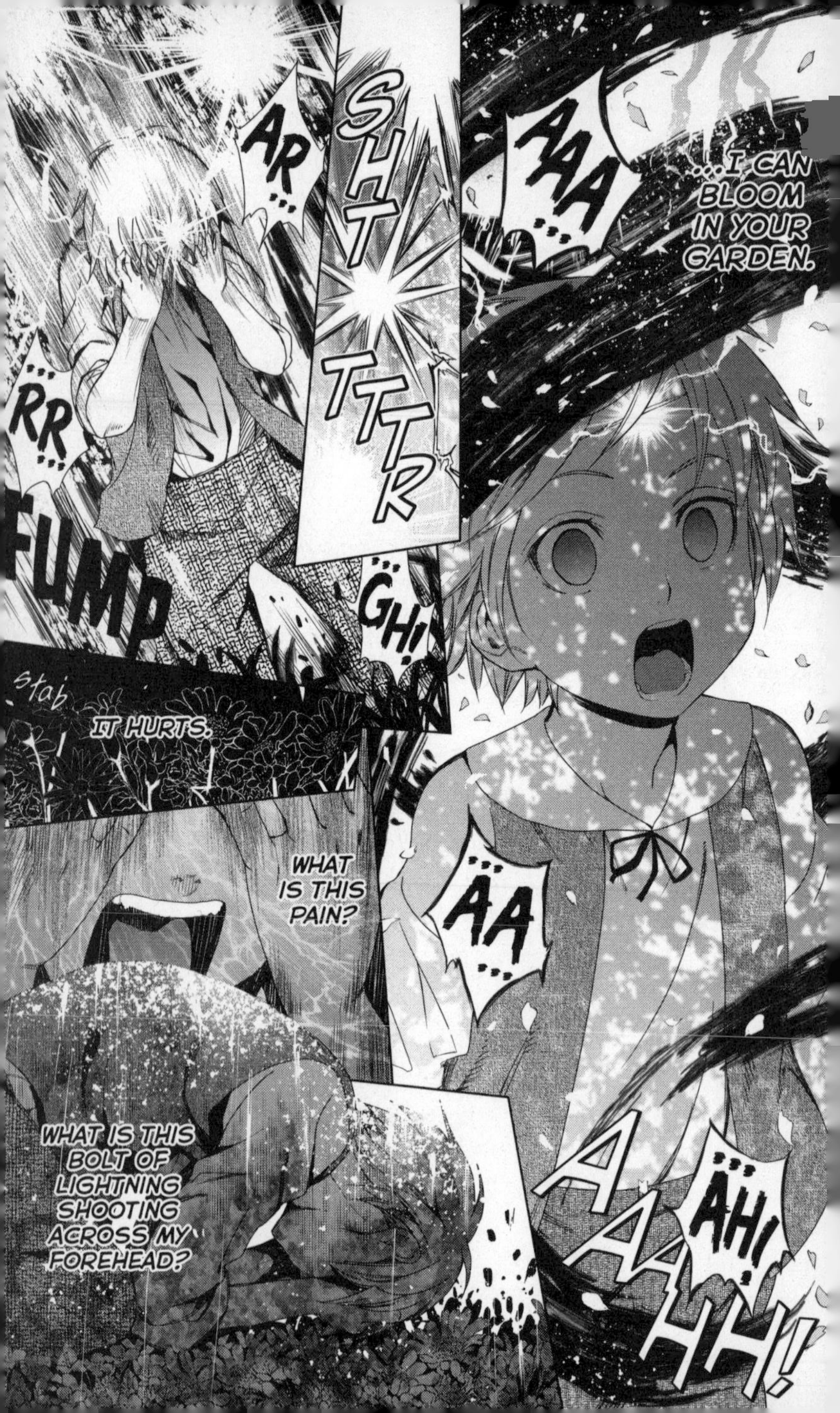
...I CAN BLOOM IN YOUR GARDEN.
AAA...
AA...
AAAAHH!
...AHI!
SHTTTTR
...AR...
...RR...
FUMP
...GHI!
stab
IT HURTS.
WHAT IS THIS PAIN?
WHAT IS THIS BOLT OF LIGHTNING SHOOTING ACROSS MY FOREHEAD?

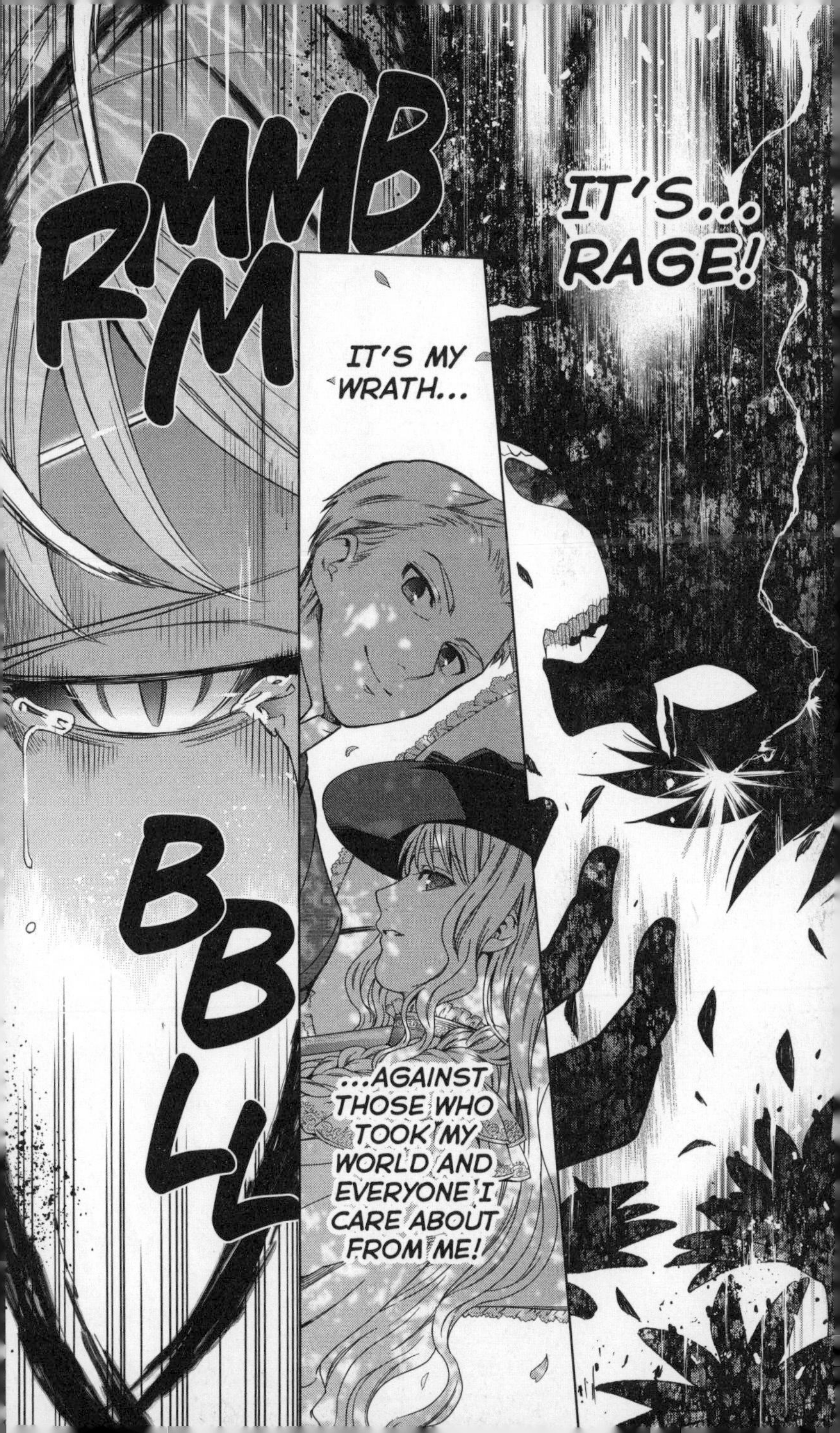
IT'S... RAGE!
IT'S MY WRATH...
...AGAINST THOSE WHO TOOK MY WORLD AND EVERYONE I CARE ABOUT FROM ME!
RMMBM
BBLL

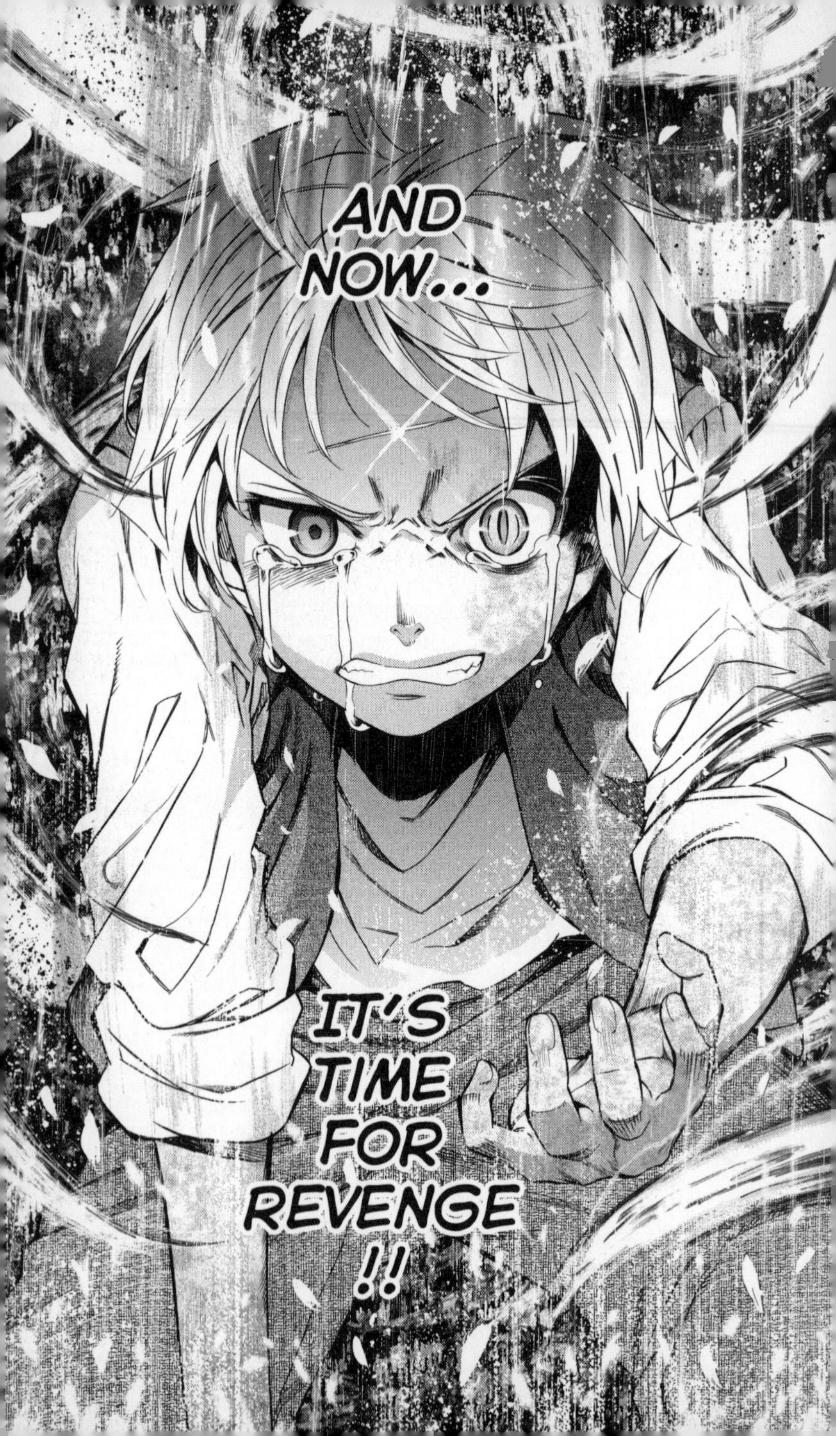
AND NOW...
IT'S TIME FOR REVENGE!!

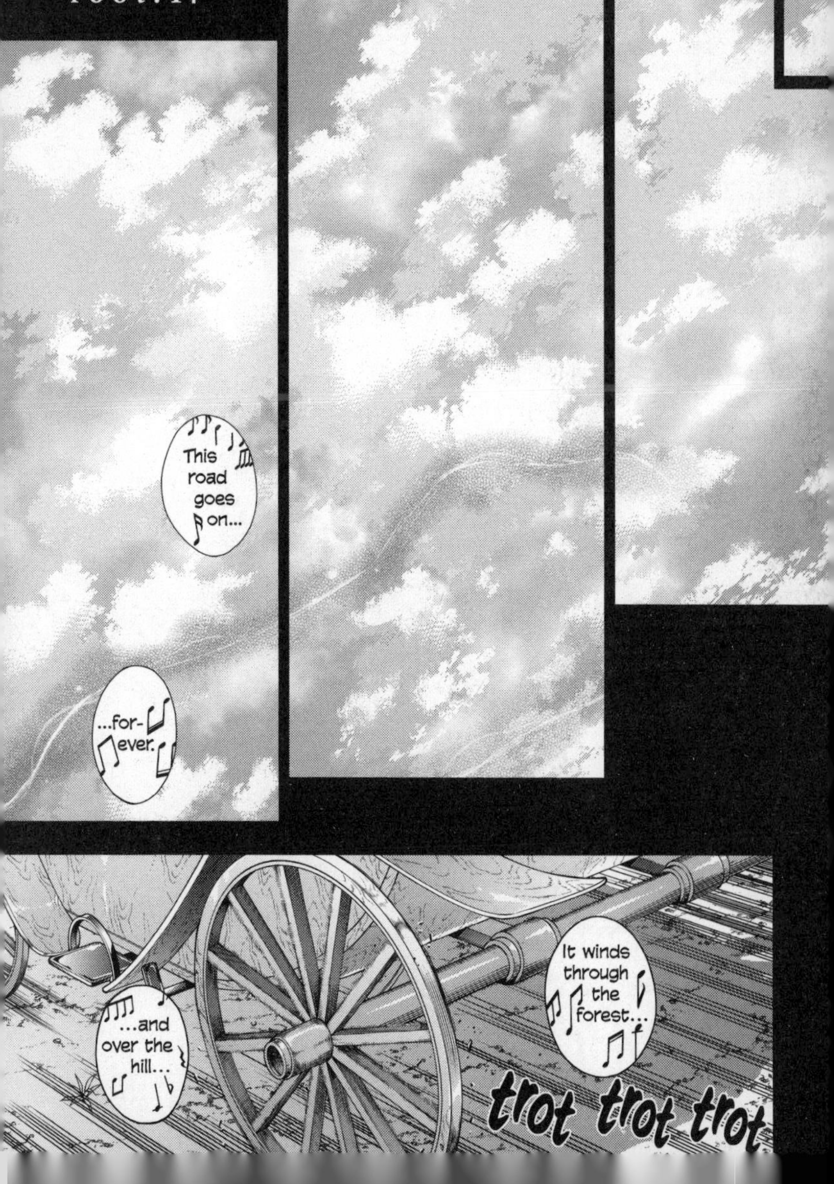
This road goes on...
...for-ever.
It winds through the forest...
...and over the hill...
trot trot trot

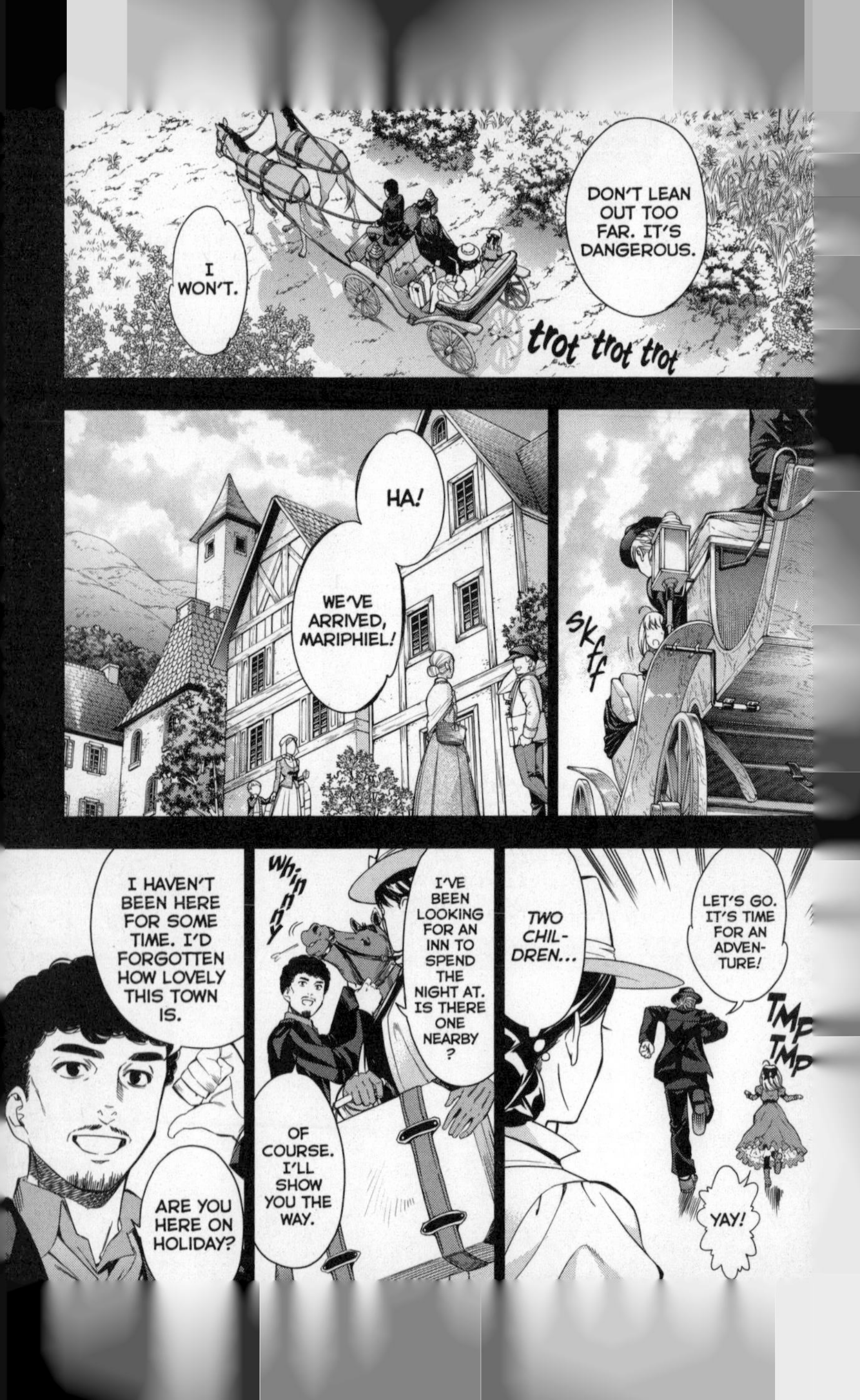
DON'T LEAN OUT TOO FAR. IT'S DANGEROUS.
I WON'T.
trot trot trot
SKFF
HA!
WE'VE ARRIVED, MARIPHIEL!
LET'S GO. IT'S TIME FOR AN ADVENTURE!
TWO CHILDREN...
TMP TMP
YAY!
I'VE BEEN LOOKING FOR AN INN TO SPEND THE NIGHT AT. IS THERE ONE NEARBY?
WHINNY
OF COURSE. I'LL SHOW YOU THE WAY.
I HAVEN'T BEEN HERE FOR SOME TIME. I'D FORGOTTEN HOW LOVELY THIS TOWN IS.
ARE YOU HERE ON HOLIDAY?

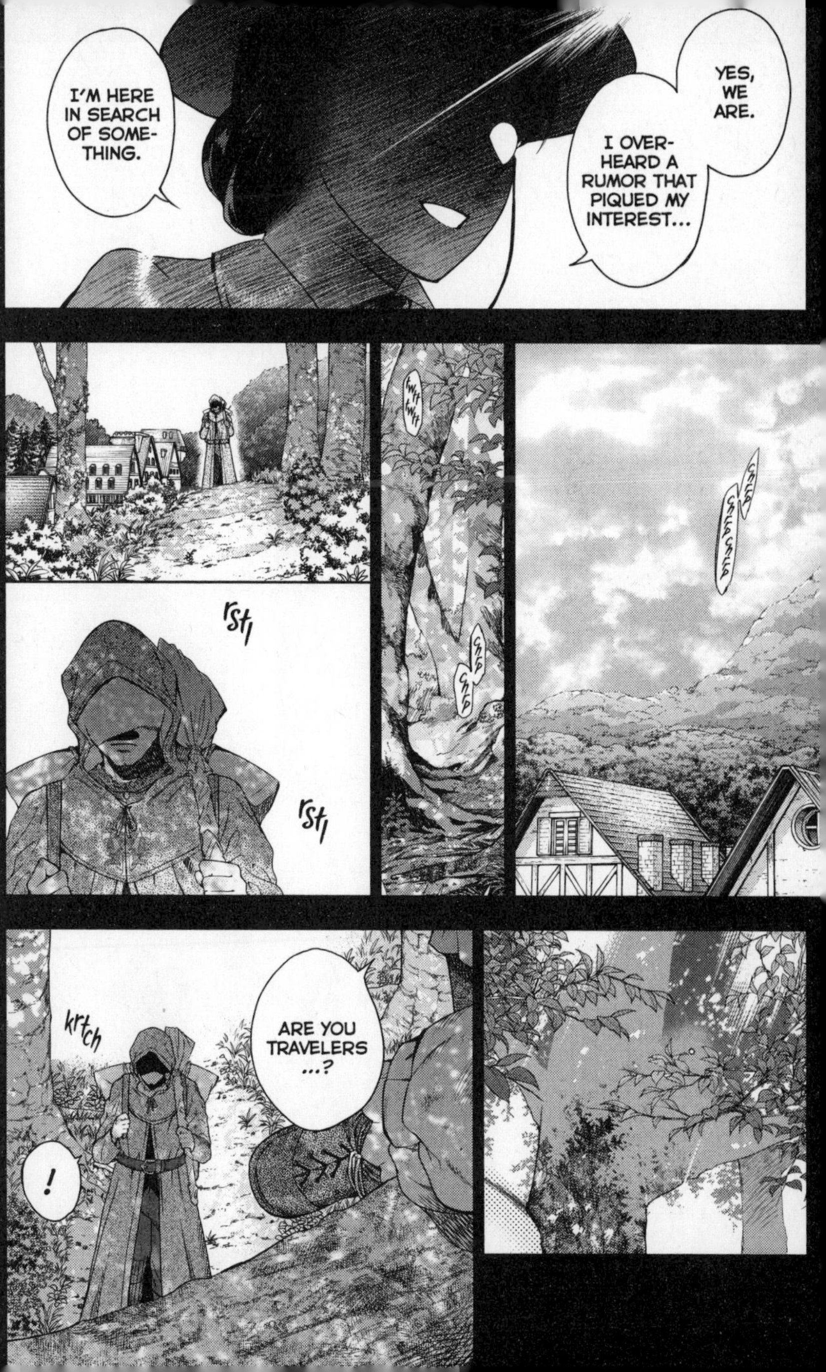
YES, WE ARE.
I OVER-HEARD A RUMOR THAT PIQUED MY INTEREST...
I'M HERE IN SEARCH OF SOME-THING.
rstl
rstl
ARE YOU TRAVELERS ...?
krtch
!

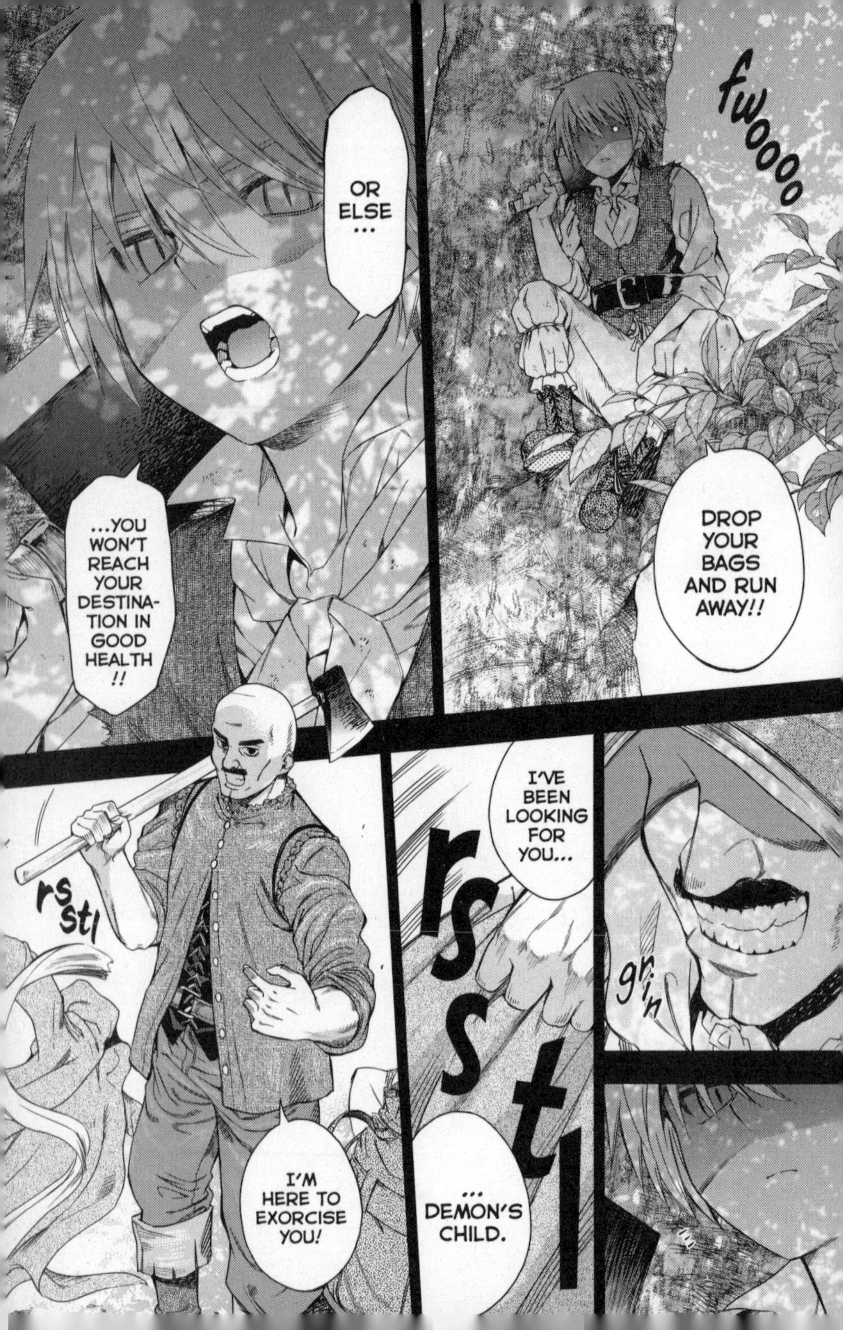
fwoooo
DROP YOUR BAGS AND RUN AWAY!!
OR ELSE...
...YOU WON'T REACH YOUR DESTINATION IN GOOD HEALTH!!
grin
I'VE BEEN LOOKING FOR YOU...
rsstl
...DEMON'S CHILD.
rsstl
I'M HERE TO EXORCISE YOU!

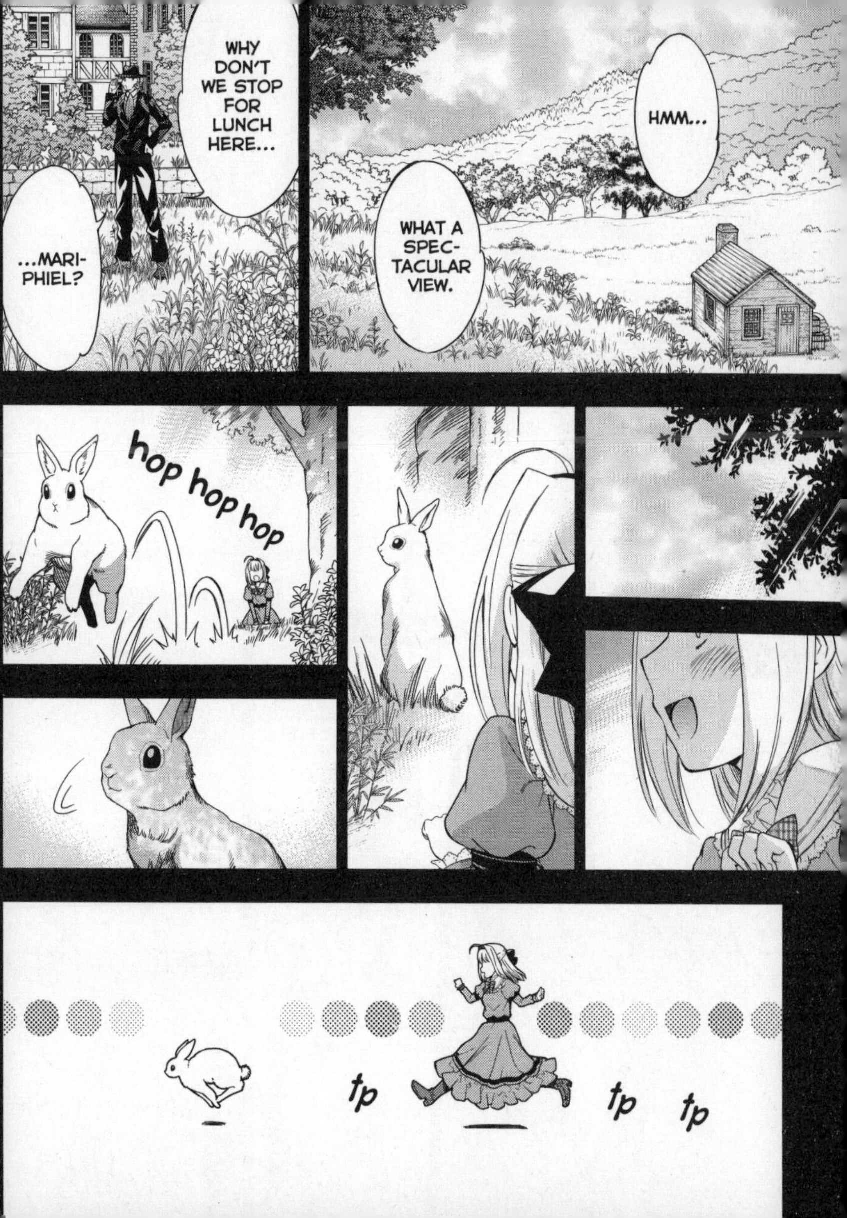
HMM...
WHAT A SPECTACULAR VIEW.
WHY DON'T WE STOP FOR LUNCH HERE...
...MARIPHIEL?
hop hop hop
tp tp
tp

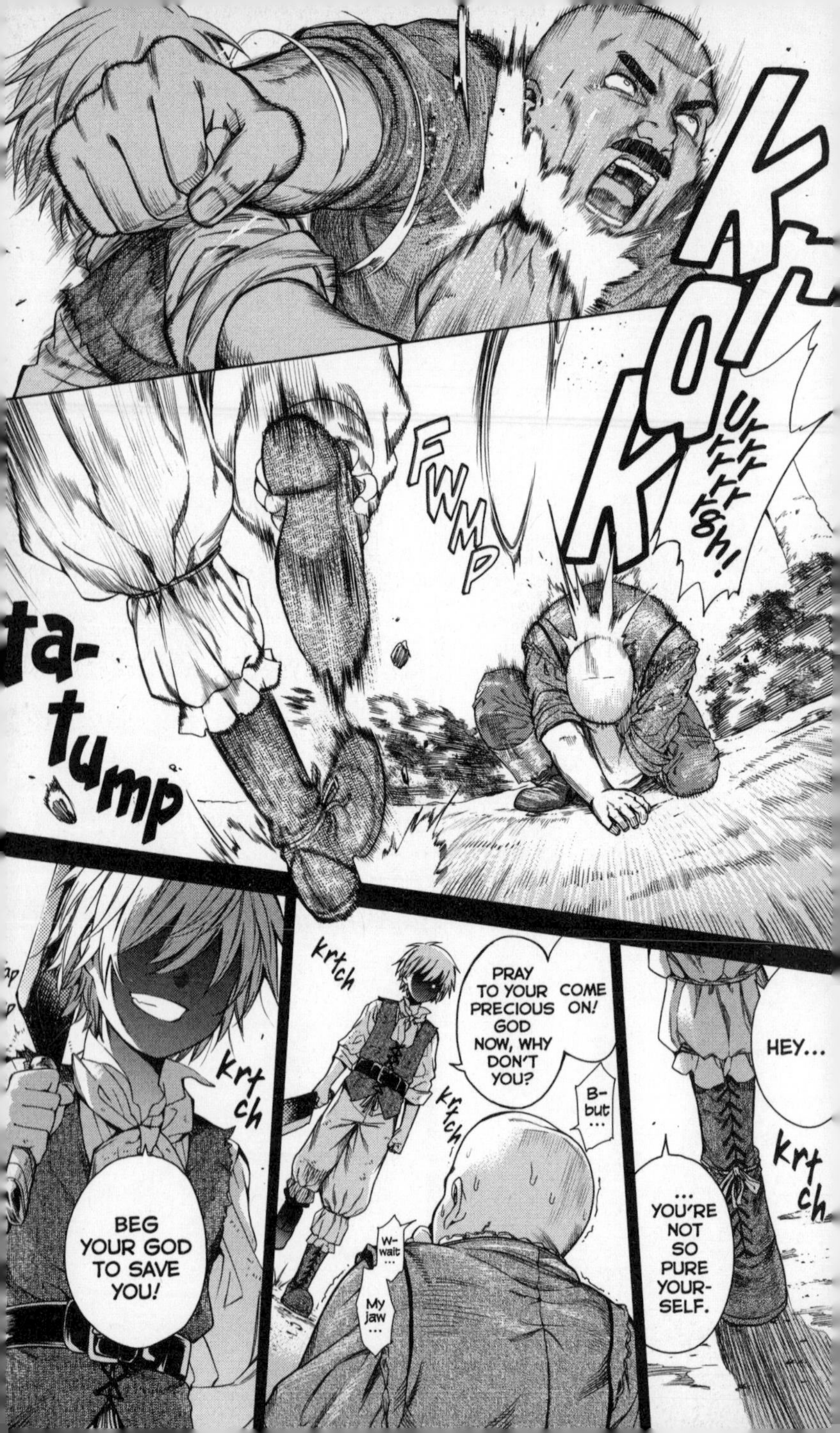
Urrrrrrrgh!
FWMP
ta-tump
HEY...
krtch
...YOU'RE NOT SO PURE YOURSELF.
krtch
PRAY TO YOUR PRECIOUS GOD NOW, WHY DON'T YOU?
COME ON!
B-but...
krtch
W-wait...
My jaw...
krtch
BEG YOUR GOD TO SAVE YOU!

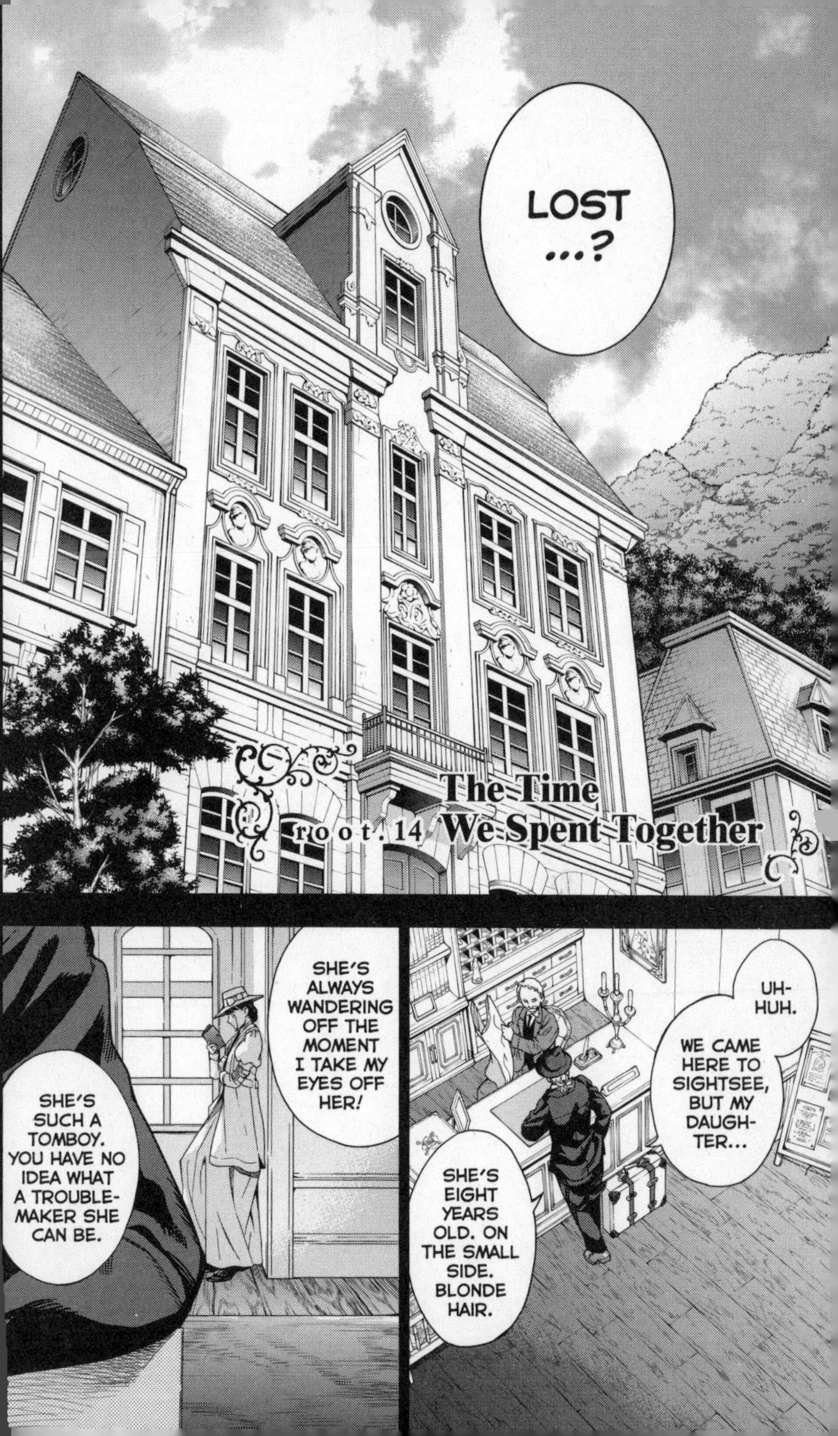
LOST ...?
root.14 The Time We Spent Together
UH-HUH.
WE CAME HERE TO SIGHTSEE, BUT MY DAUGHTER...
SHE'S EIGHT YEARS OLD. ON THE SMALL SIDE. BLONDE HAIR.
SHE'S ALWAYS WANDERING OFF THE MOMENT I TAKE MY EYES OFF HER!
SHE'S SUCH A TOMBOY. YOU HAVE NO IDEA WHAT A TROUBLE-MAKER SHE CAN BE.

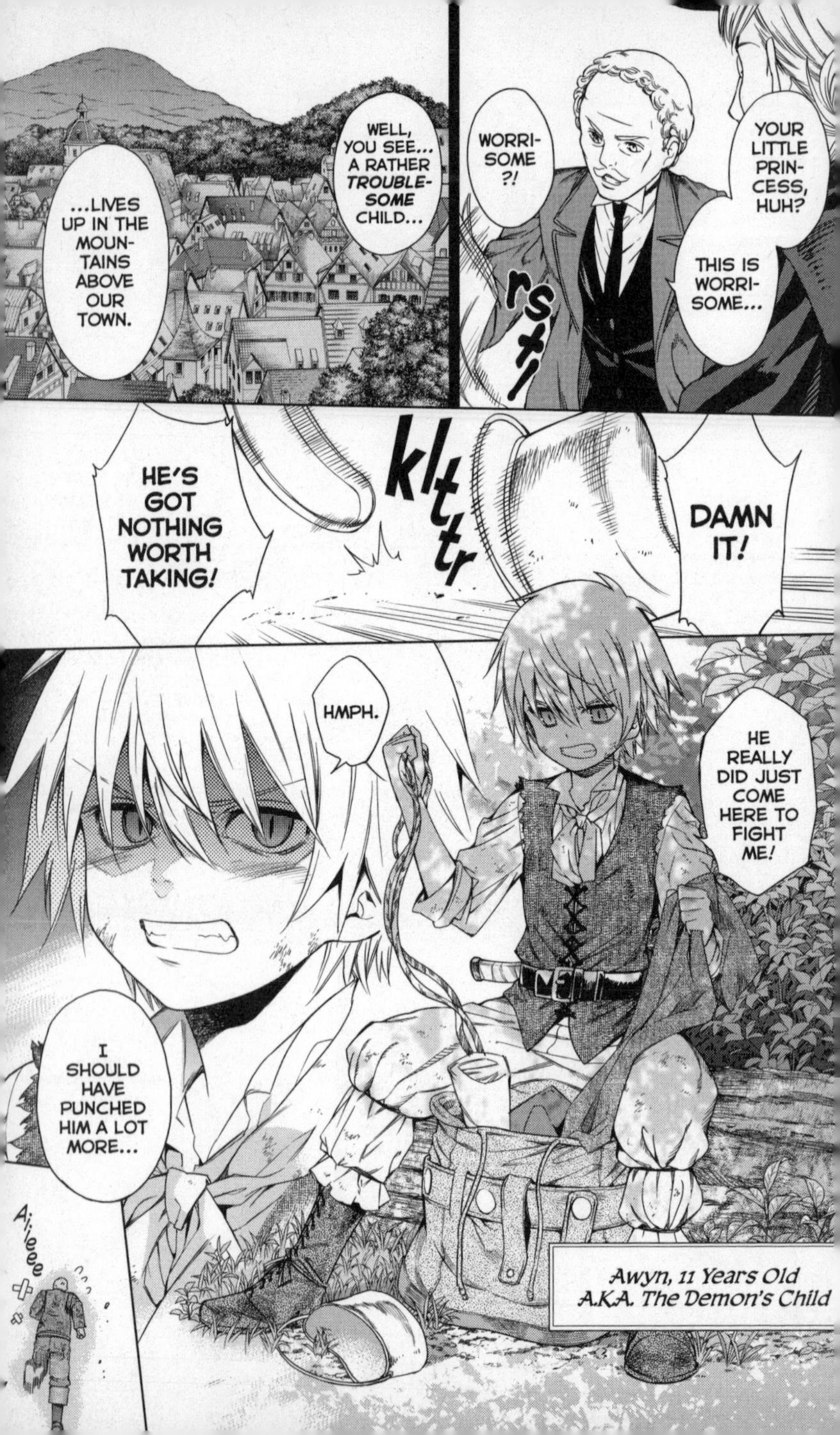
YOUR LITTLE PRINCESS, HUH?
THIS IS WORRISOME...
rstl
WORRISOME?!
WELL, YOU SEE... A RATHER *TROUBLESOME* CHILD...
...LIVES UP IN THE MOUNTAINS ABOVE OUR TOWN.
DAMN IT!
klttr
HE'S GOT NOTHING WORTH TAKING!
HE REALLY DID JUST COME HERE TO FIGHT ME!
HMPH.
I SHOULD HAVE PUNCHED HIM A LOT MORE...
Awyn, 11 Years Old
A.K.A. The Demon's Child
Aiieee

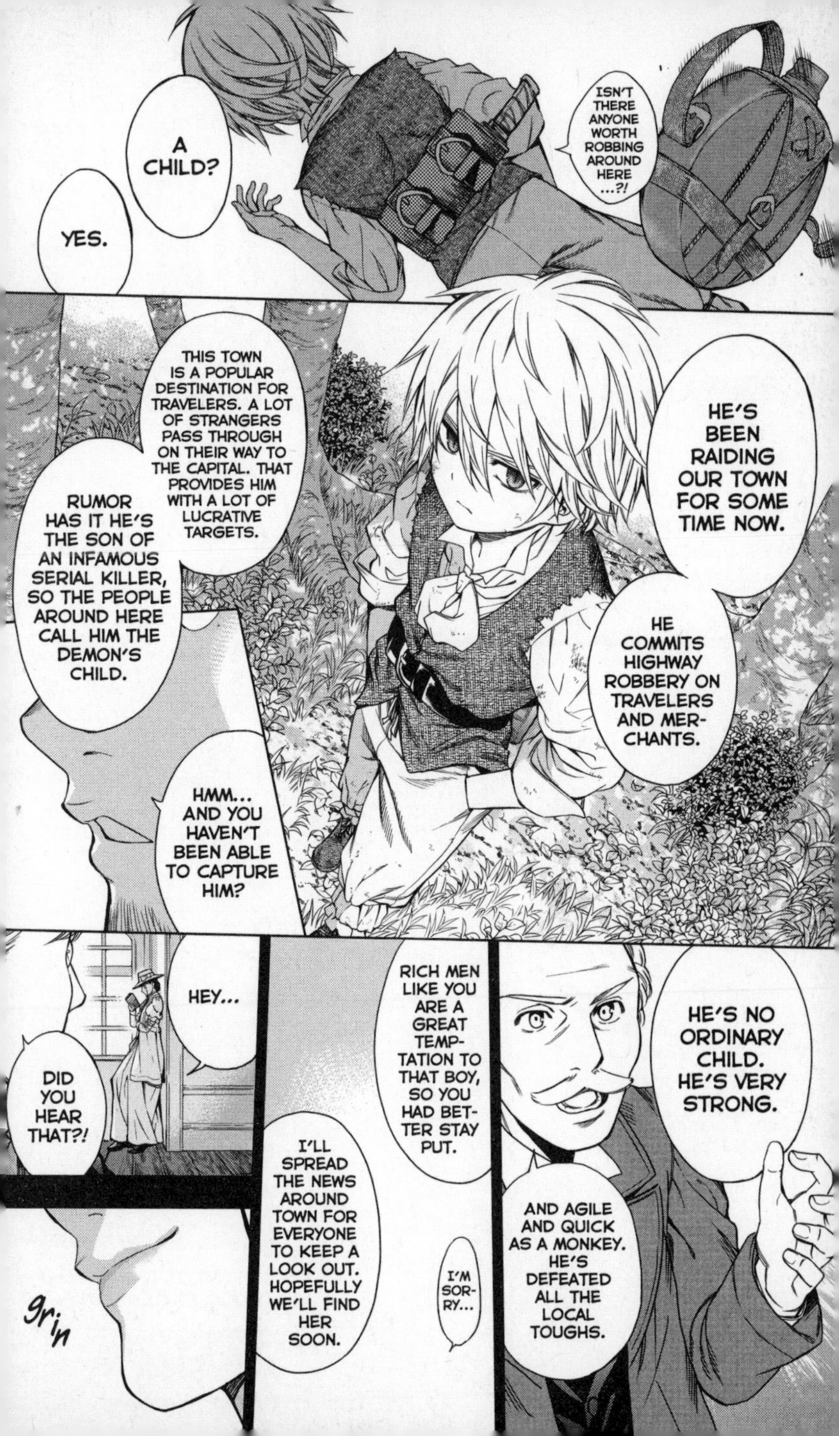
ISN'T THERE ANYONE WORTH ROBBING AROUND HERE ...?!
A CHILD?
YES.
HE'S BEEN RAIDING OUR TOWN FOR SOME TIME NOW.
HE COMMITS HIGHWAY ROBBERY ON TRAVELERS AND MER-CHANTS.
THIS TOWN IS A POPULAR DESTINATION FOR TRAVELERS. A LOT OF STRANGERS PASS THROUGH ON THEIR WAY TO THE CAPITAL. THAT PROVIDES HIM WITH A LOT OF LUCRATIVE TARGETS.
RUMOR HAS IT HE'S THE SON OF AN INFAMOUS SERIAL KILLER, SO THE PEOPLE AROUND HERE CALL HIM THE DEMON'S CHILD.
HMM... AND YOU HAVEN'T BEEN ABLE TO CAPTURE HIM?
HE'S NO ORDINARY CHILD. HE'S VERY STRONG.
AND AGILE AND QUICK AS A MONKEY. HE'S DEFEATED ALL THE LOCAL TOUGHS.
I'M SOR-RY...
RICH MEN LIKE YOU ARE A GREAT TEMP-TATION TO THAT BOY, SO YOU HAD BET-TER STAY PUT.
I'LL SPREAD THE NEWS AROUND TOWN FOR EVERYONE TO KEEP A LOOK OUT. HOPEFULLY WE'LL FIND HER SOON.
HEY...
DID YOU HEAR THAT?!
grin

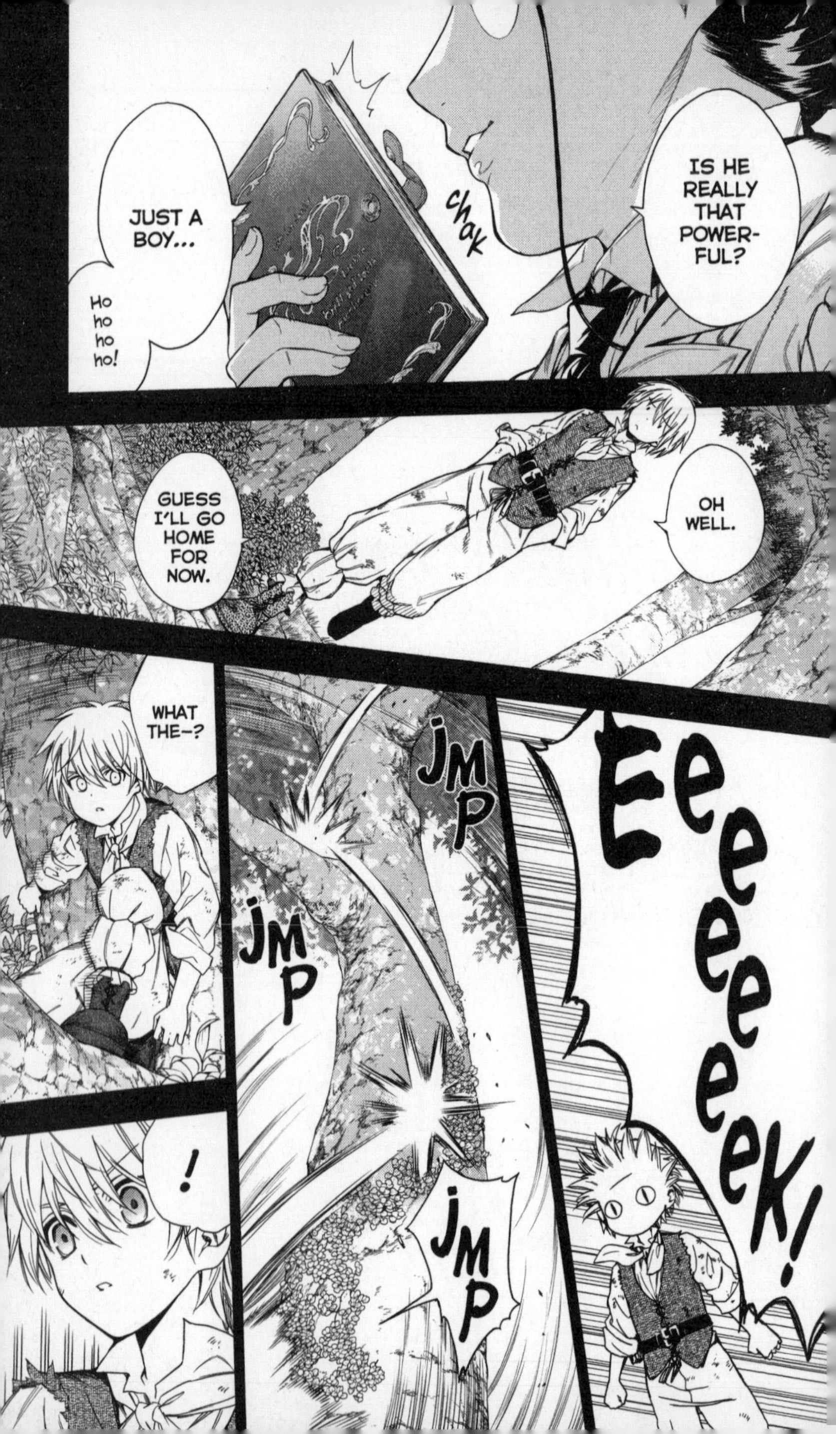
IS HE REALLY THAT POWER-FUL?
chak
JUST A BOY...
Ho ho ho ho!
OH WELL.
GUESS I'LL GO HOME FOR NOW.
Eeeeeeek!
jMP
jMP
jMP
WHAT THE-?
!

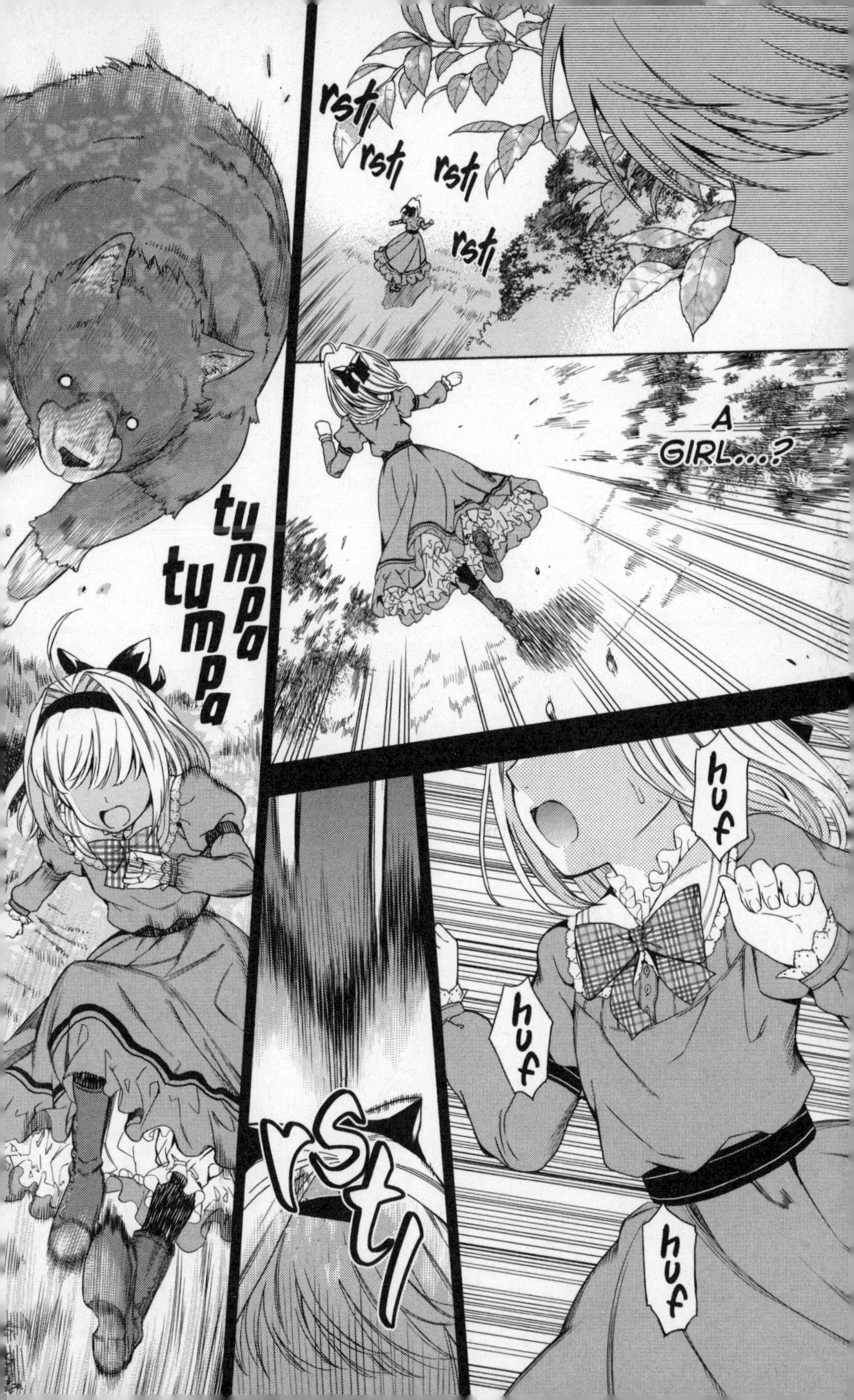
rstl
rstl
rstl
rstl
A GIRL...?
huf
huf
huf
rstl
tumpa
tumpa

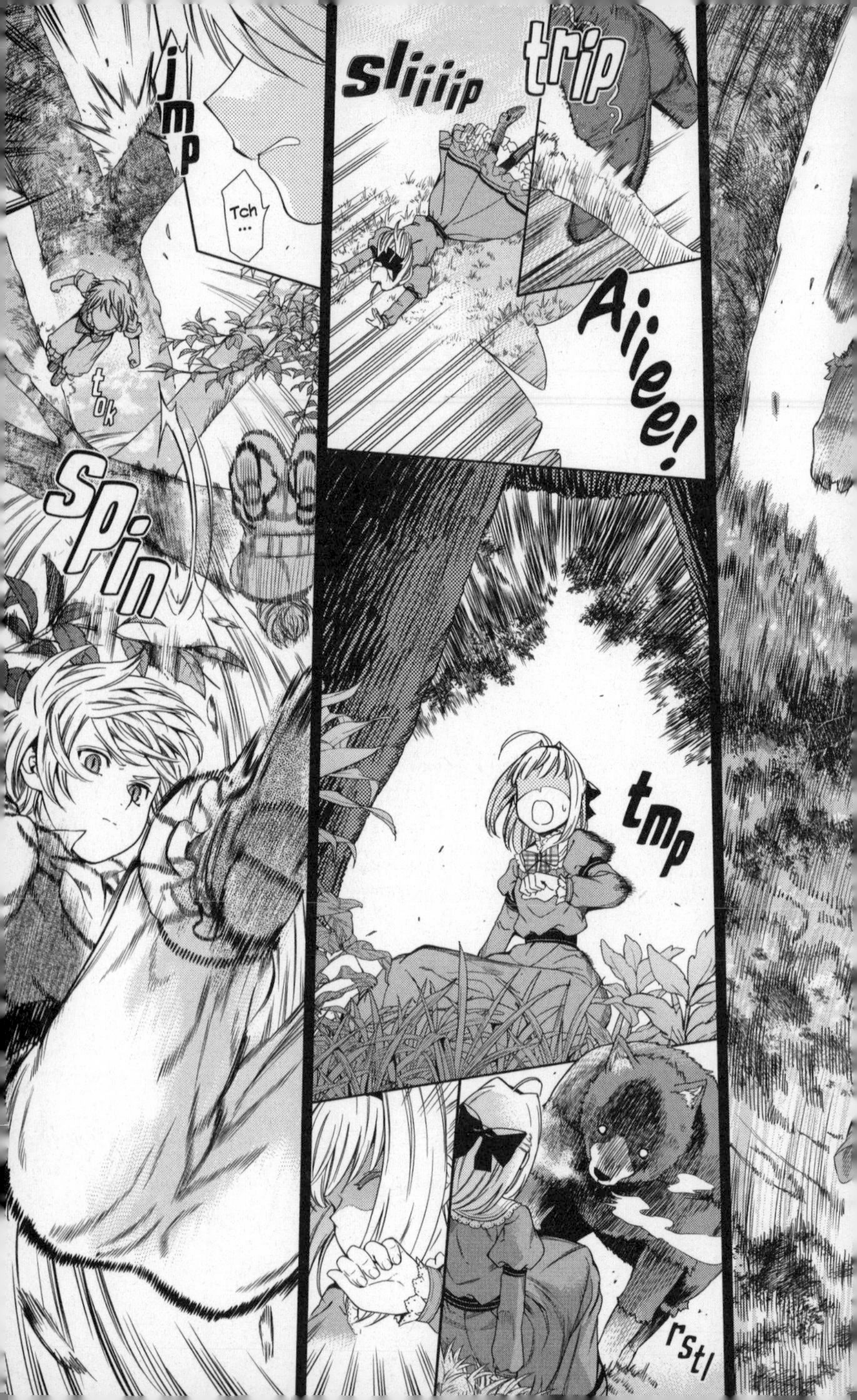
trip
Aiieee!
sliiiip
tmp
rstl
jmp
Tch...
tok
spin

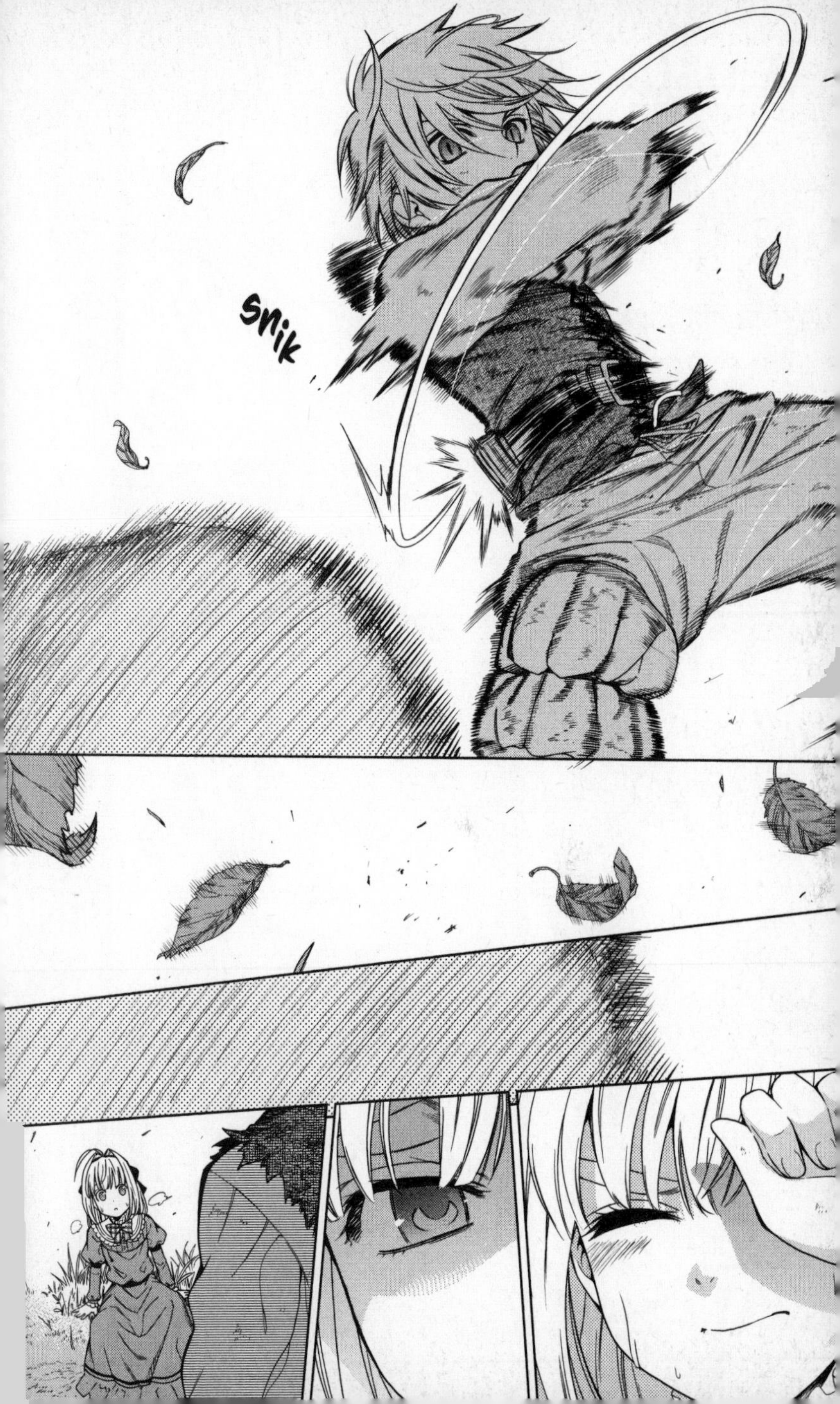
snik

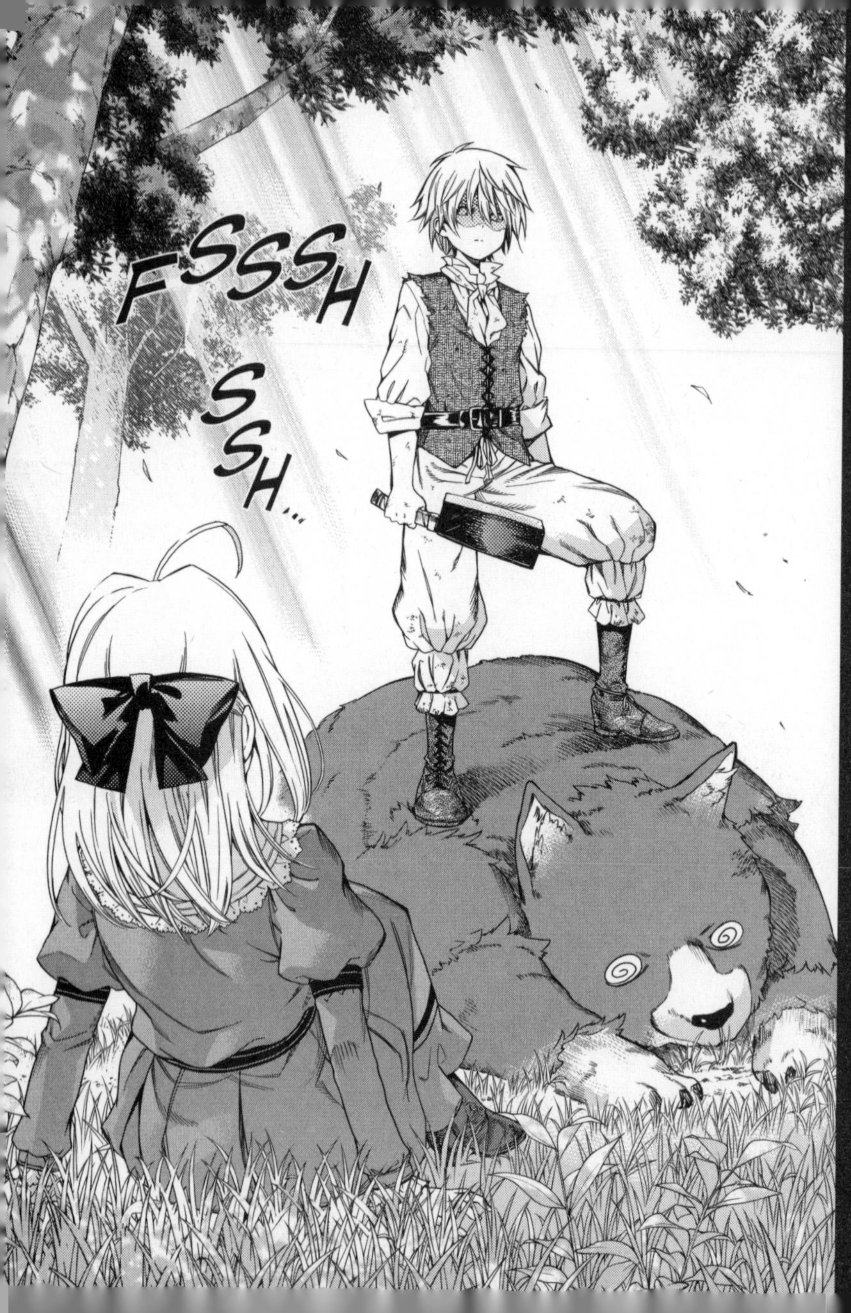
FSSSH
SSH...

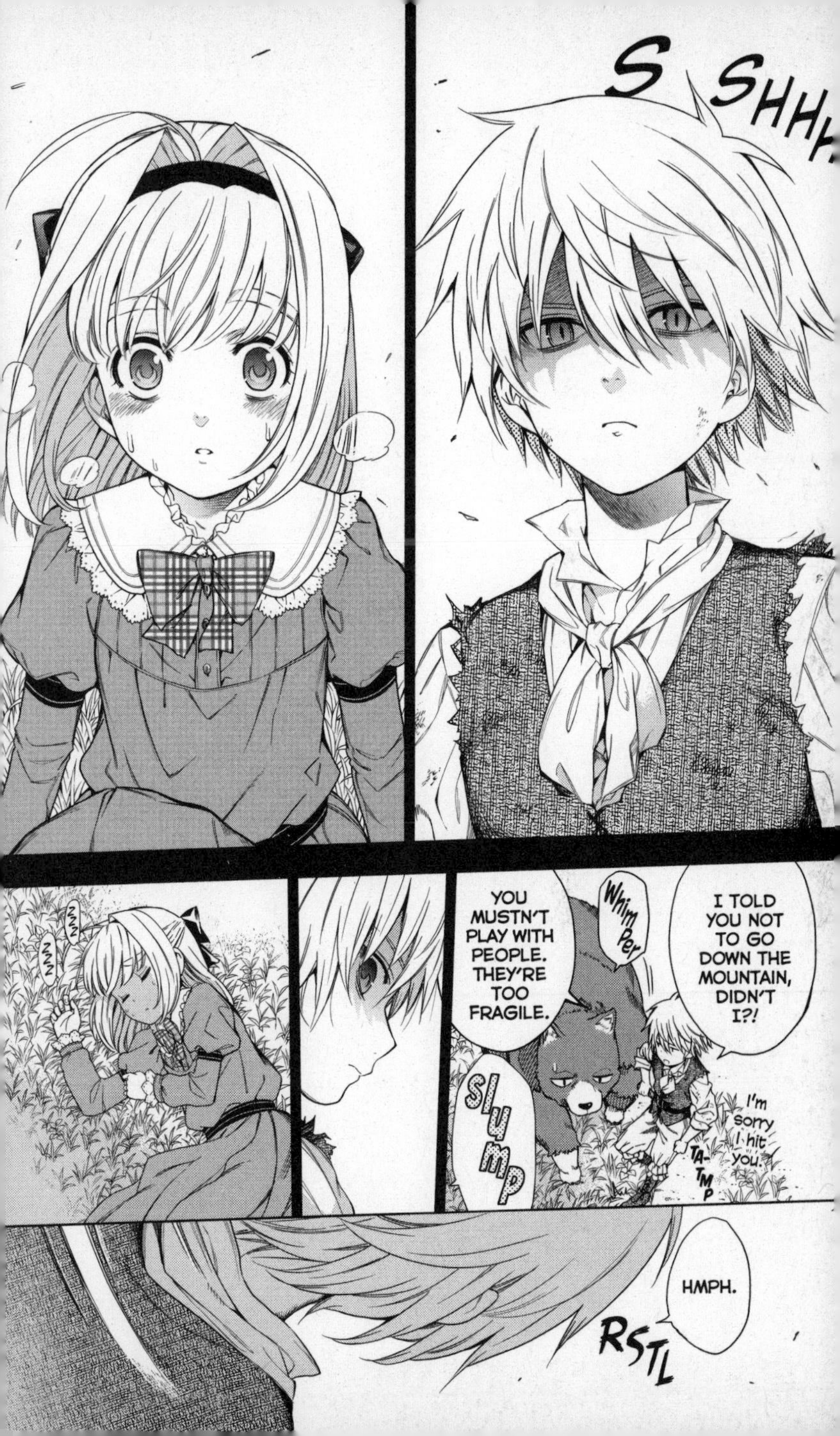
S SHH
I TOLD YOU NOT TO GO DOWN THE MOUNTAIN, DIDN'T I?!
Whimper
YOU MUSTN'T PLAY WITH PEOPLE. THEY'RE TOO FRAGILE.
Slump
I'm sorry I hit you.
TA-TMP
ZZZ
ZZZ
HMPH.
RSTL

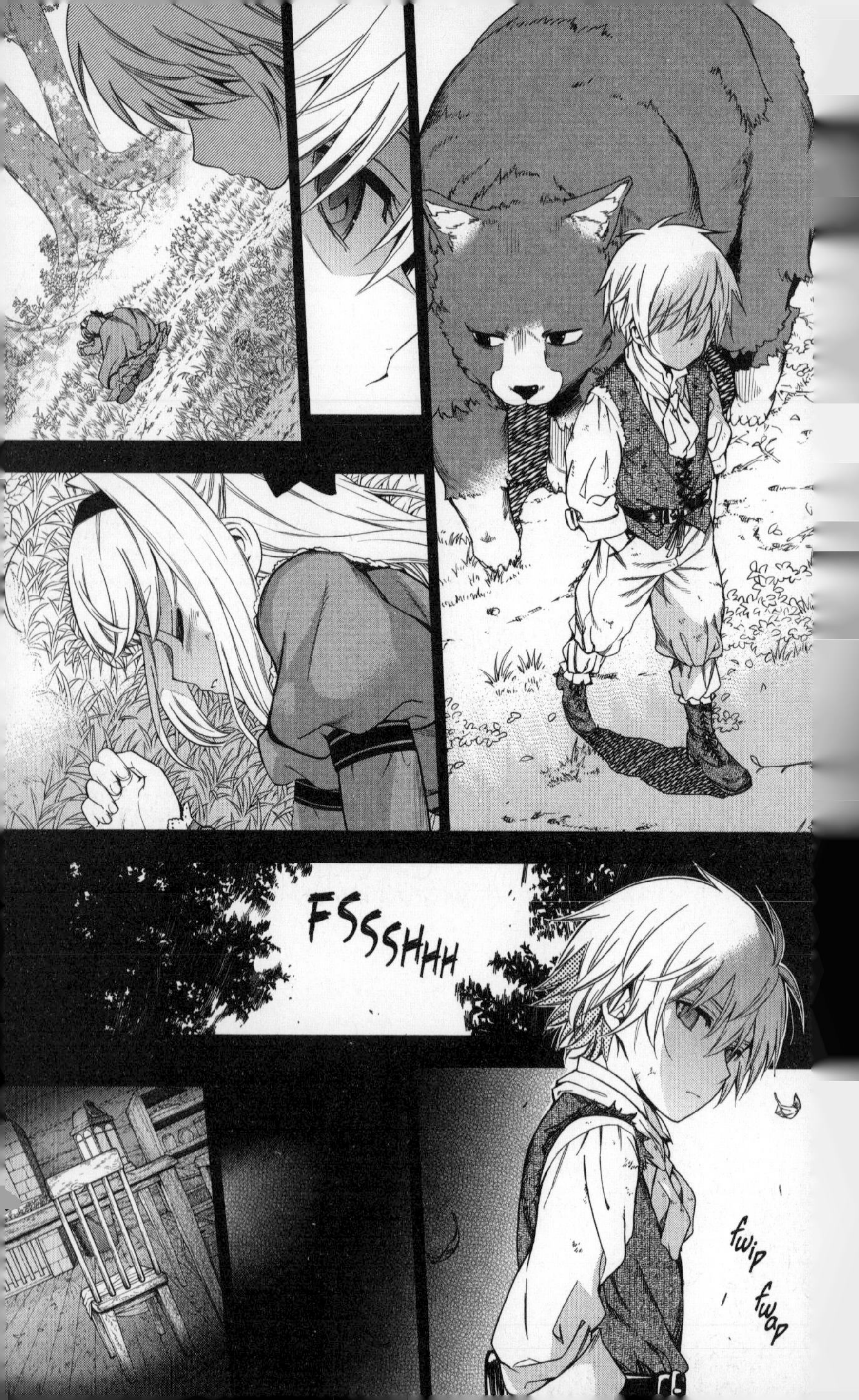
FSSSHHH
fwip
fwap

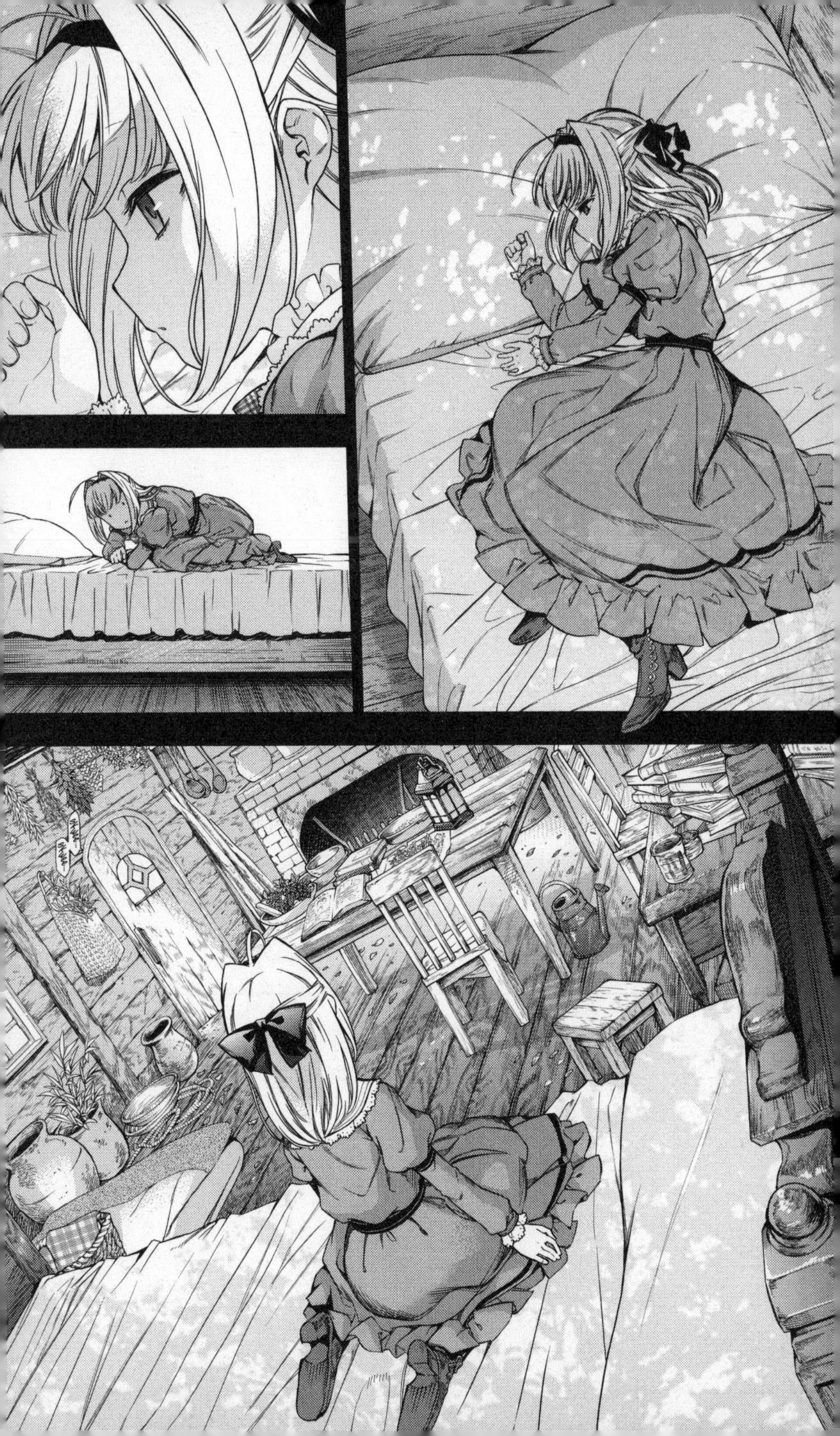
Skwaa...
Skwaa...

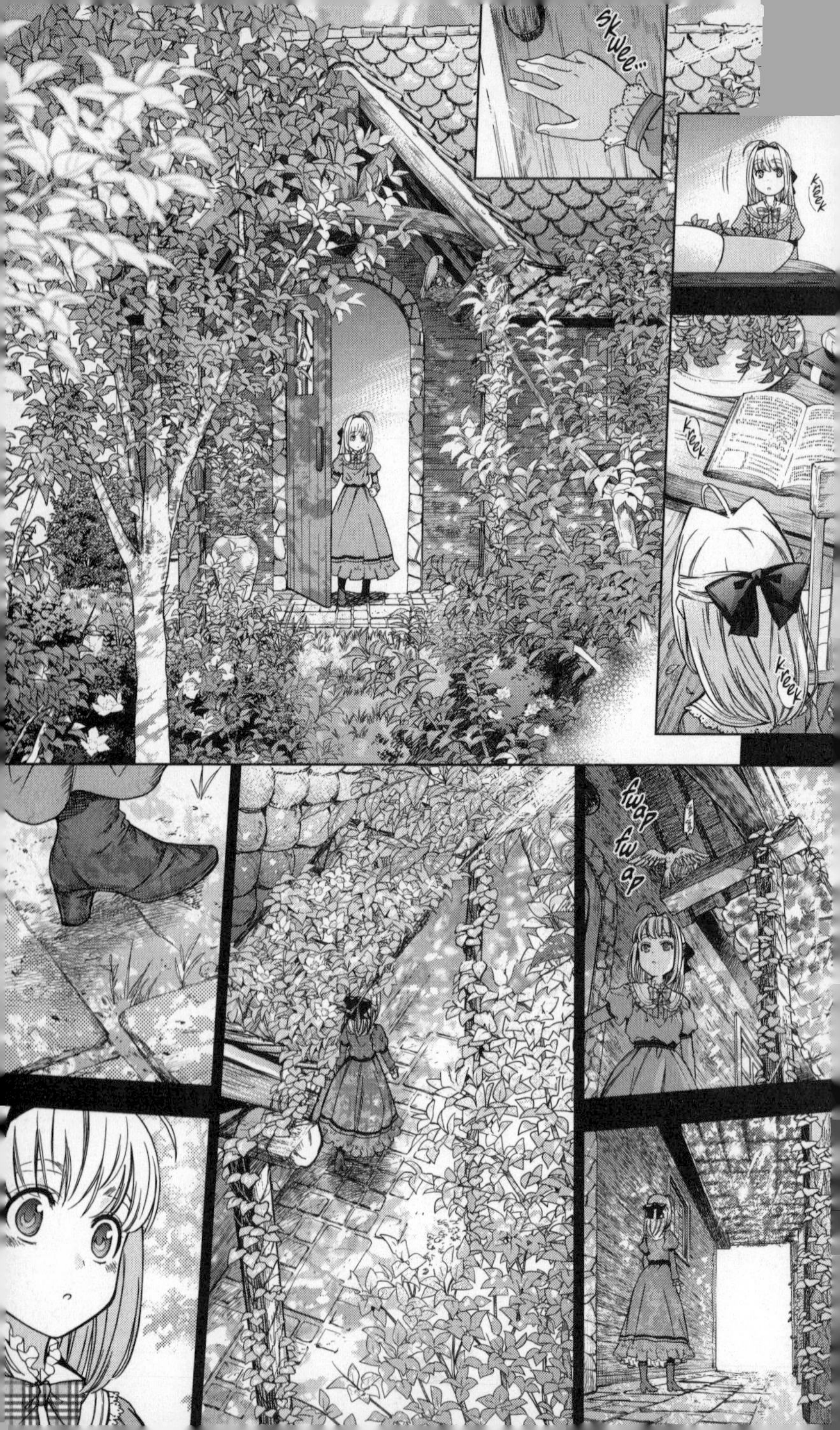
SKwee...
Kreek
Kreek
Kreek
fwap fwap

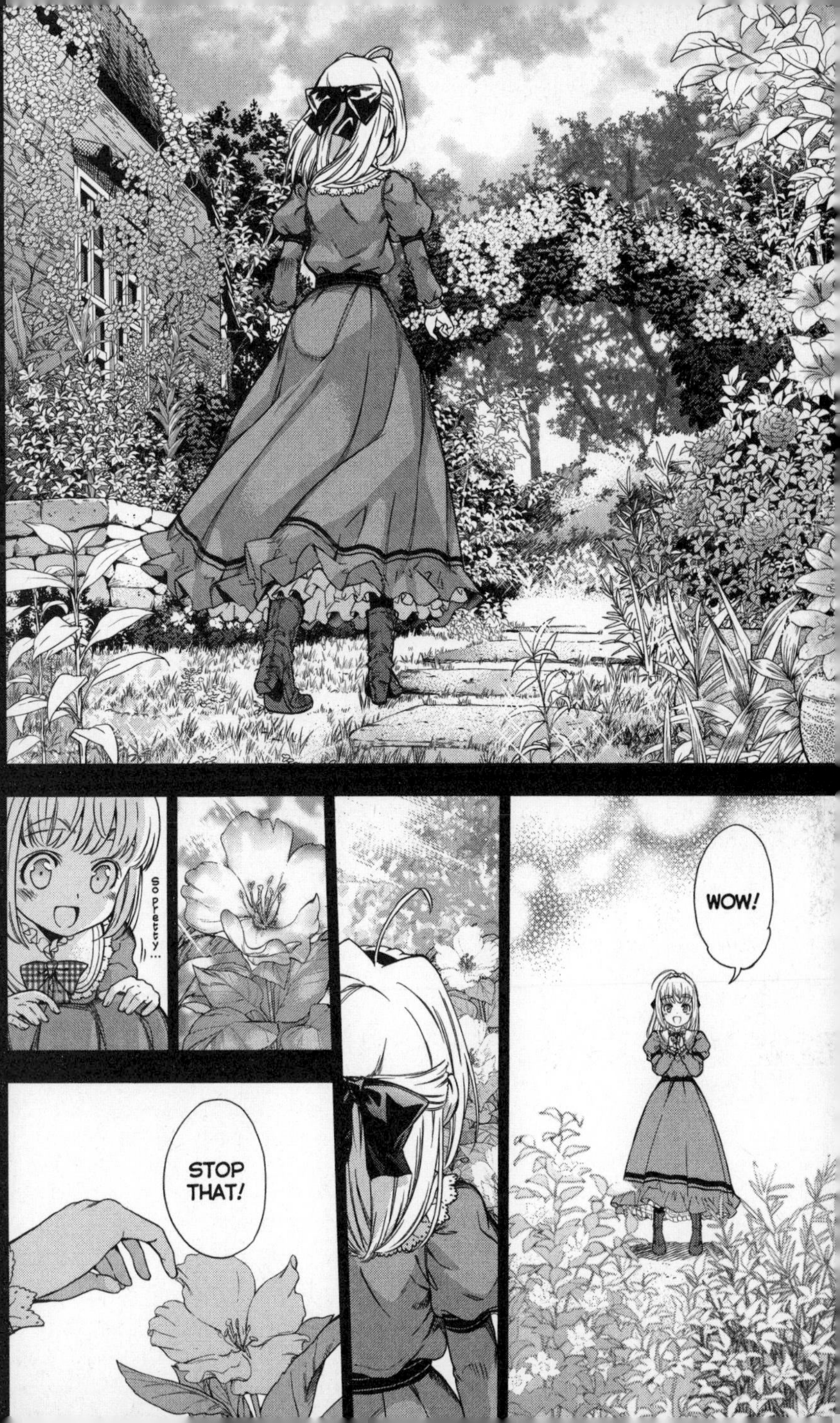
WOW!
So pretty...
STOP THAT!

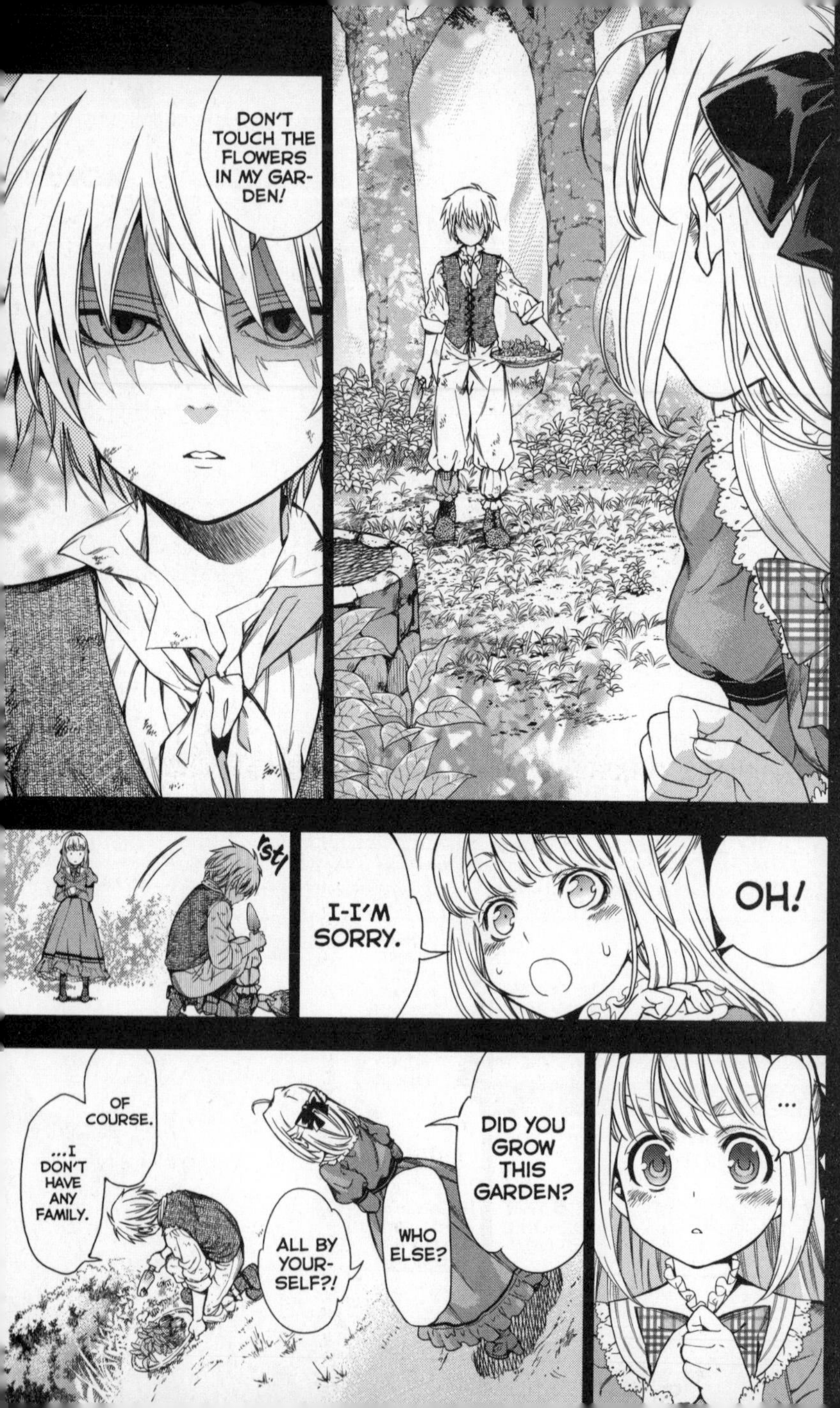
DON'T TOUCH THE FLOWERS IN MY GARDEN!
OH!
I-I'M SORRY.
...
DID YOU GROW THIS GARDEN?
WHO ELSE?
ALL BY YOURSELF?!
OF COURSE.
...I DON'T HAVE ANY FAMILY.

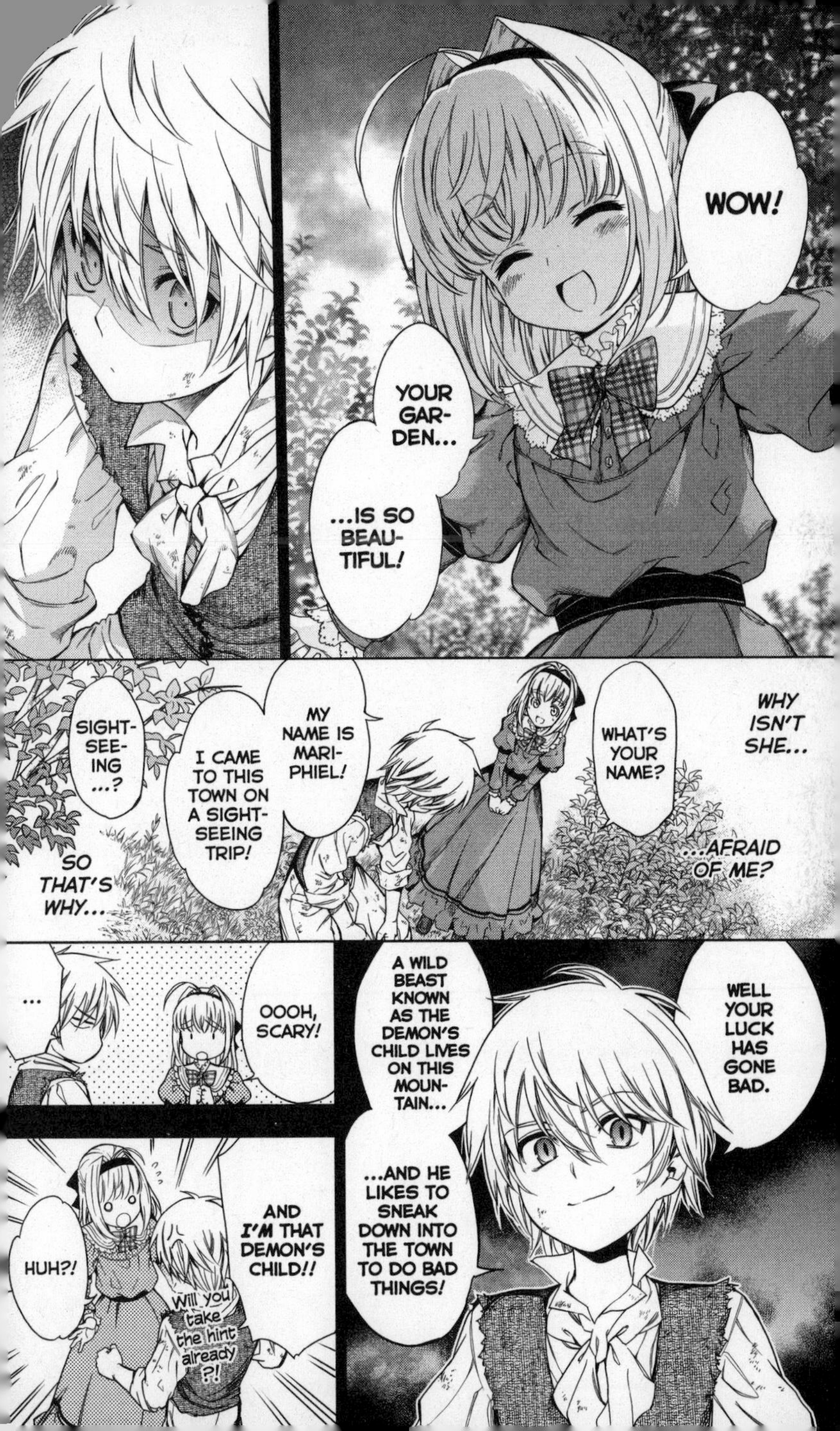
WOW!
YOUR GARDEN...
...IS SO BEAUTIFUL!
WHY ISN'T SHE...
...AFRAID OF ME?
WHAT'S YOUR NAME?
MY NAME IS MARIPHIEL!
I CAME TO THIS TOWN ON A SIGHTSEEING TRIP!
SIGHTSEEING...?
SO THAT'S WHY...
WELL YOUR LUCK HAS GONE BAD.
A WILD BEAST KNOWN AS THE DEMON'S CHILD LIVES ON THIS MOUNTAIN...
...AND HE LIKES TO SNEAK DOWN INTO THE TOWN TO DO BAD THINGS!
OOOH, SCARY!
...
AND I'M THAT DEMON'S CHILD!!
HUH?!
Will you take the hint already?!

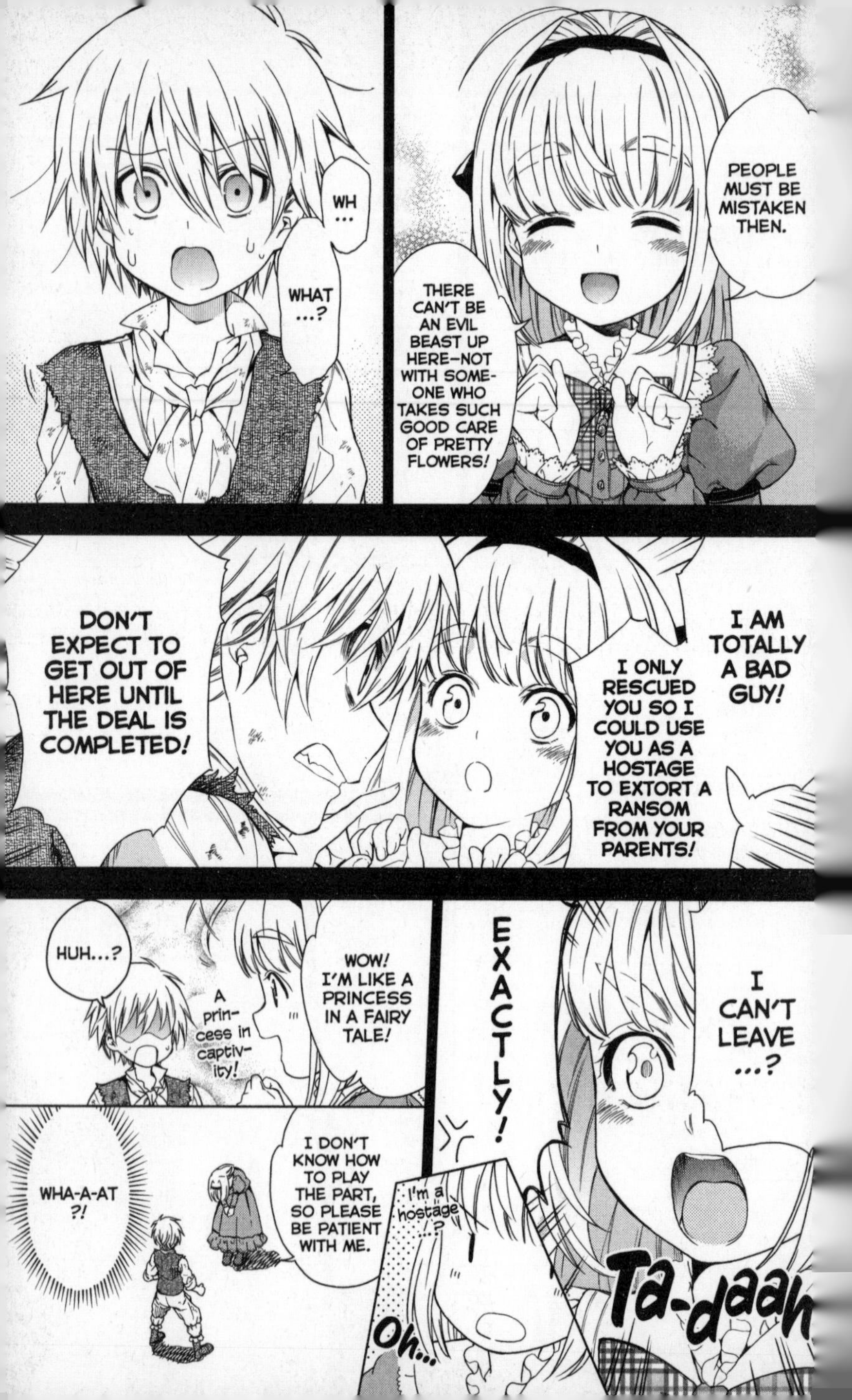
PEOPLE MUST BE MISTAKEN THEN.
THERE CAN'T BE AN EVIL BEAST UP HERE—NOT WITH SOME-ONE WHO TAKES SUCH GOOD CARE OF PRETTY FLOWERS!
WH...
WHAT...?
I AM TOTALLY A BAD GUY!
I ONLY RESCUED YOU SO I COULD USE YOU AS A HOSTAGE TO EXTORT A RANSOM FROM YOUR PARENTS!
DON'T EXPECT TO GET OUT OF HERE UNTIL THE DEAL IS COMPLETED!
I CAN'T LEAVE...?
EXACTLY!
Ta-daah
Oh...
I'm a hostage...?
WOW! I'M LIKE A PRINCESS IN A FAIRY TALE!
A prin-cess in captiv-ity!
HUH...?
I DON'T KNOW HOW TO PLAY THE PART, SO PLEASE BE PATIENT WITH ME.
WHA-A-AT?!

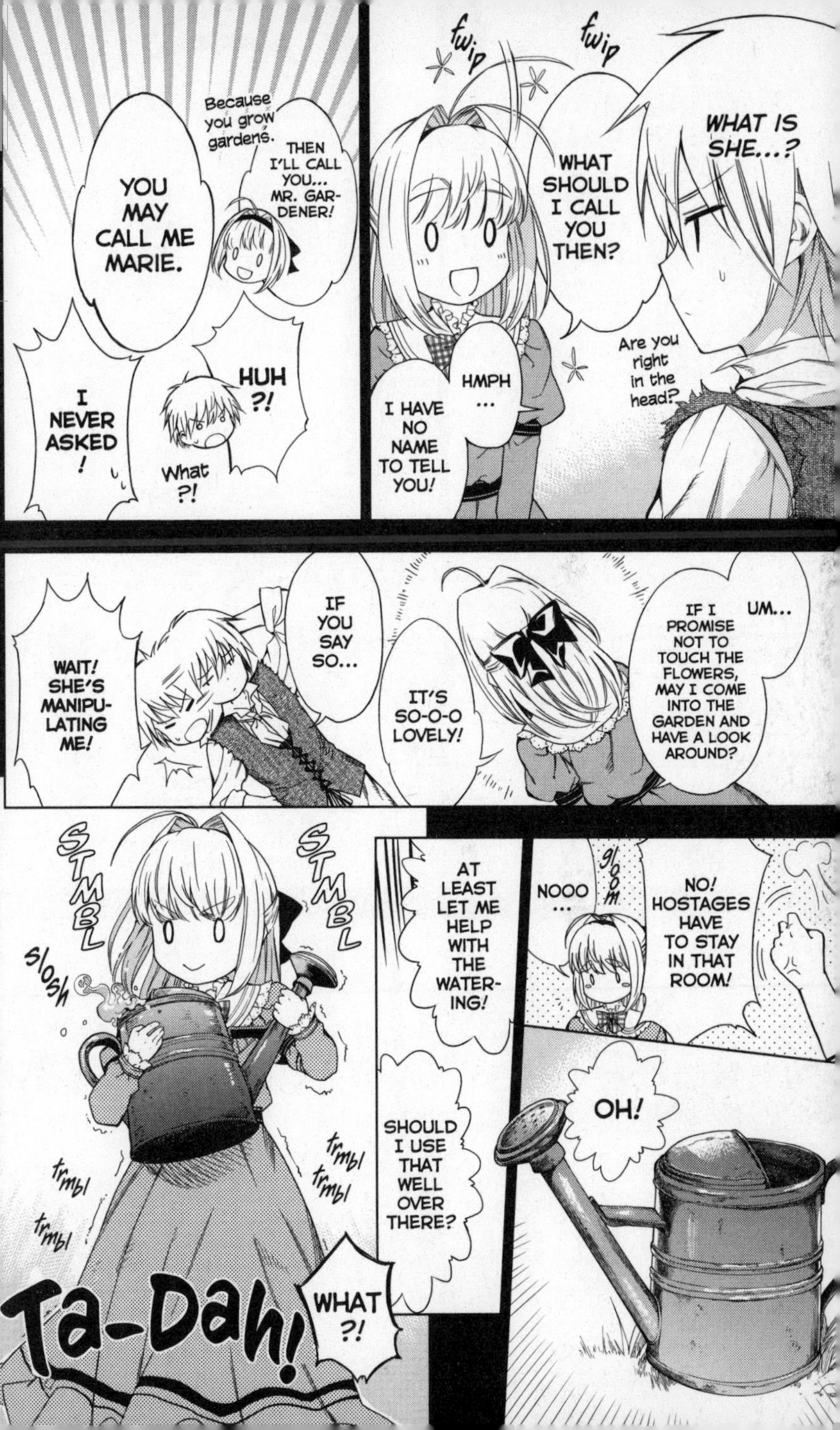
fwip
fwip
WHAT IS SHE...?
WHAT SHOULD I CALL YOU THEN?
Are you right in the head?
HMPH ...
I HAVE NO NAME TO TELL YOU!
THEN I'LL CALL YOU... MR. GARDENER!
Because you grow gardens.
YOU MAY CALL ME MARIE.
HUH ?!
What ?!
I NEVER ASKED!
UM...
IF I PROMISE NOT TO TOUCH THE FLOWERS, MAY I COME INTO THE GARDEN AND HAVE A LOOK AROUND?
IT'S SO-O-O LOVELY!
IF YOU SAY SO...
WAIT! SHE'S MANIPULATING ME!
NO! HOSTAGES HAVE TO STAY IN THAT ROOM!
gloom
NOOO ...
OH!
AT LEAST LET ME HELP WITH THE WATERING!
SHOULD I USE THAT WELL OVER THERE?
WHAT ?!
STMBL
STMBL
slosh
trmbl
trmbl
trmbl
trmbl
Ta-Dah!

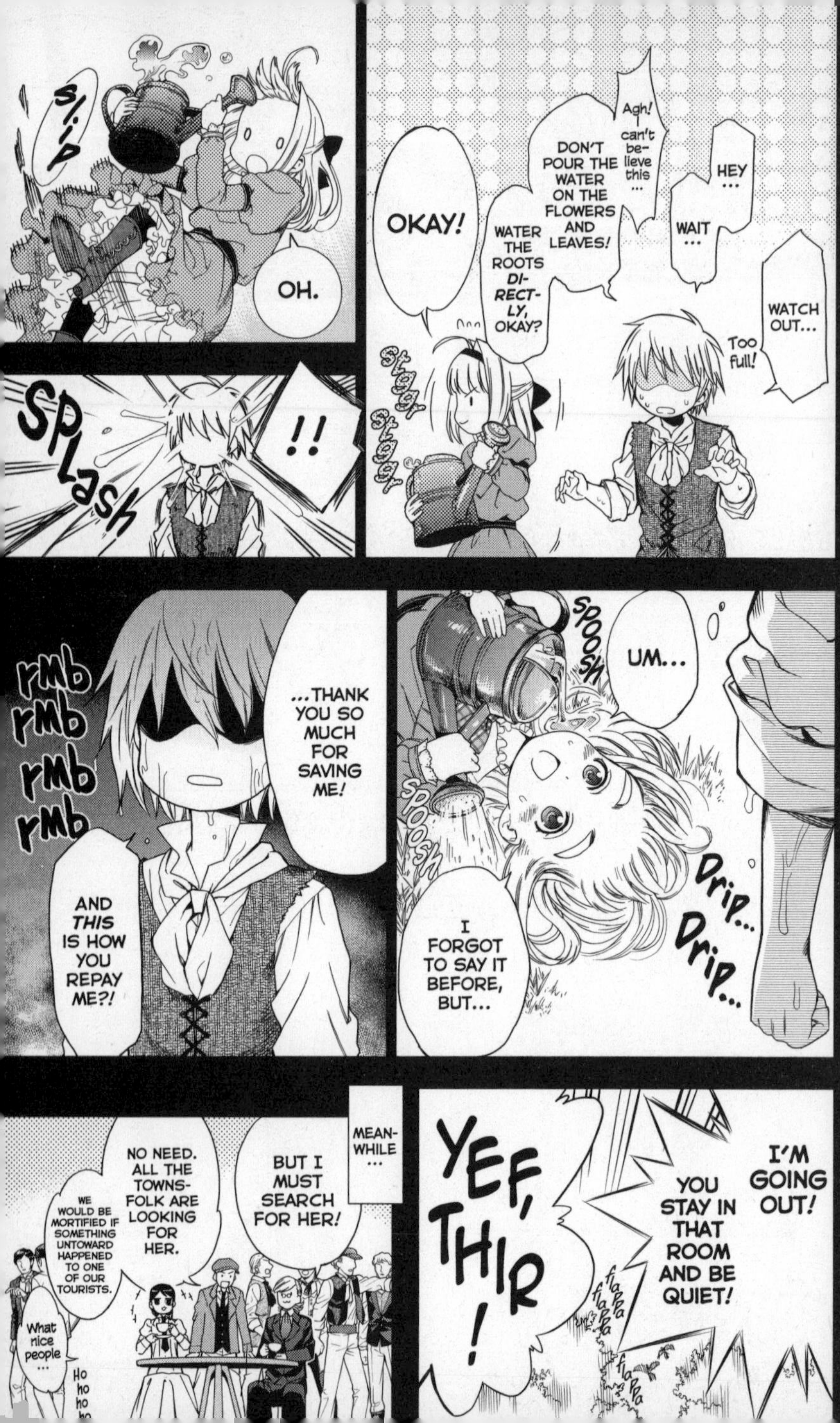
HEY... WAIT...
WATCH OUT... Too full!
Agh! I can't believe this...
DON'T POUR THE WATER ON THE FLOWERS AND LEAVES!
WATER THE ROOTS DIRECTLY, OKAY?
OKAY!
stggr stggr
slip
OH.
SPLASH
!!
UM...
SPOOSH
Drip... Drip...
I FORGOT TO SAY IT BEFORE, BUT...
SPOOSH
rmb rmb rmb rmb
...THANK YOU SO MUCH FOR SAVING ME!
AND THIS IS HOW YOU REPAY ME?!
I'M GOING OUT!
YOU STAY IN THAT ROOM AND BE QUIET!
YEF, THIR!
flappa flappa flappa
MEANWHILE...
BUT I MUST SEARCH FOR HER!
NO NEED. ALL THE TOWNSFOLK ARE LOOKING FOR HER.
WE WOULD BE MORTIFIED IF SOMETHING UNTOWARD HAPPENED TO ONE OF OUR TOURISTS.
What nice people...
Ho ho ho

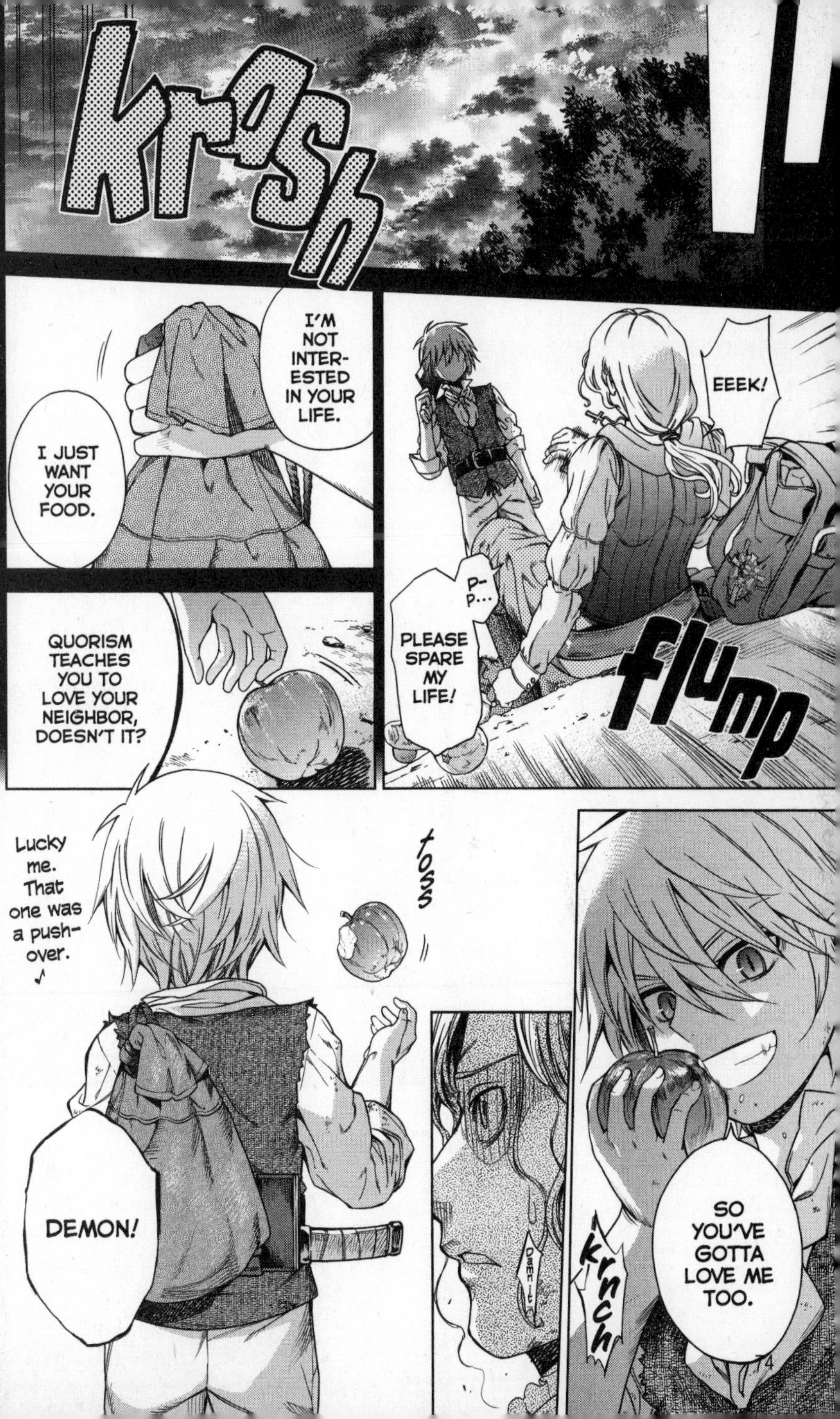
krash
EEEK!
P-P...
PLEASE SPARE MY LIFE!
flump
I'M NOT INTERESTED IN YOUR LIFE.
I JUST WANT YOUR FOOD.
QUORISM TEACHES YOU TO LOVE YOUR NEIGHBOR, DOESN'T IT?
SO YOU'VE GOTTA LOVE ME TOO.
krnch
Damn it
toss
Lucky me. That one was a push-over. ♪
DEMON!

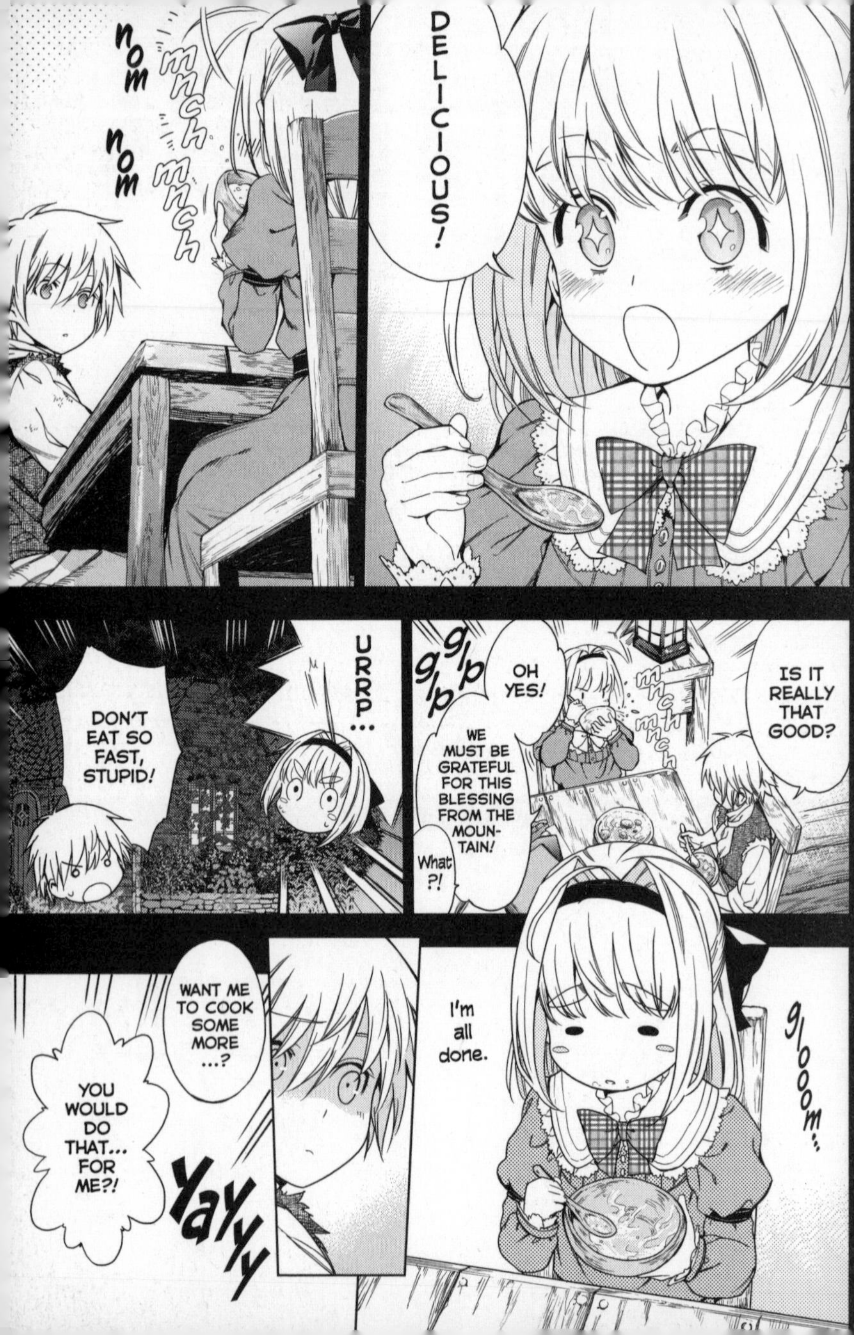
DELICIOUS!
mnch mnch
nom nom
IS IT REALLY THAT GOOD?
OH YES!
WE MUST BE GRATEFUL FOR THIS BLESSING FROM THE MOUN-TAIN!
What?!
mnch mnch
glp glp
URRP...
DON'T EAT SO FAST, STUPID!
glooom...
I'm all done.
WANT ME TO COOK SOME MORE ...?
YOU WOULD DO THAT... FOR ME?!
Yayyy

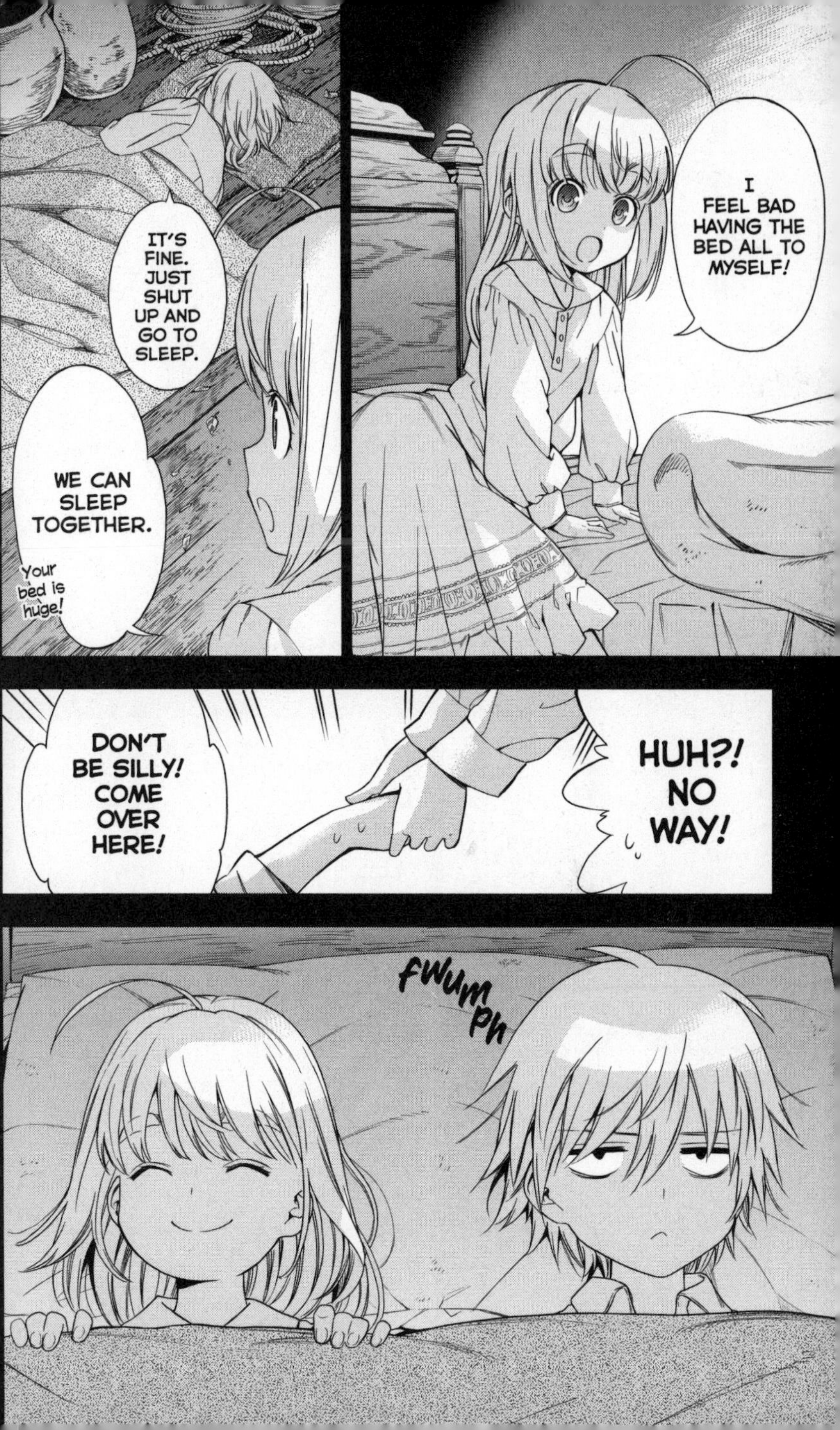
I FEEL BAD HAVING THE BED ALL TO MYSELF!
IT'S FINE. JUST SHUT UP AND GO TO SLEEP.
WE CAN SLEEP TOGETHER.
Your bed is huge!
HUH?! NO WAY!
DON'T BE SILLY! COME OVER HERE!
fwumph

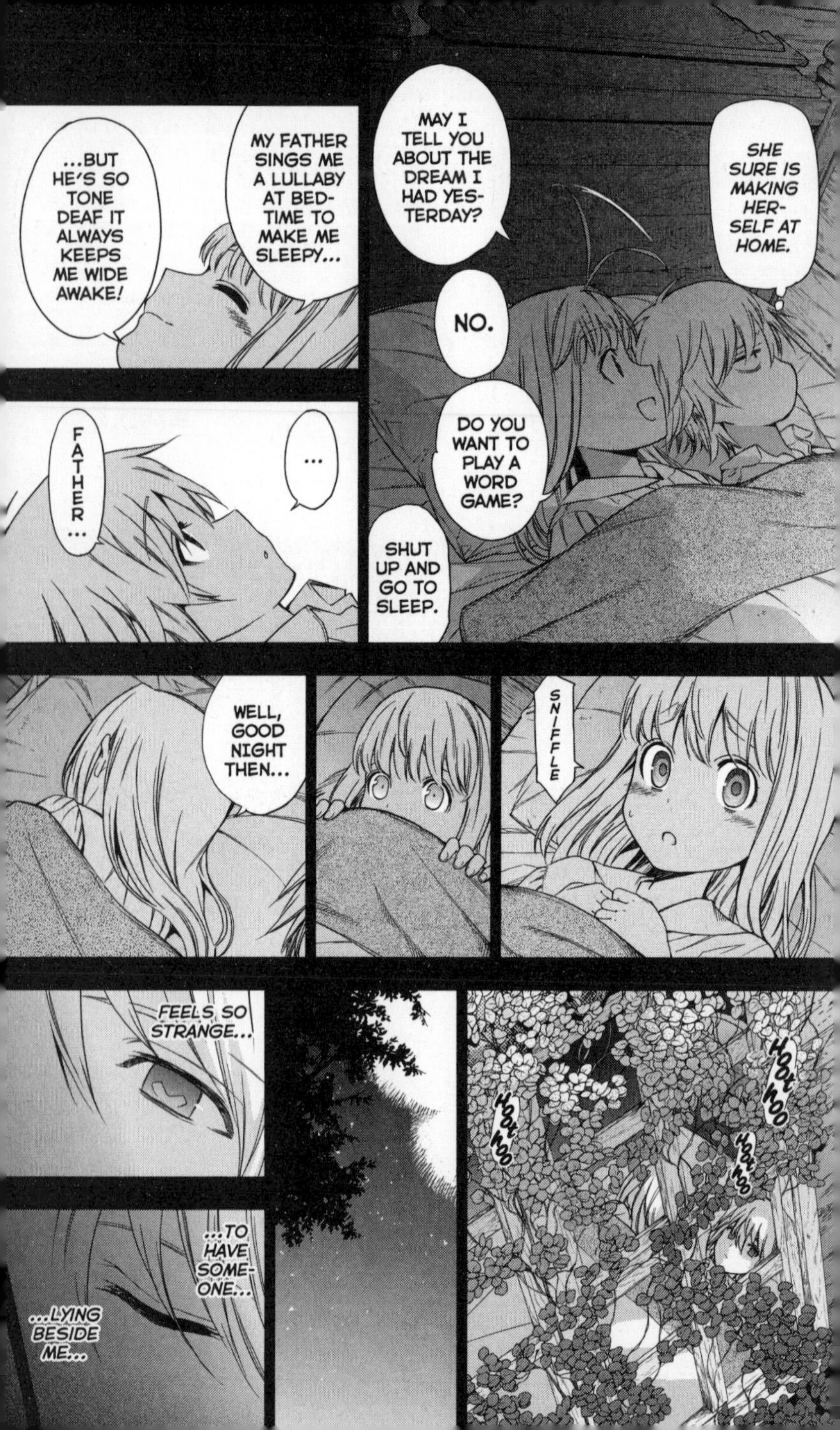
SHE SURE IS MAKING HER-SELF AT HOME.
MAY I TELL YOU ABOUT THE DREAM I HAD YES-TERDAY?
NO.
DO YOU WANT TO PLAY A WORD GAME?
SHUT UP AND GO TO SLEEP.
MY FATHER SINGS ME A LULLABY AT BED-TIME TO MAKE ME SLEEPY...
...BUT HE'S SO TONE DEAF IT ALWAYS KEEPS ME WIDE AWAKE!
...
FATHER...
SNIFFLE
WELL, GOOD NIGHT THEN...
HOOT HOO
HOOT HOO
HOOT HOO
FEELS SO STRANGE...
...TO HAVE SOME-ONE...
...LYING BESIDE ME...

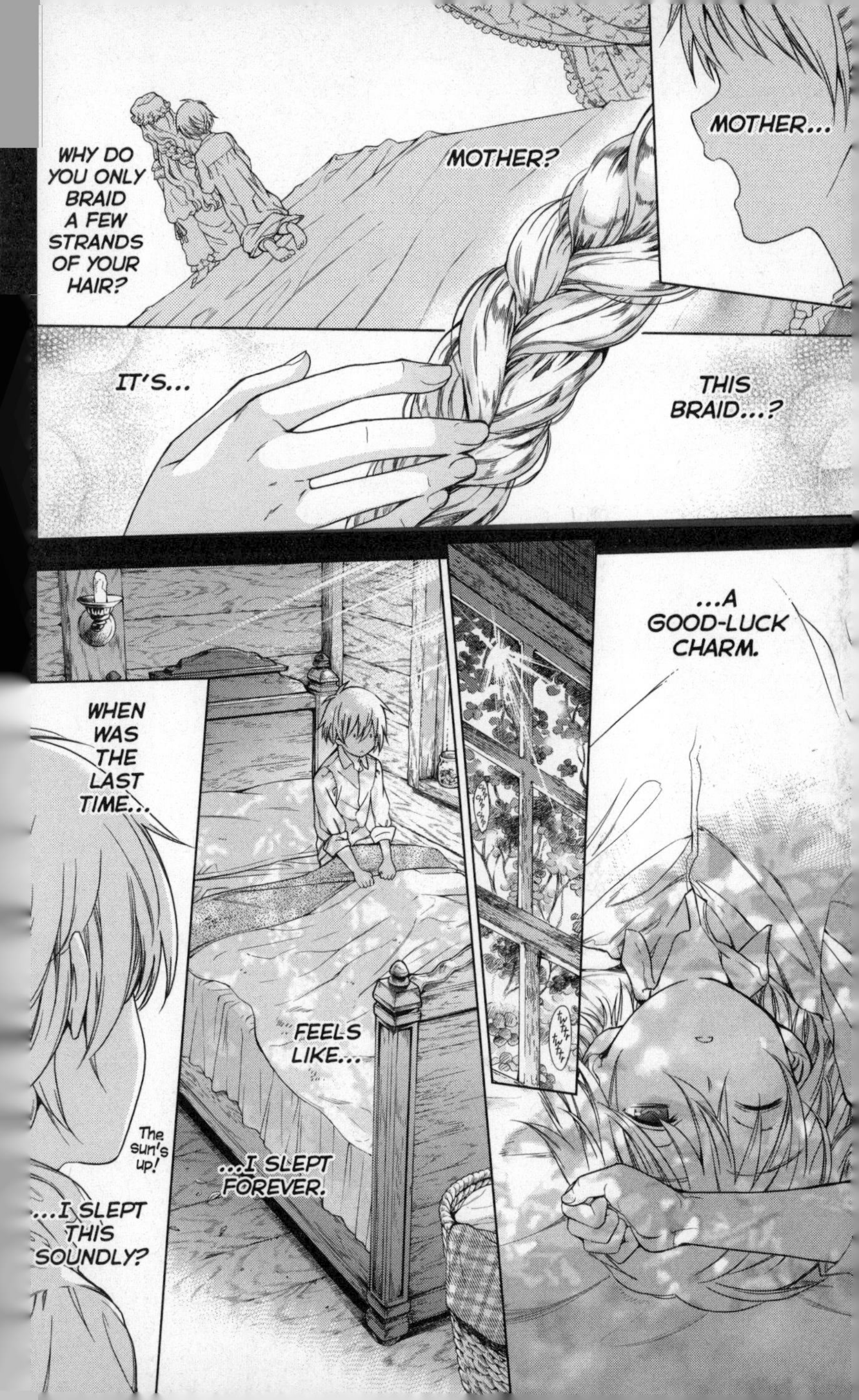
MOTHER...
MOTHER?
WHY DO YOU ONLY BRAID A FEW STRANDS OF YOUR HAIR?
THIS BRAID...?
IT'S...
...A GOOD-LUCK CHARM.
FEELS LIKE...
...I SLEPT FOREVER.
WHEN WAS THE LAST TIME...
The sun's up!
...I SLEPT THIS SOUNDLY?

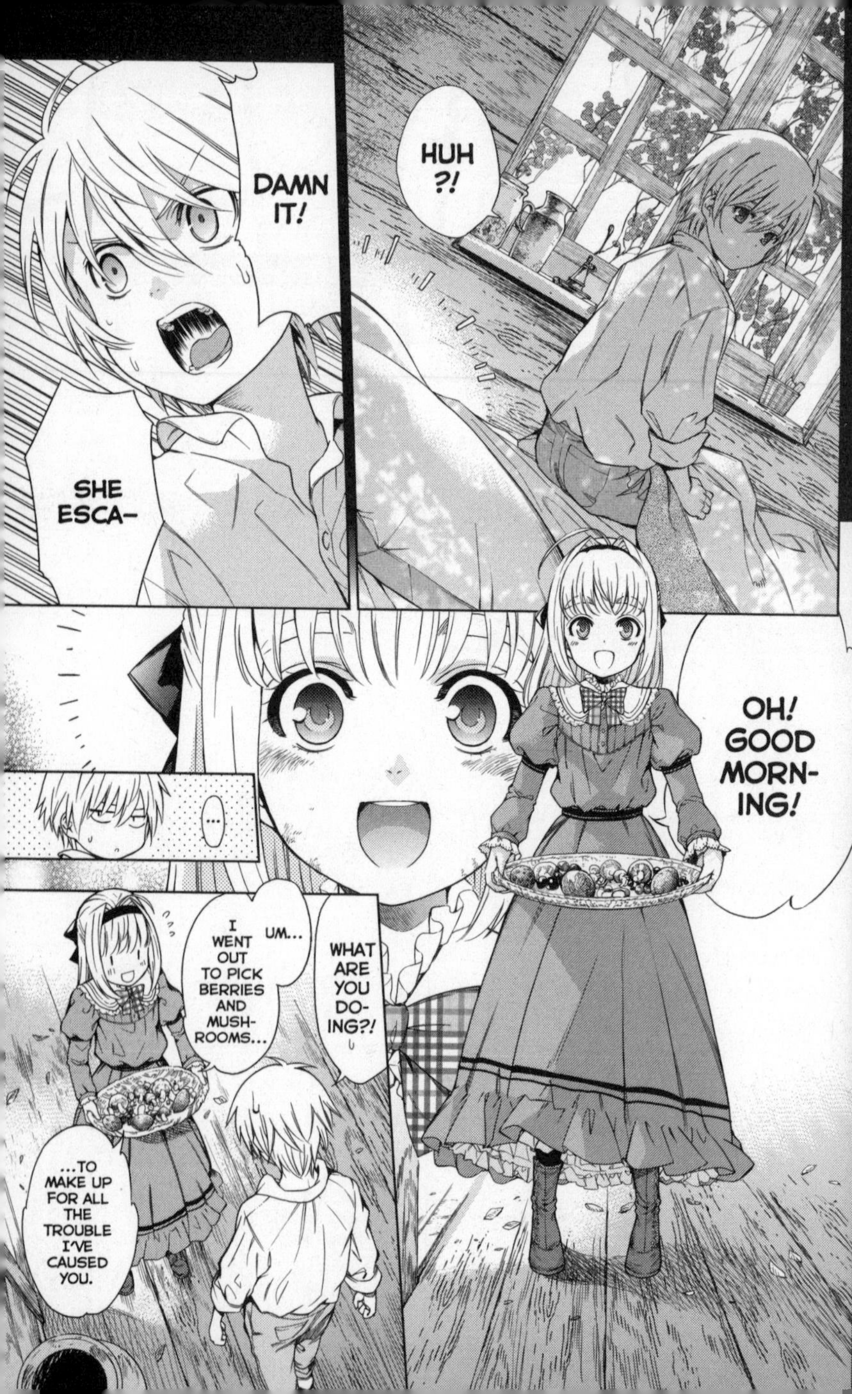
HUH ?!
DAMN IT!
SHE ESCA-
OH! GOOD MORNING!
...
WHAT ARE YOU DOING?!
UM... I WENT OUT TO PICK BERRIES AND MUSHROOMS...
...TO MAKE UP FOR ALL THE TROUBLE I'VE CAUSED YOU.

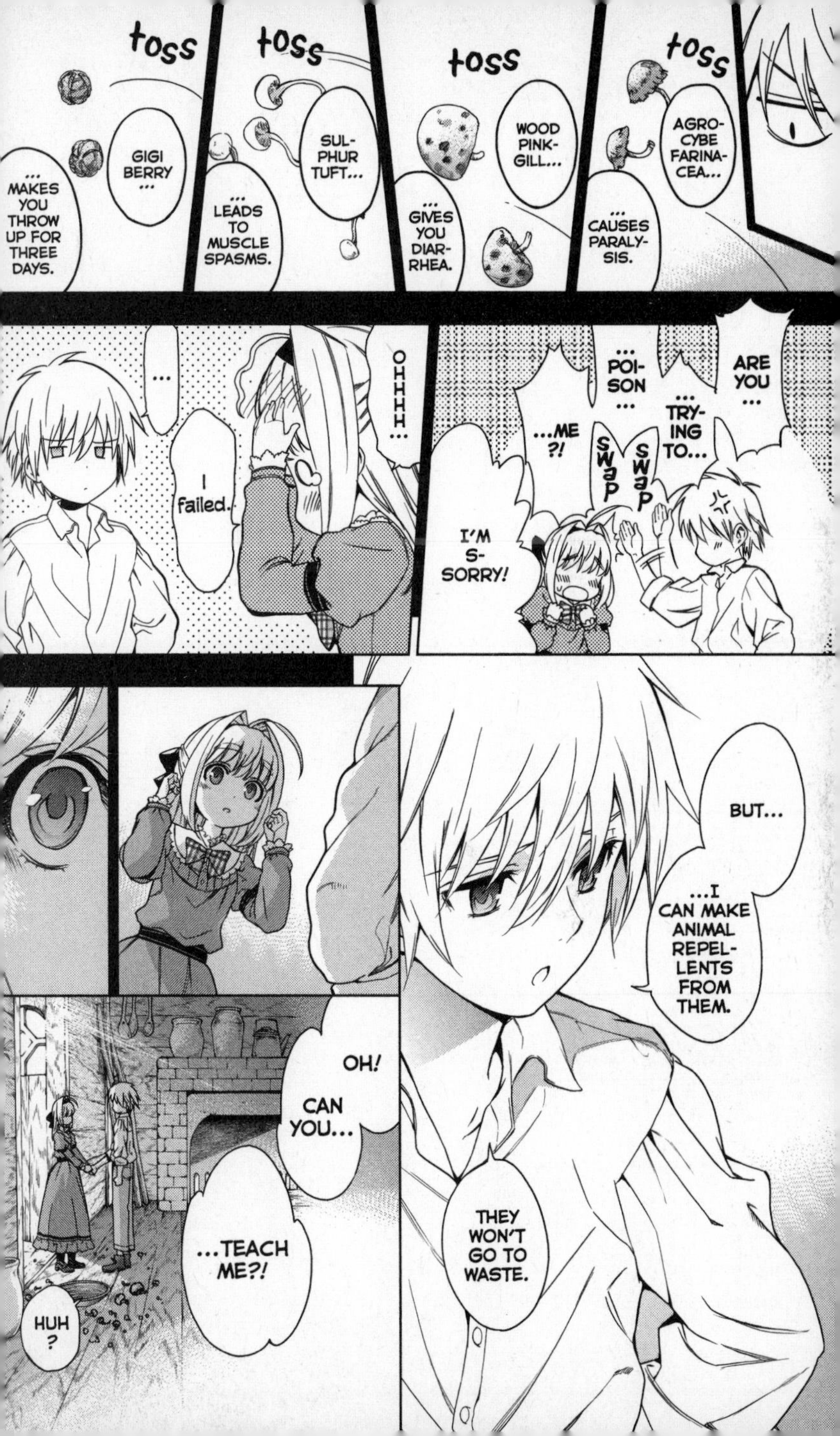
toss
AGRO-CYBE FARINA-CEA...
...CAUSES PARALY-SIS.
toss
WOOD PINK-GILL...
...GIVES YOU DIAR-RHEA.
toss
SUL-PHUR TUFT...
...LEADS TO MUSCLE SPASMS.
toss
GIGI BERRY...
...MAKES YOU THROW UP FOR THREE DAYS.
ARE YOU...
...TRY-ING TO...
...POI-SON...
...ME ?!
swap
swap
I'M S-SORRY!
OHHHH...
...
I failed.
BUT...
...I CAN MAKE ANIMAL REPEL-LENTS FROM THEM.
THEY WON'T GO TO WASTE.
OH!
CAN YOU...
...TEACH ME?!
HUH ?

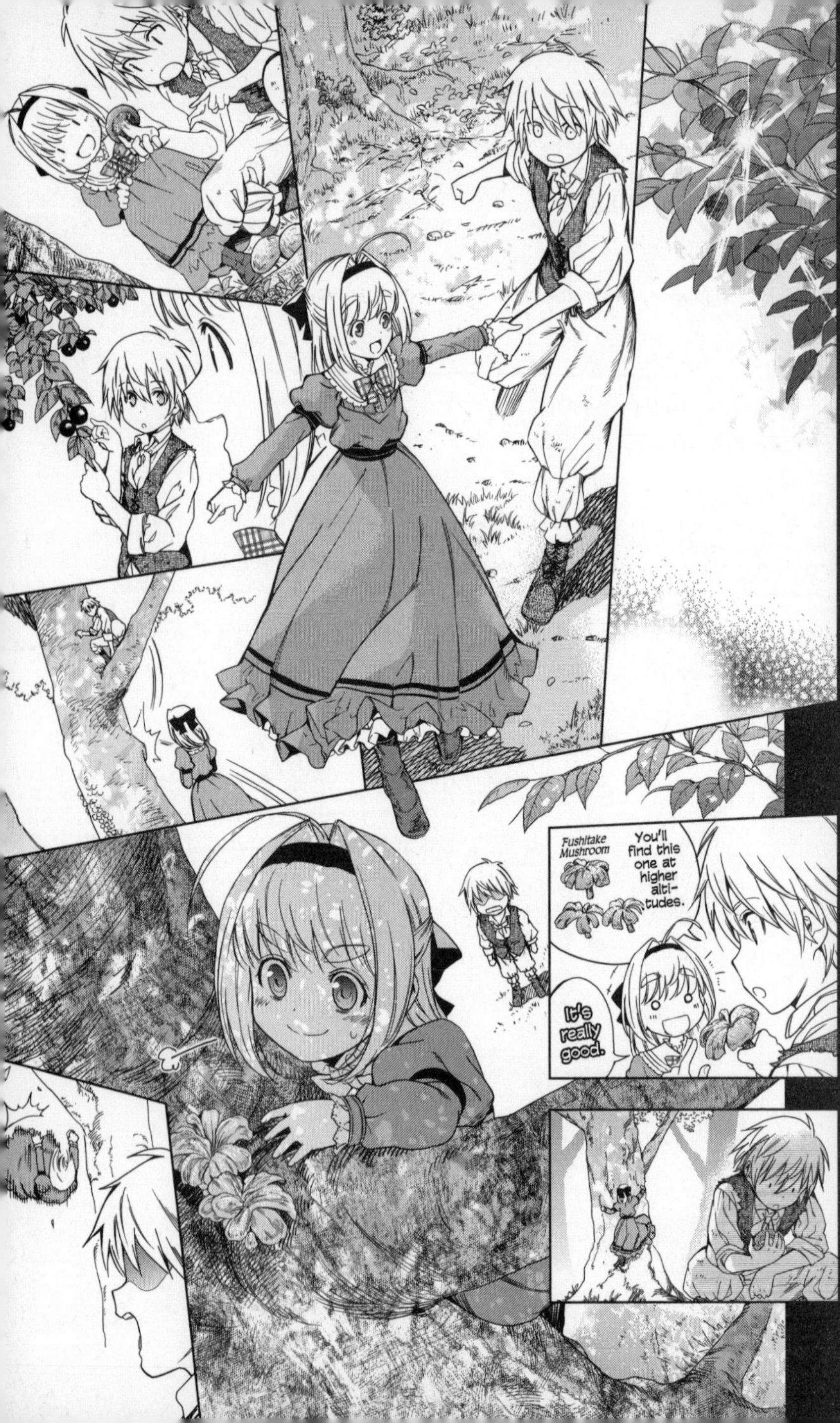

Fushitake Mushroom
You'll find this one at higher alti-tudes.
It's really good.

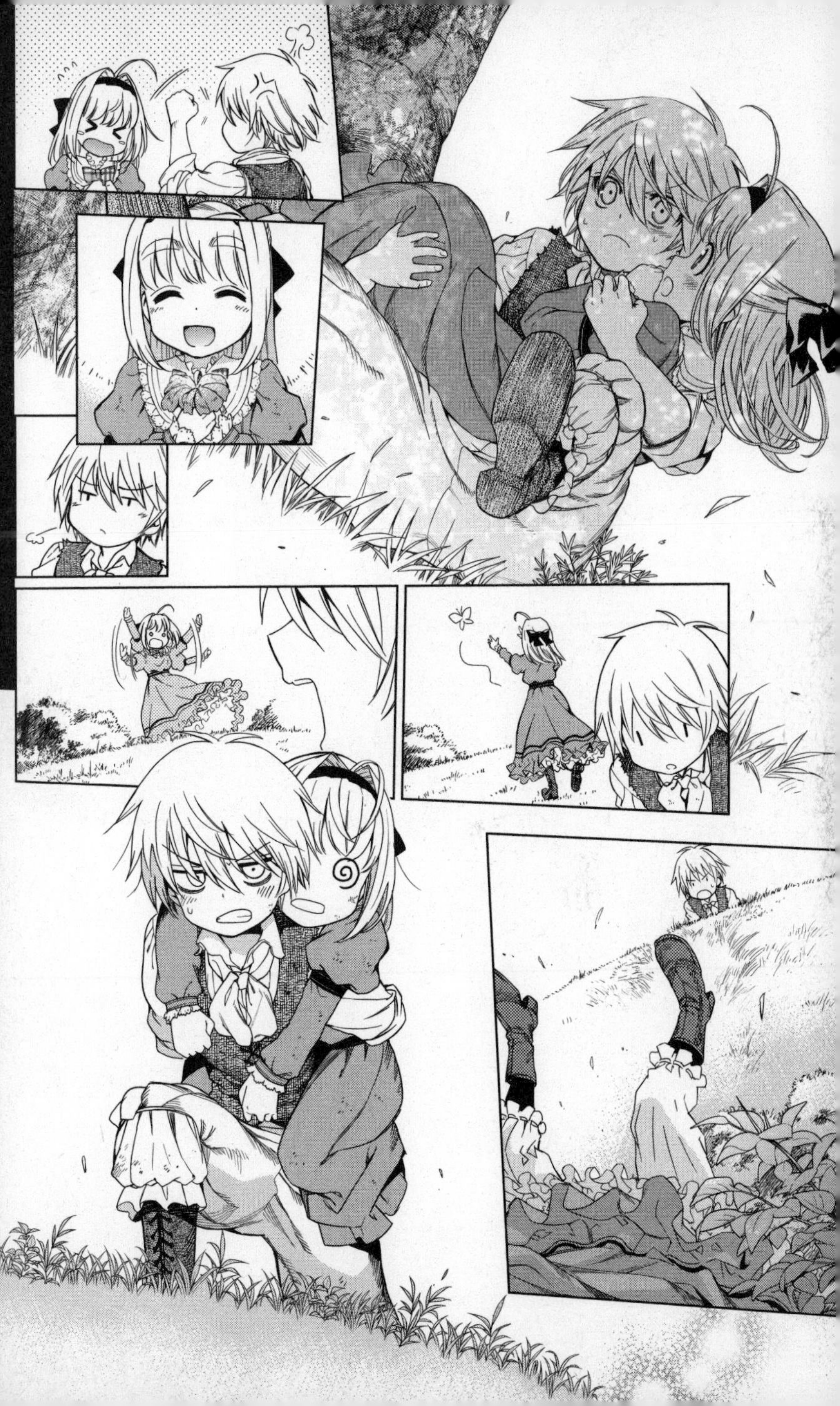

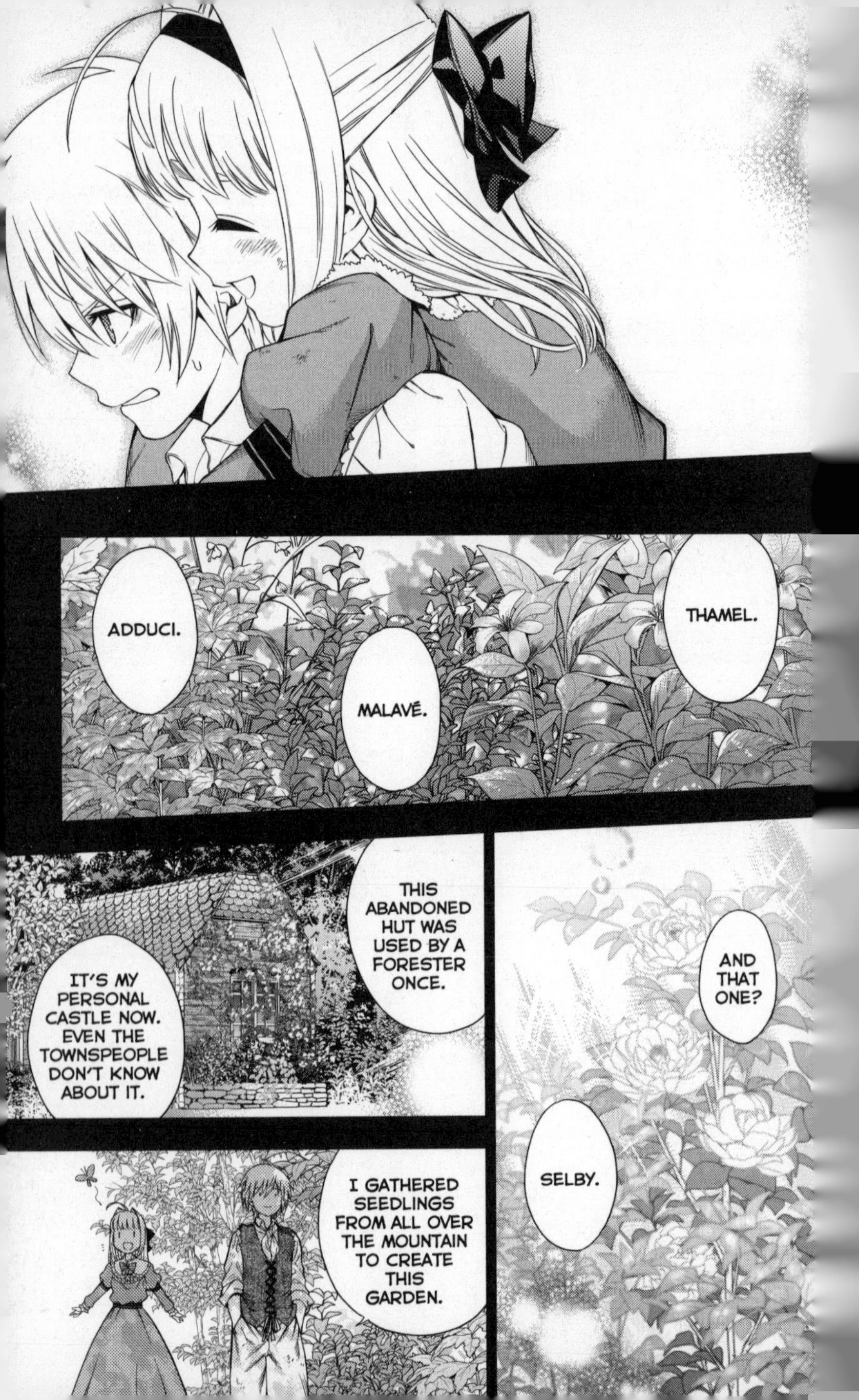
THAMEL.
MALAVÉ.
ADDUCI.
AND THAT ONE?
SELBY.
THIS ABANDONED HUT WAS USED BY A FORESTER ONCE.
IT'S MY PERSONAL CASTLE NOW. EVEN THE TOWNSPEOPLE DON'T KNOW ABOUT IT.
I GATHERED SEEDLINGS FROM ALL OVER THE MOUNTAIN TO CREATE THIS GARDEN.

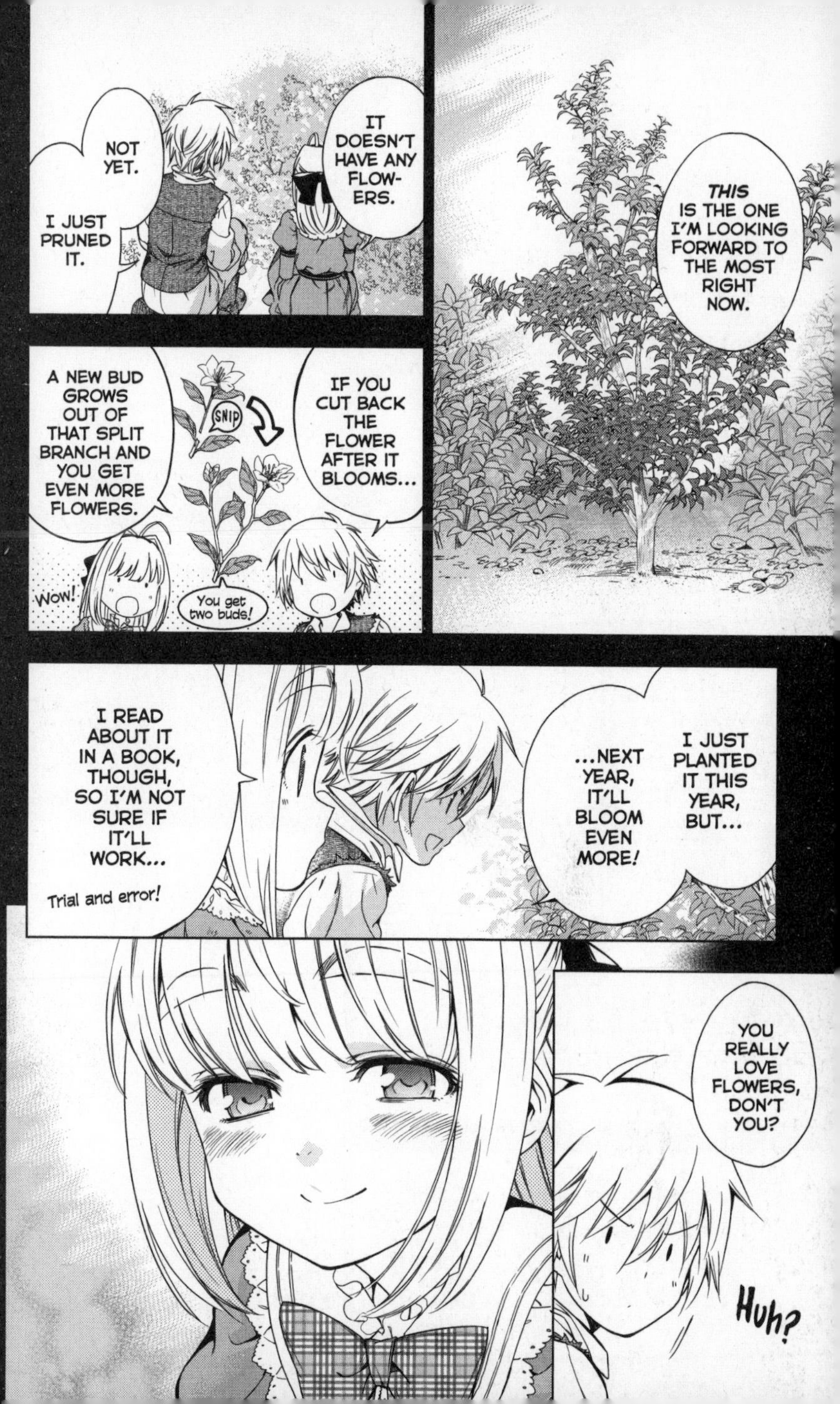
THIS IS THE ONE I'M LOOKING FORWARD TO THE MOST RIGHT NOW.
IT DOESN'T HAVE ANY FLOW-ERS.
NOT YET.
I JUST PRUNED IT.
IF YOU CUT BACK THE FLOWER AFTER IT BLOOMS...
SNIP
A NEW BUD GROWS OUT OF THAT SPLIT BRANCH AND YOU GET EVEN MORE FLOWERS.
You get two buds!
Wow!
I JUST PLANTED IT THIS YEAR, BUT...
...NEXT YEAR, IT'LL BLOOM EVEN MORE!
I READ ABOUT IT IN A BOOK, THOUGH, SO I'M NOT SURE IF IT'LL WORK...
Trial and error!
YOU REALLY LOVE FLOWERS, DON'T YOU?
Huh?

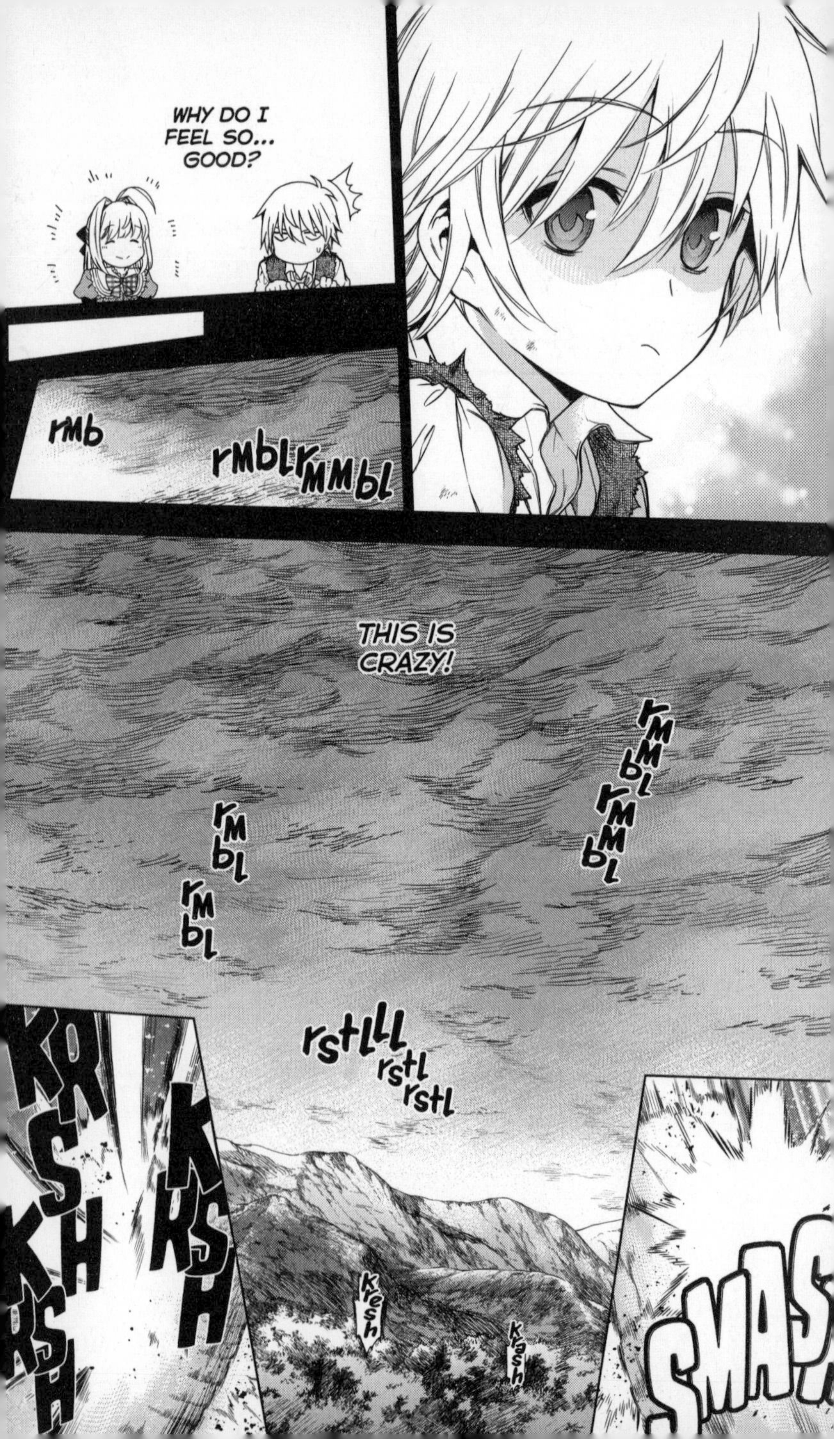
WHY DO I FEEL SO... GOOD?
rmb
rmblrmmbl
THIS IS CRAZY!
rmmbl rmmbl
rmbl
rmbl
rstLLL rstl rstl
SMAS
krash!
kresh
KRSH
KRSH
KRSH

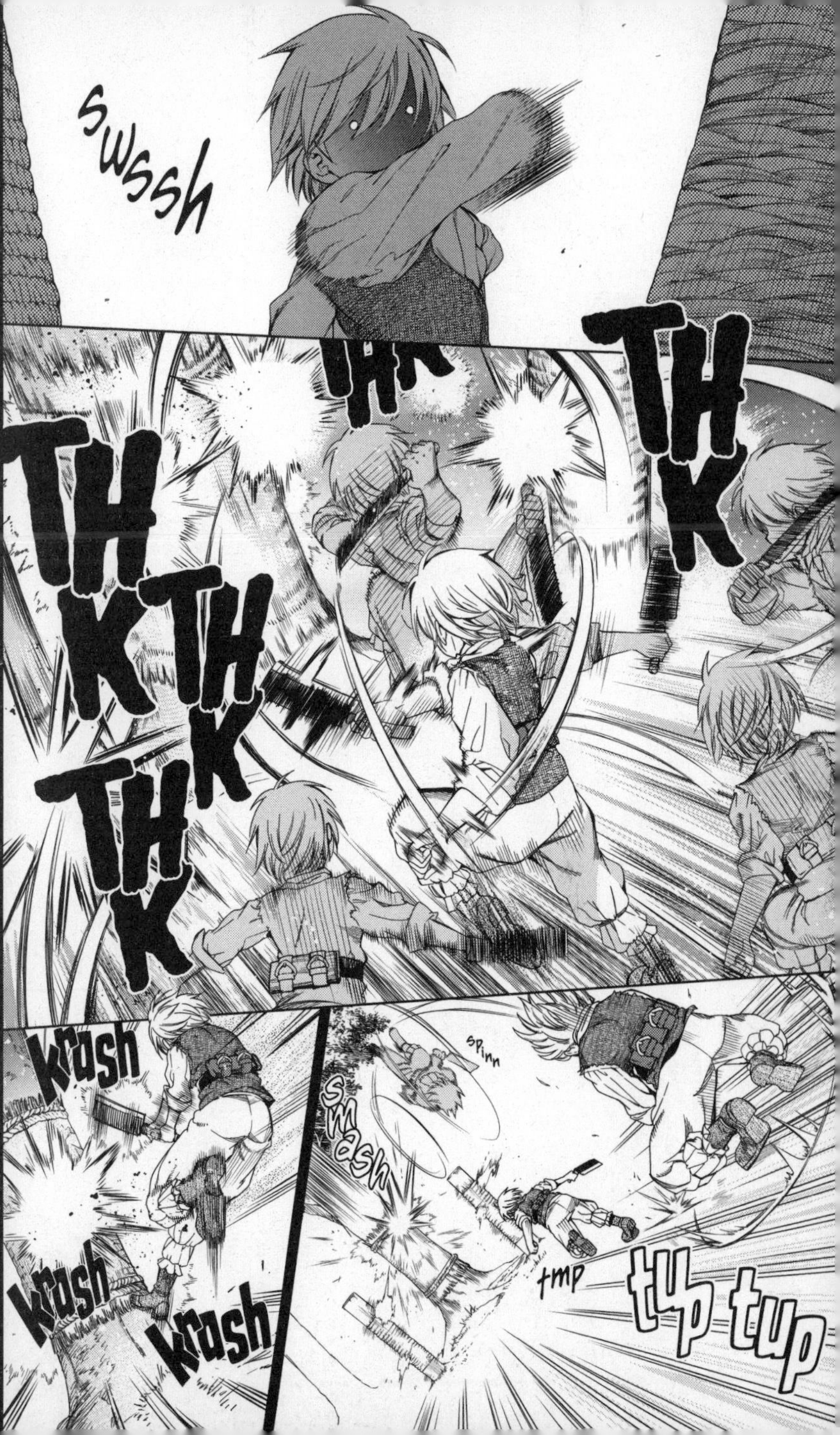
swssh
THK
THK
THK
THK
spinn
smash
tmp
tup tup
krash
krash
krash

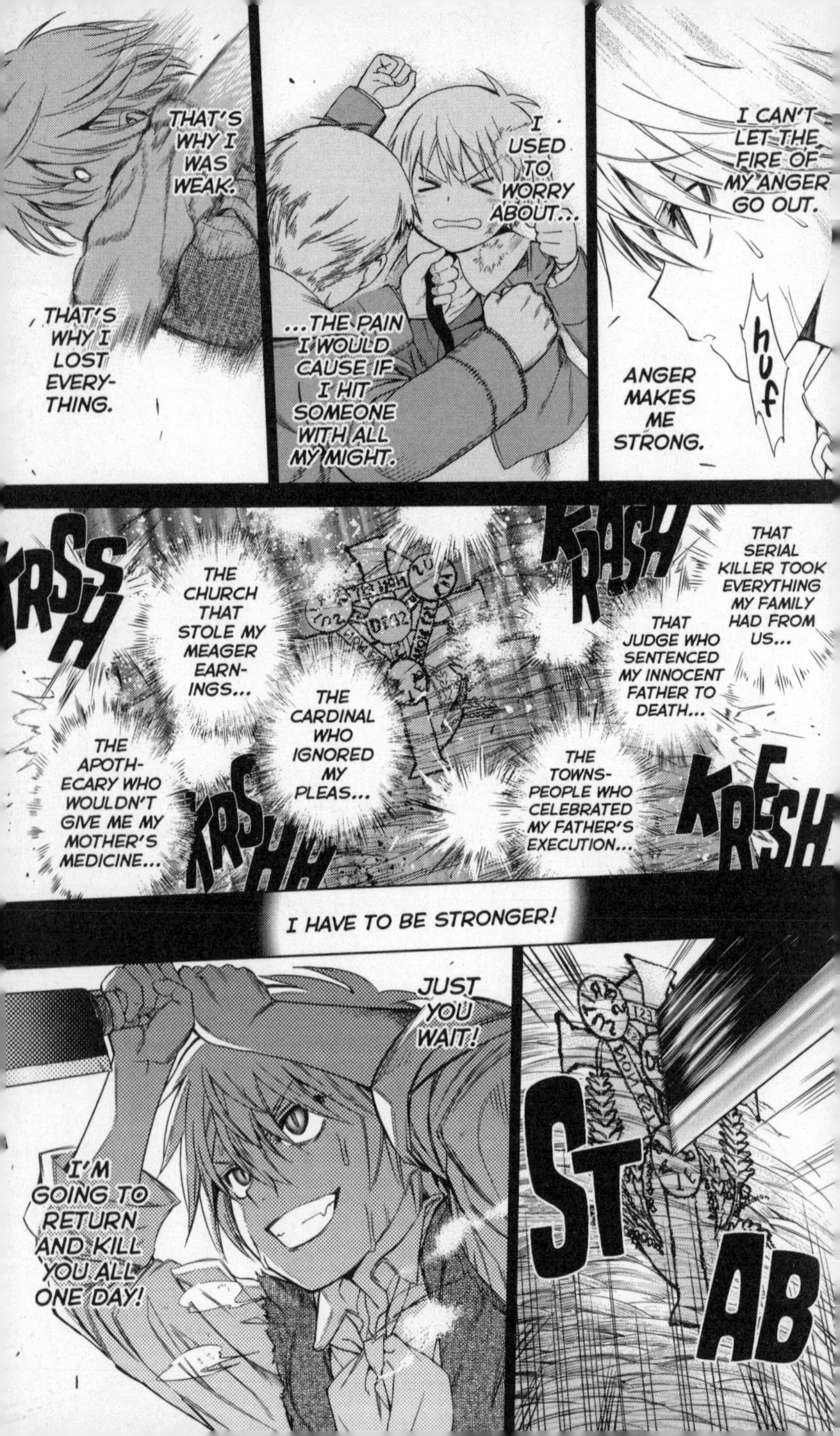
I CAN'T LET THE FIRE OF MY ANGER GO OUT.
huf
ANGER MAKES ME STRONG.
I USED TO WORRY ABOUT...
...THE PAIN I WOULD CAUSE IF I HIT SOMEONE WITH ALL MY MIGHT.
THAT'S WHY I WAS WEAK.
THAT'S WHY I LOST EVERY-THING.
THAT SERIAL KILLER TOOK EVERYTHING MY FAMILY HAD FROM US...
KRASH
THAT JUDGE WHO SENTENCED MY INNOCENT FATHER TO DEATH...
KRESH
THE TOWNS-PEOPLE WHO CELEBRATED MY FATHER'S EXECUTION...
THE CHURCH THAT STOLE MY MEAGER EARN-INGS...
THE CARDINAL WHO IGNORED MY PLEAS...
KRSSH
THE APOTH-ECARY WHO WOULDN'T GIVE ME MY MOTHER'S MEDICINE...
KRSHH
I HAVE TO BE STRONGER!
STAB
JUST YOU WAIT!
I'M GOING TO RETURN AND KILL YOU ALL ONE DAY!

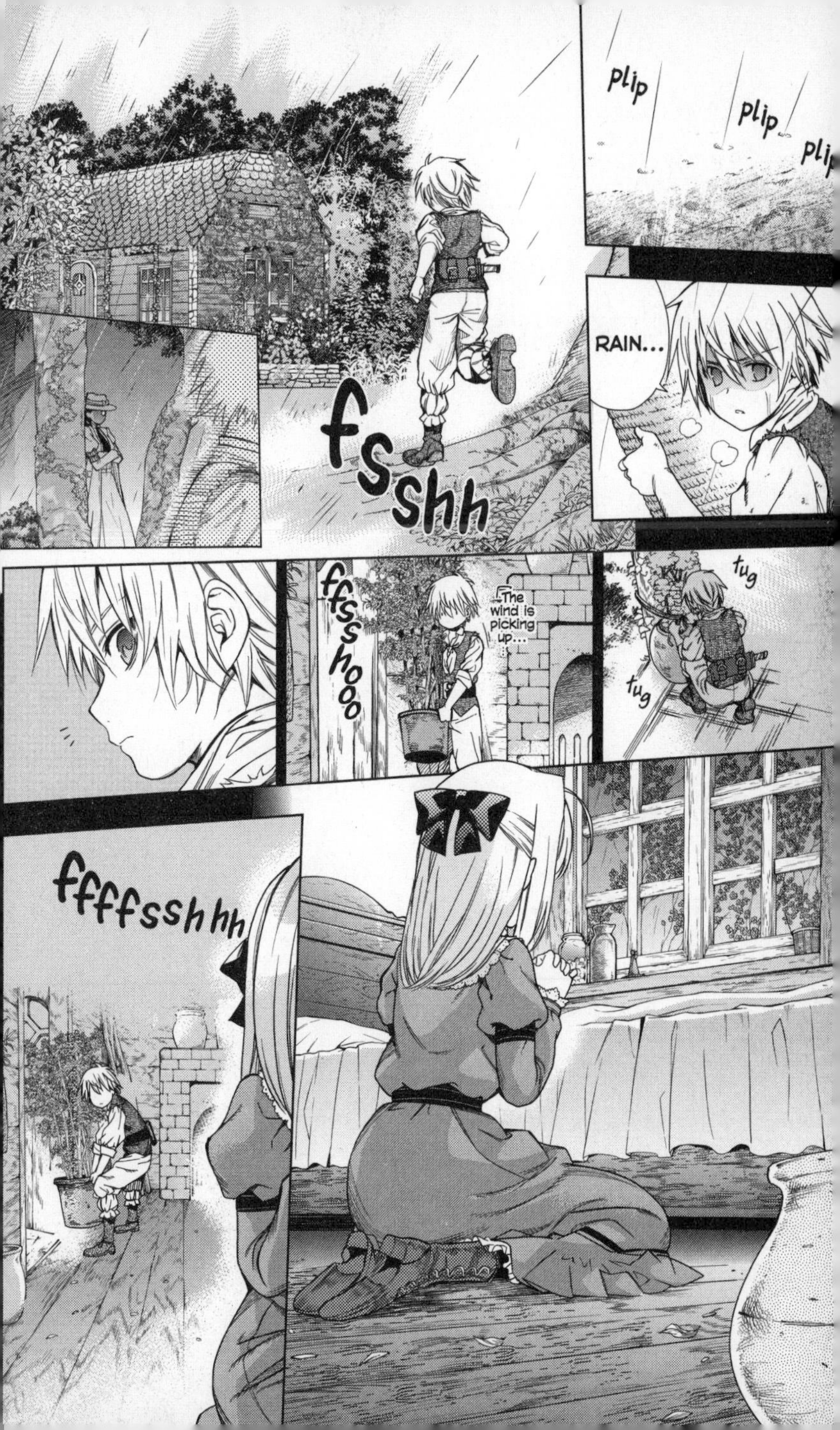
plip
plip
pli
RAIN...
fsshh
tug
tug
ffsshooo
...The wind is picking up...
ffffsshhh

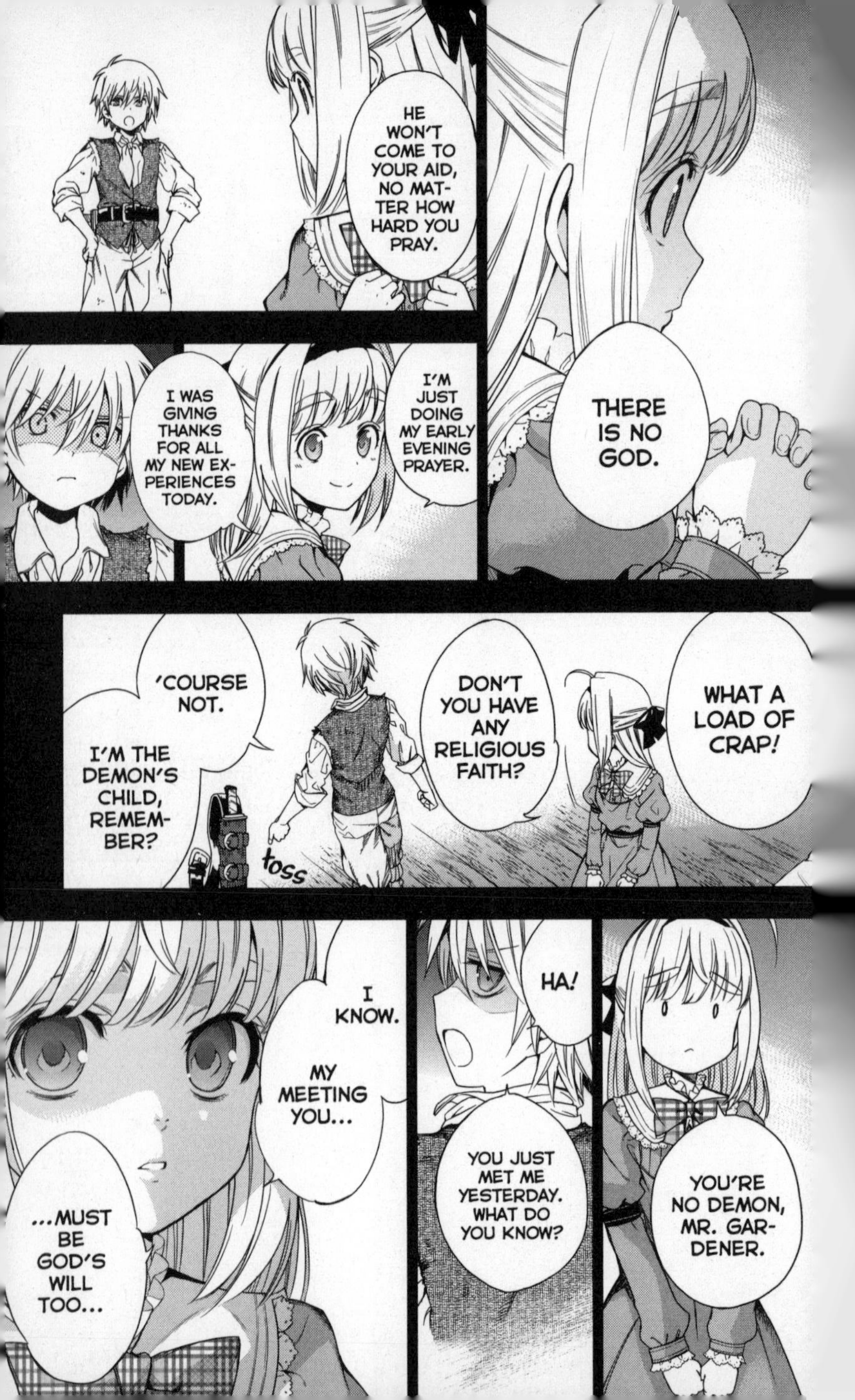
THERE IS NO GOD.
HE WON'T COME TO YOUR AID, NO MAT-TER HOW HARD YOU PRAY.
I'M JUST DOING MY EARLY EVENING PRAYER.
I WAS GIVING THANKS FOR ALL MY NEW EX-PERIENCES TODAY.
WHAT A LOAD OF CRAP!
DON'T YOU HAVE ANY RELIGIOUS FAITH?
'COURSE NOT.
I'M THE DEMON'S CHILD, REMEM-BER?
toss
YOU'RE NO DEMON, MR. GAR-DENER.
HA!
YOU JUST MET ME YESTERDAY. WHAT DO YOU KNOW?
I KNOW.
MY MEETING YOU...
...MUST BE GOD'S WILL TOO...

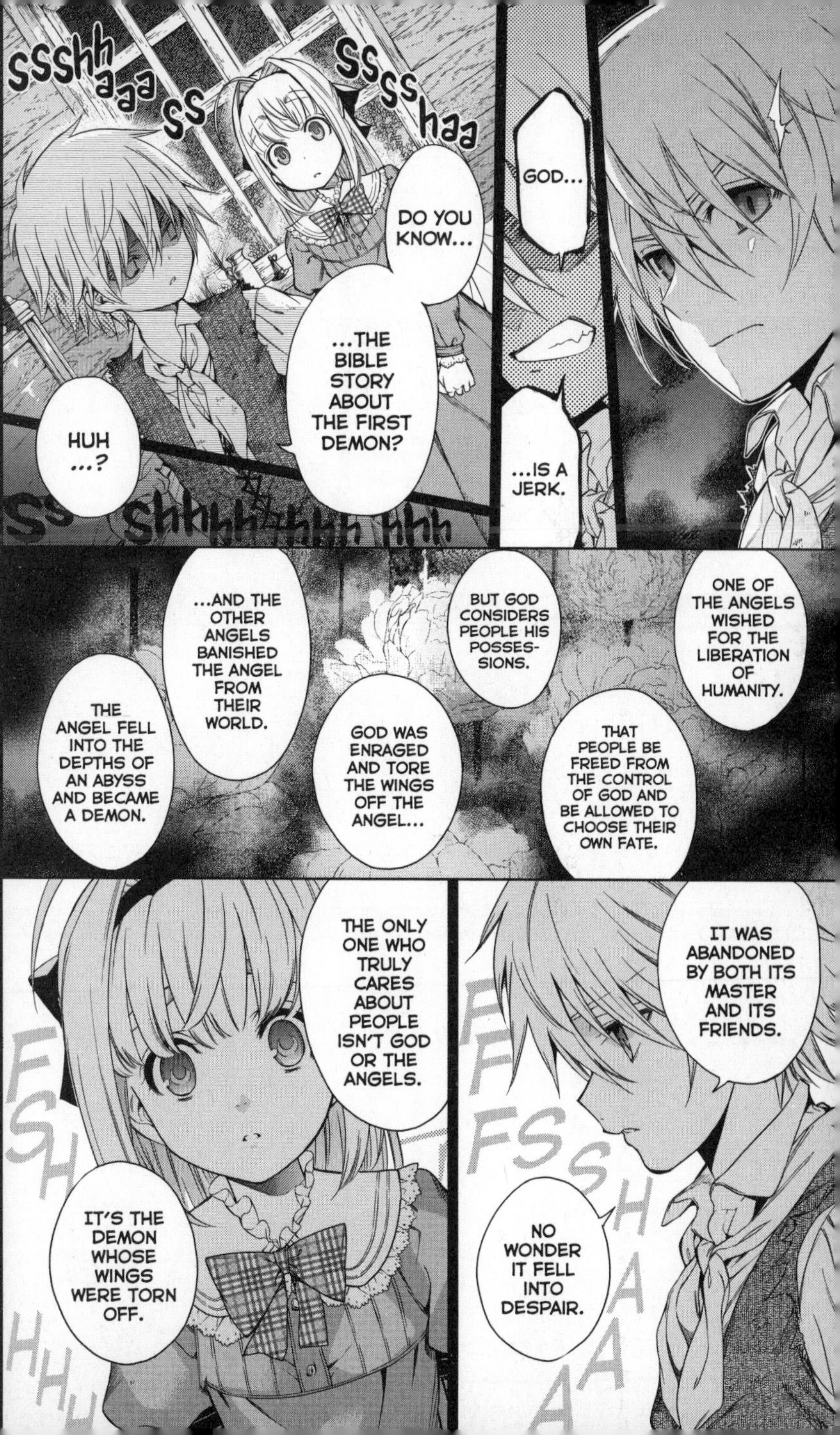
GOD...
...IS A JERK.
SSShhaaa SS
SSSShaa
DO YOU KNOW...
...THE BIBLE STORY ABOUT THE FIRST DEMON?
HUH ...?
ONE OF THE ANGELS WISHED FOR THE LIBERATION OF HUMANITY.
THAT PEOPLE BE FREED FROM THE CONTROL OF GOD AND BE ALLOWED TO CHOOSE THEIR OWN FATE.
BUT GOD CONSIDERS PEOPLE HIS POSSES-SIONS.
GOD WAS ENRAGED AND TORE THE WINGS OFF THE ANGEL...
...AND THE OTHER ANGELS BANISHED THE ANGEL FROM THEIR WORLD.
THE ANGEL FELL INTO THE DEPTHS OF AN ABYSS AND BECAME A DEMON.
IT WAS ABANDONED BY BOTH ITS MASTER AND ITS FRIENDS.
NO WONDER IT FELL INTO DESPAIR.
THE ONLY ONE WHO TRULY CARES ABOUT PEOPLE ISN'T GOD OR THE ANGELS.
IT'S THE DEMON WHOSE WINGS WERE TORN OFF.

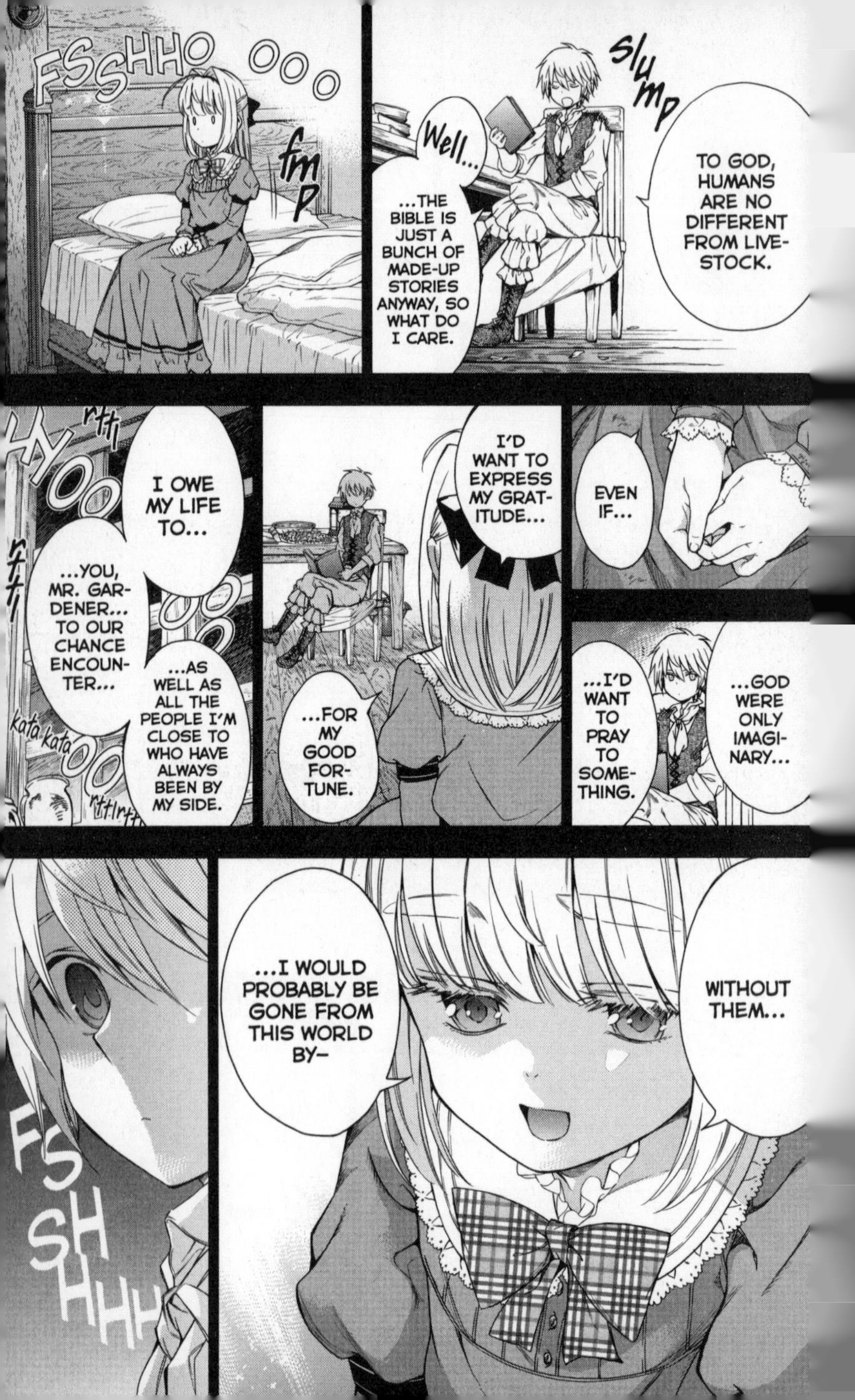
slump
TO GOD, HUMANS ARE NO DIFFERENT FROM LIVE-STOCK.
Well...
...THE BIBLE IS JUST A BUNCH OF MADE-UP STORIES ANYWAY, SO WHAT DO I CARE.
FSSHHOOOO
fmp
EVEN IF...
...GOD WERE ONLY IMAGINARY...
...I'D WANT TO PRAY TO SOMETHING.
I'D WANT TO EXPRESS MY GRATITUDE...
...FOR MY GOOD FORTUNE.
HYOOOOOO
I OWE MY LIFE TO...
...YOU, MR. GARDENER... TO OUR CHANCE ENCOUNTER...
...AS WELL AS ALL THE PEOPLE I'M CLOSE TO WHO HAVE ALWAYS BEEN BY MY SIDE.
kata kata
WITHOUT THEM...
...I WOULD PROBABLY BE GONE FROM THIS WORLD BY–
FSSHHHH

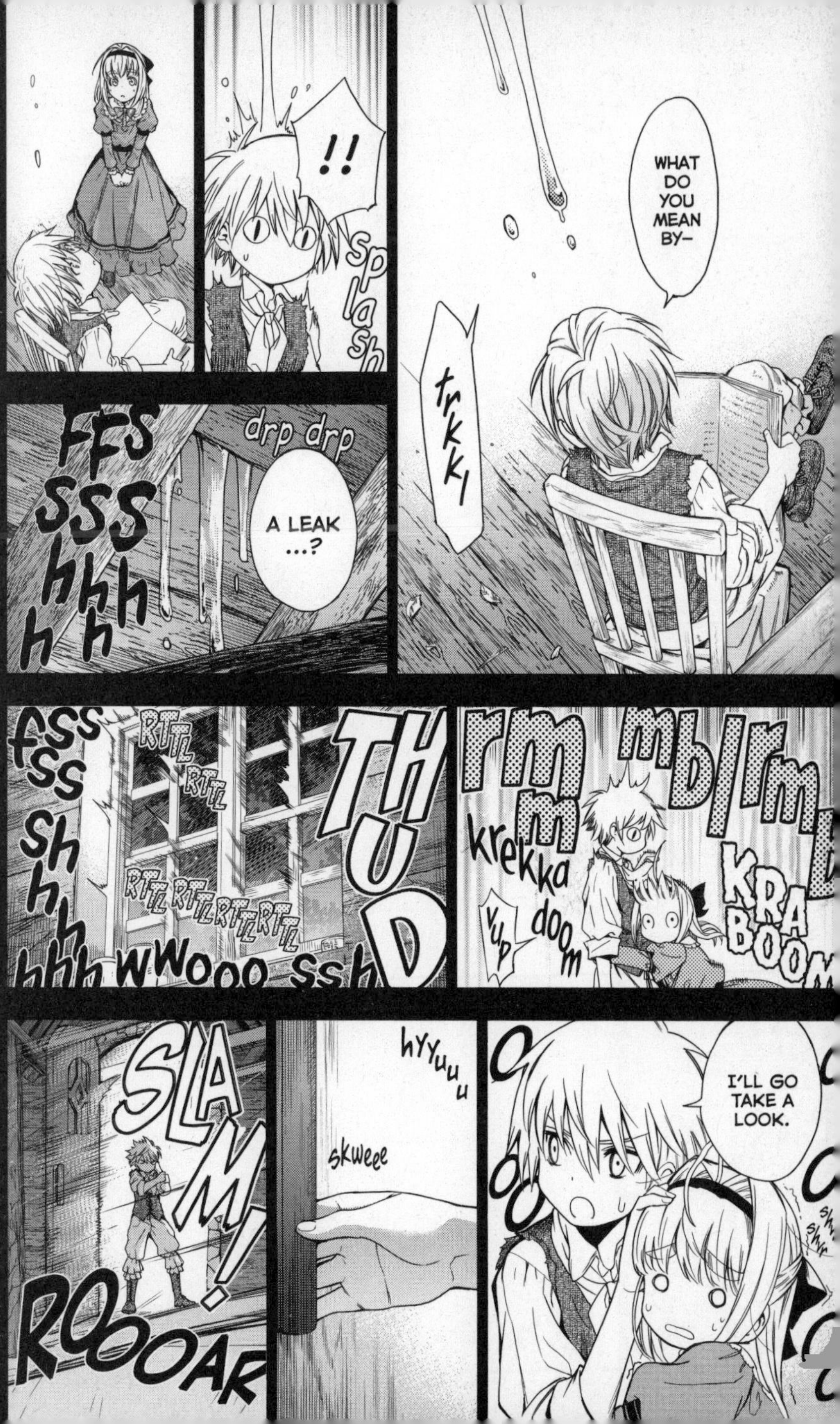
WHAT DO YOU MEAN BY–
trkkkl
!!
splash
drp drp
A LEAK ...?
FFSSSShhhhh
rmmm blrm
krekka doom
vup
KRABOOM
THUD
fsss sshhhhh
RTTL RTTL
RTTL RTTL RTTL RTTL
wwooo ssh
I'LL GO TAKE A LOOK.
hyyuuu
skweee
SLAM!
ROOOAR

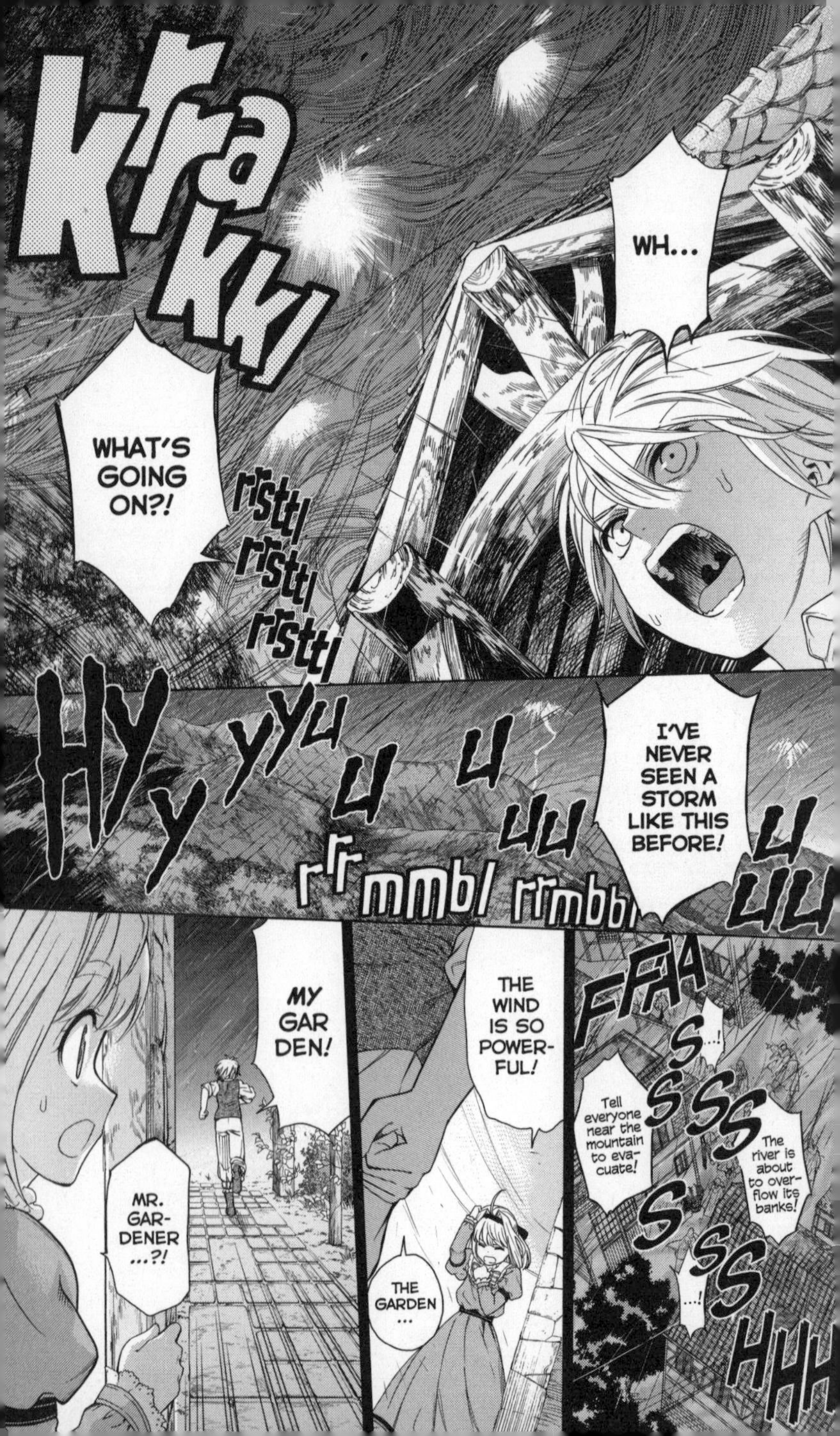
WH...
K-RA KKK!
WHAT'S GOING ON?!
rrsttl rrsttl rrsttl
I'VE NEVER SEEN A STORM LIKE THIS BEFORE!
HYYYUUUUUUUUU
rrrmmbl rrmbbl
FFAASSSSSSSSHHH
Tell everyone near the mountain to evacuate!
...!
The river is about to overflow its banks!
...!
THE WIND IS SO POWERFUL!
THE GARDEN...
MY GARDEN!
MR. GARDENER...?!

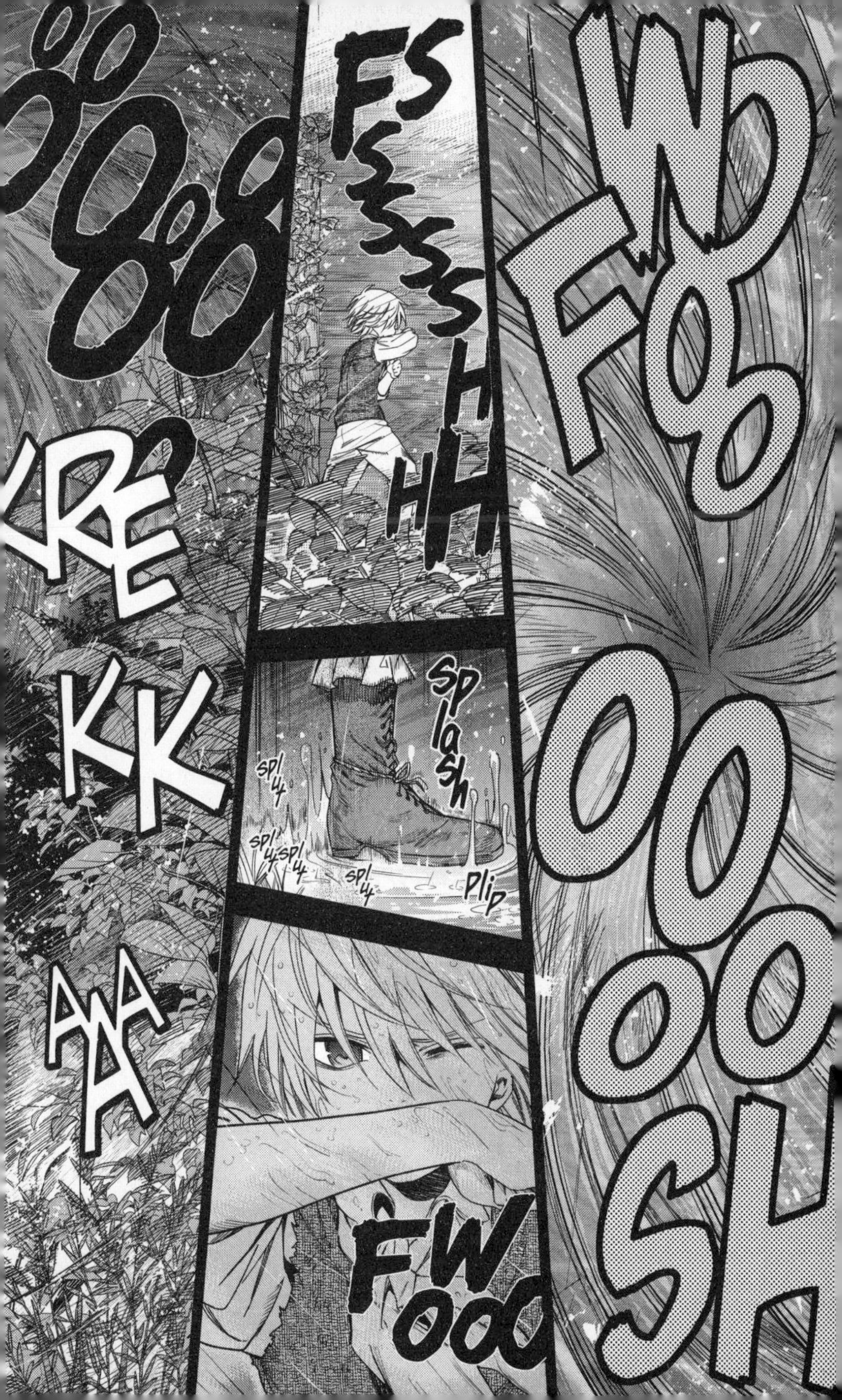
FSSSSSHHH
splash
Plip
FWOOO
KREEKK
AAAA

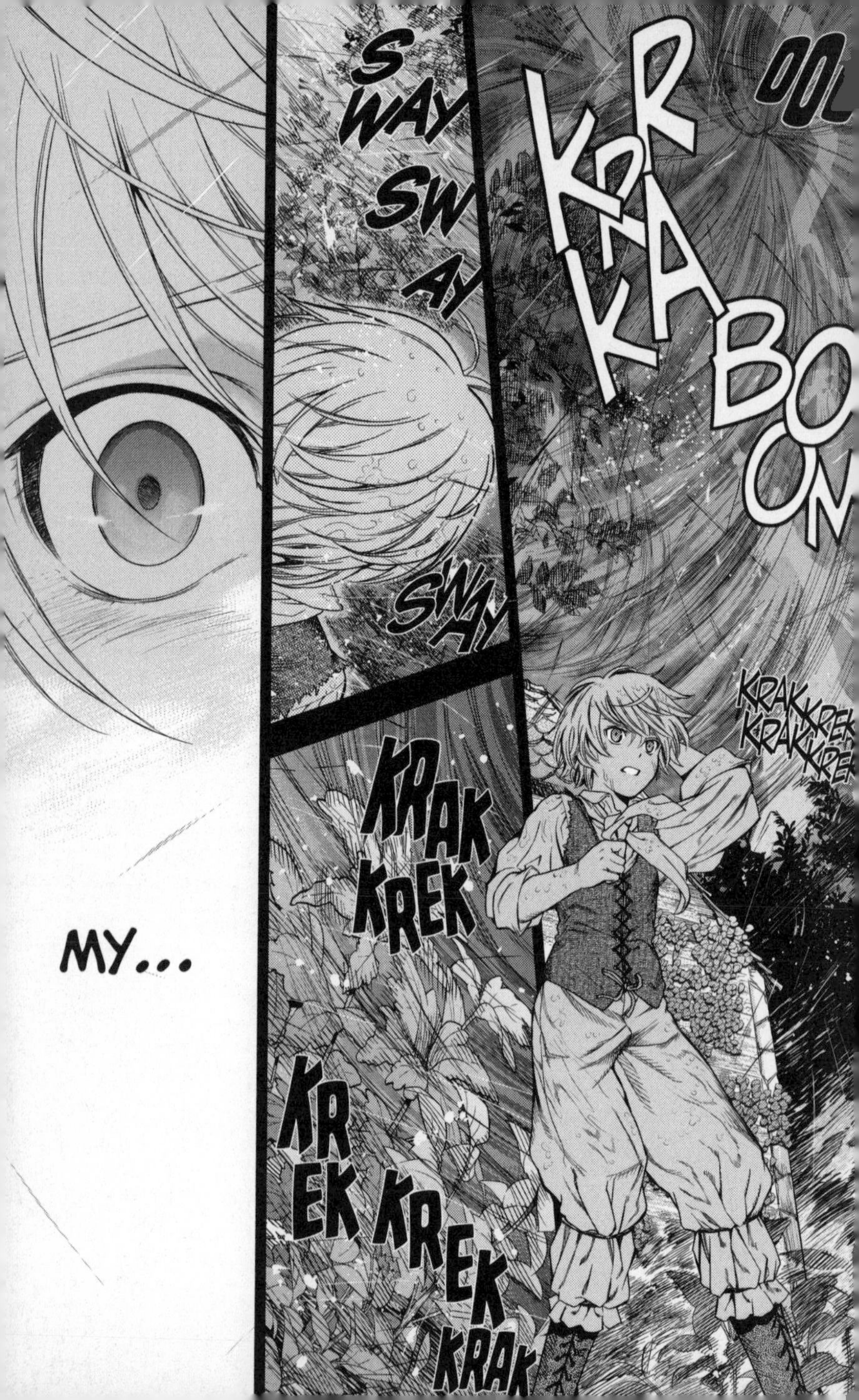
KRAKABOOM
SWAY SWAY SWAY
SWAY
KRAKKREK KRAKKREK
KRAK KREK
KREK KREK KRAK
MY...

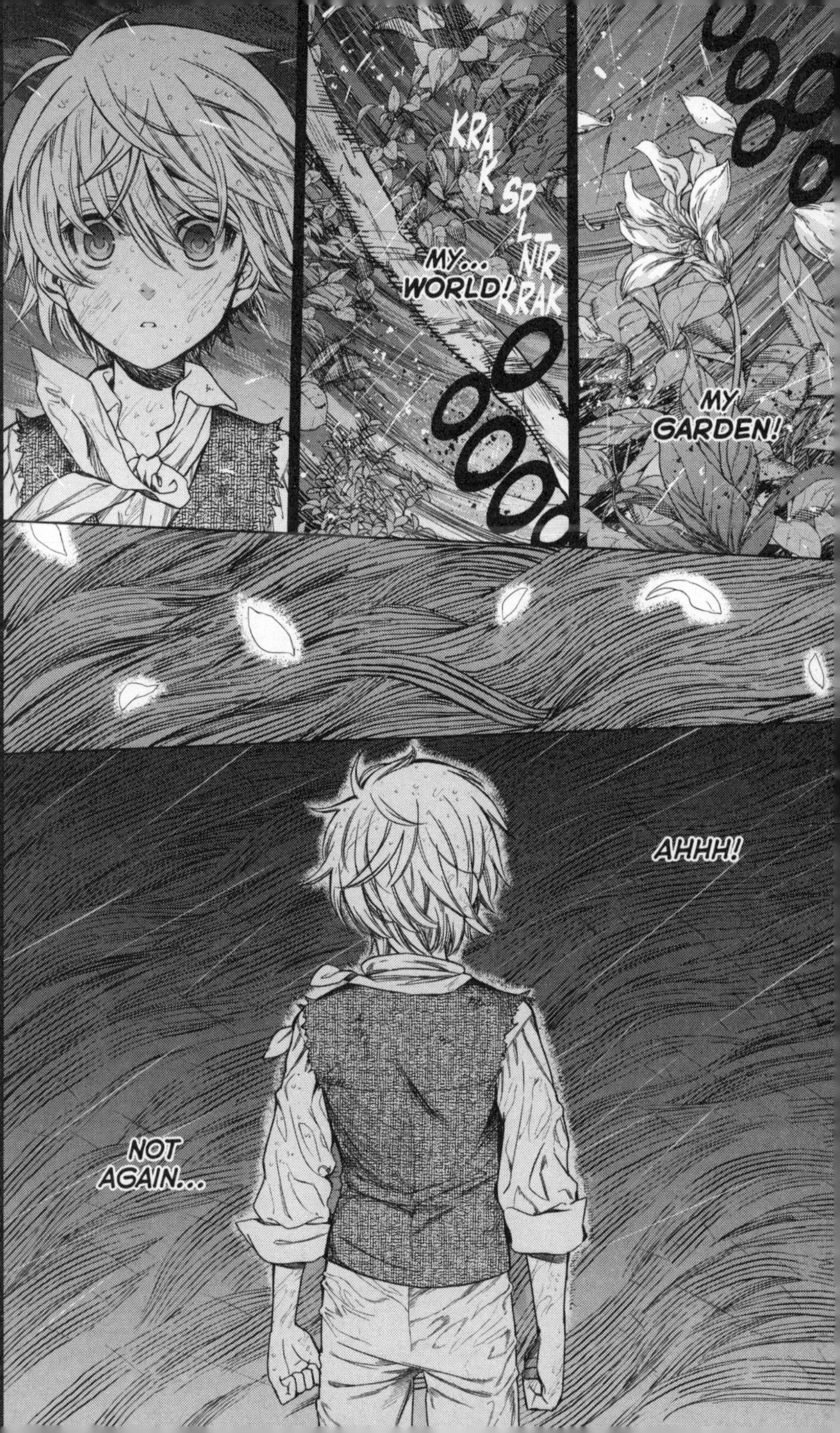

MY GARDEN!
KRAK SPLNTR KRAK
MY... WORLD!
AHHH!
NOT AGAIN...

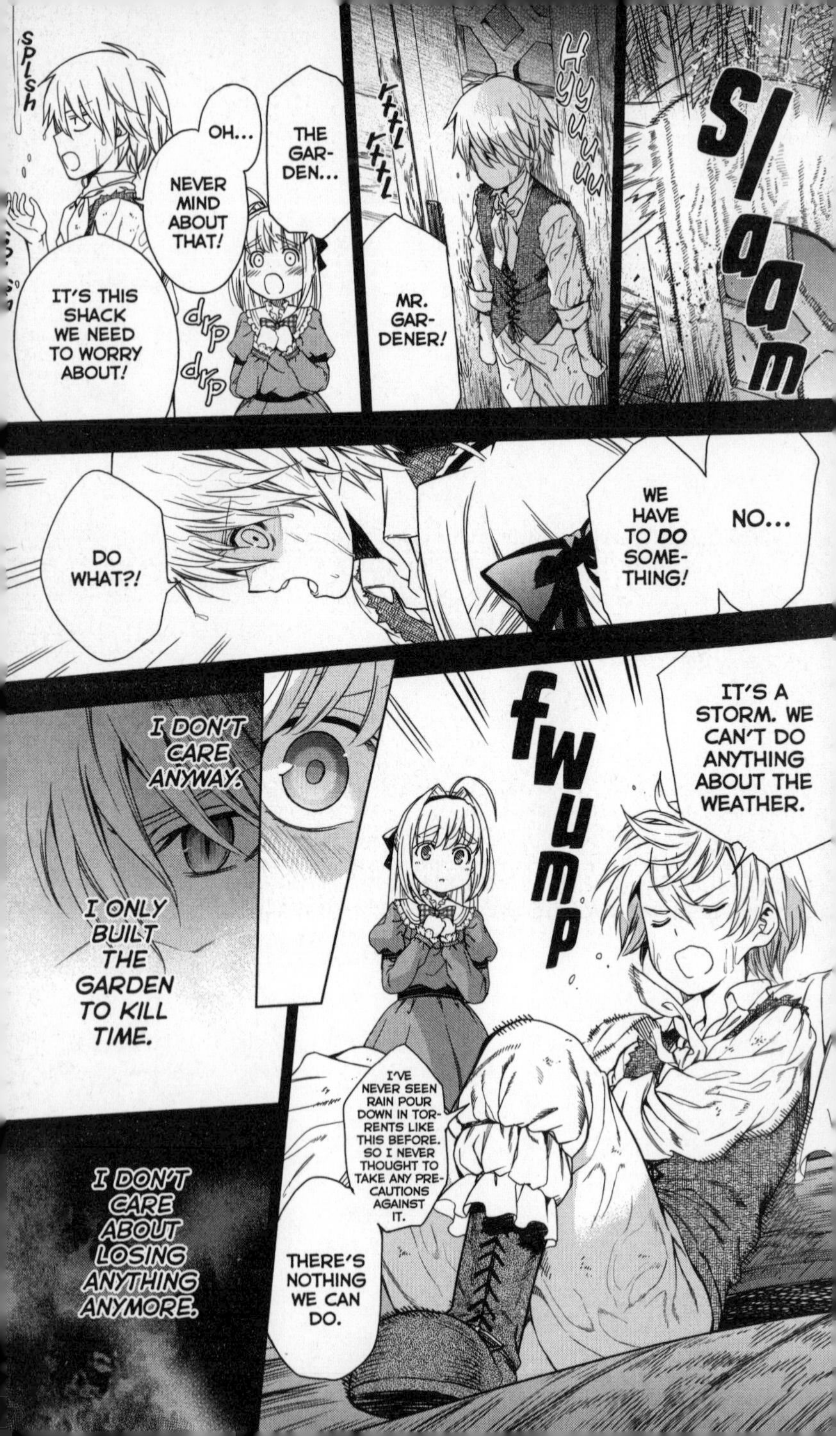
Slaam
Hyyuuuu
rttl rttl
MR. GARDENER!
THE GARDEN...
OH...
NEVER MIND ABOUT THAT!
IT'S THIS SHACK WE NEED TO WORRY ABOUT!
drp drp
splsh
NO...
WE HAVE TO DO SOMETHING!
DO WHAT?!
IT'S A STORM. WE CAN'T DO ANYTHING ABOUT THE WEATHER.
fwump
I'VE NEVER SEEN RAIN POUR DOWN IN TORRENTS LIKE THIS BEFORE. SO I NEVER THOUGHT TO TAKE ANY PRECAUTIONS AGAINST IT.
THERE'S NOTHING WE CAN DO.
I DON'T CARE ANYWAY.
I ONLY BUILT THE GARDEN TO KILL TIME.
I DON'T CARE ABOUT LOSING ANYTHING ANYMORE.

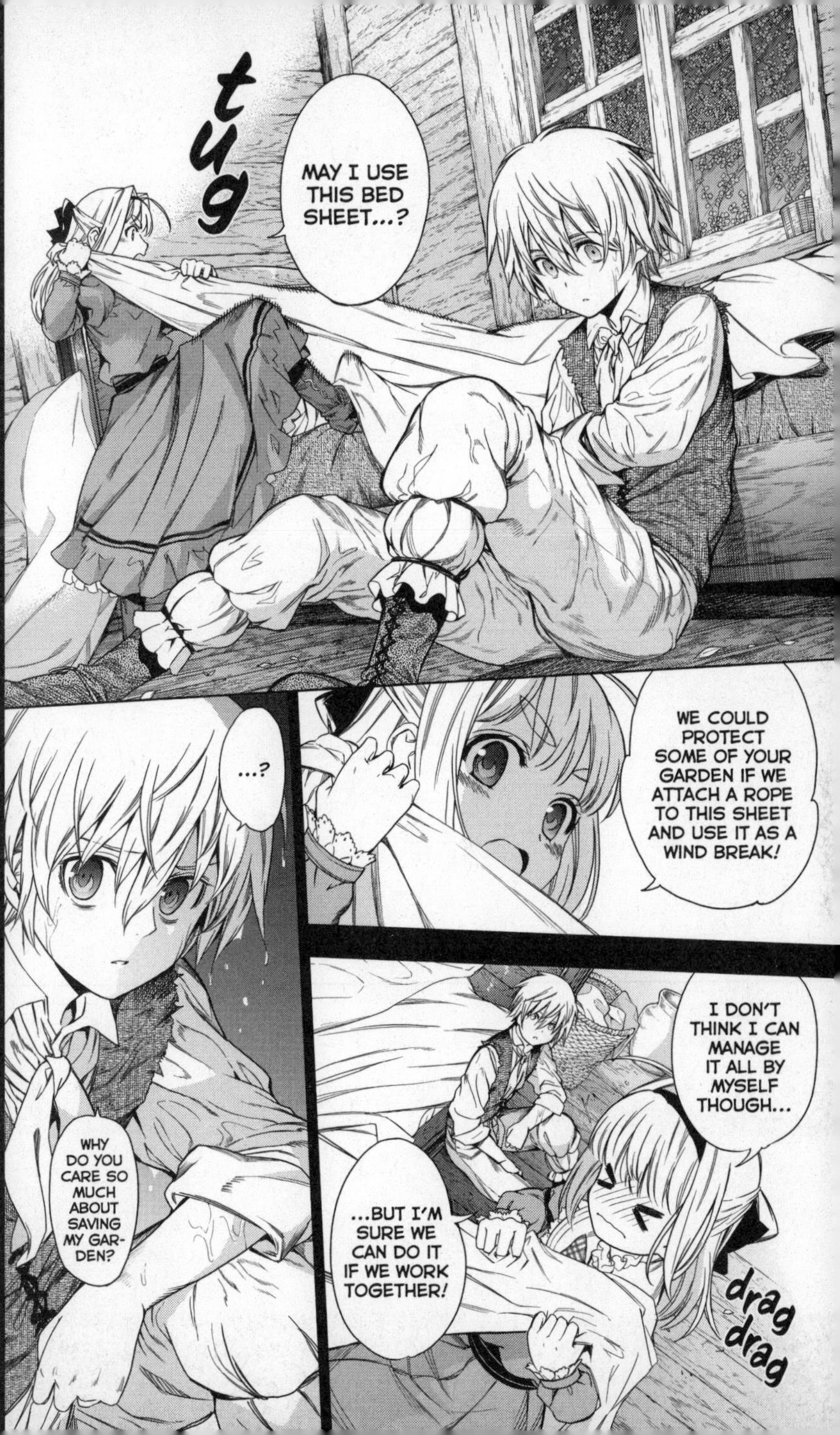
MAY I USE THIS BED SHEET...?
tug
WE COULD PROTECT SOME OF YOUR GARDEN IF WE ATTACH A ROPE TO THIS SHEET AND USE IT AS A WIND BREAK!
I DON'T THINK I CAN MANAGE IT ALL BY MYSELF THOUGH...
...BUT I'M SURE WE CAN DO IT IF WE WORK TOGETHER!
drag drag
...?
WHY DO YOU CARE SO MUCH ABOUT SAVING MY GAR-DEN?

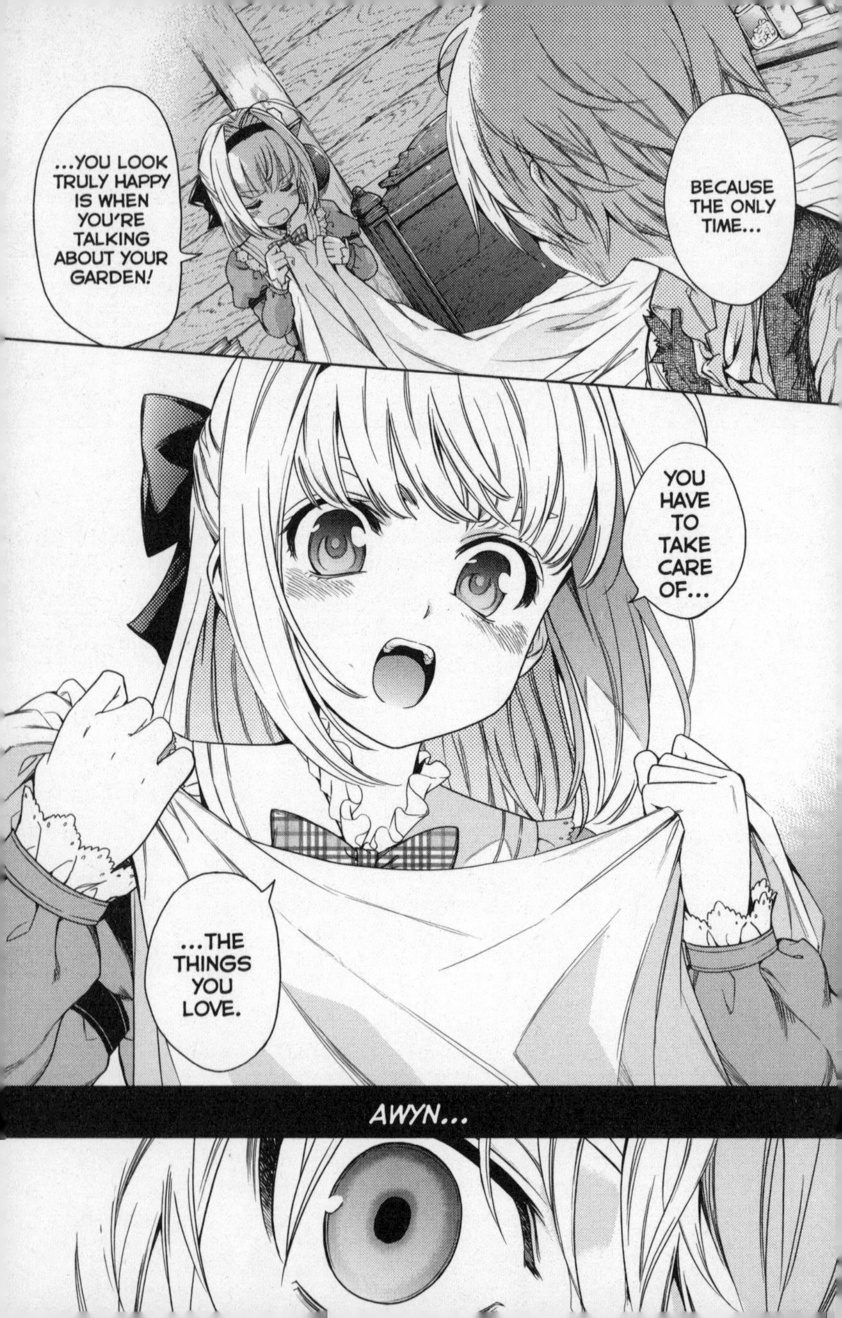
BECAUSE THE ONLY TIME...
...YOU LOOK TRULY HAPPY IS WHEN YOU'RE TALKING ABOUT YOUR GARDEN!
YOU HAVE TO TAKE CARE OF...
...THE THINGS YOU LOVE.
AWYN...

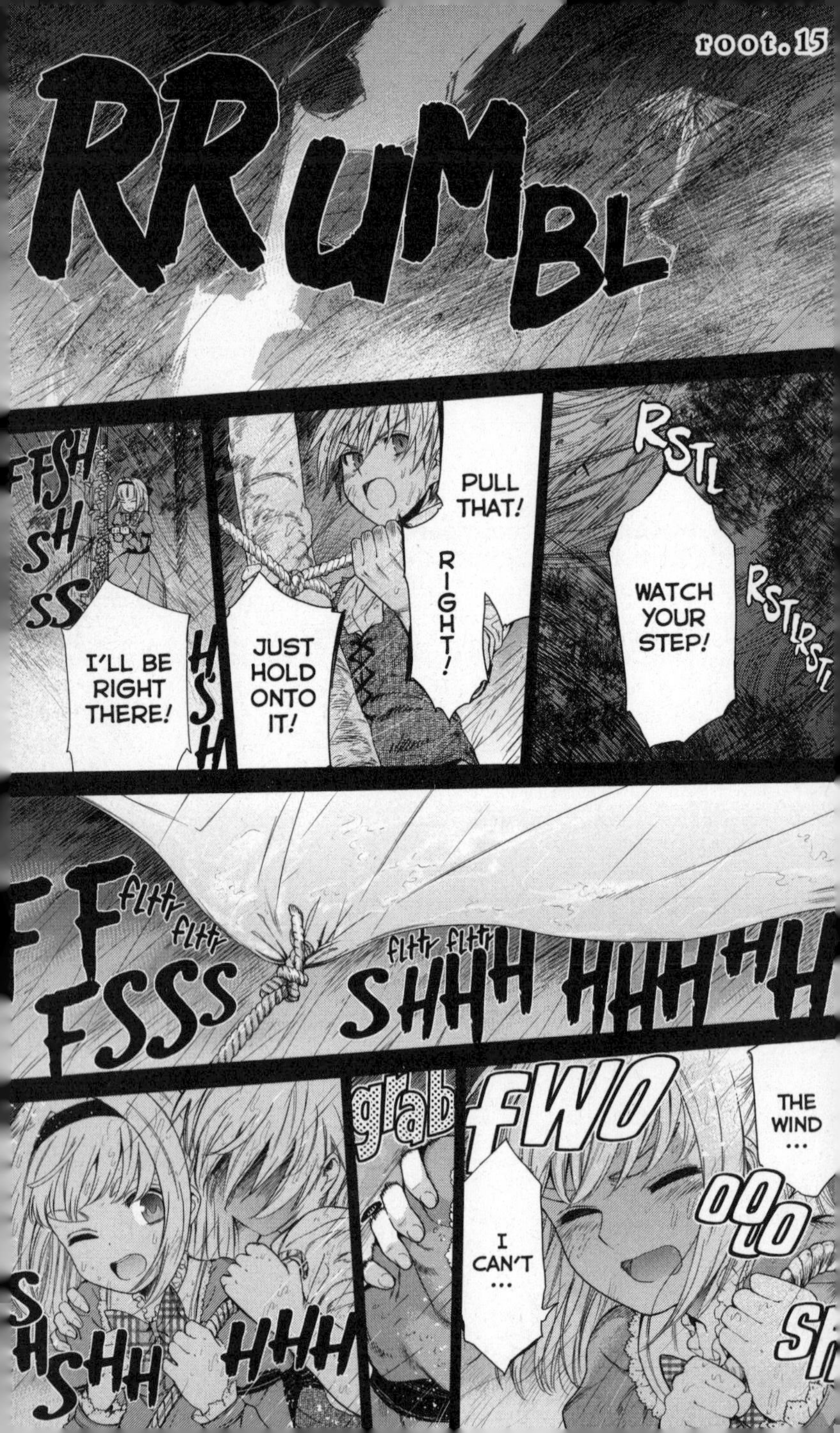
root. 15
RRUMBL
RSTL
WATCH YOUR STEP!
RSTLRSTL
PULL THAT!
RIGHT!
JUST HOLD ONTO IT!
HSH
FFSH SH SSS
I'LL BE RIGHT THERE!
SHHH HHHHH
fltr fltr
FF FSSS
fltr fltr
THE WIND...
FWO
OOO
SH
I CAN'T...
grab
SHSHH HHH

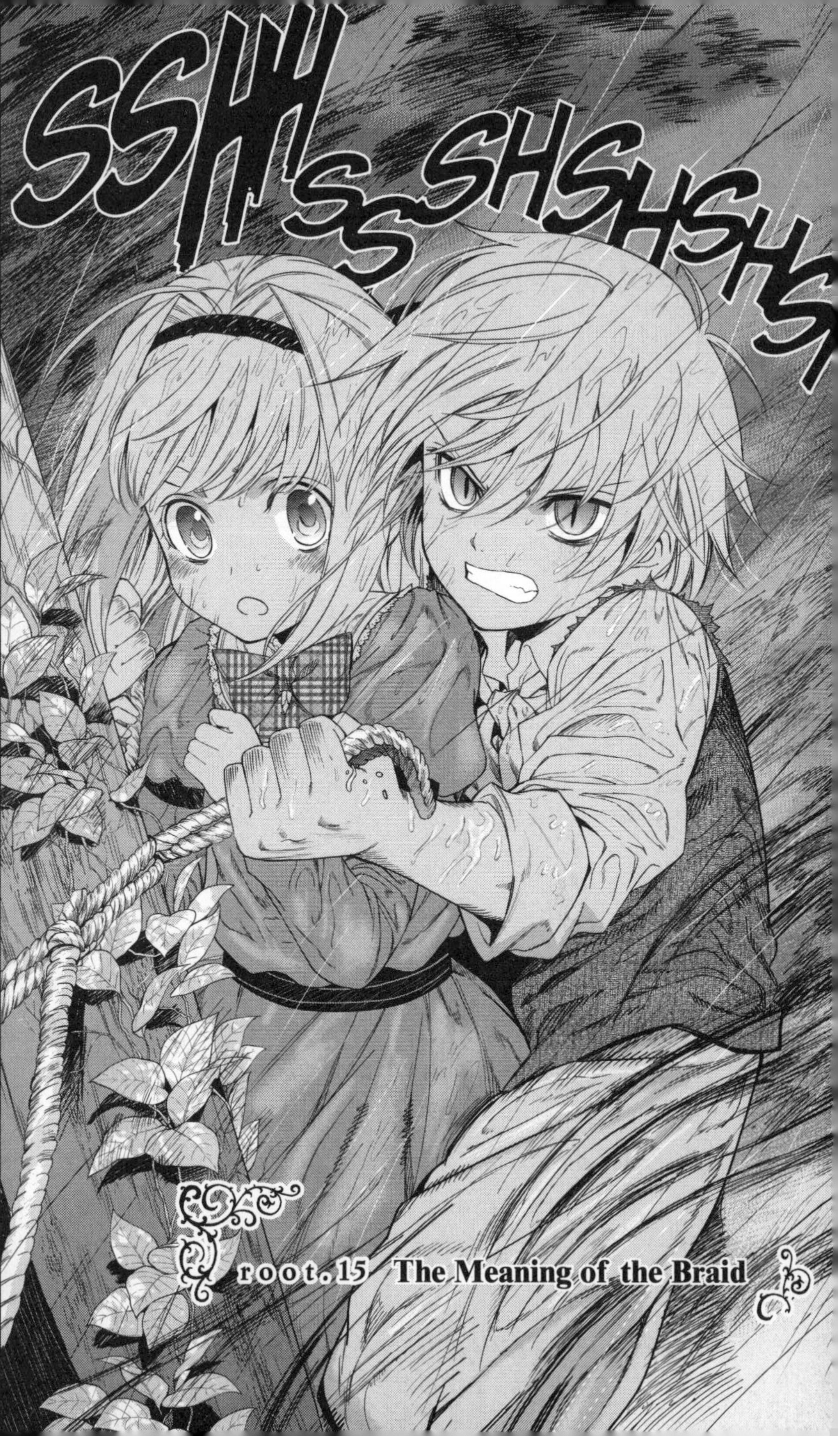
SSHHH
SSSHSHSHSHSH
root. 15 The Meaning of the Braid

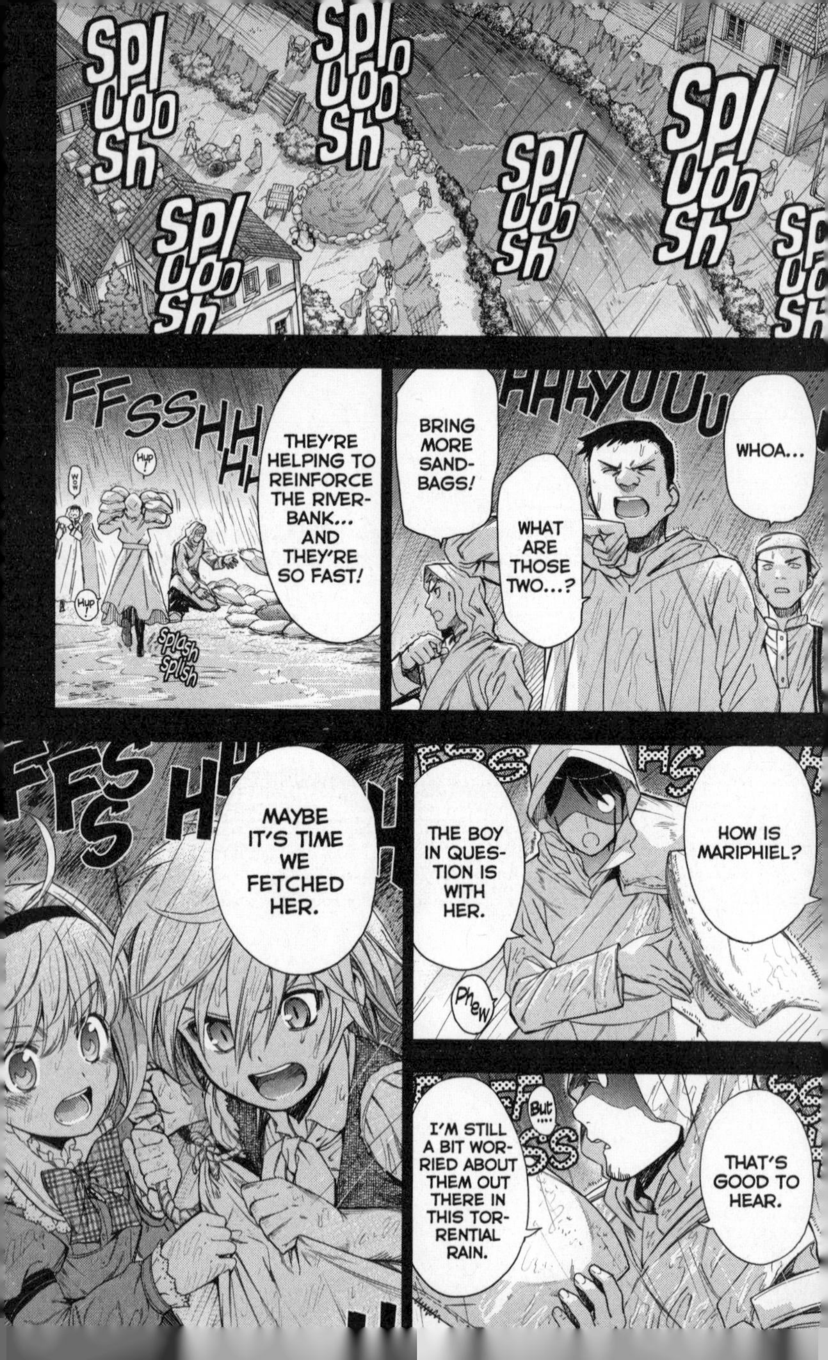
Splooosh
Splooosh
Splooosh
Splooosh
Splooosh
Splooosh
HHHYUUU
WHOA...
BRING MORE SAND-BAGS!
WHAT ARE THOSE TWO...?
FFSSHHH
THEY'RE HELPING TO REINFORCE THE RIVER-BANK... AND THEY'RE SO FAST!
Hup!
WOW
Hup!
Splash splish
HOW IS MARIPHIEL?
THE BOY IN QUES-TION IS WITH HER.
Phew
THAT'S GOOD TO HEAR.
But...
I'M STILL A BIT WOR-RIED ABOUT THEM OUT THERE IN THIS TOR-RENTIAL RAIN.
FFSSHH
MAYBE IT'S TIME WE FETCHED HER.

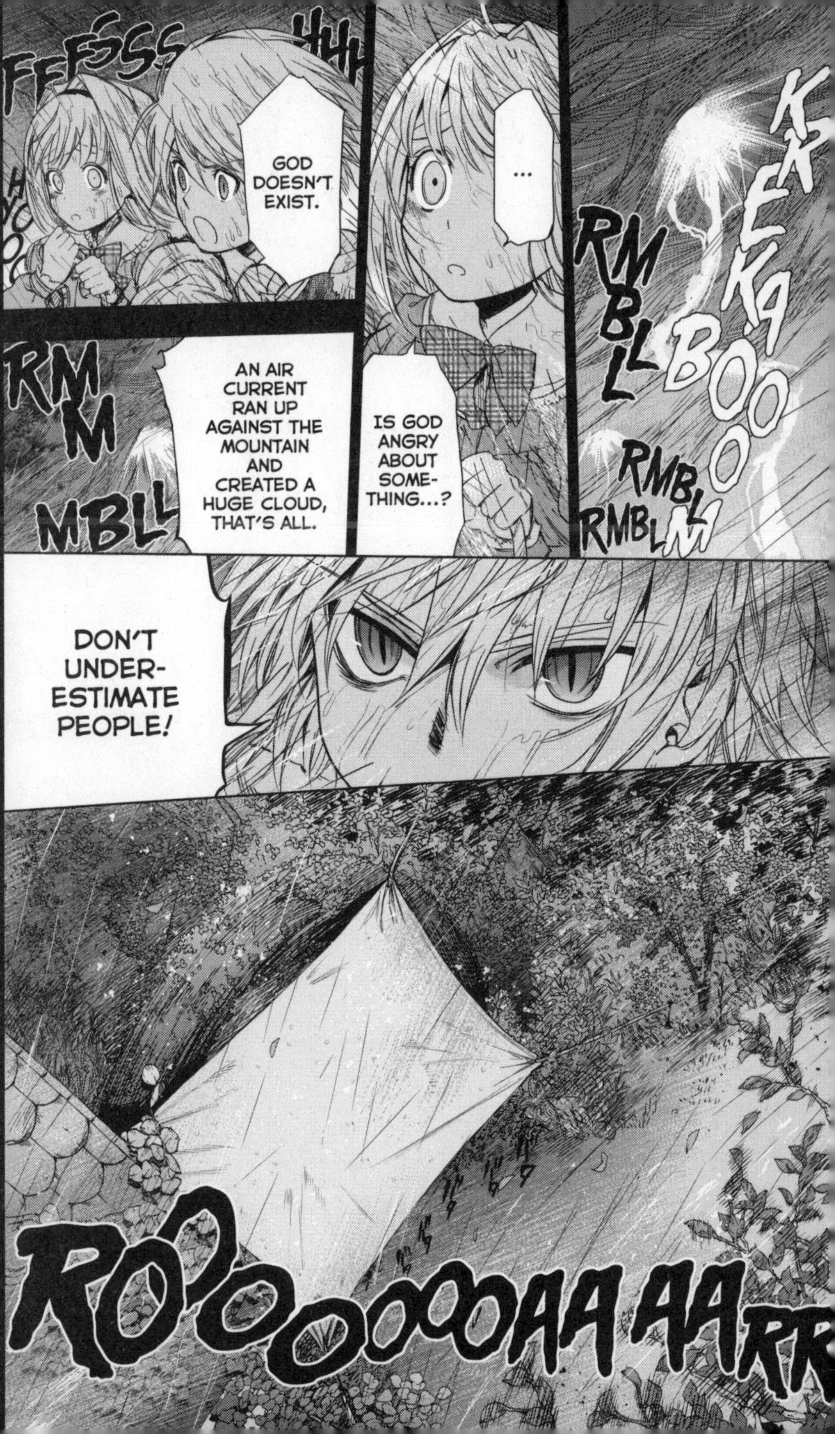
KRACKABOOOM
RMBLL
RMBLM
RMBLM
...
IS GOD ANGRY ABOUT SOME-THING...?
FFFSSS
HHH
HYOOO
GOD DOESN'T EXIST.
RMMMBLL
AN AIR CURRENT RAN UP AGAINST THE MOUNTAIN AND CREATED A HUGE CLOUD, THAT'S ALL.
DON'T UNDER-ESTIMATE PEOPLE!
ROOOOOAAAARR

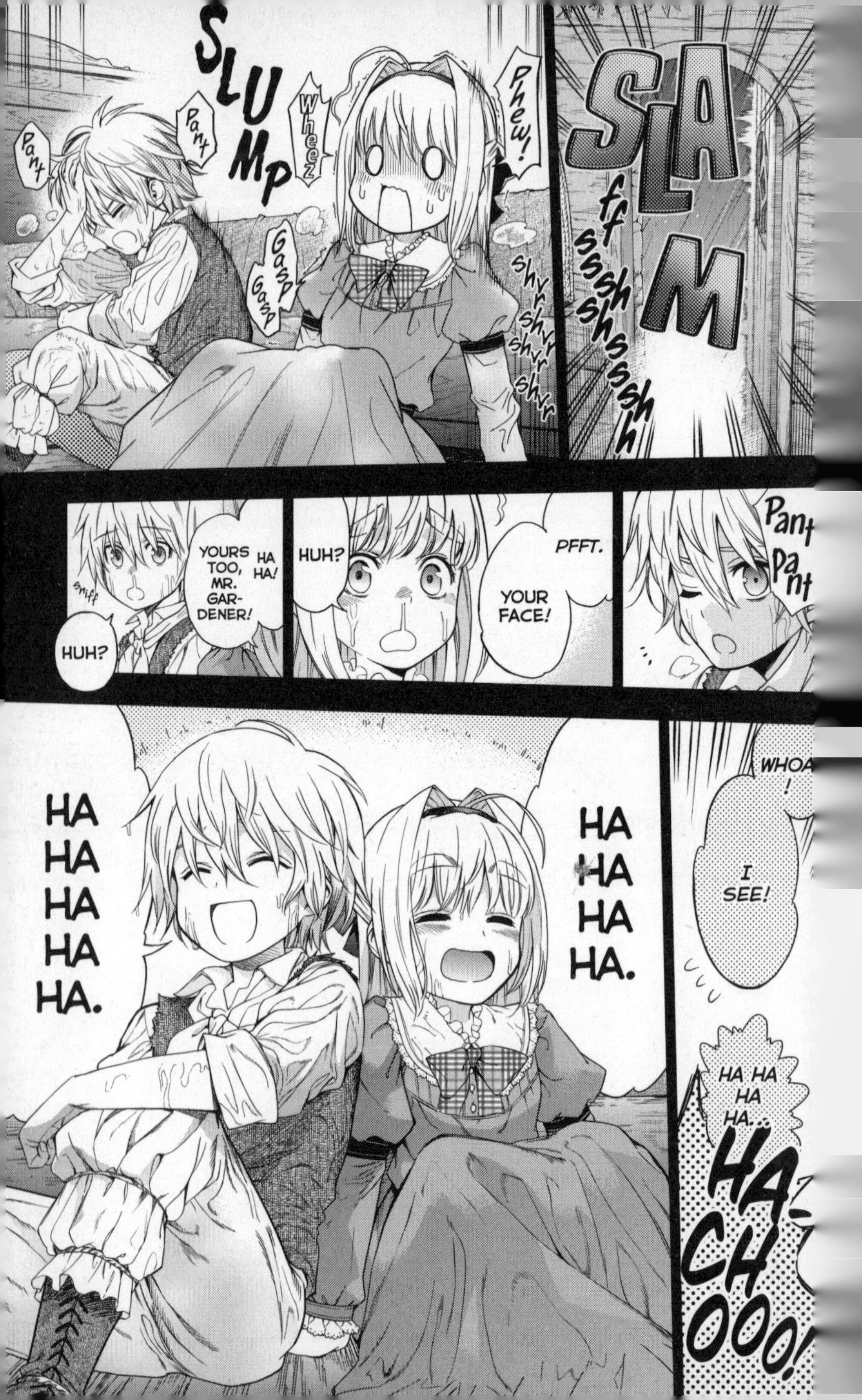
SLAM
ffssshshssssh
Phew!
wheez
SLUMP
Pant
Pant
Gasp Gasp
shvr shvr shvr shvr
Pant pant
...
PFFT.
YOUR FACE!
HUH?
HA HA!
YOURS TOO, MR. GARDENER!
sniff
HUH?
WHOA!
I SEE!
HA HA HA HA...
HA-CHOOO!
HA HA HA HA.
HA HA HA HA HA.

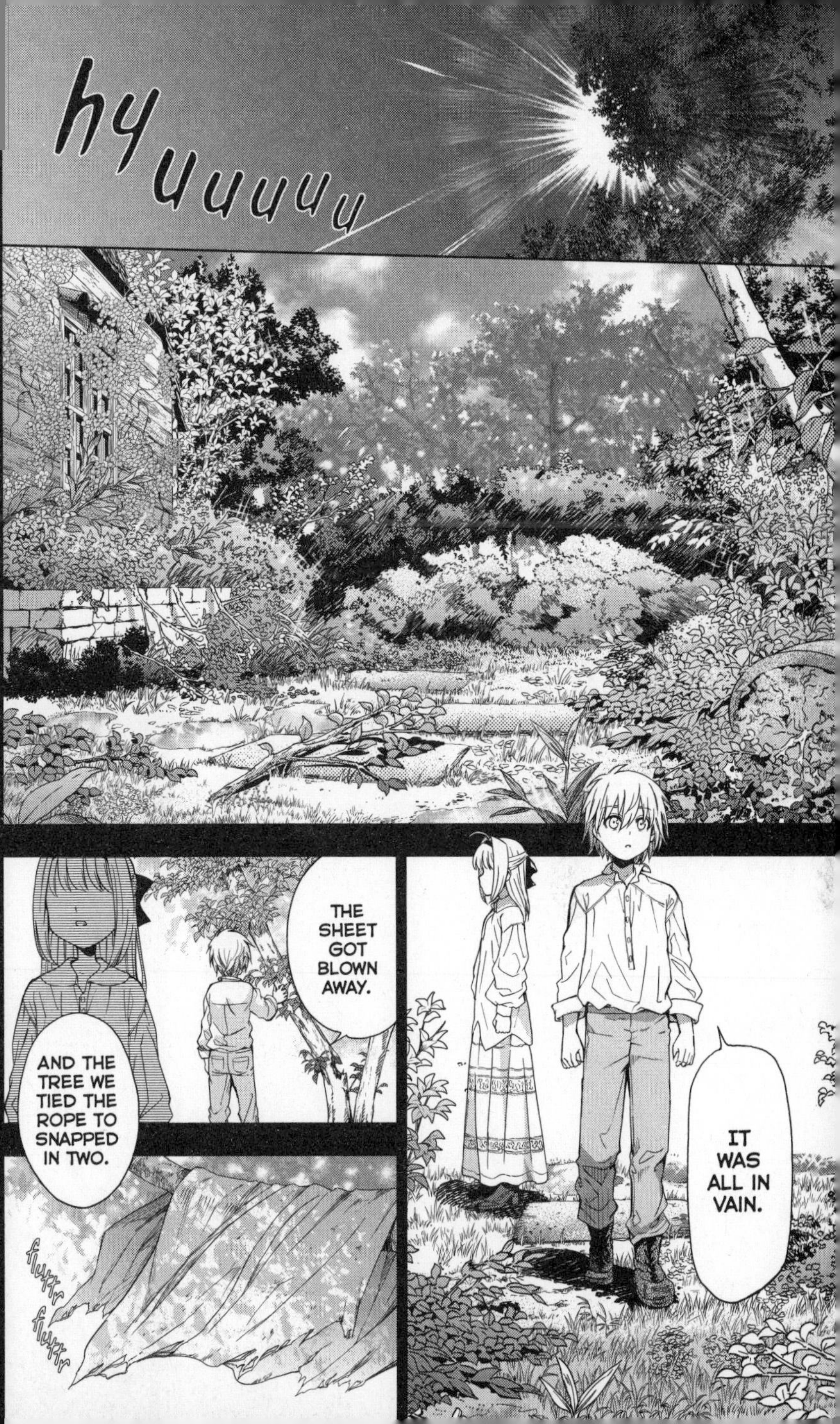
hyuuuuuu
IT WAS ALL IN VAIN.
THE SHEET GOT BLOWN AWAY.
AND THE TREE WE TIED THE ROPE TO SNAPPED IN TWO.
flutter flutter

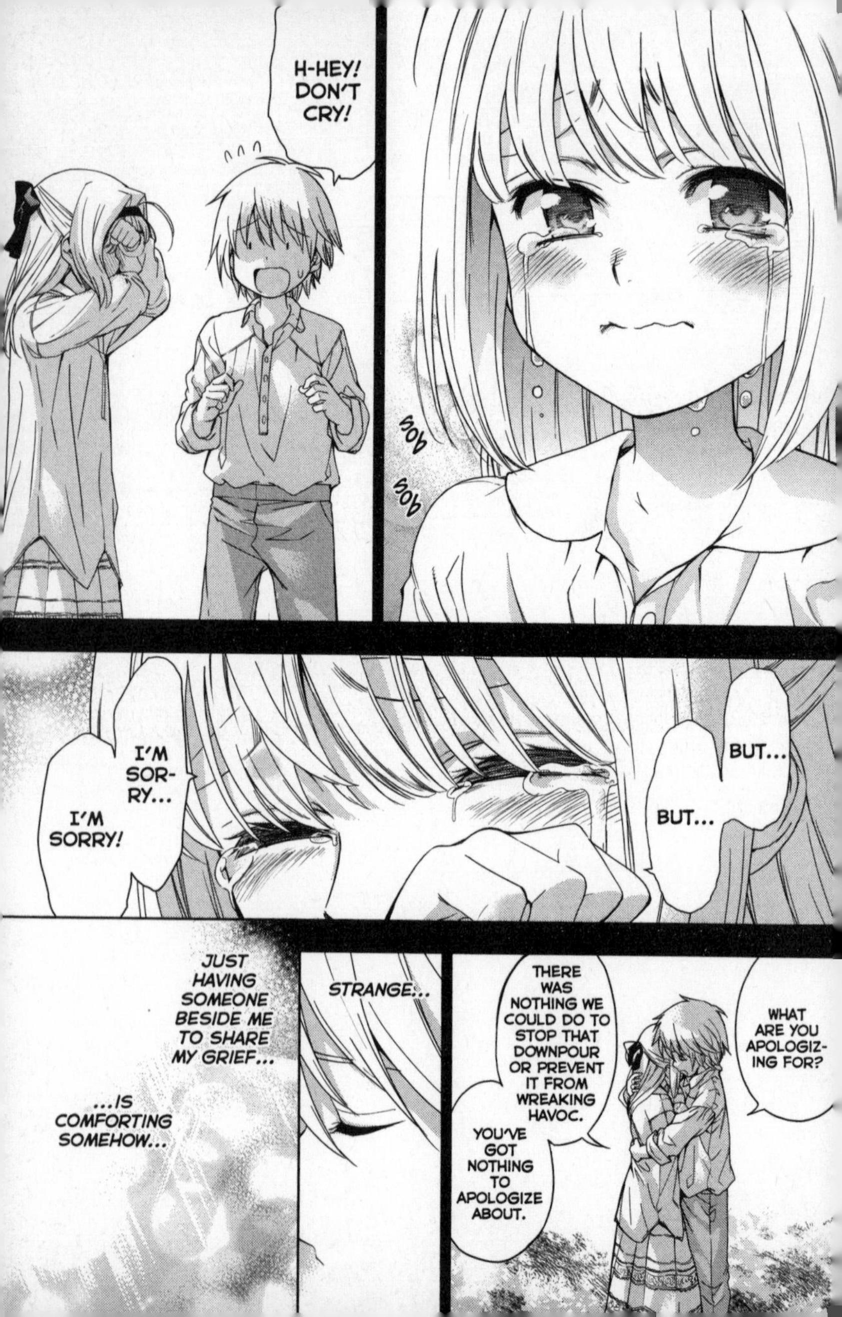
sob
sob
H-HEY! DON'T CRY!
BUT...
BUT...
I'M SORRY...
I'M SORRY!
WHAT ARE YOU APOLOGIZING FOR?
THERE WAS NOTHING WE COULD DO TO STOP THAT DOWNPOUR OR PREVENT IT FROM WREAKING HAVOC.
YOU'VE GOT NOTHING TO APOLOGIZE ABOUT.
STRANGE...
JUST HAVING SOMEONE BESIDE ME TO SHARE MY GRIEF...
...IS COMFORTING SOMEHOW...

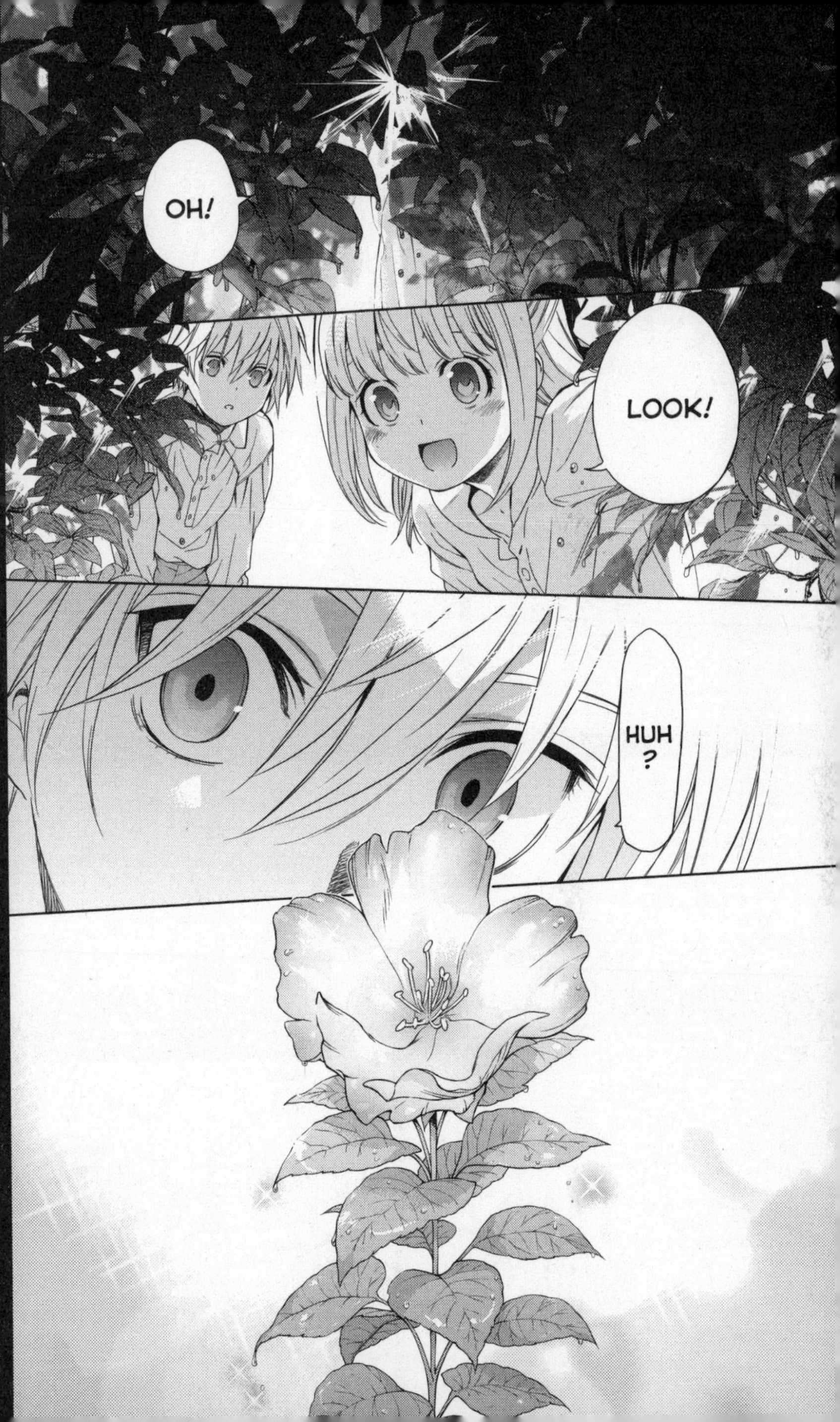
OH!
LOOK!
HUH?

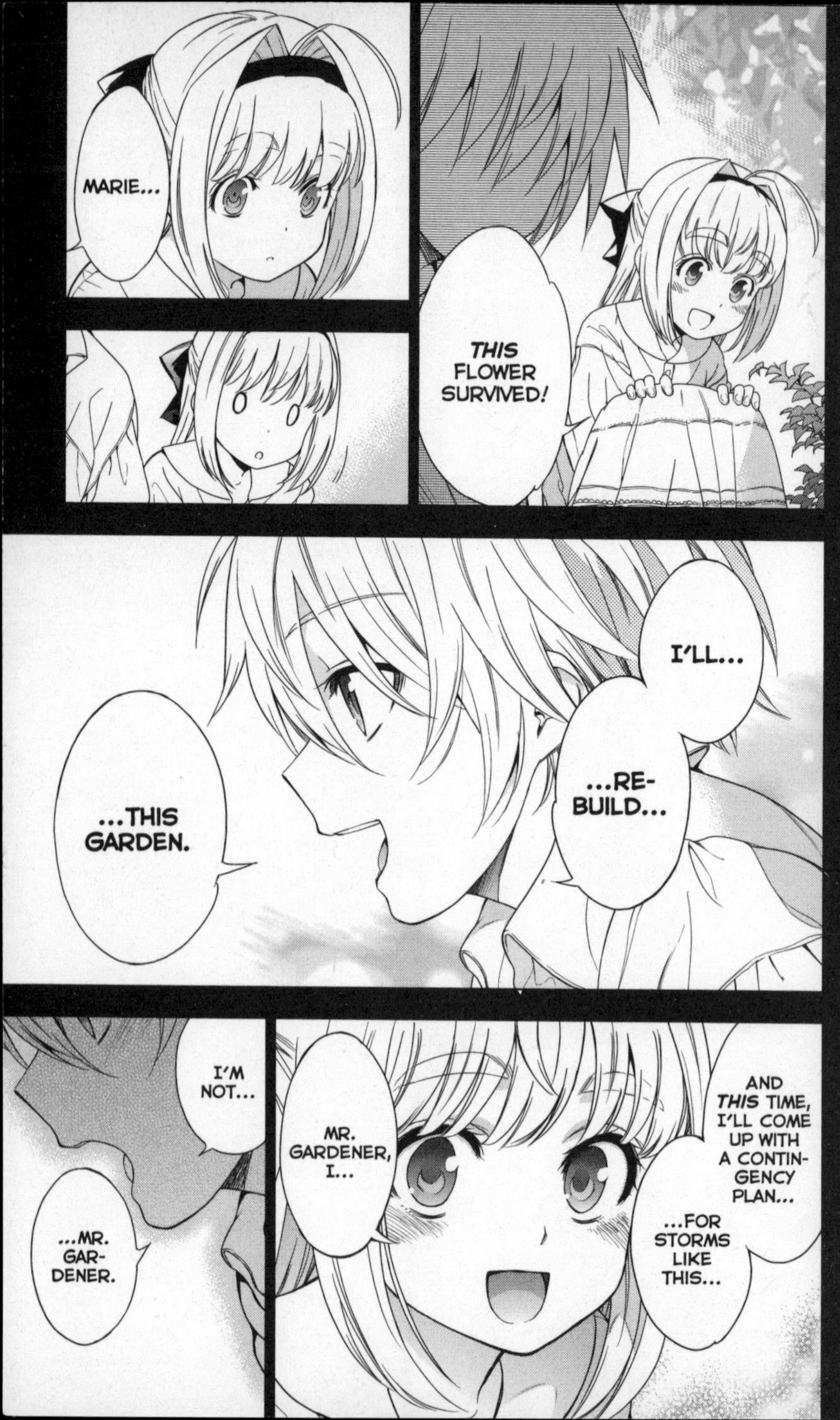
THIS FLOWER SURVIVED!
MARIE...
I'LL...
...RE-BUILD...
...THIS GARDEN.
AND THIS TIME, I'LL COME UP WITH A CONTIN-GENCY PLAN...
...FOR STORMS LIKE THIS...
MR. GARDENER, I...
I'M NOT...
...MR. GAR-DENER.

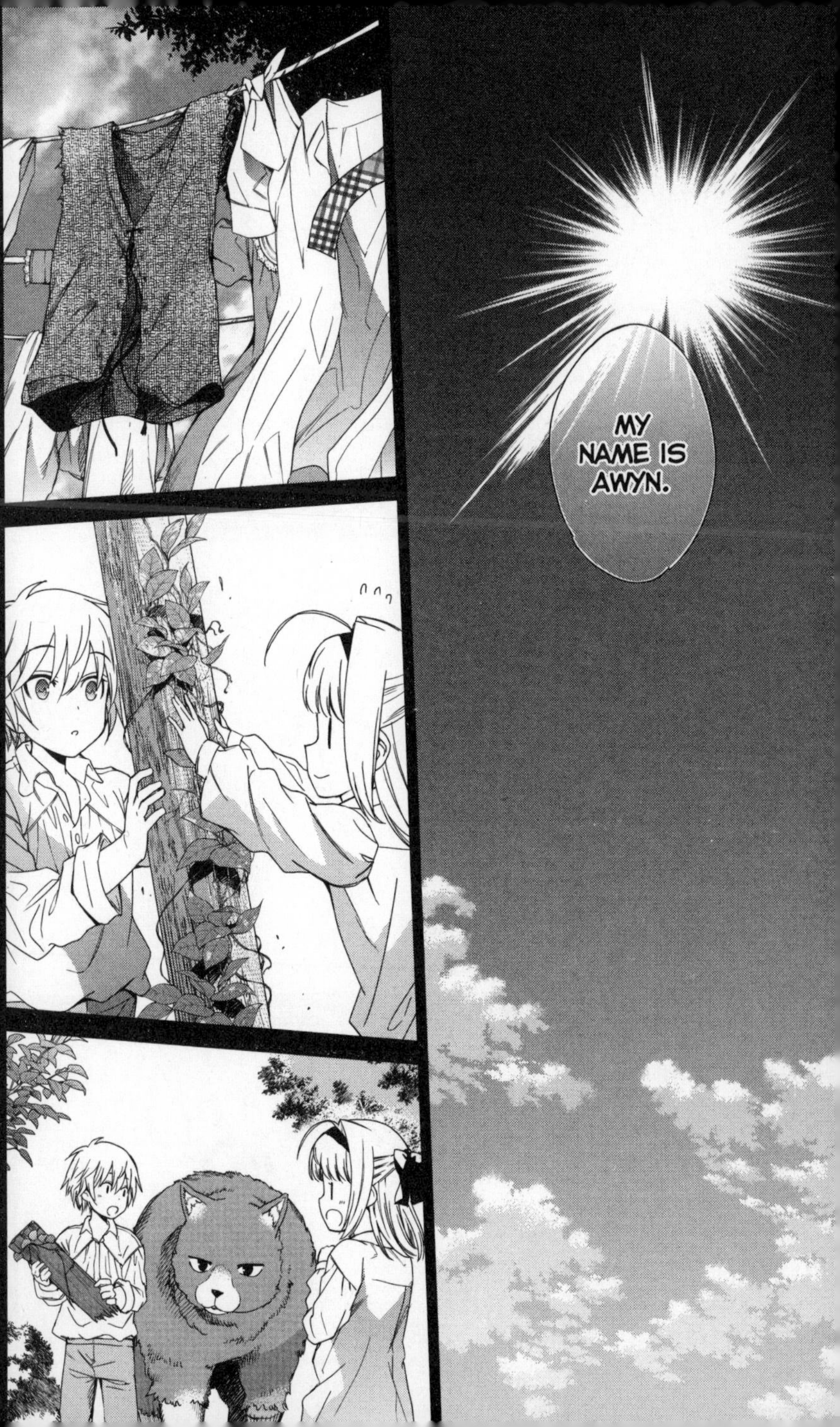
MY NAME IS AWYN.

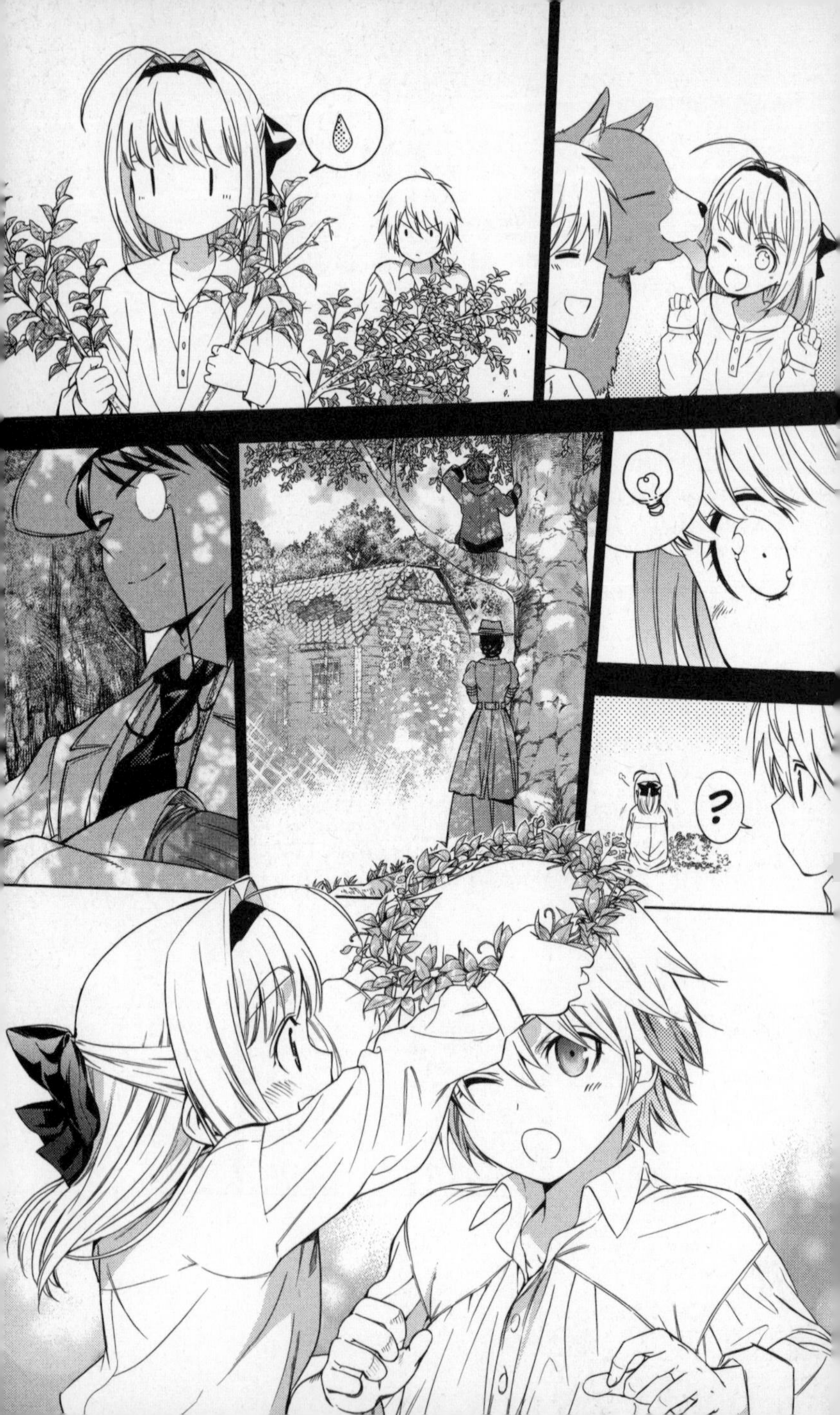
?

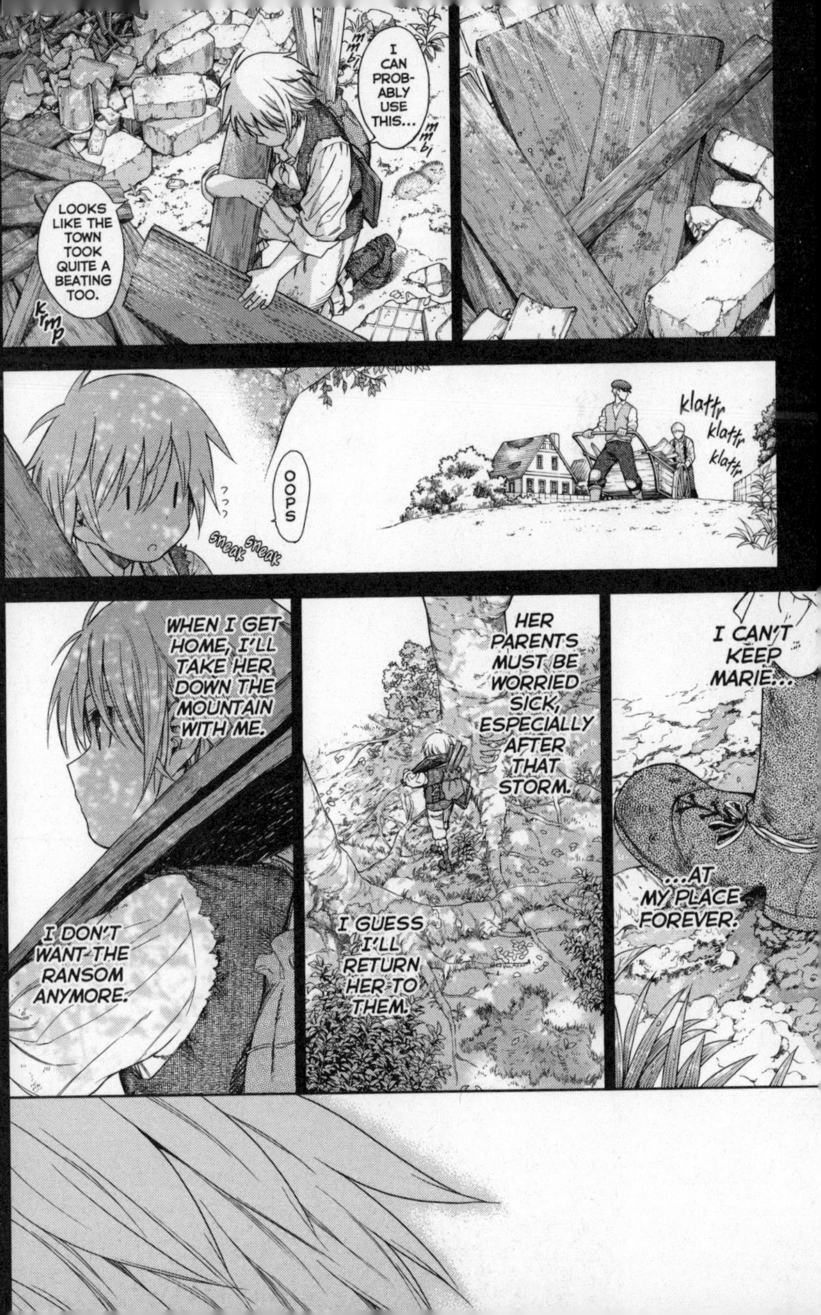
mmbi mmbi
I CAN PROBABLY USE THIS...
LOOKS LIKE THE TOWN TOOK QUITE A BEATING TOO.
krmp
klattr klattr klattr
OOPS
???
sneak sneak
I CAN'T KEEP MARIE...
...AT MY PLACE FOREVER.
HER PARENTS MUST BE WORRIED SICK, ESPECIALLY AFTER THAT STORM.
I GUESS I'LL RETURN HER TO THEM.
WHEN I GET HOME, I'LL TAKE HER DOWN THE MOUNTAIN WITH ME.
I DON'T WANT THE RANSOM ANYMORE.

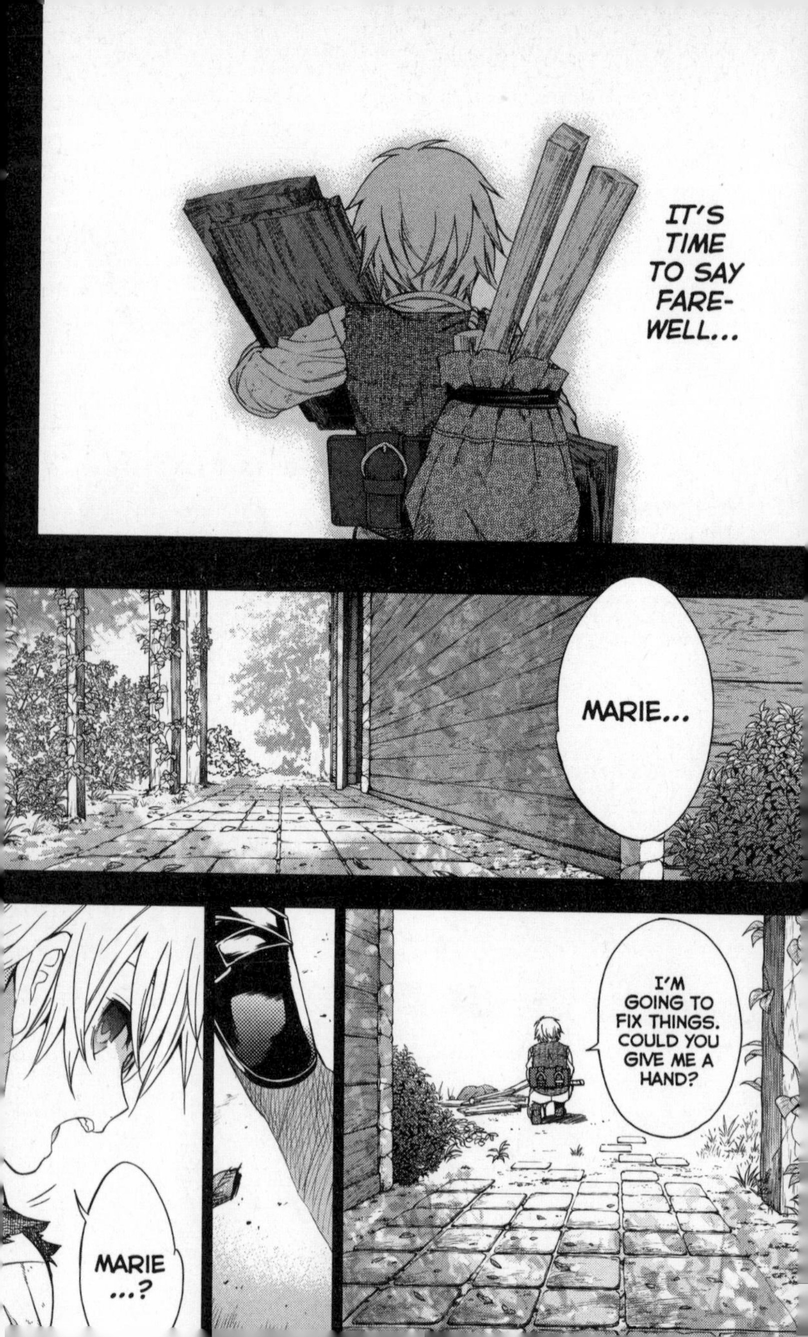
IT'S TIME TO SAY FARE-WELL...
MARIE...
I'M GOING TO FIX THINGS. COULD YOU GIVE ME A HAND?
MARIE ...?

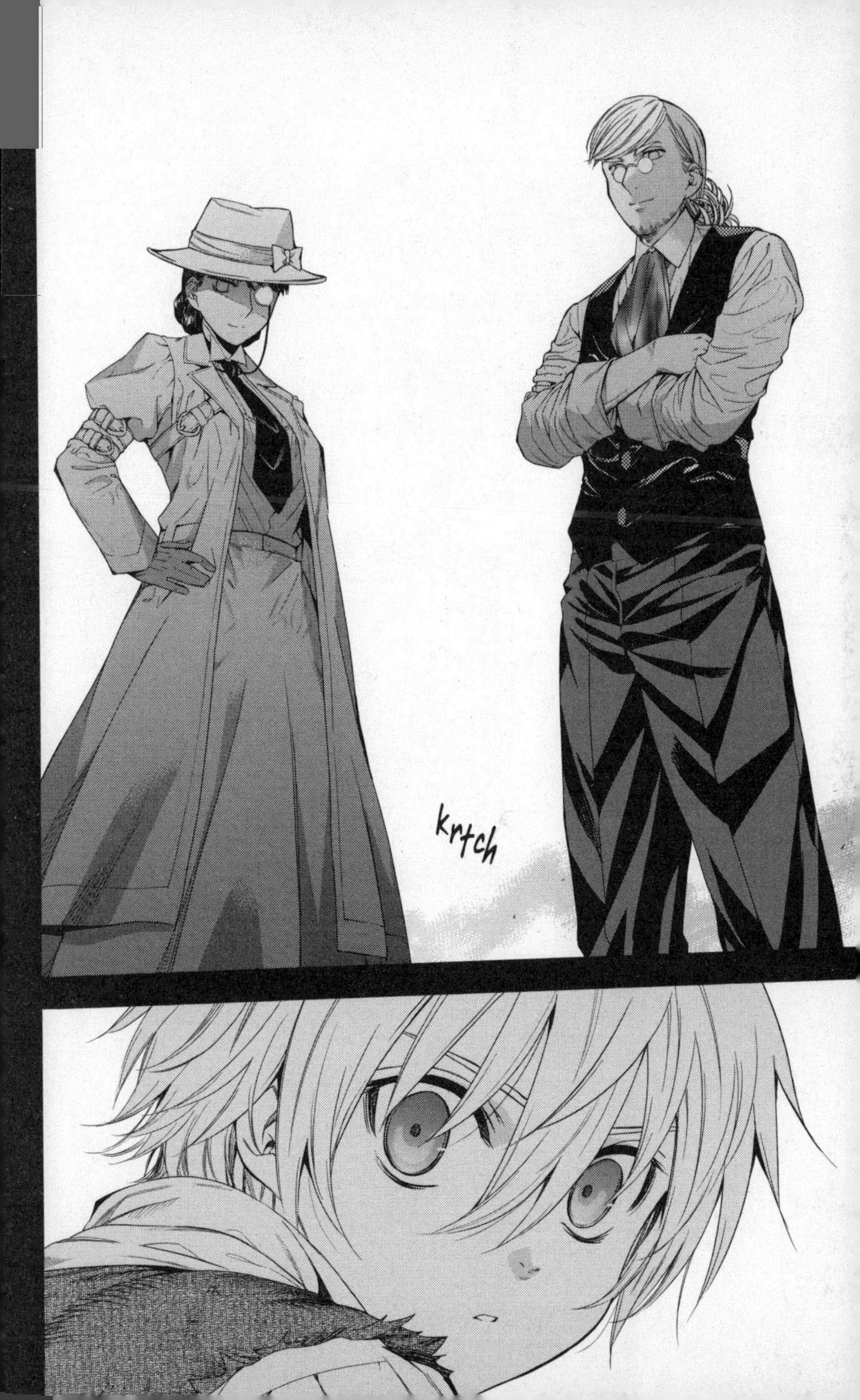
krtch

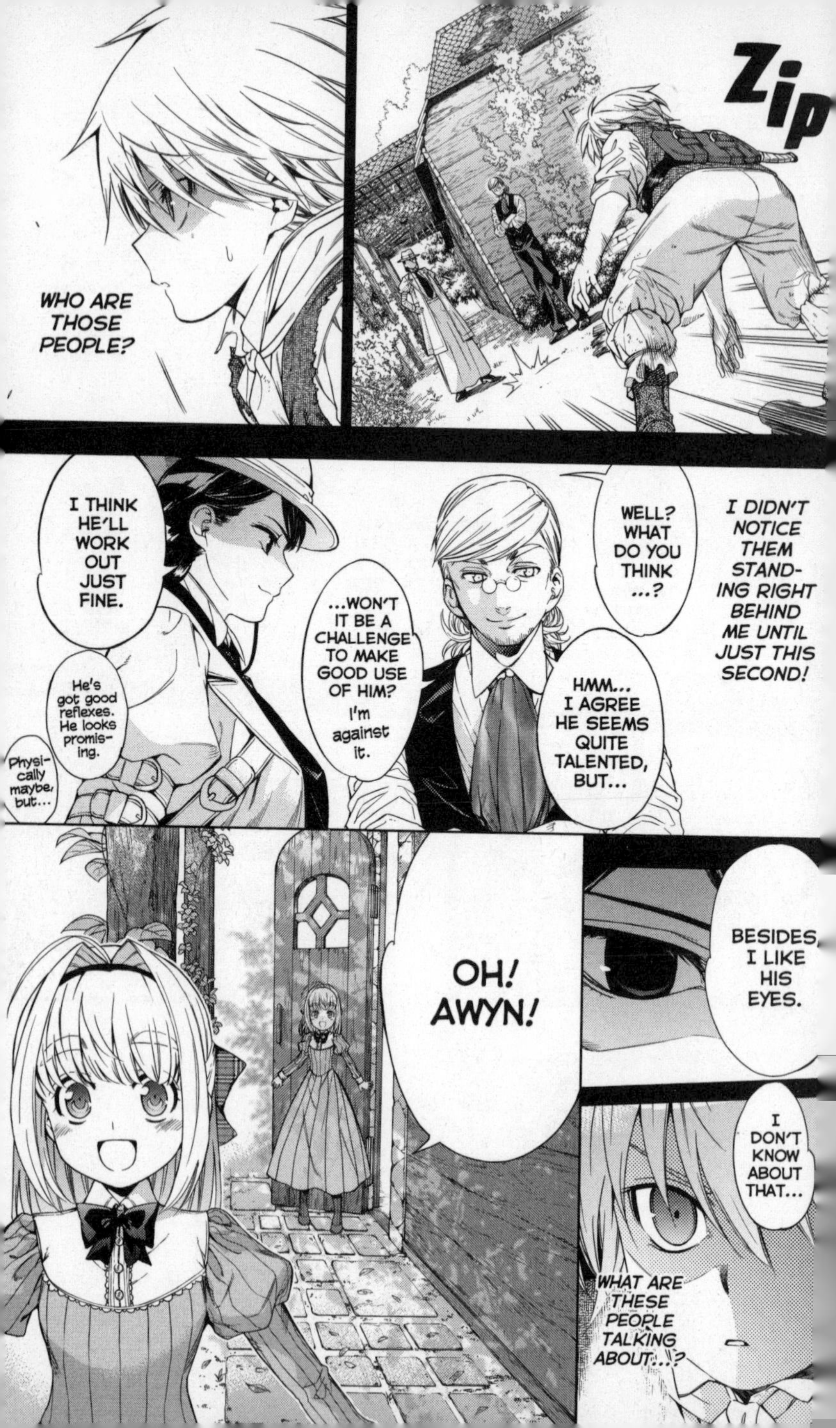
Zip
WHO ARE THOSE PEOPLE?
I DIDN'T NOTICE THEM STANDING RIGHT BEHIND ME UNTIL JUST THIS SECOND!
WELL? WHAT DO YOU THINK ...?
HMM... I AGREE HE SEEMS QUITE TALENTED, BUT...
...WON'T IT BE A CHALLENGE TO MAKE GOOD USE OF HIM?
I'm against it.
I THINK HE'LL WORK OUT JUST FINE.
He's got good reflexes. He looks promising.
Physically maybe, but...
BESIDES, I LIKE HIS EYES.
I DON'T KNOW ABOUT THAT...
WHAT ARE THESE PEOPLE TALKING ABOUT...?
OH! AWYN!

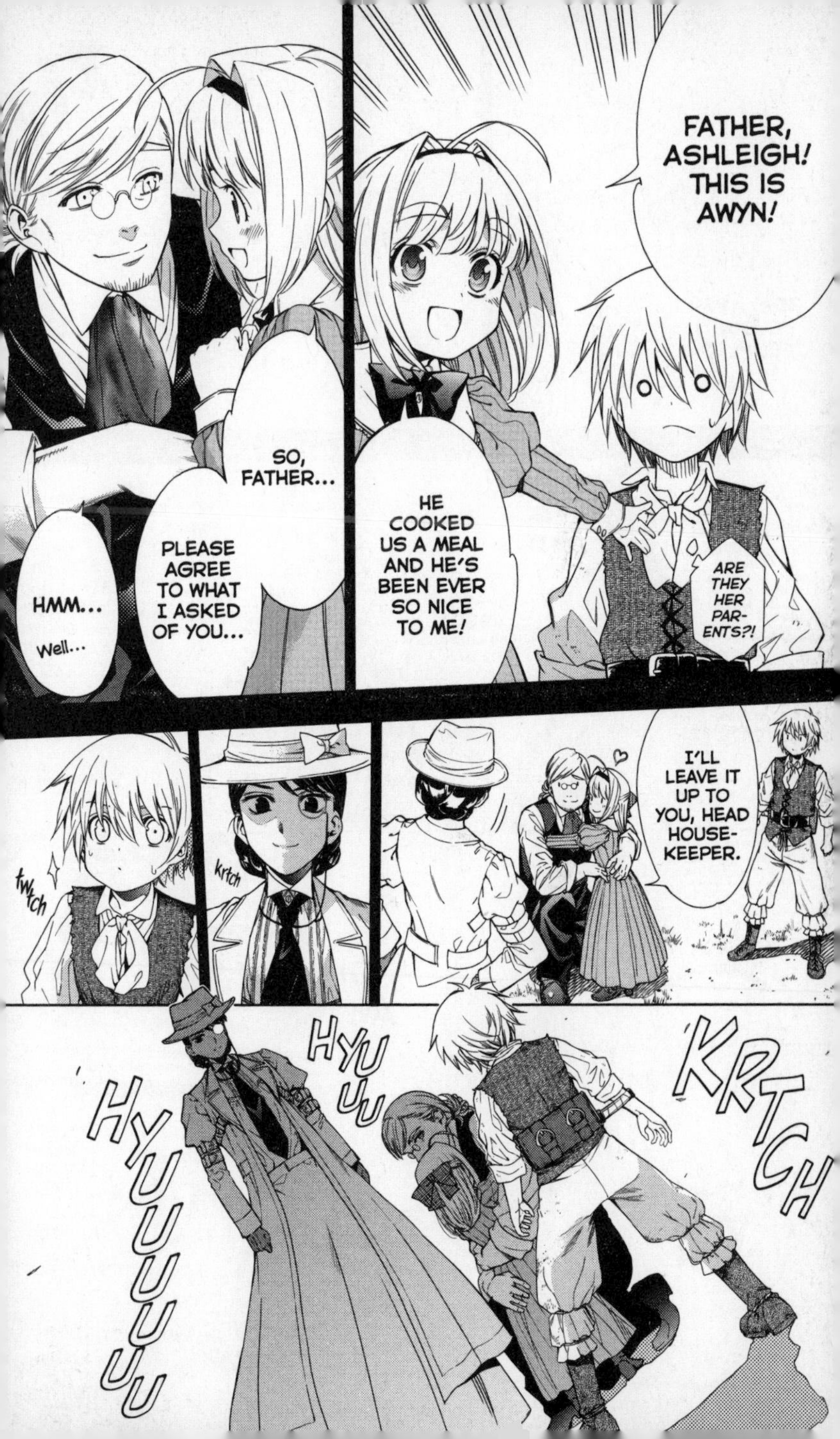
FATHER, ASHLEIGH! THIS IS AWYN!
HE COOKED US A MEAL AND HE'S BEEN EVER SO NICE TO ME!
ARE THEY HER PAR-ENTS?!
SO, FATHER...
PLEASE AGREE TO WHAT I ASKED OF YOU...
HMM...
Well...
I'LL LEAVE IT UP TO YOU, HEAD HOUSE-KEEPER.
krtch
twitch
KRTCH
HYUUU
HYUUUUUUU

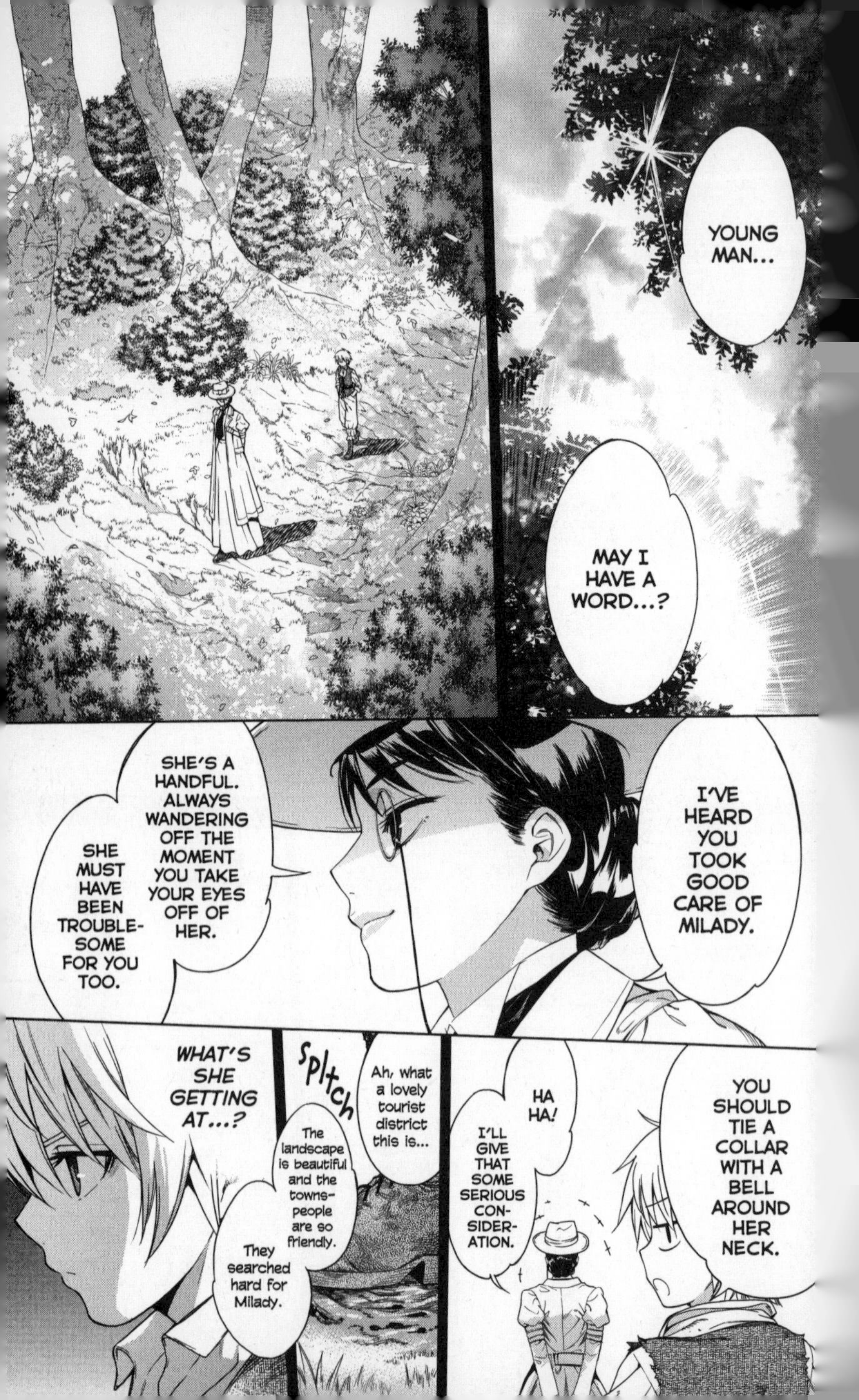
YOUNG MAN...
MAY I HAVE A WORD...?
I'VE HEARD YOU TOOK GOOD CARE OF MILADY.
SHE'S A HANDFUL. ALWAYS WANDERING OFF THE MOMENT YOU TAKE YOUR EYES OFF OF HER.
SHE MUST HAVE BEEN TROUBLE-SOME FOR YOU TOO.
YOU SHOULD TIE A COLLAR WITH A BELL AROUND HER NECK.
HA HA!
I'LL GIVE THAT SOME SERIOUS CON-SIDER-ATION.
Splitch
Ah, what a lovely tourist district this is...
The landscape is beautiful and the towns-people are so friendly.
They searched hard for Milady.
WHAT'S SHE GETTING AT...?

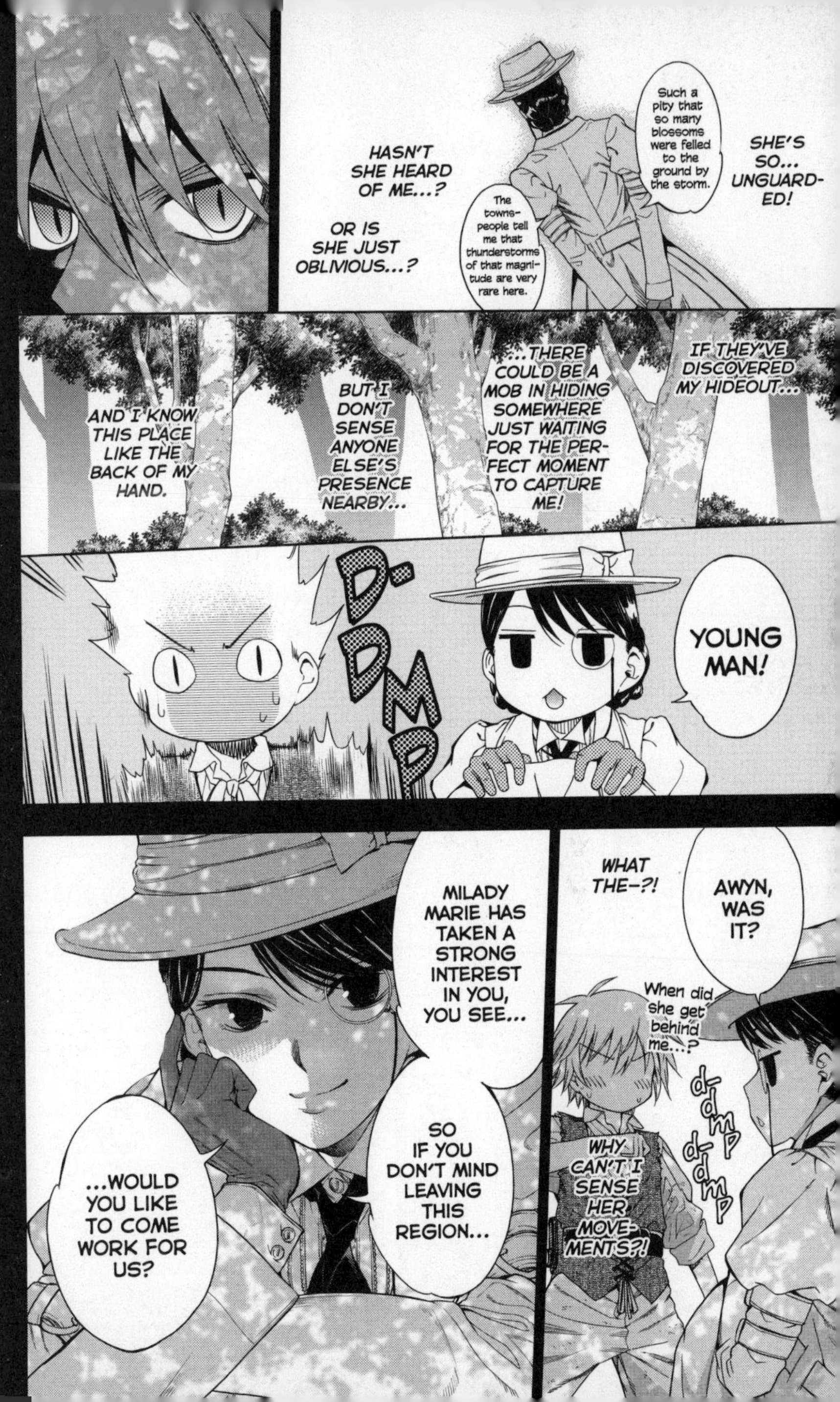
SHE'S SO... UNGUARDED!
Such a pity that so many blossoms were felled to the ground by the storm.
The towns-people tell me that thunderstorms of that magnitude are very rare here.
HASN'T SHE HEARD OF ME...?
OR IS SHE JUST OBLIVIOUS...?
IF THEY'VE DISCOVERED MY HIDEOUT...
...THERE COULD BE A MOB IN HIDING SOMEWHERE JUST WAITING FOR THE PERFECT MOMENT TO CAPTURE ME!
BUT I DON'T SENSE ANYONE ELSE'S PRESENCE NEARBY...
AND I KNOW THIS PLACE LIKE THE BACK OF MY HAND.
YOUNG MAN!
D-DMP
AWYN, WAS IT?
WHAT THE-?!
When did she get behind me...?
d-dmp d-dmp
WHY CAN'T I SENSE HER MOVEMENTS?!
MILADY MARIE HAS TAKEN A STRONG INTEREST IN YOU, YOU SEE...
SO IF YOU DON'T MIND LEAVING THIS REGION...
...WOULD YOU LIKE TO COME WORK FOR US?

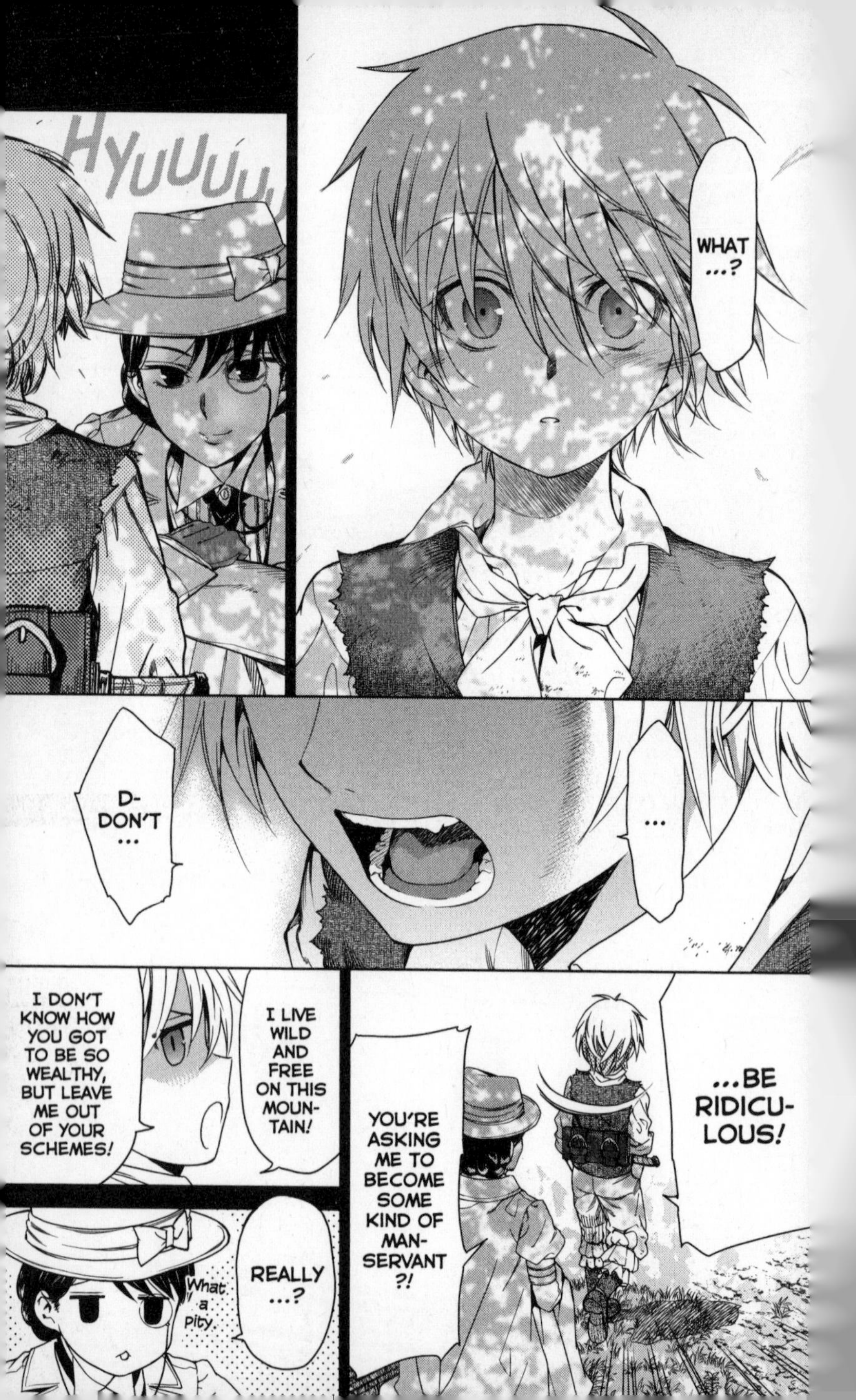
WHAT ...?
HYUUUU
...
D- DON'T ...
...BE RIDICULOUS!
YOU'RE ASKING ME TO BECOME SOME KIND OF MAN-SERVANT?!
I LIVE WILD AND FREE ON THIS MOUNTAIN!
I DON'T KNOW HOW YOU GOT TO BE SO WEALTHY, BUT LEAVE ME OUT OF YOUR SCHEMES!
REALLY ...?
What a pity.

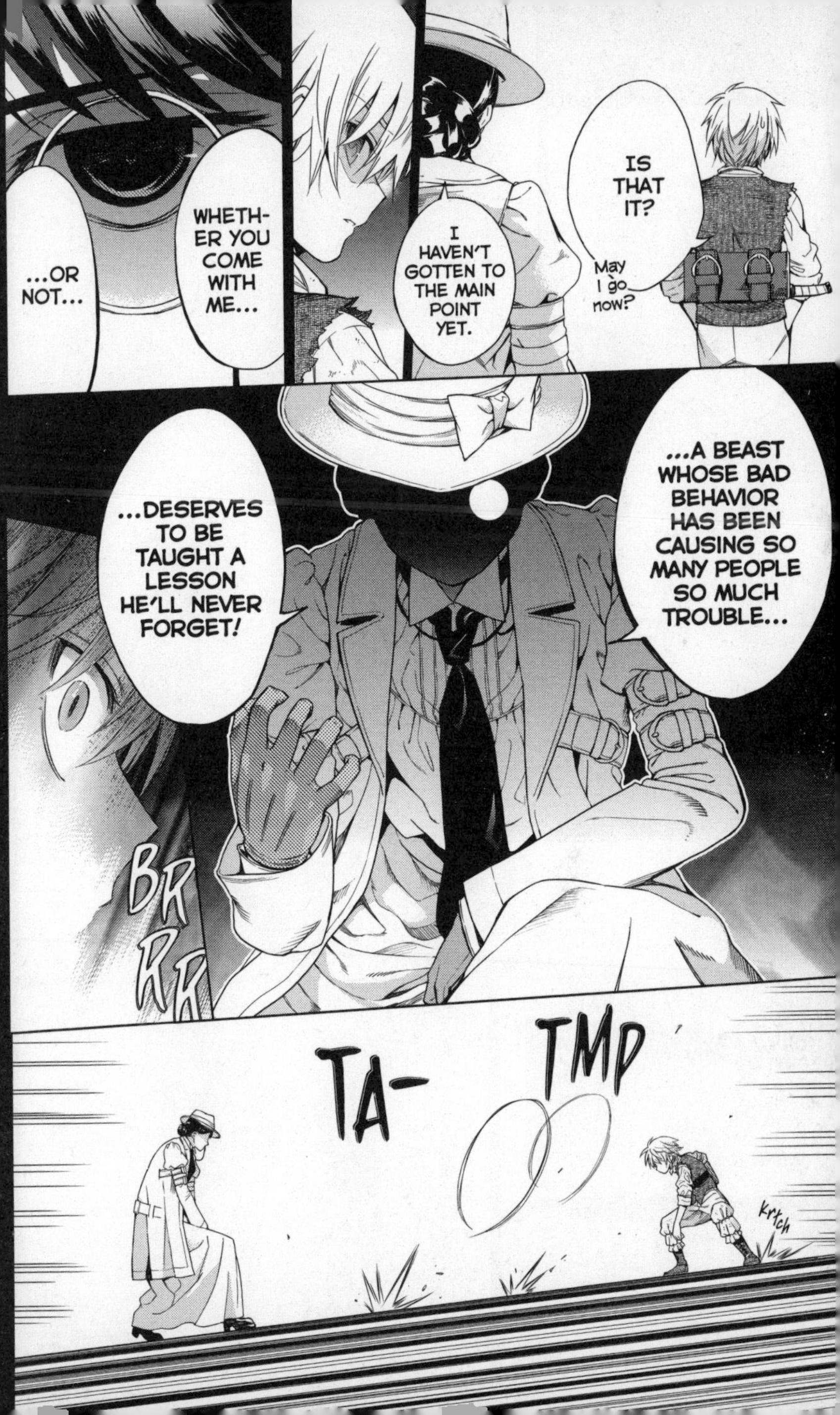
IS THAT IT?
May I go now?
I HAVEN'T GOTTEN TO THE MAIN POINT YET.
WHETH-ER YOU COME WITH ME...
...OR NOT...
...A BEAST WHOSE BAD BEHAVIOR HAS BEEN CAUSING SO MANY PEOPLE SO MUCH TROUBLE...
...DESERVES TO BE TAUGHT A LESSON HE'LL NEVER FORGET!
BRRR
TA- TMP
krtch

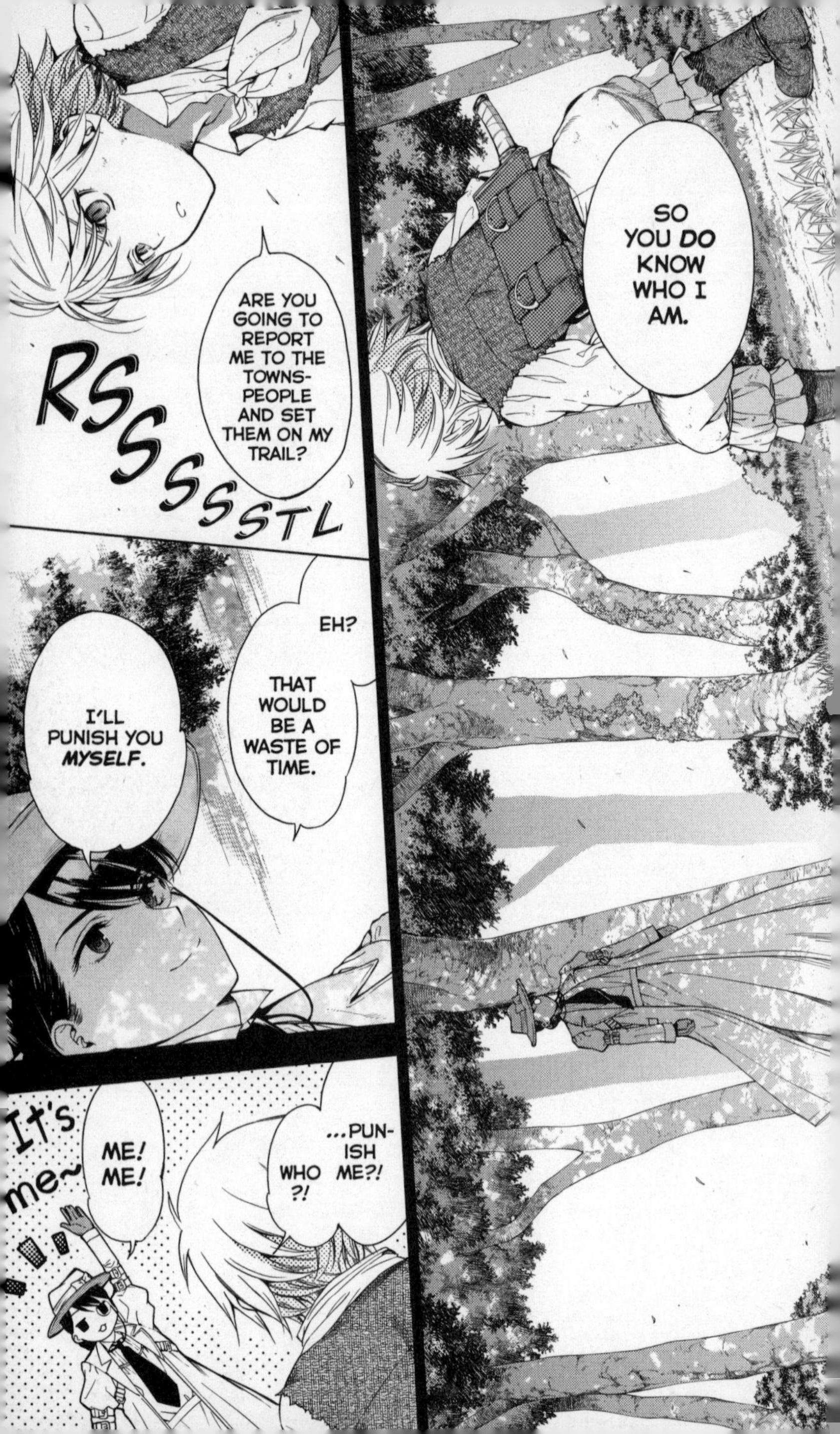
SO YOU DO KNOW WHO I AM.
ARE YOU GOING TO REPORT ME TO THE TOWNS-PEOPLE AND SET THEM ON MY TRAIL?
RSSSSSTL
EH?
THAT WOULD BE A WASTE OF TIME.
I'LL PUNISH YOU MYSELF.
...PUN-ISH ME?!
WHO ?!
ME! ME!
It's me~

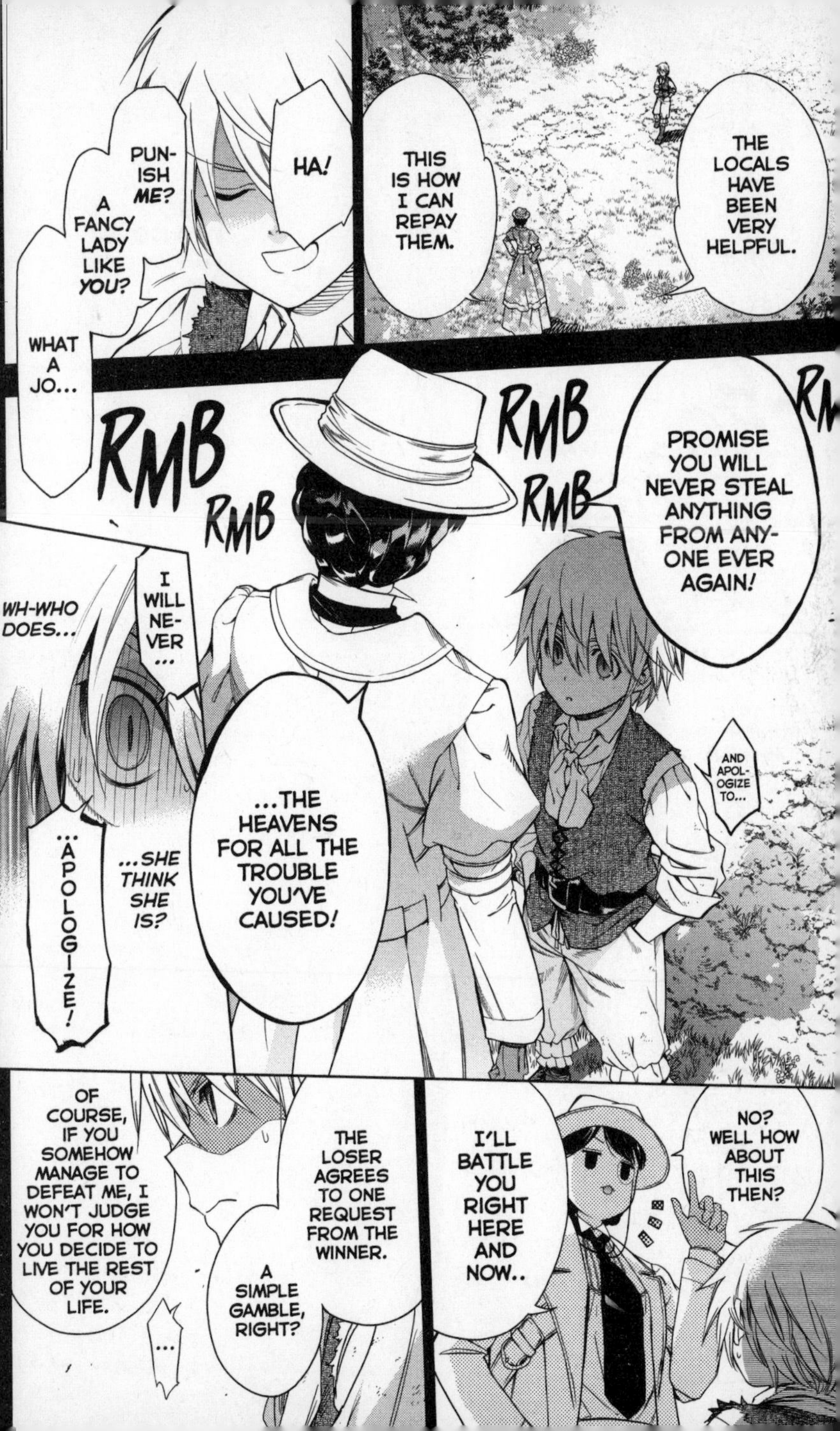
THE LOCALS HAVE BEEN VERY HELPFUL.
THIS IS HOW I CAN REPAY THEM.
HA!
PUN-ISH ME?
A FANCY LADY LIKE YOU?
WHAT A JO...
RMB
PROMISE YOU WILL NEVER STEAL ANYTHING FROM ANY-ONE EVER AGAIN!
RMB
RMB
RMB
AND APOL-OGIZE TO...
...THE HEAVENS FOR ALL THE TROUBLE YOU'VE CAUSED!
I WILL NE-VER...
WH-WHO DOES...
...SHE THINK SHE IS?
...APOLOGIZE!
NO? WELL HOW ABOUT THIS THEN?
I'LL BATTLE YOU RIGHT HERE AND NOW..
THE LOSER AGREES TO ONE REQUEST FROM THE WINNER.
A SIMPLE GAMBLE, RIGHT?
OF COURSE, IF YOU SOMEHOW MANAGE TO DEFEAT ME, I WON'T JUDGE YOU FOR HOW YOU DECIDE TO LIVE THE REST OF YOUR LIFE.
...

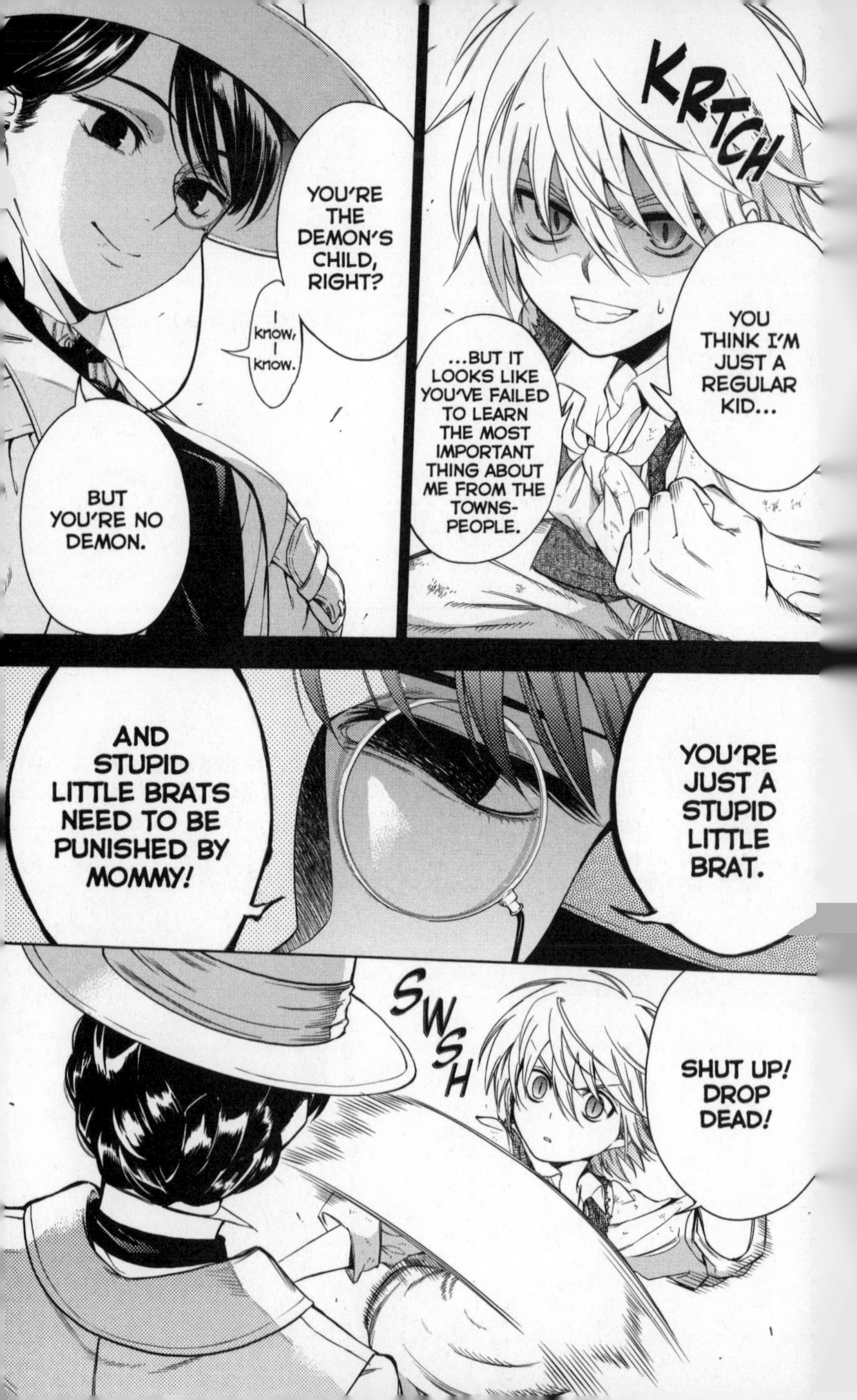
KRTCH
YOU THINK I'M JUST A REGULAR KID...
...BUT IT LOOKS LIKE YOU'VE FAILED TO LEARN THE MOST IMPORTANT THING ABOUT ME FROM THE TOWNSPEOPLE.
YOU'RE THE DEMON'S CHILD, RIGHT?
I know, I know.
BUT YOU'RE NO DEMON.
YOU'RE JUST A STUPID LITTLE BRAT.
AND STUPID LITTLE BRATS NEED TO BE PUNISHED BY MOMMY!
SHUT UP! DROP DEAD!
SWSH

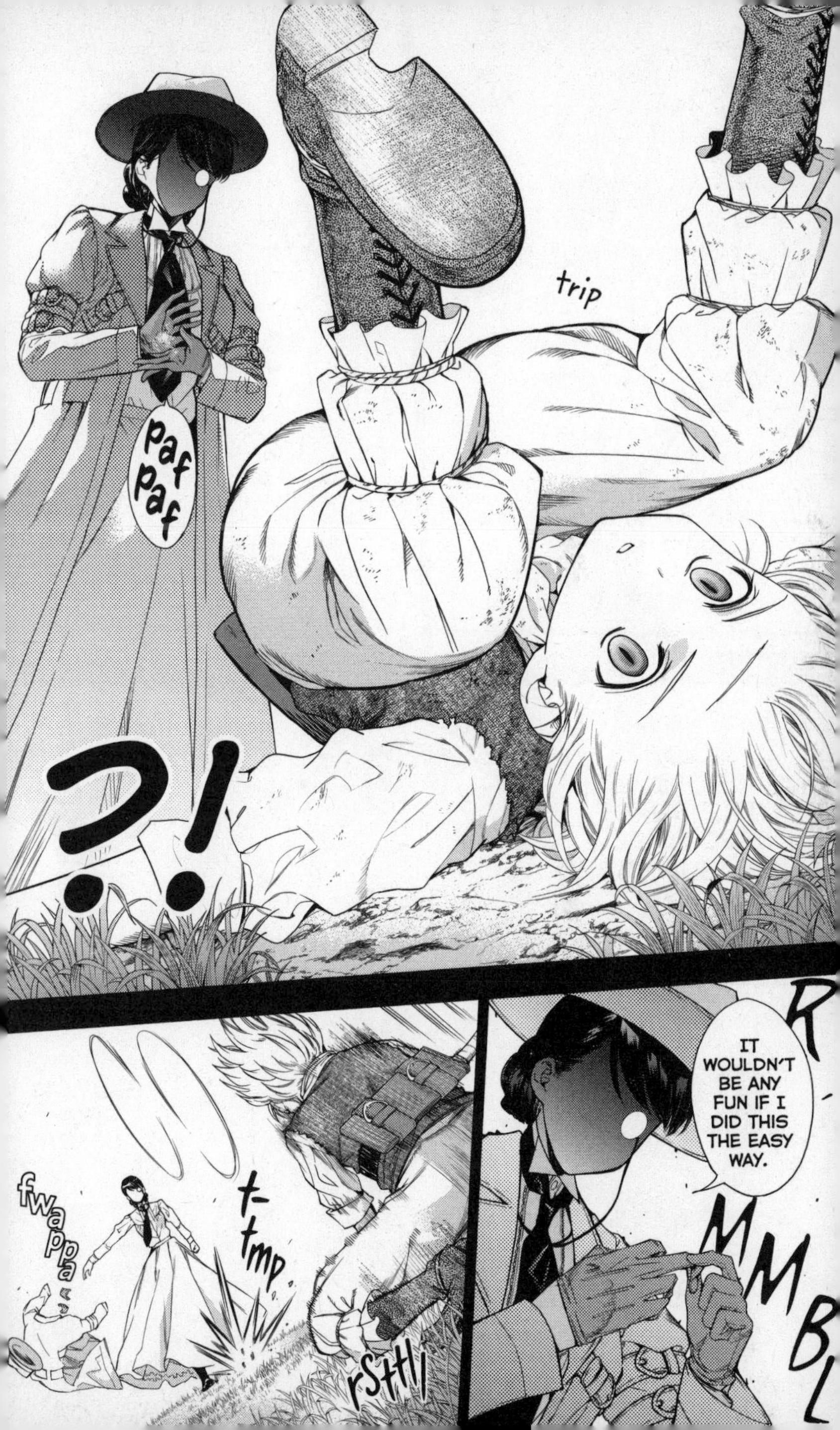
trip
paf paf
?!
IT WOULDN'T BE ANY FUN IF I DID THIS THE EASY WAY.
R-MMBL
t-tmp.
fwappa
rStl

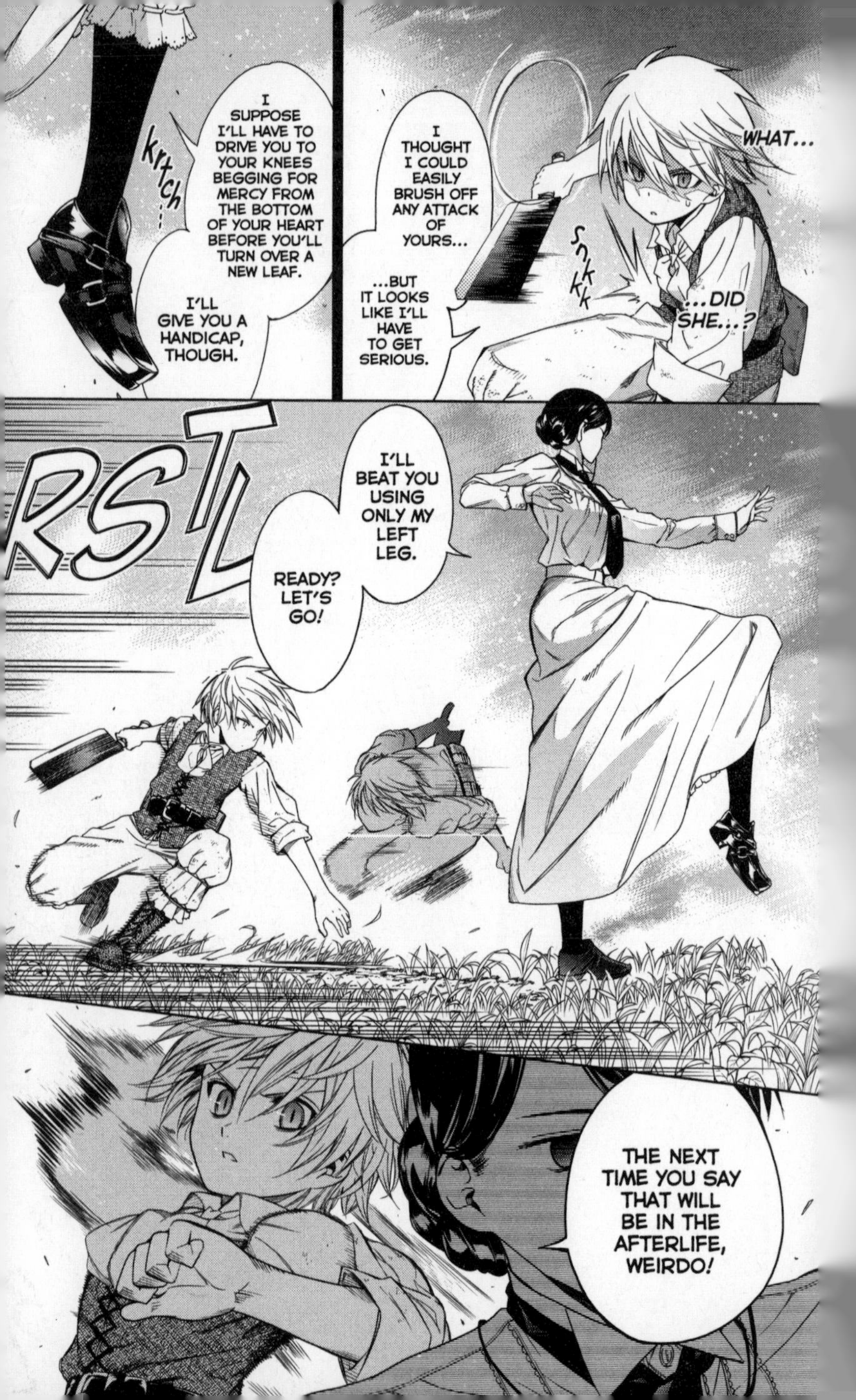
WHAT...
I THOUGHT I COULD EASILY BRUSH OFF ANY ATTACK OF YOURS...
Snkkk
...DID SHE...?
...BUT IT LOOKS LIKE I'LL HAVE TO GET SERIOUS.
I SUPPOSE I'LL HAVE TO DRIVE YOU TO YOUR KNEES BEGGING FOR MERCY FROM THE BOTTOM OF YOUR HEART BEFORE YOU'LL TURN OVER A NEW LEAF.
krtch
I'LL GIVE YOU A HANDICAP, THOUGH.
I'LL BEAT YOU USING ONLY MY LEFT LEG.
READY? LET'S GO!
RSTL
THE NEXT TIME YOU SAY THAT WILL BE IN THE AFTERLIFE, WEIRDO!

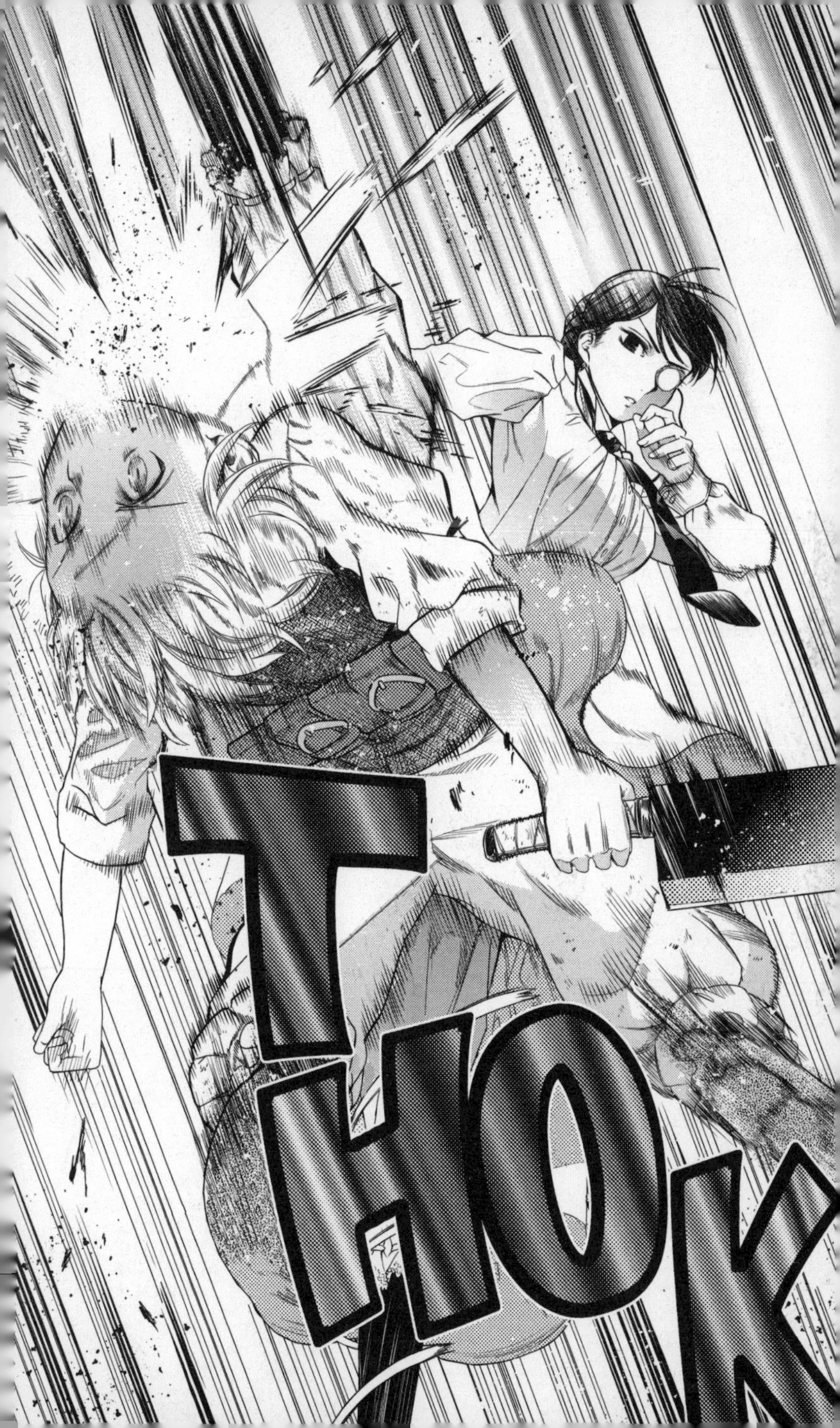
THOK

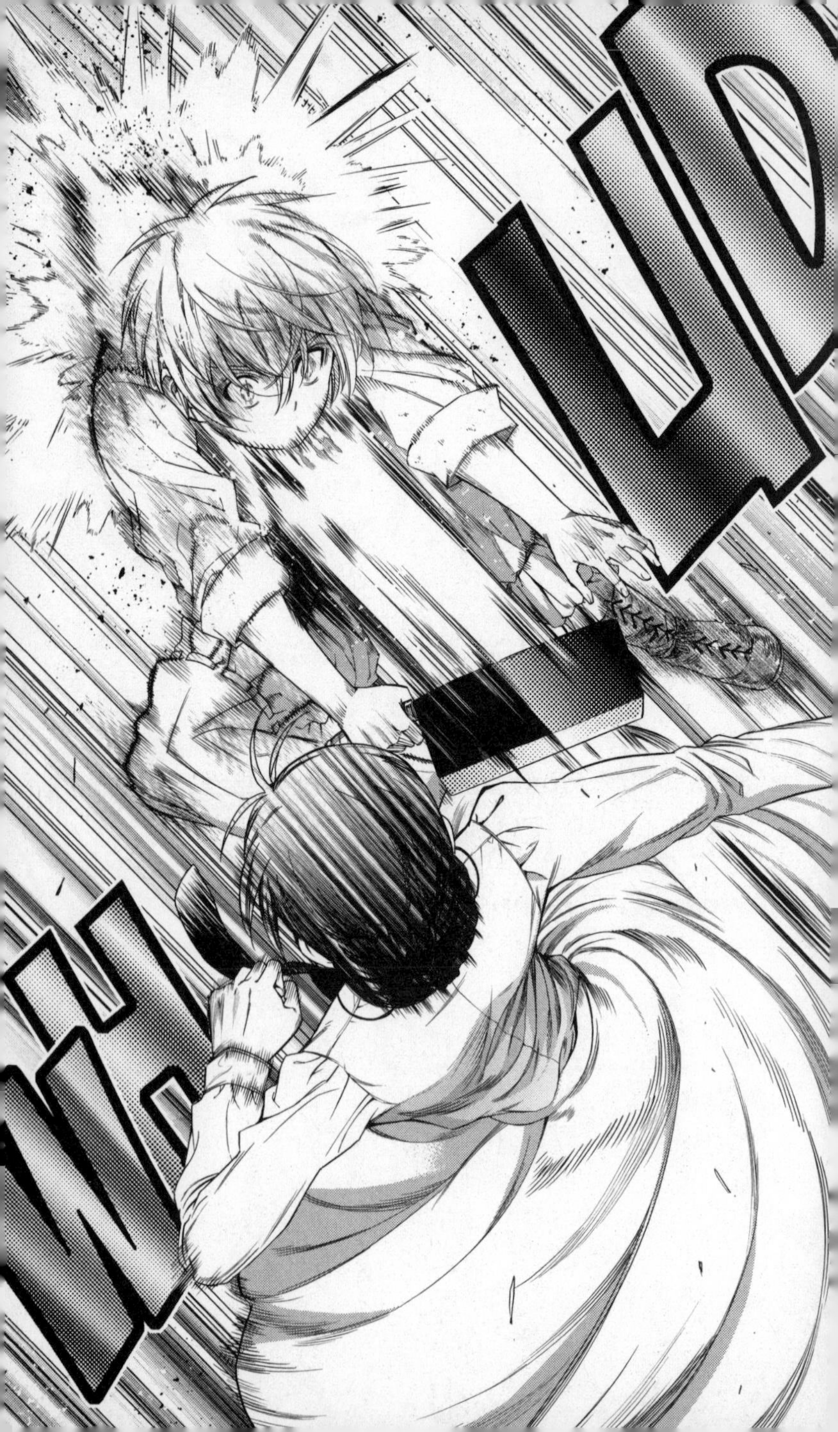

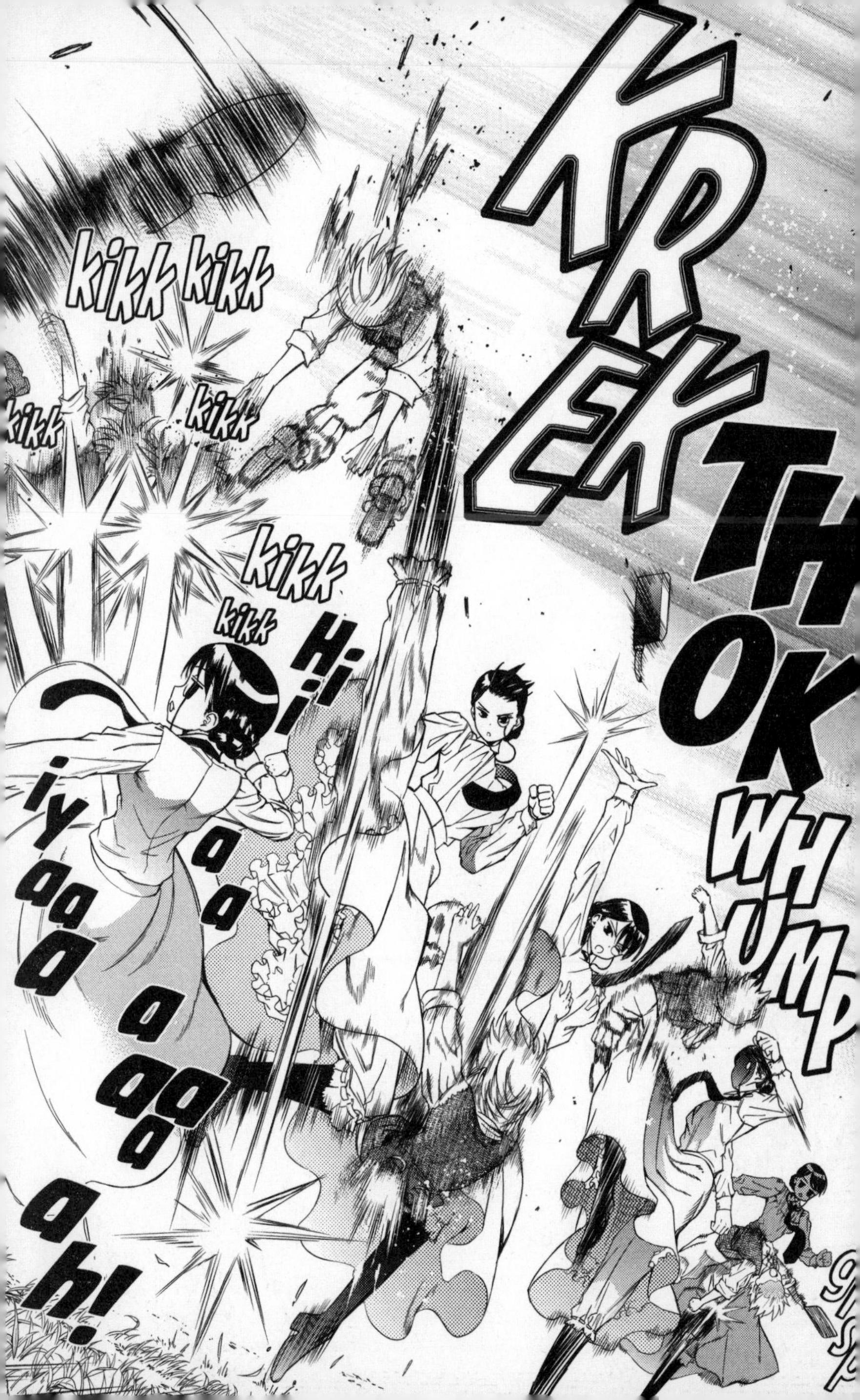
THOK
WHUMP
kikk kikk
kikk
kikk
kikk
kikk
Hiiiaaaaah!
iyaaaaaaah!

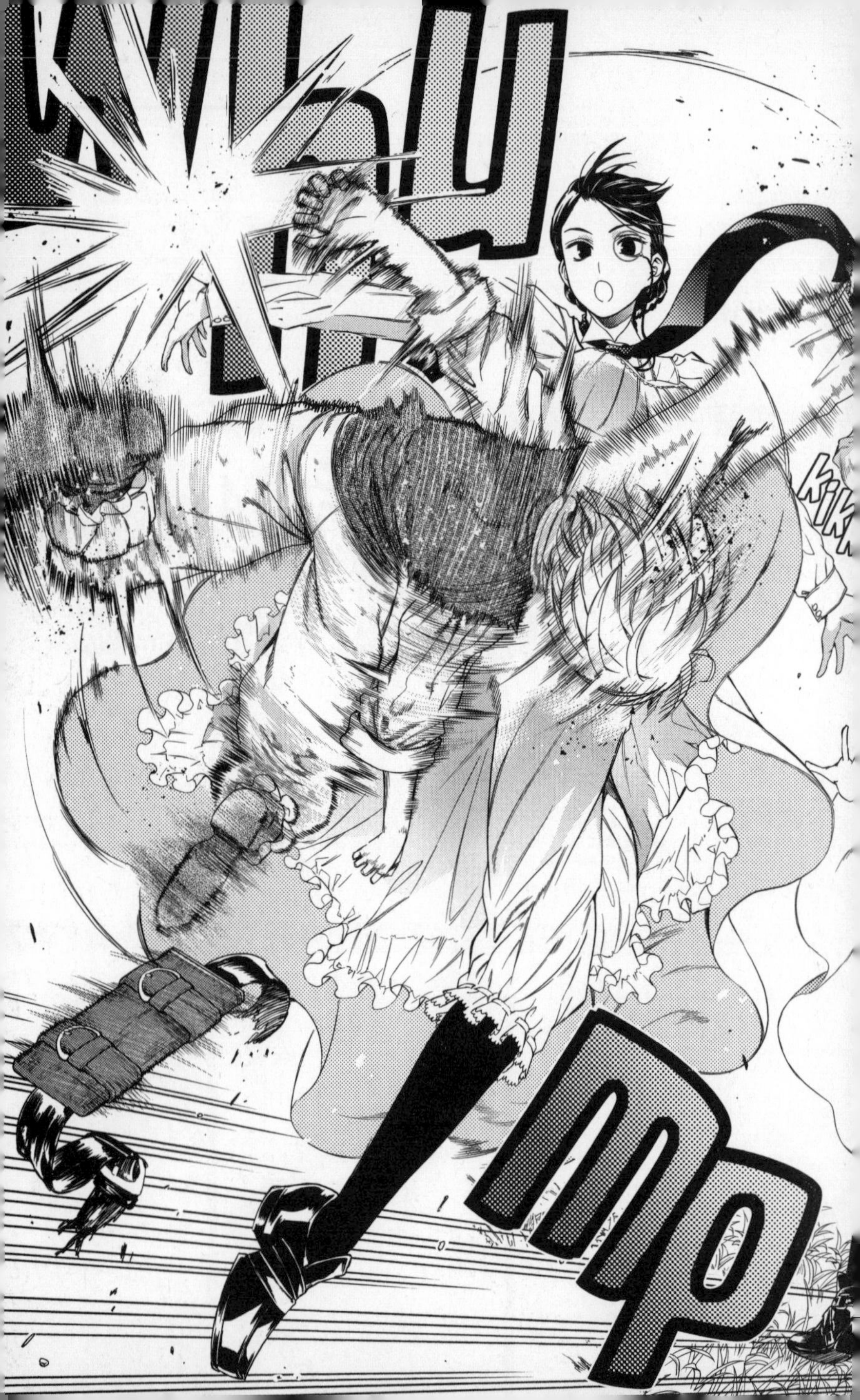
KiK
mp

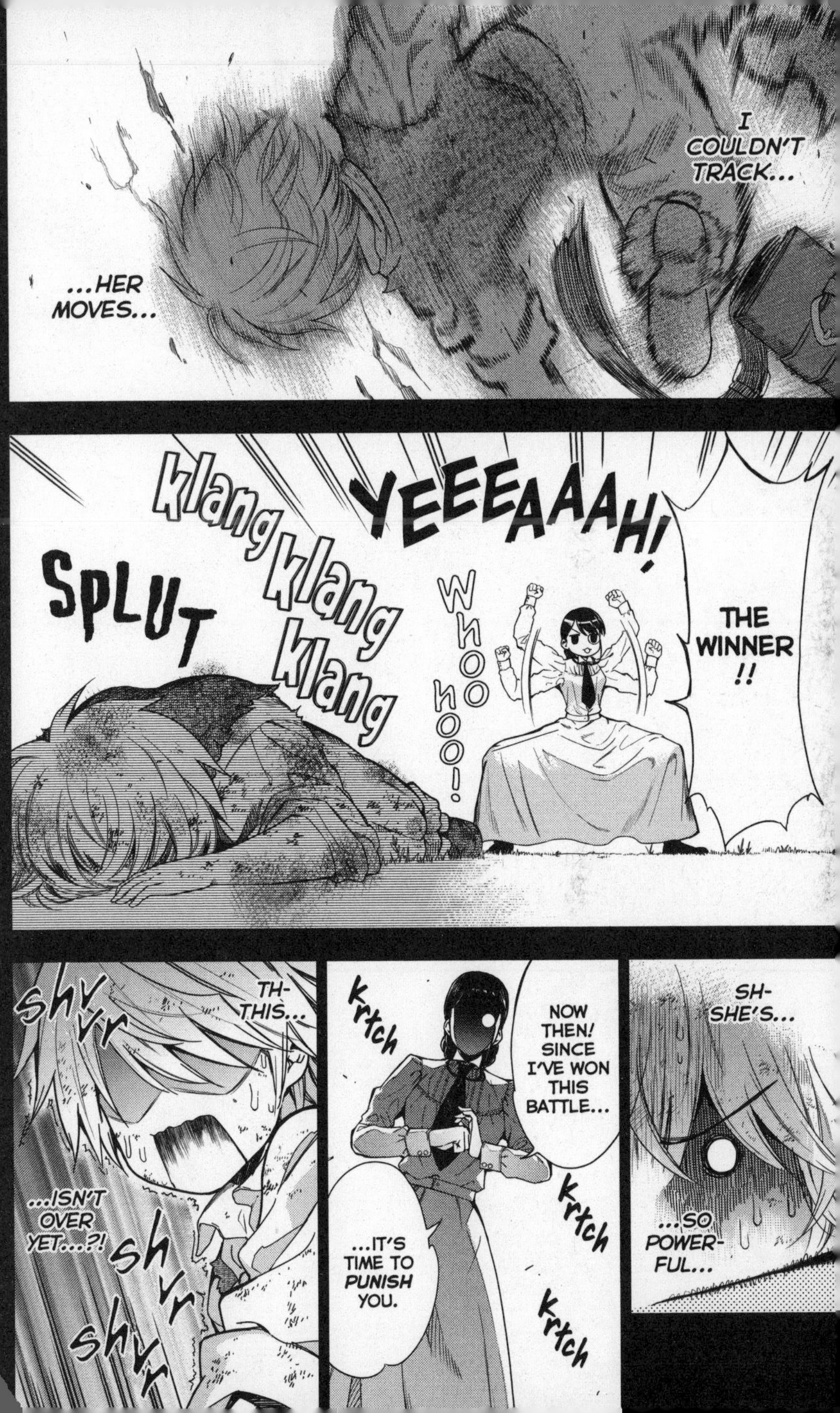
I COULDN'T TRACK...
...HER MOVES...
THE WINNER!!
YEEEAAAAH!
Whoo hooo!
klang klang klang
SPLUT
SH- SHE'S...
...SO POWER-FUL...
NOW THEN! SINCE I'VE WON THIS BATTLE...
krtch
...IT'S TIME TO PUNISH YOU.
krtch
krtch
TH- THIS...
shvr
...ISN'T OVER YET...?!
shvr
shvr

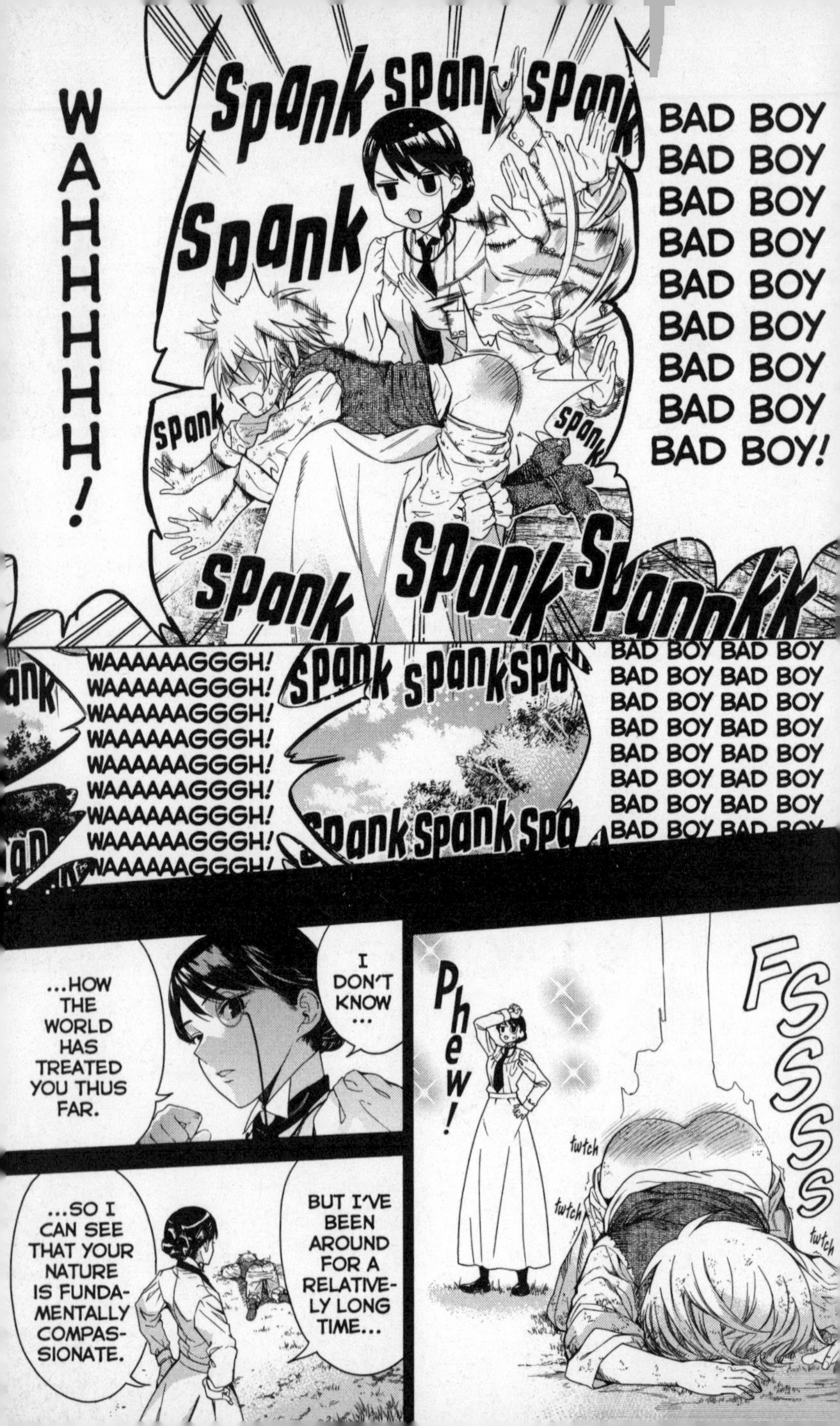
BAD BOY BAD BOY BAD BOY BAD BOY BAD BOY BAD BOY BAD BOY BAD BOY BAD BOY!
Spank spank spank
Spank
spank
spank
Spank Spank Spannkk
WAHHHHH!
BAD BOY BAD BOY BAD BOY BAD BOY BAD BOY BAD BOY BAD BOY BAD BOY BAD BOY BAD BOY BAD BOY BAD BOY BAD BOY BAD BOY
spank spank spa
Spank Spank Spa
WAAAAAAGGGH! WAAAAAAGGGH! WAAAAAAGGGH! WAAAAAAGGGH! WAAAAAAGGGH! WAAAAAAGGGH! WAAAAAAGGGH! WAAAAAAGGGH!
FSSSSS
twtch
twtch
twtch
Phew!
I DON'T KNOW...
...HOW THE WORLD HAS TREATED YOU THUS FAR.
BUT I'VE BEEN AROUND FOR A RELATIVELY LONG TIME...
...SO I CAN SEE THAT YOUR NATURE IS FUNDAMENTALLY COMPASSIONATE.

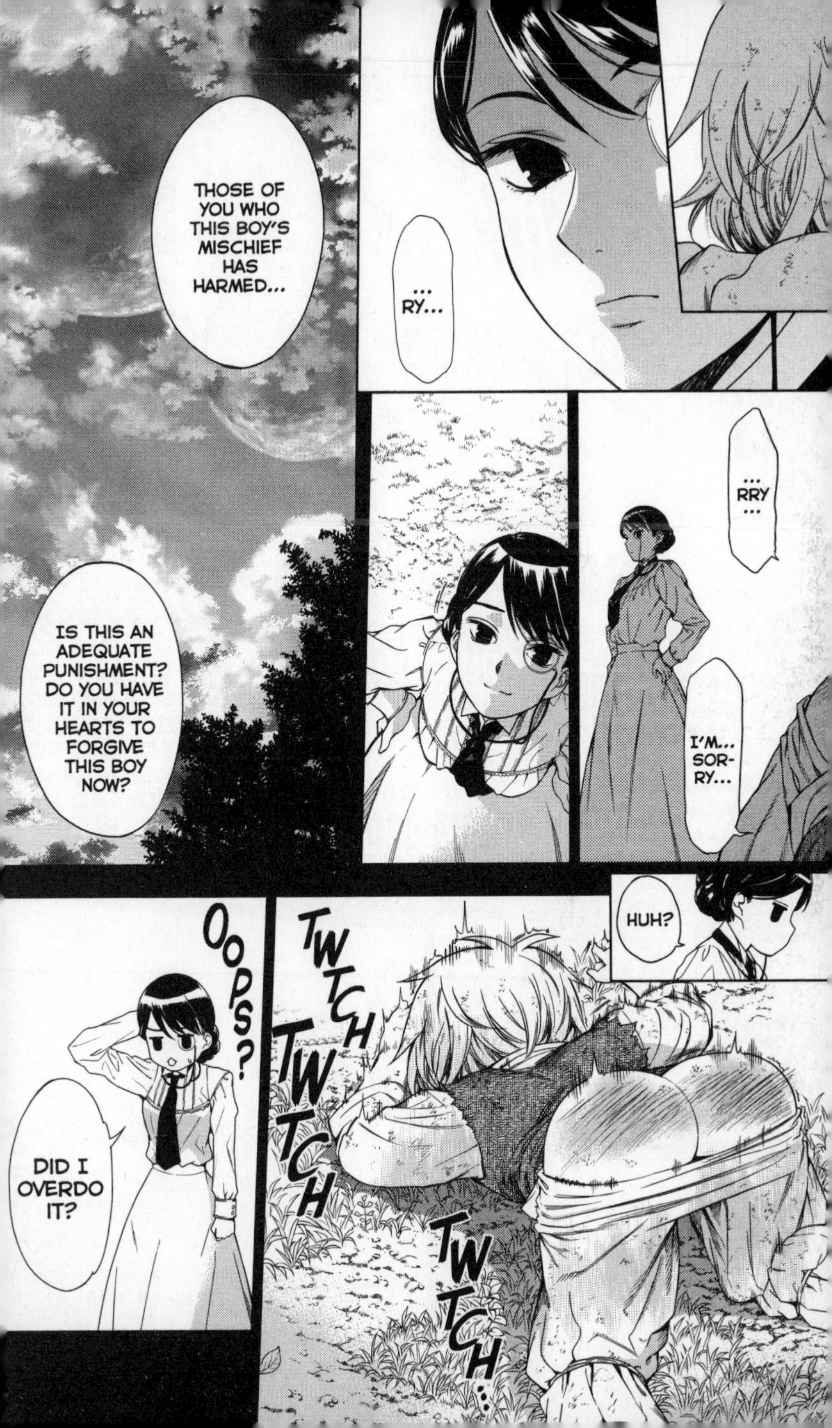
...RY...
...RRY...
I'M... SOR-RY...
THOSE OF YOU WHO THIS BOY'S MISCHIEF HAS HARMED...
IS THIS AN ADEQUATE PUNISHMENT? DO YOU HAVE IT IN YOUR HEARTS TO FORGIVE THIS BOY NOW?
HUH?
TWTCH
TWTCH
TWTCH...
OOPS?
DID I OVERDO IT?

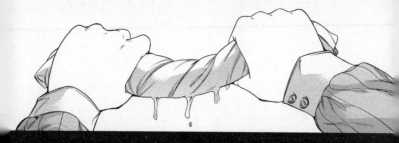

I FEEL HOT...

SO HOT...

FATHER...

MOTHER...

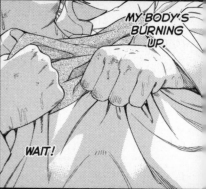

MY BODY'S BURNING UP.

WAIT!

SHAAAA

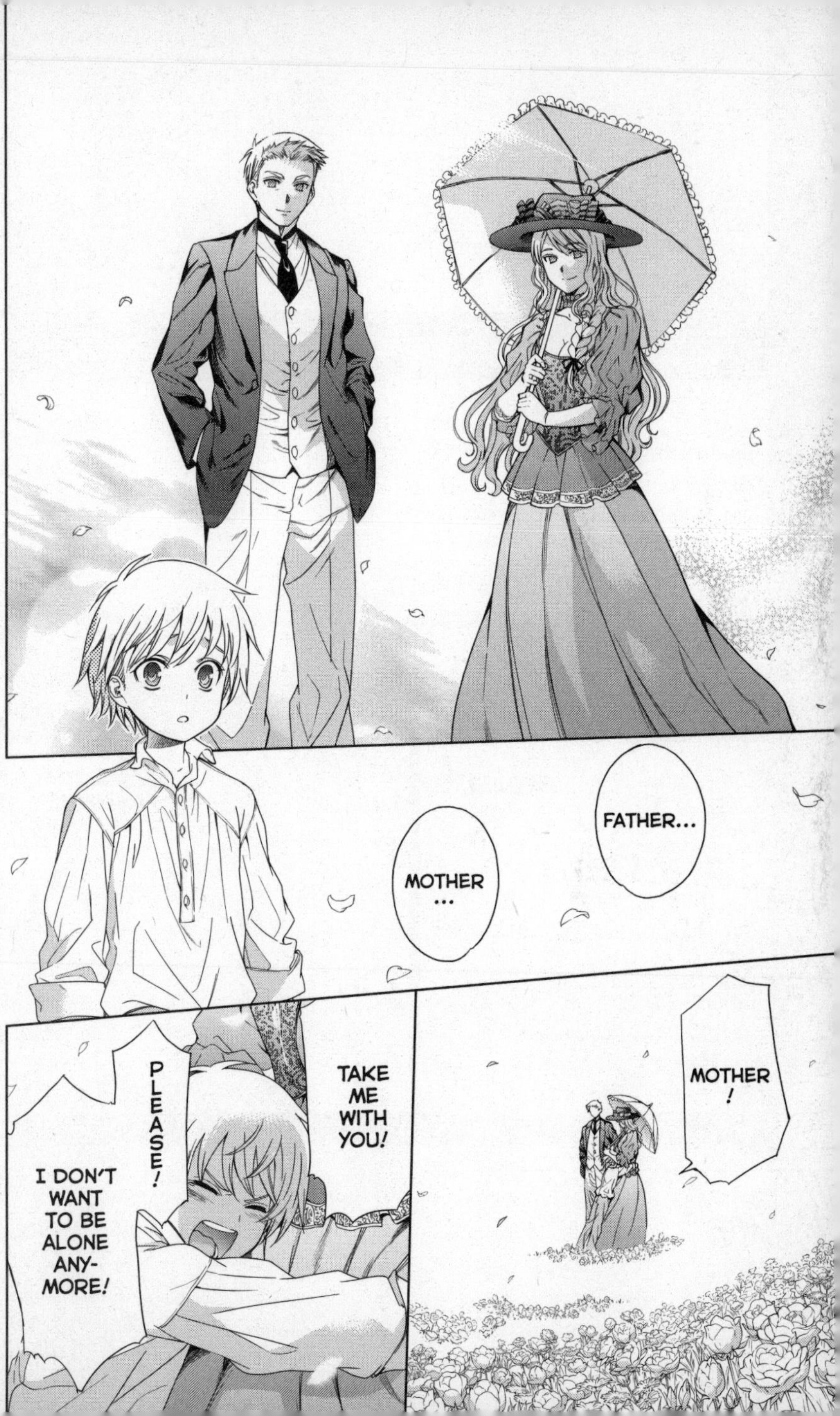
FATHER...
MOTHER...
MOTHER!
TAKE ME WITH YOU!
PLEASE!
I DON'T WANT TO BE ALONE ANY-MORE!

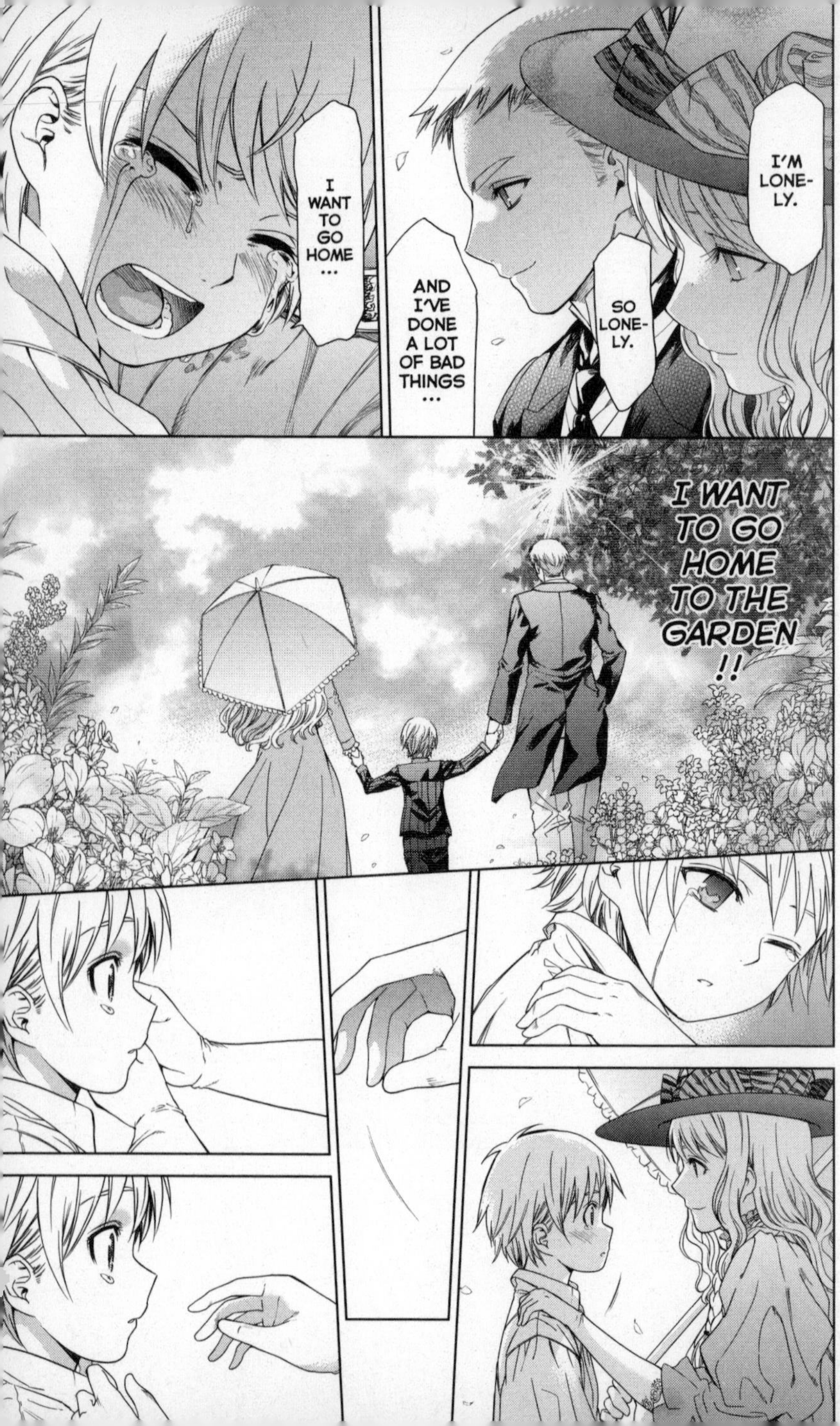
I'M LONELY.
SO LONELY.
AND I'VE DONE A LOT OF BAD THINGS...
I WANT TO GO HOME...
I WANT TO GO HOME TO THE GARDEN!!

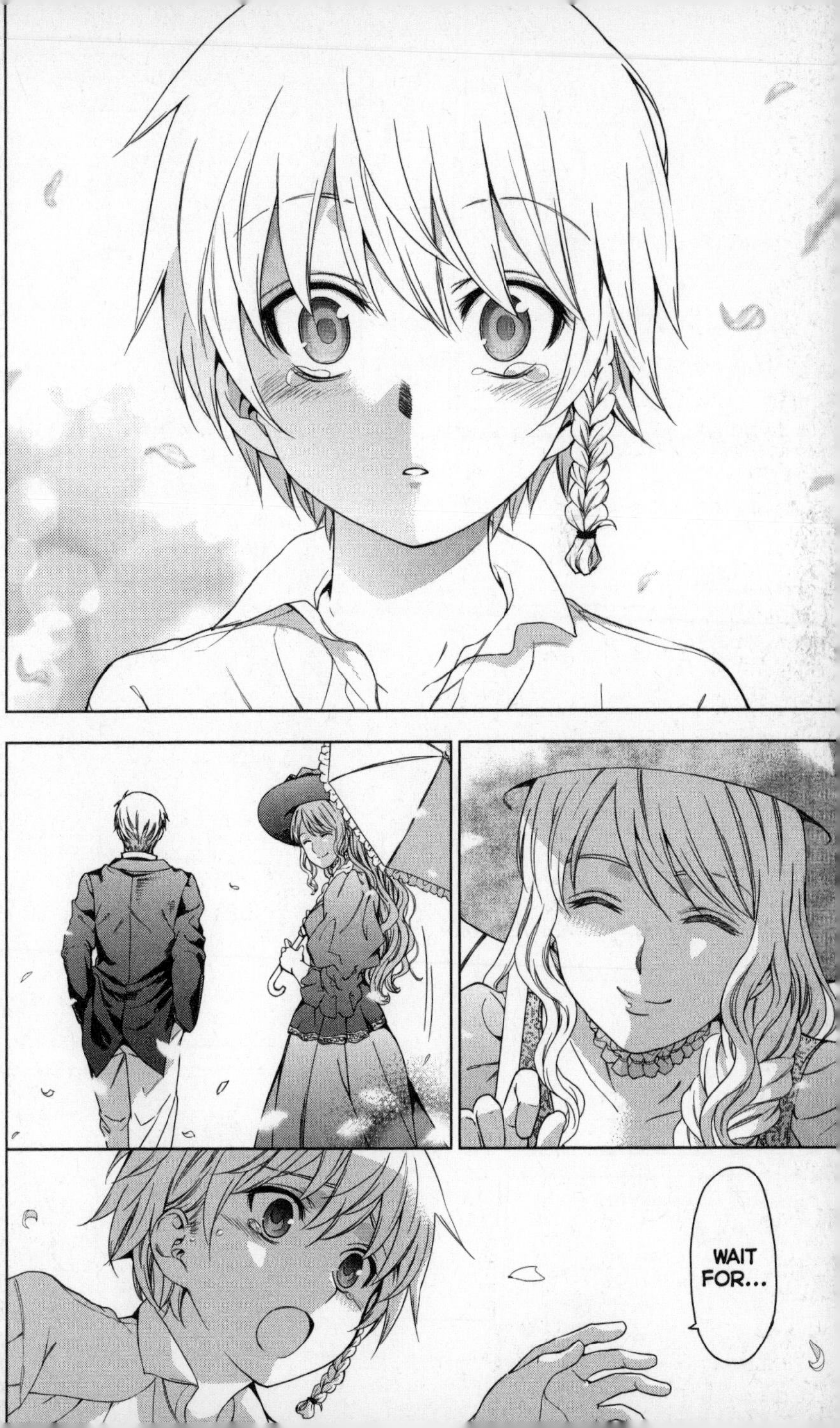
WAIT FOR...

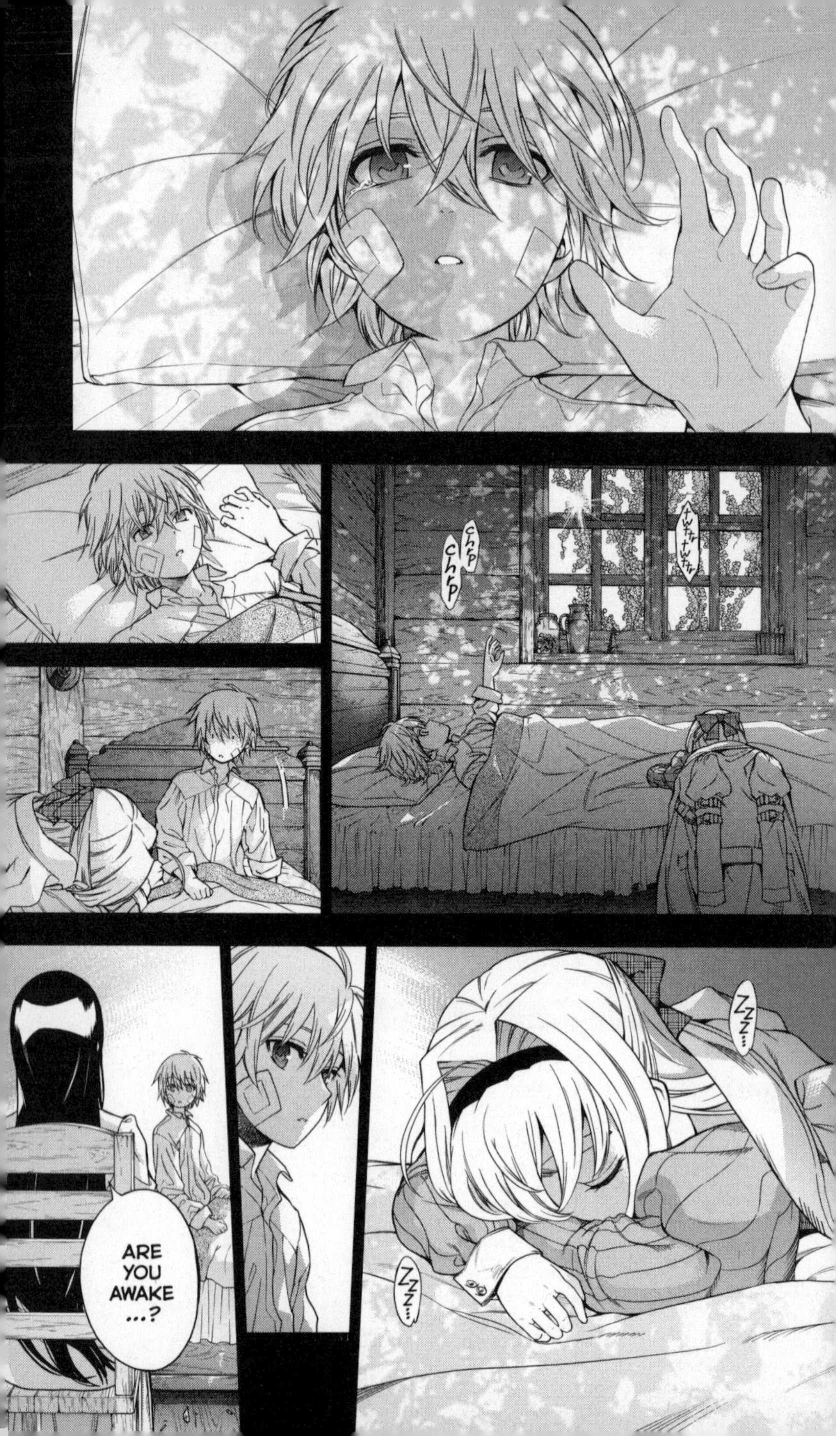
chrp
chrp
Zzz...
Zzz...
ARE YOU AWAKE ...?

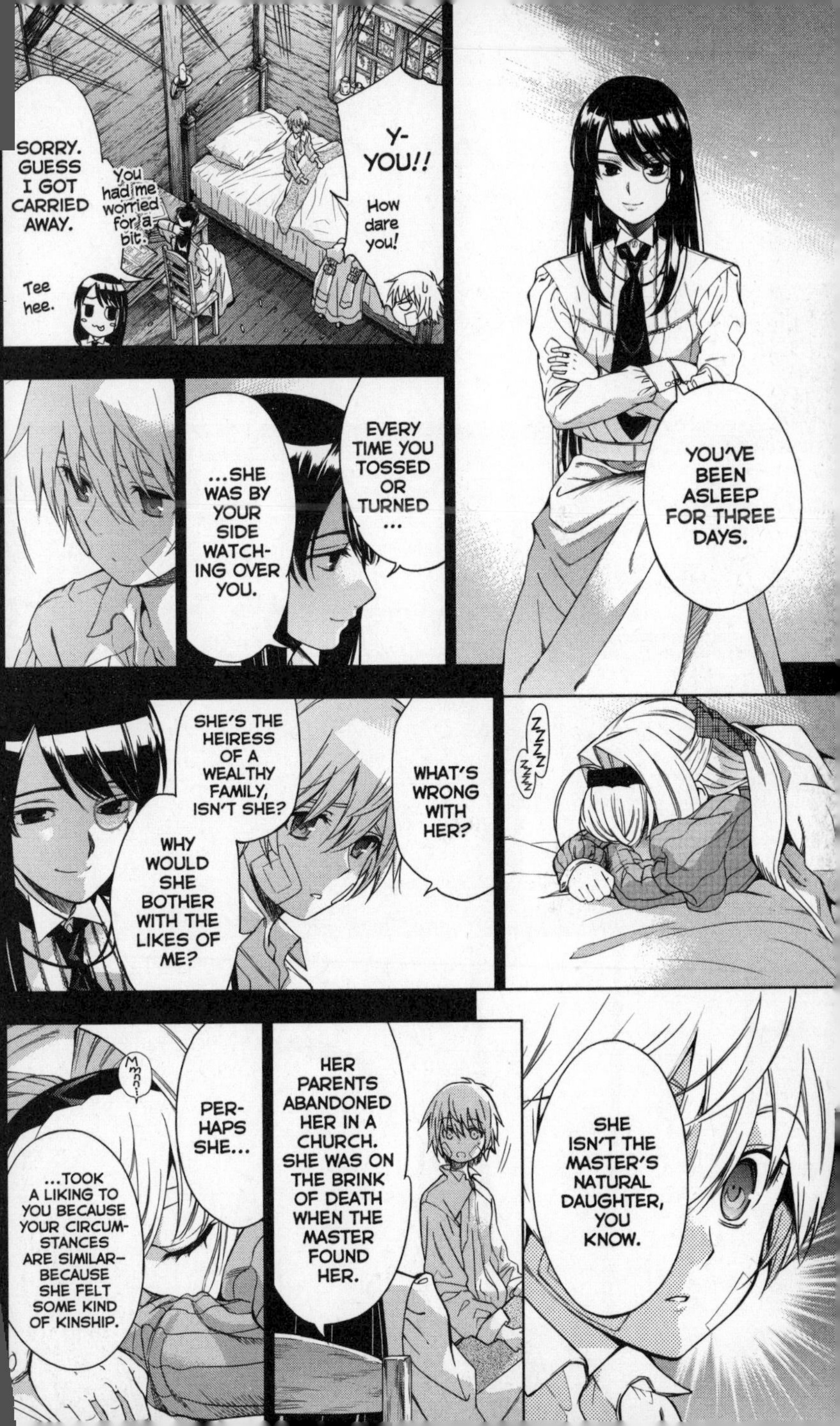
YOU'VE BEEN ASLEEP FOR THREE DAYS.
Y- YOU!!
How dare you!
SORRY. GUESS I GOT CARRIED AWAY.
You had me worried for a bit.
Tee hee.
EVERY TIME YOU TOSSED OR TURNED...
...SHE WAS BY YOUR SIDE WATCHING OVER YOU.
ZZZZ ZZZZ
WHAT'S WRONG WITH HER?
SHE'S THE HEIRESS OF A WEALTHY FAMILY, ISN'T SHE?
WHY WOULD SHE BOTHER WITH THE LIKES OF ME?
SHE ISN'T THE MASTER'S NATURAL DAUGHTER, YOU KNOW.
HER PARENTS ABANDONED HER IN A CHURCH. SHE WAS ON THE BRINK OF DEATH WHEN THE MASTER FOUND HER.
PER-HAPS SHE...
Mmn...
...TOOK A LIKING TO YOU BECAUSE YOUR CIRCUM-STANCES ARE SIMILAR—BECAUSE SHE FELT SOME KIND OF KINSHIP.

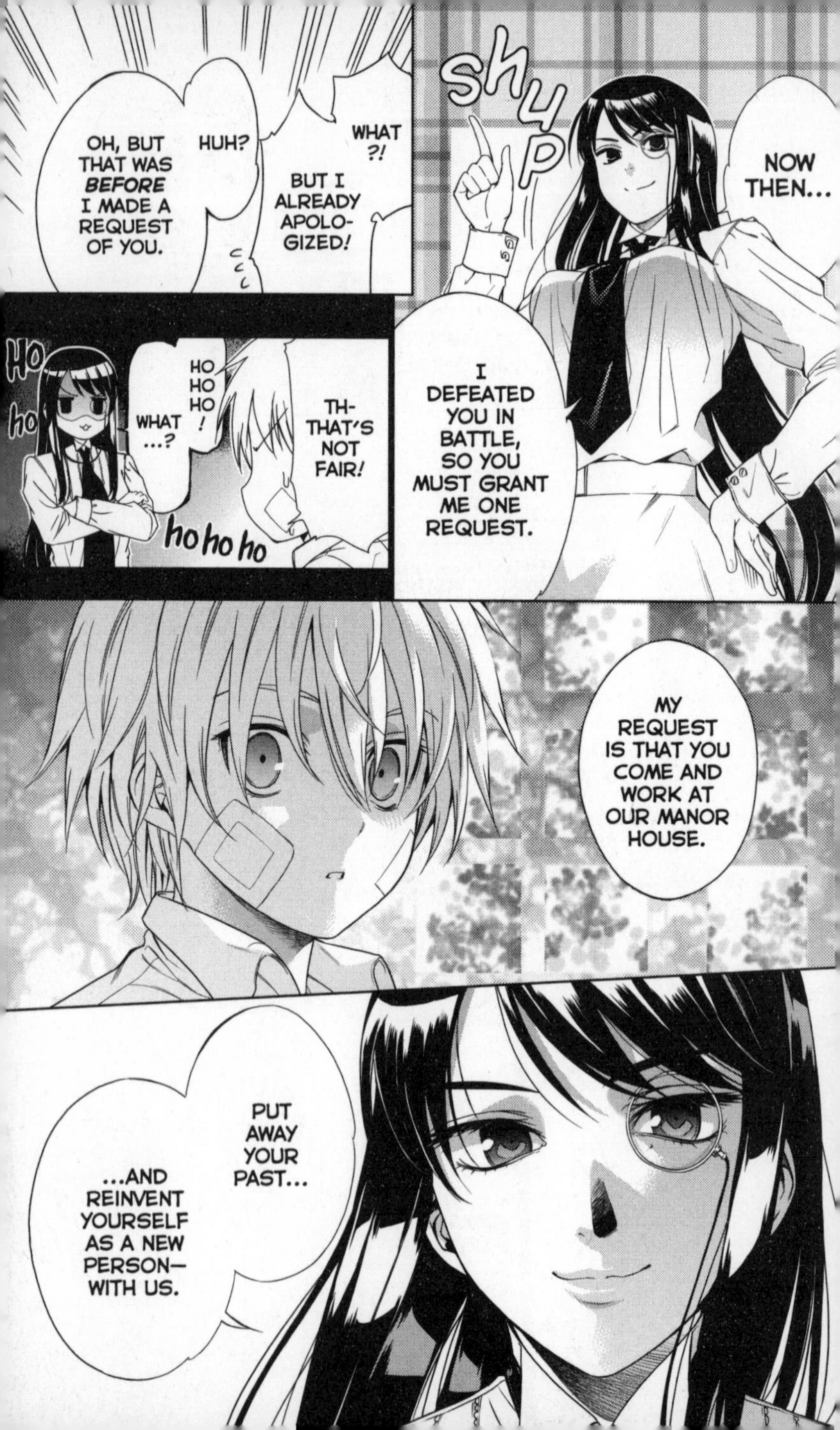
NOW THEN...
SHUP
I DEFEATED YOU IN BATTLE, SO YOU MUST GRANT ME ONE REQUEST.
WHAT ?!
BUT I ALREADY APOLOGIZED!
HUH?
OH, BUT THAT WAS *BEFORE* I MADE A REQUEST OF YOU.
TH-THAT'S NOT FAIR!
HO HO HO!
WHAT ...?
HO ho
ho ho ho
MY REQUEST IS THAT YOU COME AND WORK AT OUR MANOR HOUSE.
PUT AWAY YOUR PAST...
...AND REINVENT YOURSELF AS A NEW PERSON—WITH US.

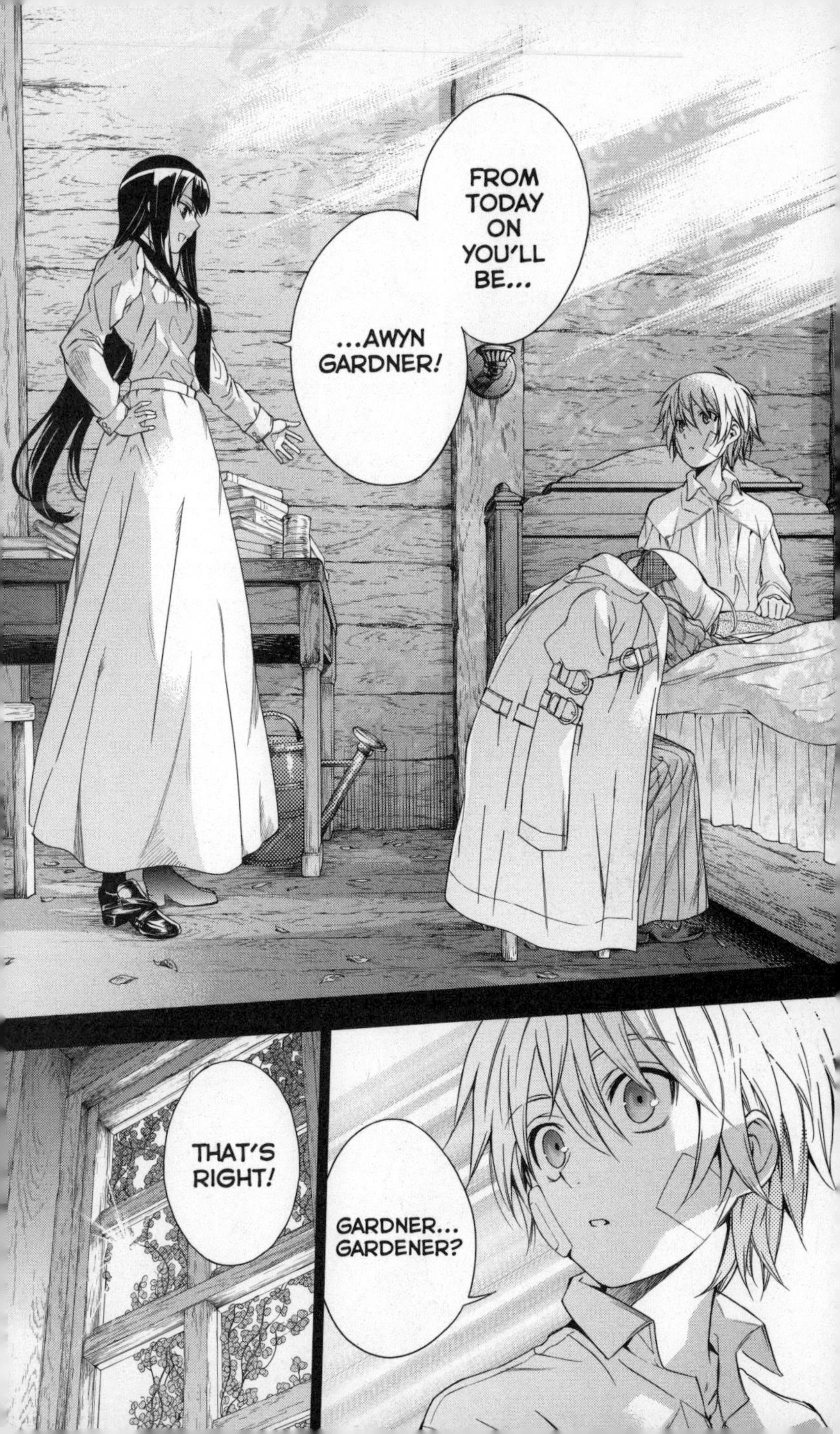
FROM TODAY ON YOU'LL BE...
...AWYN GARDNER!
GARDNER... GARDENER?
THAT'S RIGHT!

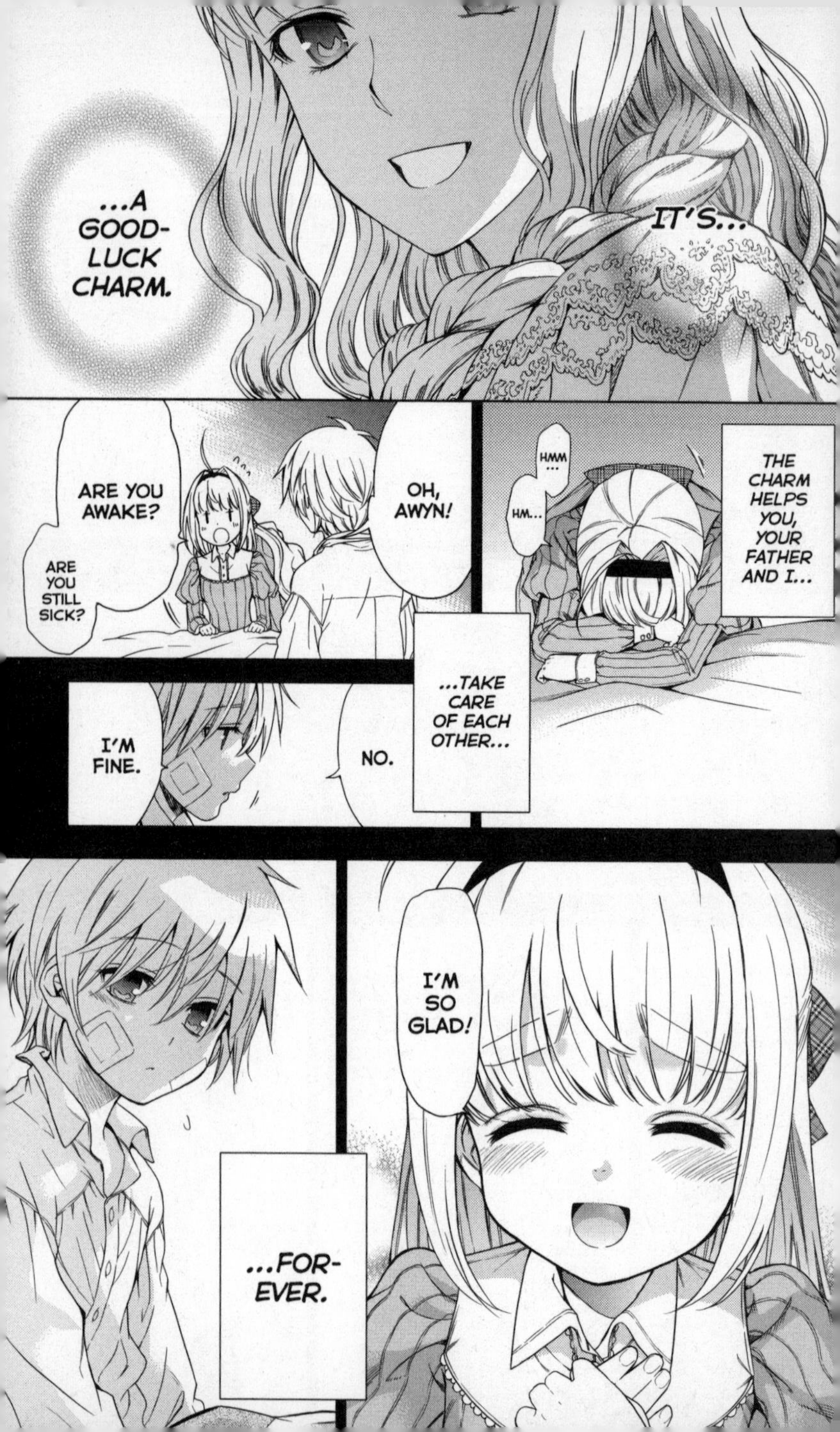
IT'S...
...A GOOD-LUCK CHARM.
THE CHARM HELPS YOU, YOUR FATHER AND I...
HMM...
HM...
OH, AWYN!
ARE YOU AWAKE?
ARE YOU STILL SICK?
...TAKE CARE OF EACH OTHER...
NO.
I'M FINE.
I'M SO GLAD!
...FOR-EVER.

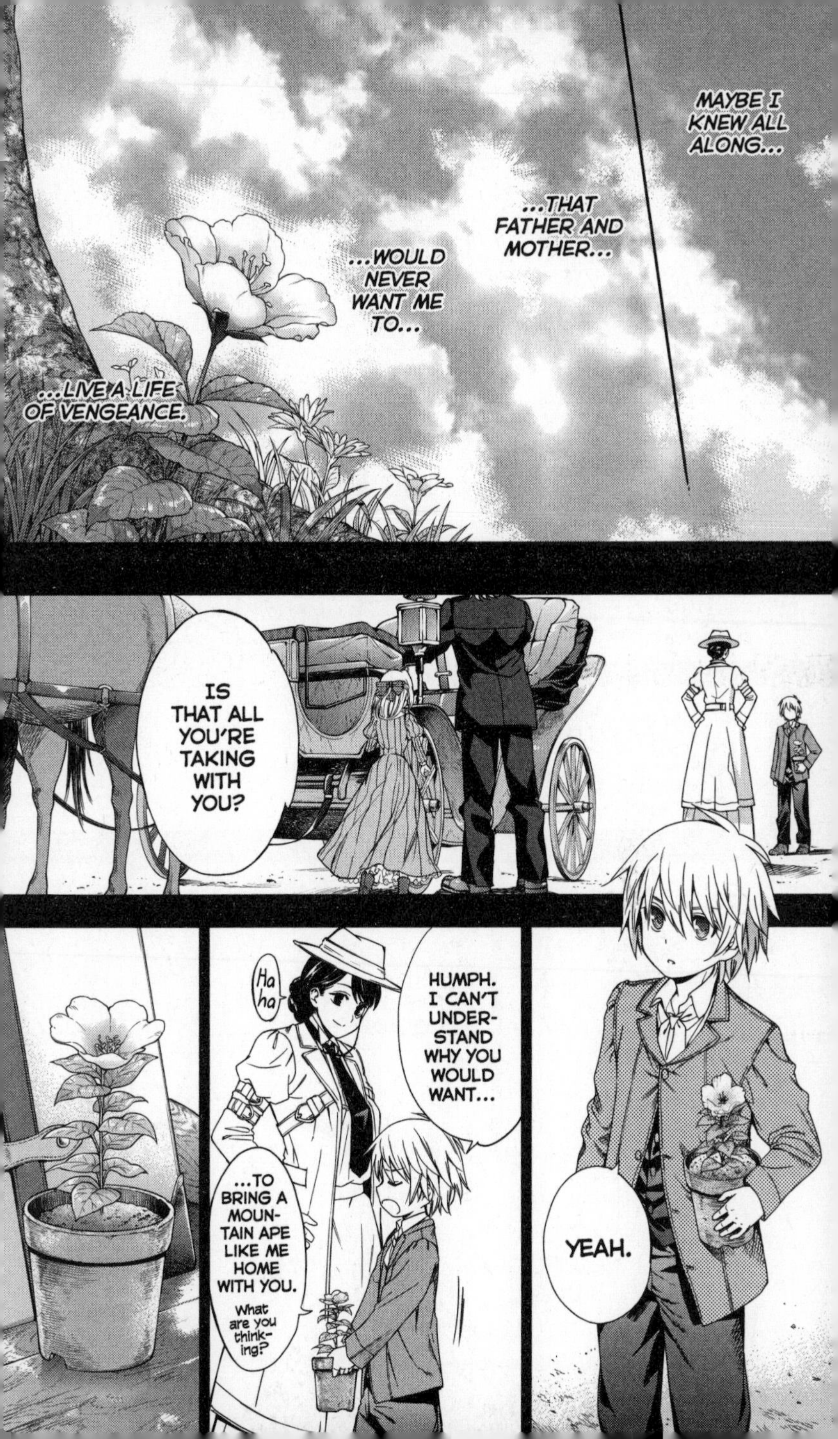
MAYBE I KNEW ALL ALONG...
...THAT FATHER AND MOTHER...
...WOULD NEVER WANT ME TO...
...LIVE A LIFE OF VENGEANCE.
IS THAT ALL YOU'RE TAKING WITH YOU?
YEAH.
HUMPH. I CAN'T UNDER-STAND WHY YOU WOULD WANT...
Ha ha
...TO BRING A MOUN-TAIN APE LIKE ME HOME WITH YOU.
What are you think-ing?

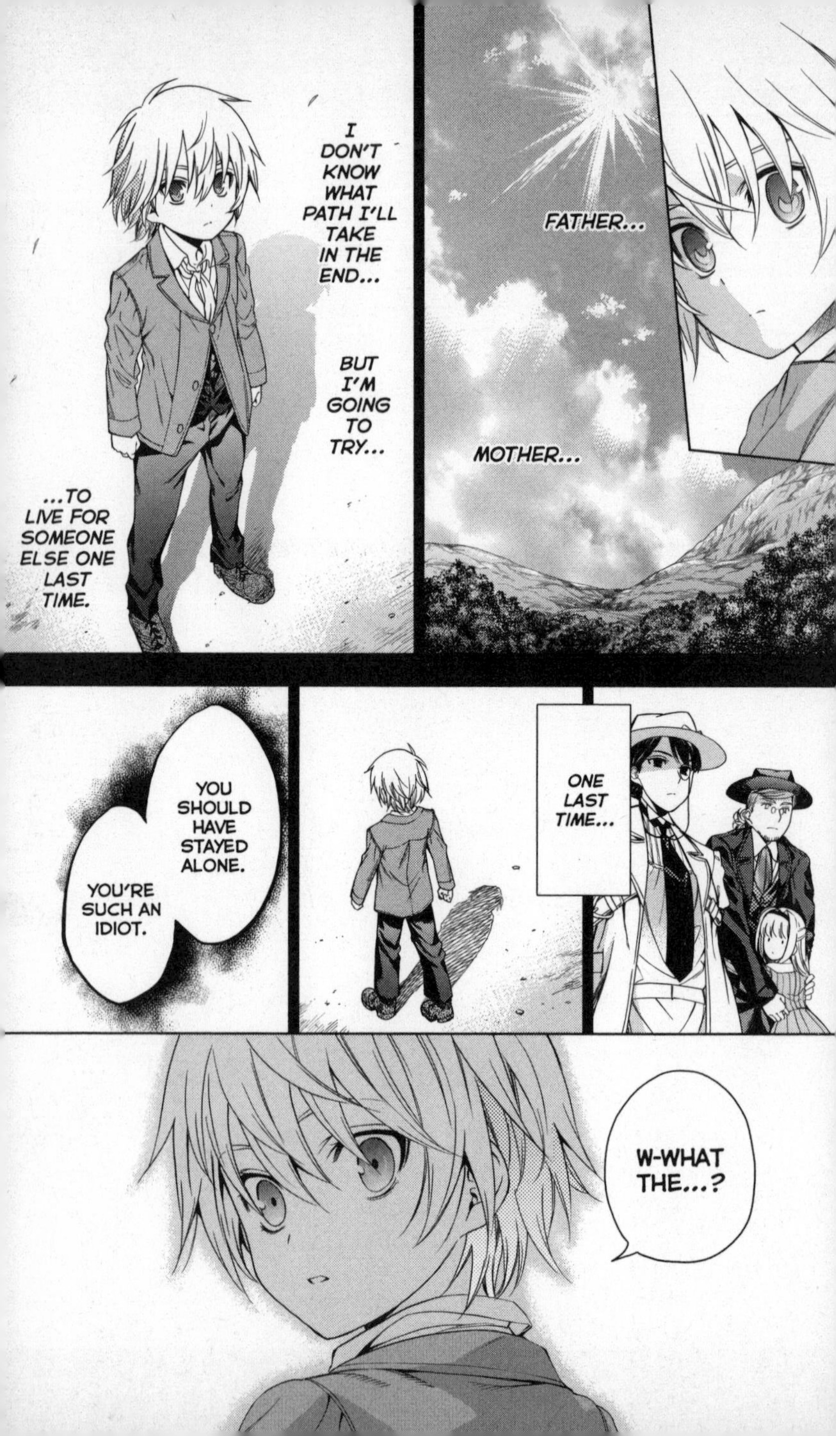
FATHER...
MOTHER...
I DON'T KNOW WHAT PATH I'LL TAKE IN THE END...
BUT I'M GOING TO TRY...
...TO LIVE FOR SOMEONE ELSE ONE LAST TIME.
ONE LAST TIME...
YOU SHOULD HAVE STAYED ALONE.
YOU'RE SUCH AN IDIOT.
W-WHAT THE...?

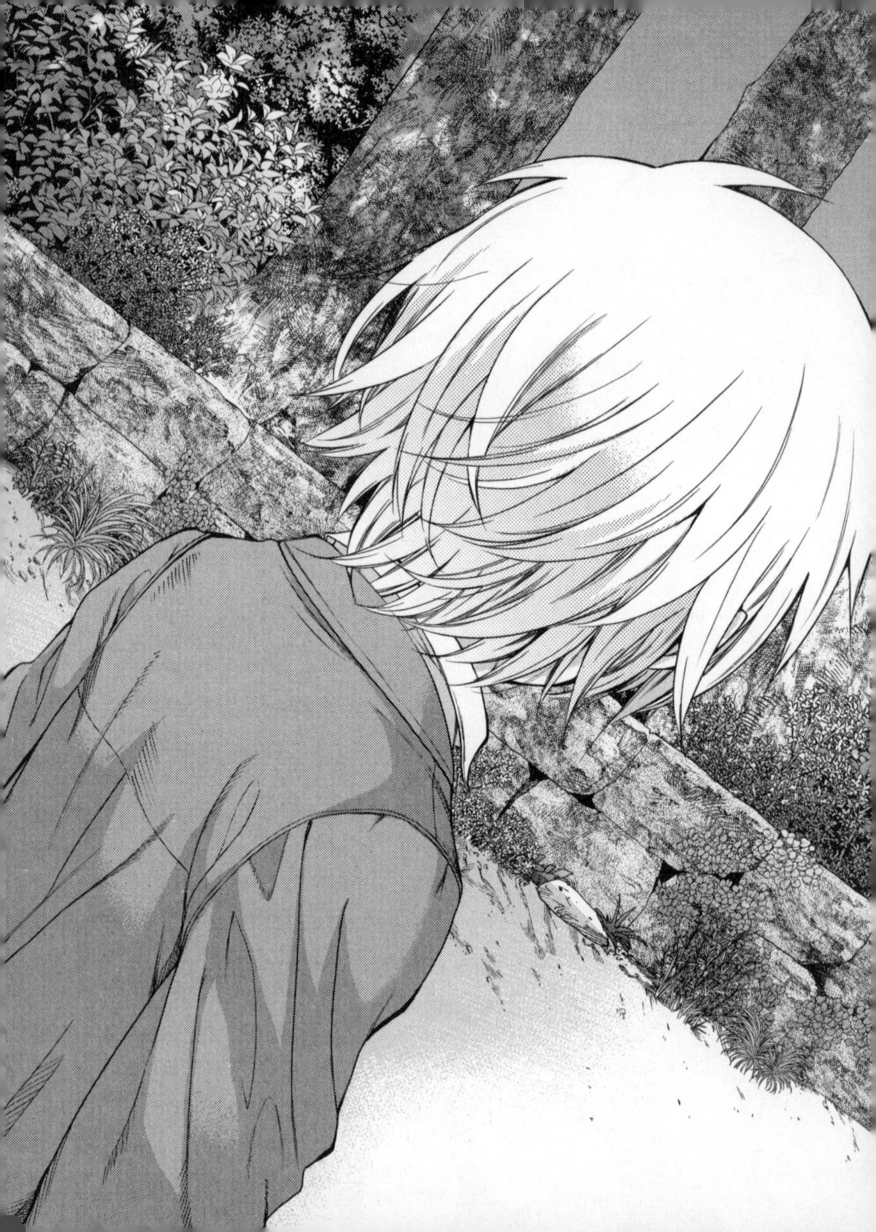

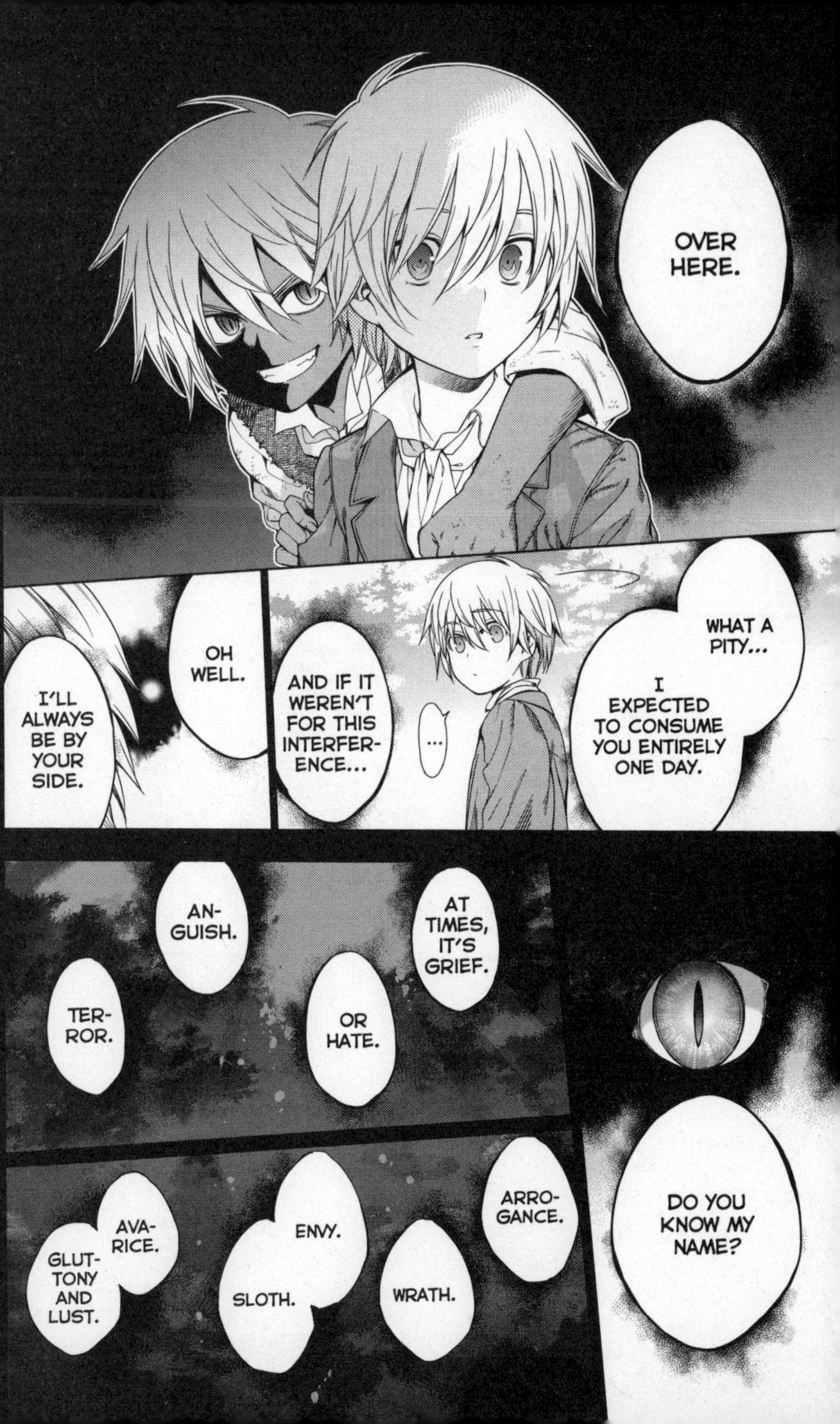
OVER HERE.
WHAT A PITY...
I EXPECTED TO CONSUME YOU ENTIRELY ONE DAY.
...
AND IF IT WEREN'T FOR THIS INTERFERENCE...
OH WELL.
I'LL ALWAYS BE BY YOUR SIDE.
DO YOU KNOW MY NAME?
AT TIMES, IT'S GRIEF.
ANGUISH.
OR HATE.
TERROR.
ARROGANCE.
ENVY.
WRATH.
SLOTH.
AVARICE.
GLUTTONY AND LUST.

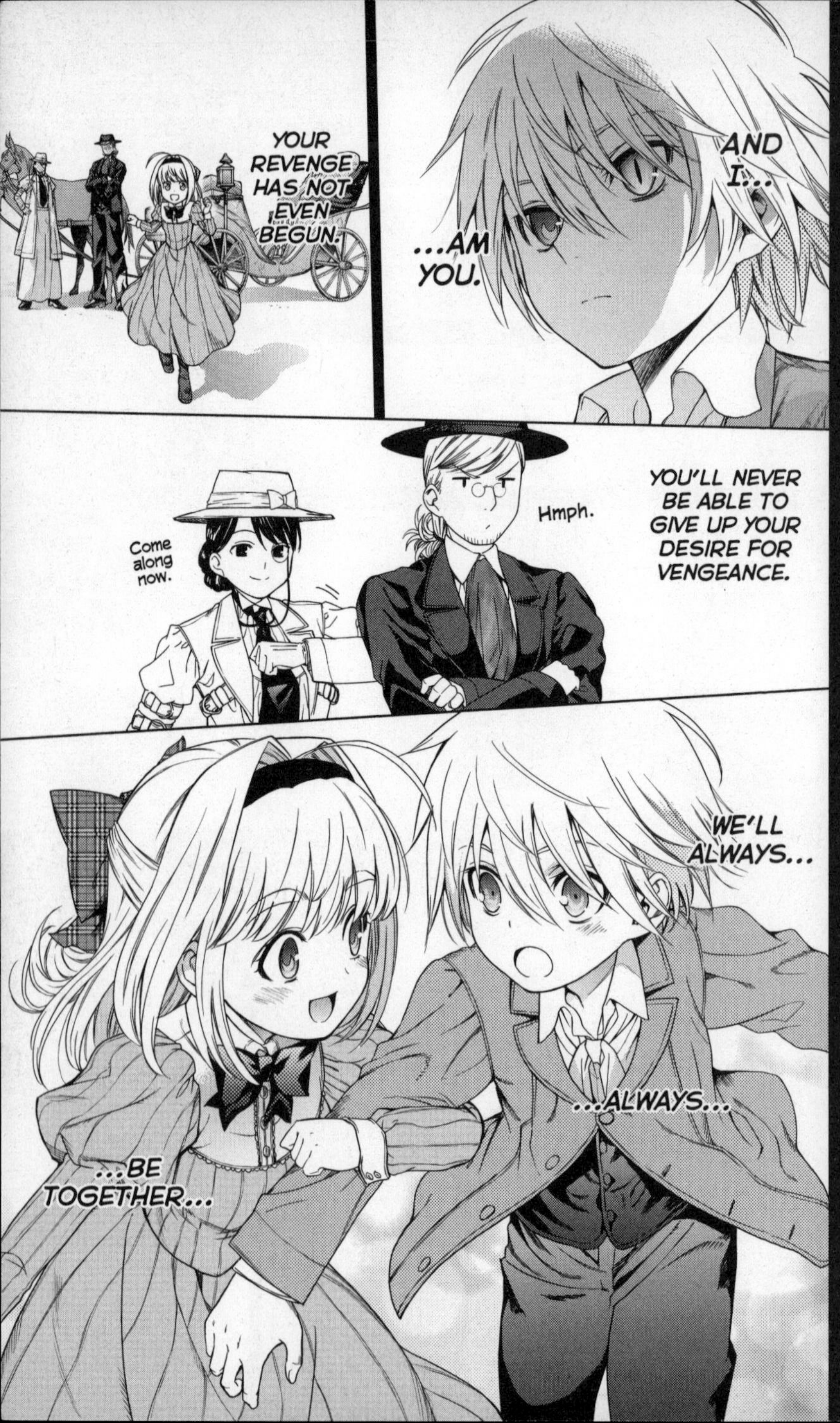
AND I...
...AM YOU.
YOUR REVENGE HAS NOT EVEN BEGUN.
YOU'LL NEVER BE ABLE TO GIVE UP YOUR DESIRE FOR VENGEANCE.
Hmph.
Come along now.
WE'LL ALWAYS...
...ALWAYS...
...BE TOGETHER...

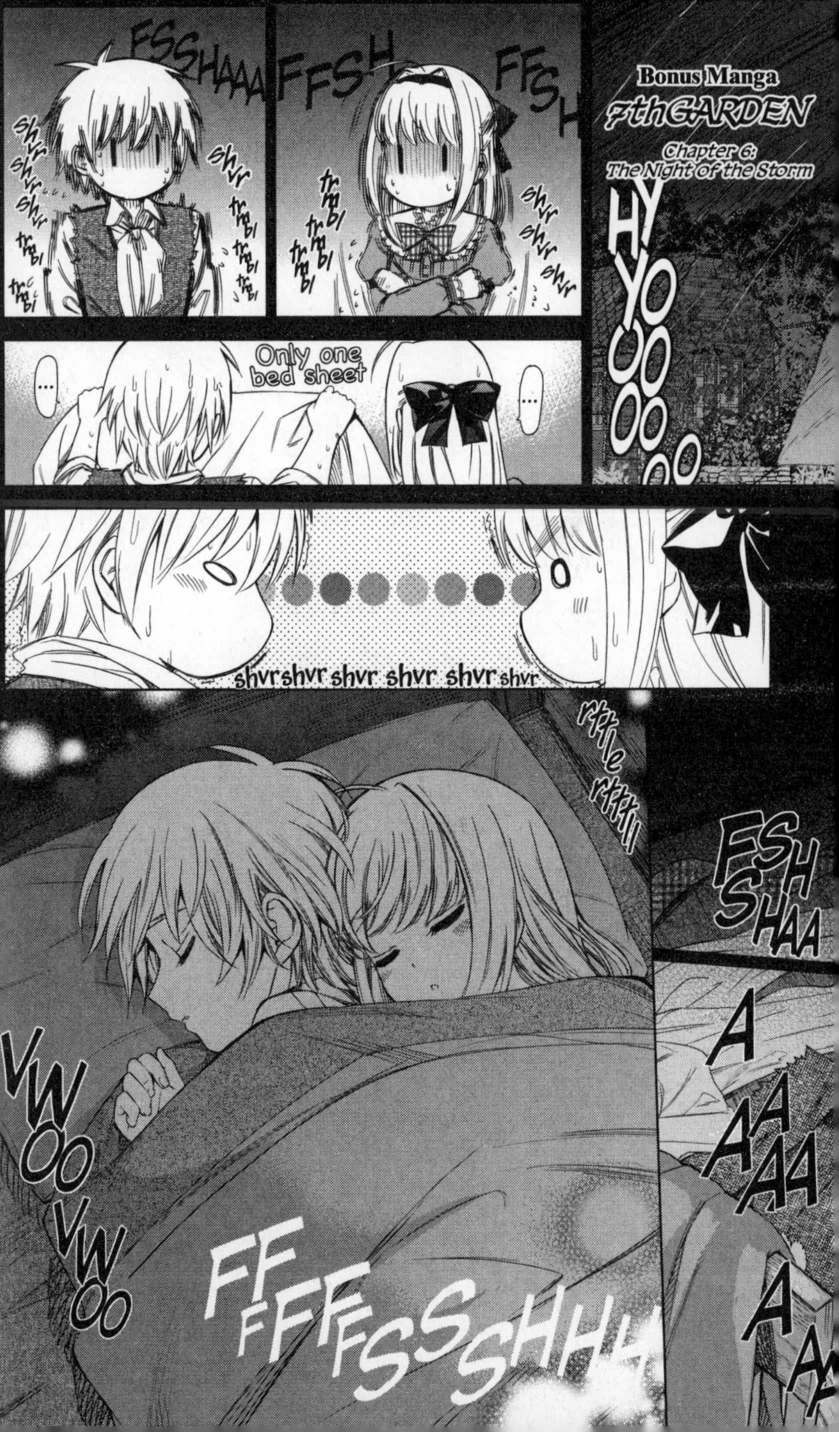
Bonus Manga
7thGARDEN
Chapter 6: The Night of the Storm
HYYOOOOOO
FFSH
FFSH
trmbl
shvr shvr shvr
FSSHAAA
shvr shvr shvr shvr
shvr
trmbl
...
Only one bed sheet
...
shvrshvr shvr shvr shvr shvr
rttle rtttll
FSHSHAA
AAAAAAA
VWOOVWOO
FFFFFFSSSHHH

root. 16 The Miniature Garden of Tomorrow

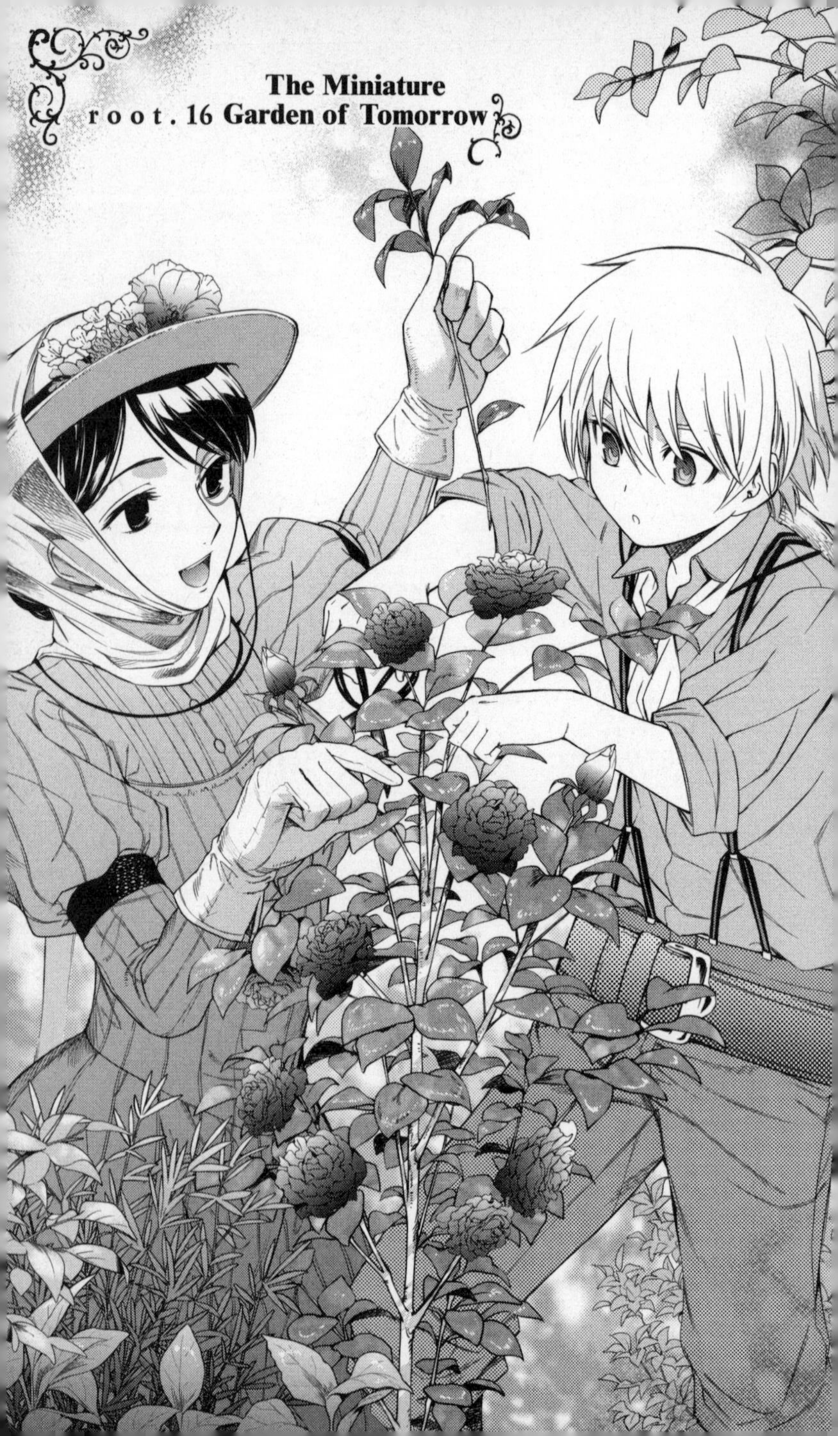

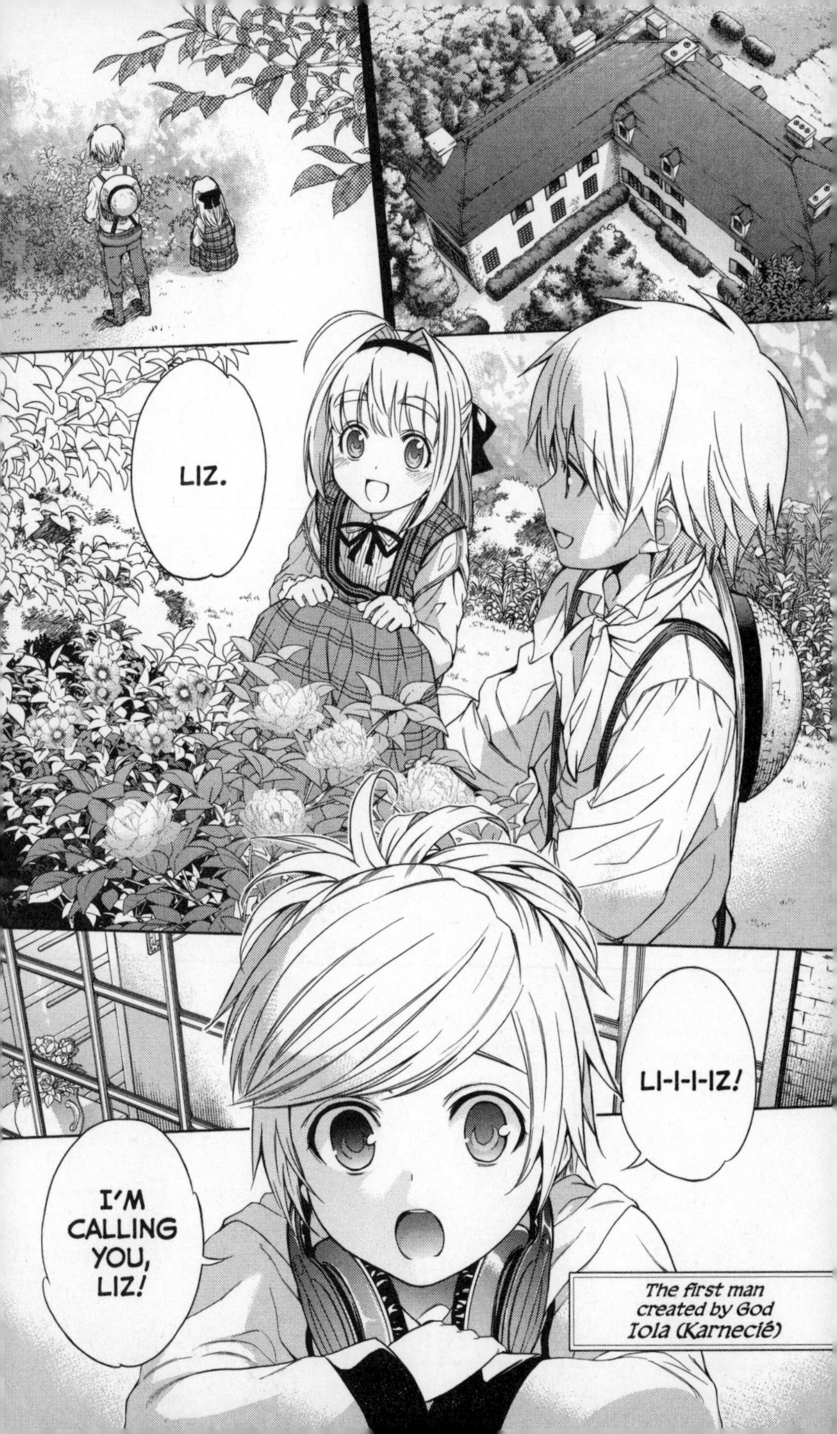
LIZ.
LI-I-I-IZ!
I'M CALLING YOU, LIZ!
The first man created by God Iola (Karnecié)

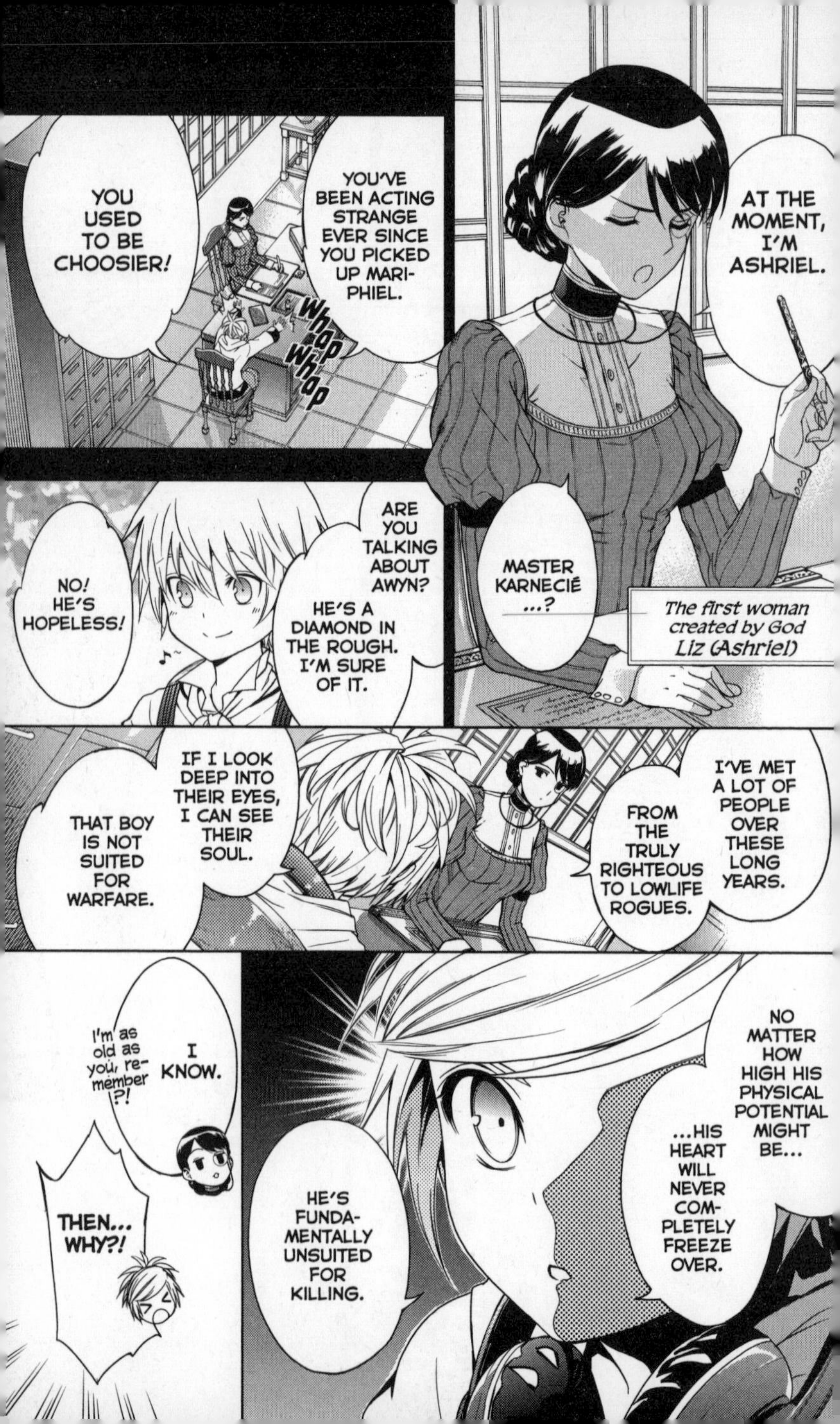

AT THE MOMENT, I'M ASHRIEL.
MASTER KARNECIÉ ...?
The first woman created by God Liz (Ashriel)
YOU'VE BEEN ACTING STRANGE EVER SINCE YOU PICKED UP MARI-PHIEL.
Whap Whap Whap
YOU USED TO BE CHOOSIER!
ARE YOU TALKING ABOUT AWYN?
HE'S A DIAMOND IN THE ROUGH. I'M SURE OF IT.
NO! HE'S HOPELESS!
I'VE MET A LOT OF PEOPLE OVER THESE LONG YEARS.
FROM THE TRULY RIGHTEOUS TO LOWLIFE ROGUES.
IF I LOOK DEEP INTO THEIR EYES, I CAN SEE THEIR SOUL.
THAT BOY IS NOT SUITED FOR WARFARE.
NO MATTER HOW HIGH HIS PHYSICAL POTENTIAL MIGHT BE...
...HIS HEART WILL NEVER COM-PLETELY FREEZE OVER.
HE'S FUNDA-MENTALLY UNSUITED FOR KILLING.
I KNOW.
I'm as old as you, re-member ?!
THEN... WHY?!

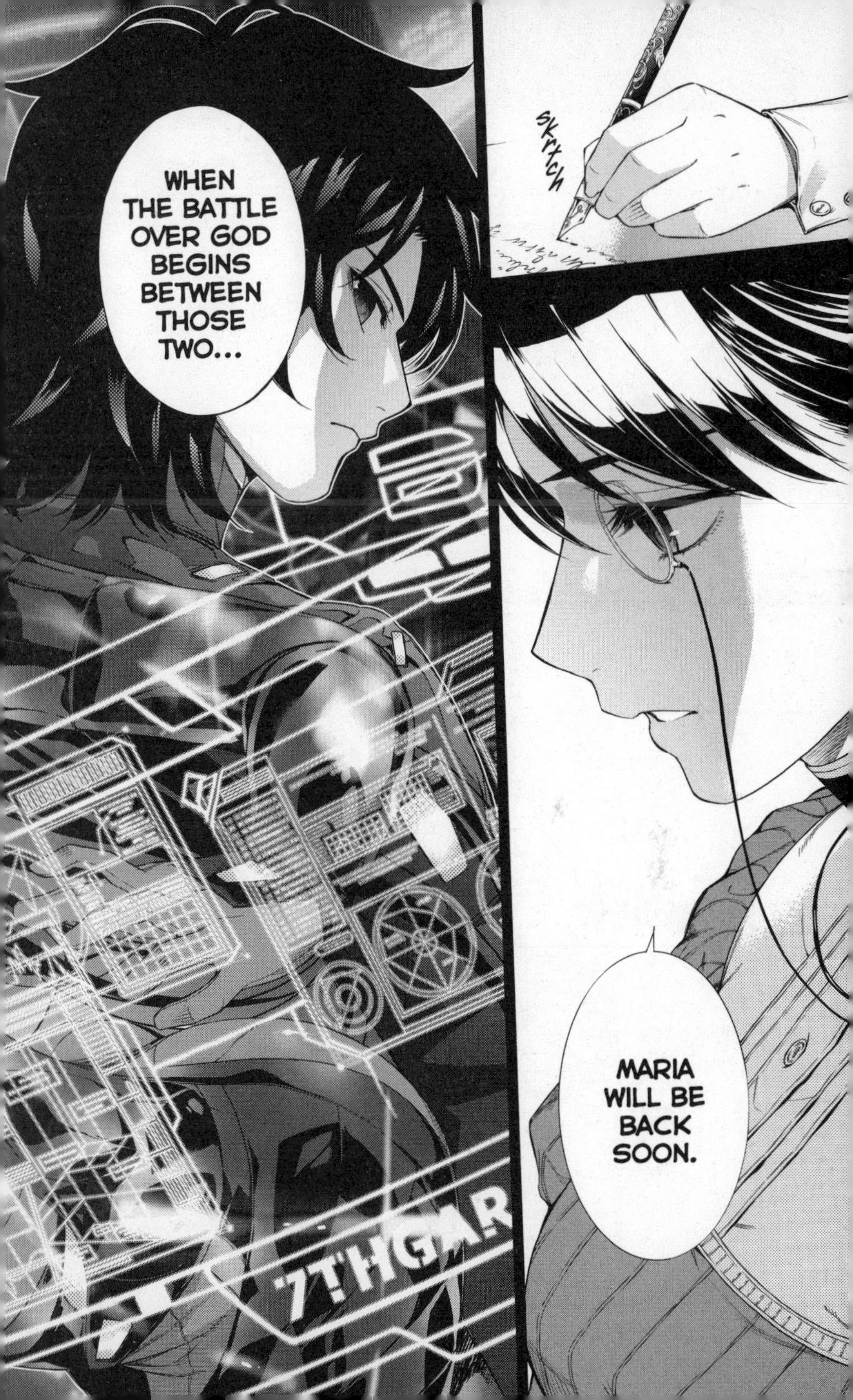
SKRXTCH
MARIA WILL BE BACK SOON.
WHEN THE BATTLE OVER GOD BEGINS BETWEEN THOSE TWO...

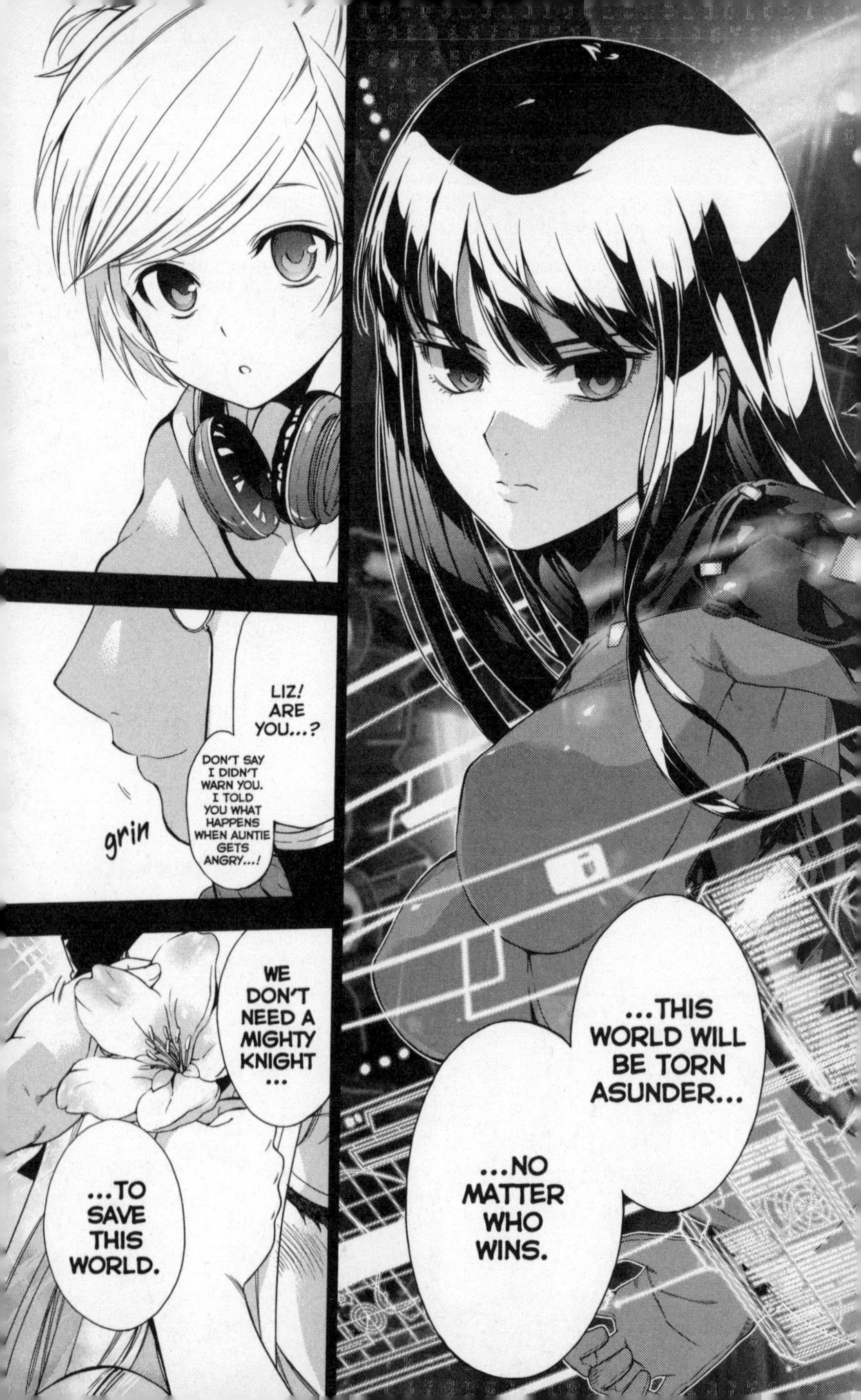
...THIS WORLD WILL BE TORN ASUNDER...
...NO MATTER WHO WINS.
LIZ! ARE YOU...?
DON'T SAY I DIDN'T WARN YOU. I TOLD YOU WHAT HAPPENS WHEN AUNTIE GETS ANGRY...!
grin
WE DON'T NEED A MIGHTY KNIGHT ...
...TO SAVE THIS WORLD.

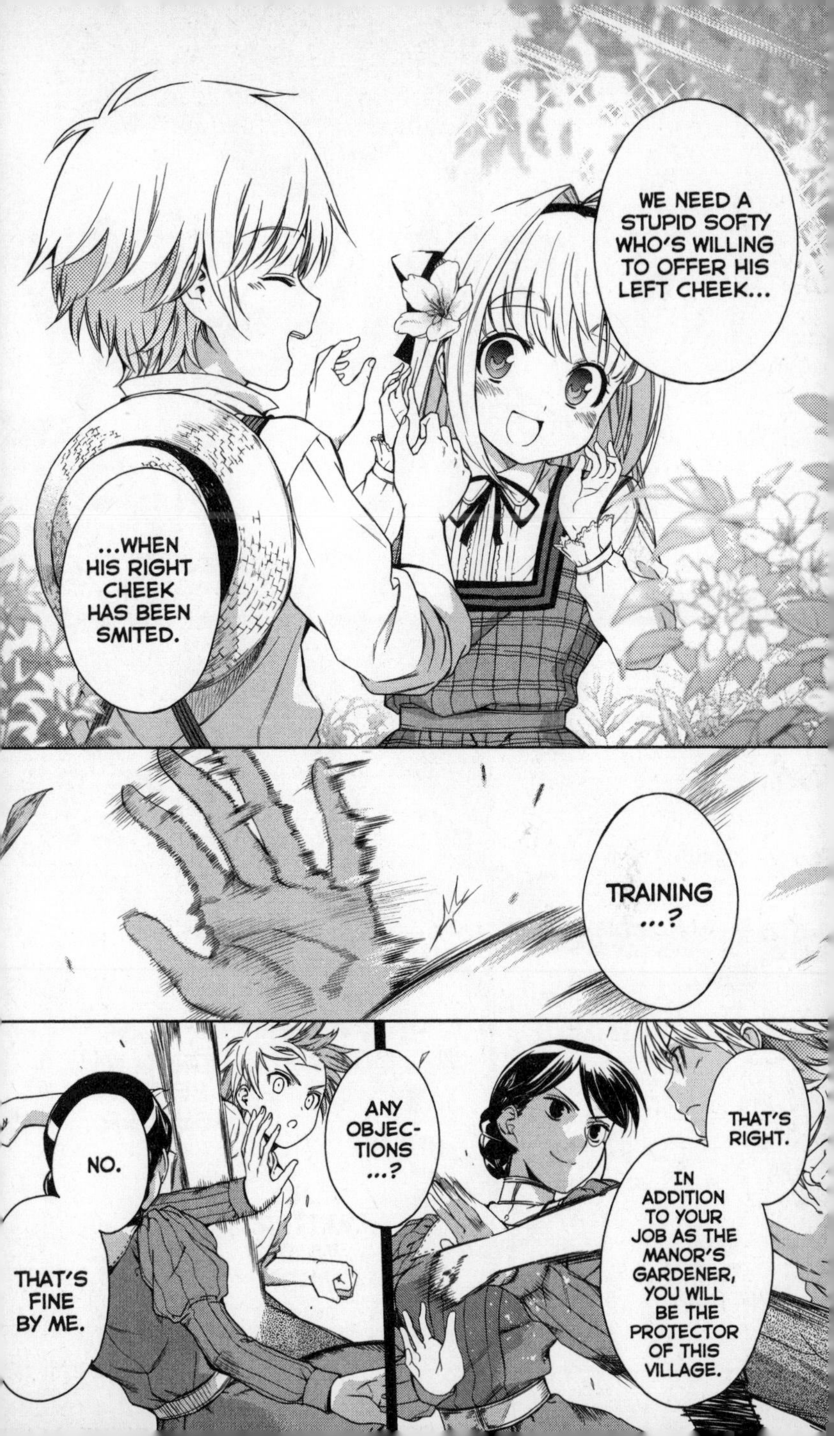
WE NEED A STUPID SOFTY WHO'S WILLING TO OFFER HIS LEFT CHEEK...
...WHEN HIS RIGHT CHEEK HAS BEEN SMITED.
TRAINING ...?
THAT'S RIGHT.
IN ADDITION TO YOUR JOB AS THE MANOR'S GARDENER, YOU WILL BE THE PROTECTOR OF THIS VILLAGE.
ANY OBJEC-TIONS ...?
NO.
THAT'S FINE BY ME.

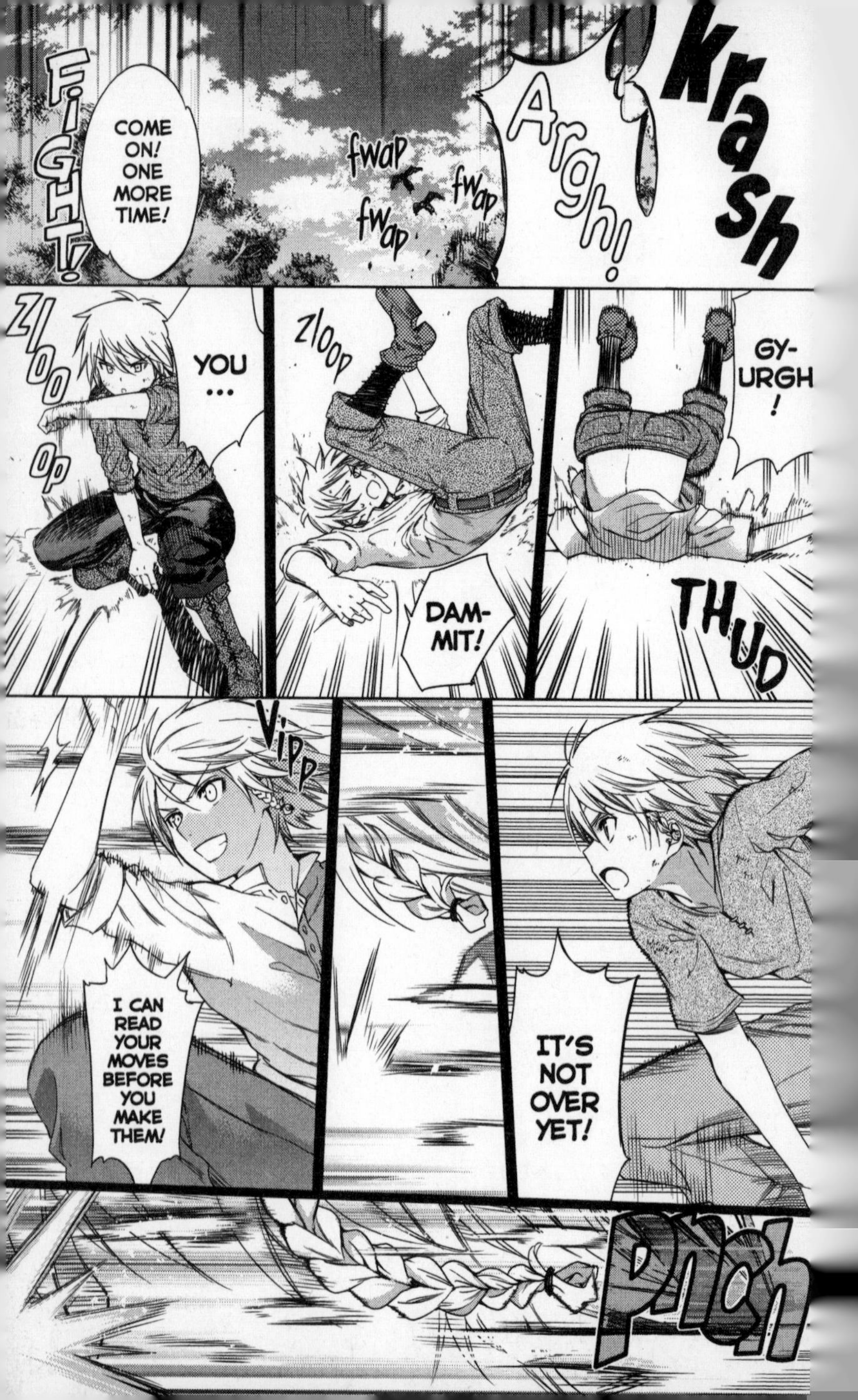
Krash
Argh!
fwap
fwap
fwap
COME ON! ONE MORE TIME!
FIGHT!
GY-URGH!
THUD
zloop
DAM-MIT!
Zlooop
YOU...
IT'S NOT OVER YET!
Vipp
I CAN READ YOUR MOVES BEFORE YOU MAKE THEM!
Pnch

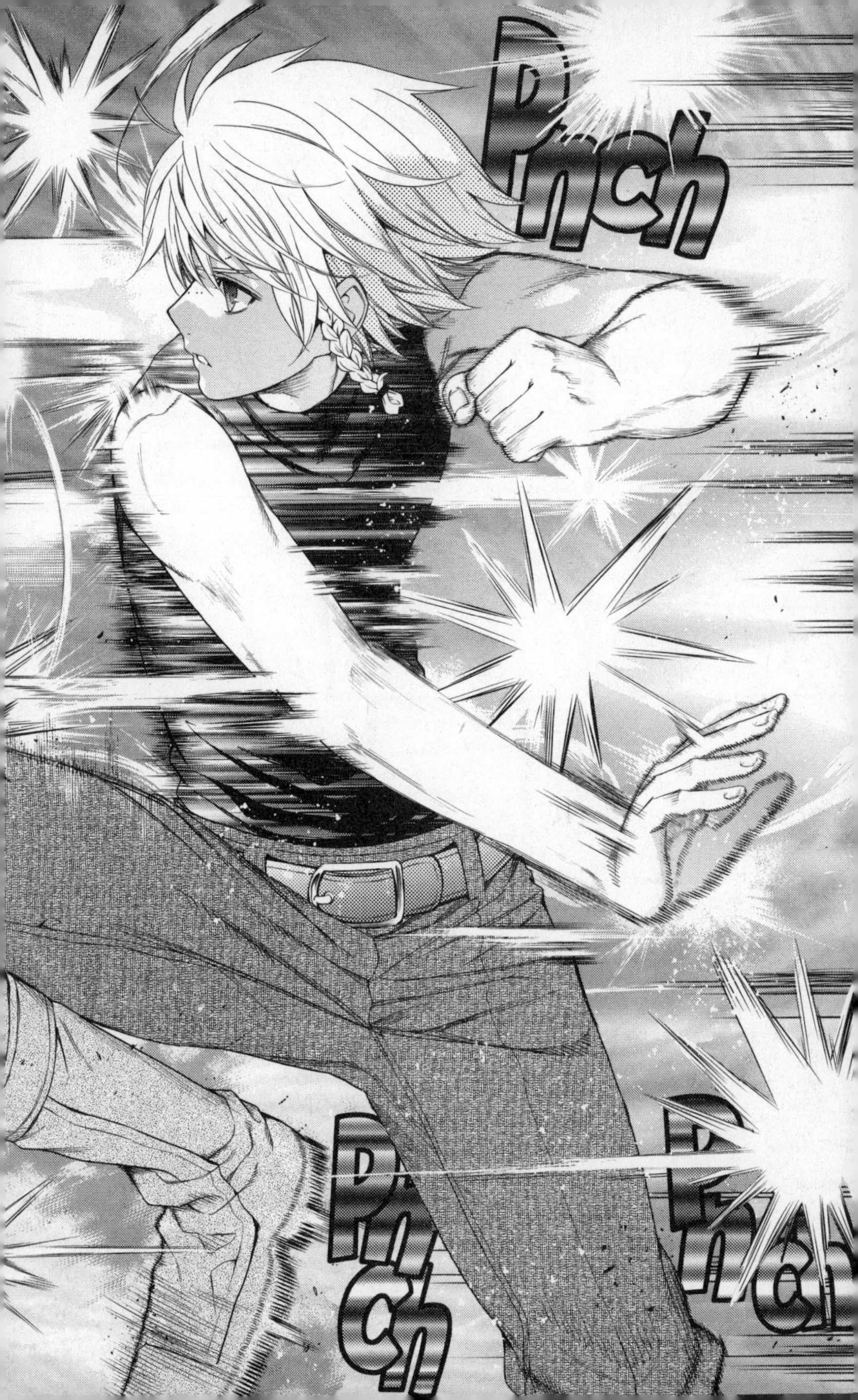
Pnch
Pnch

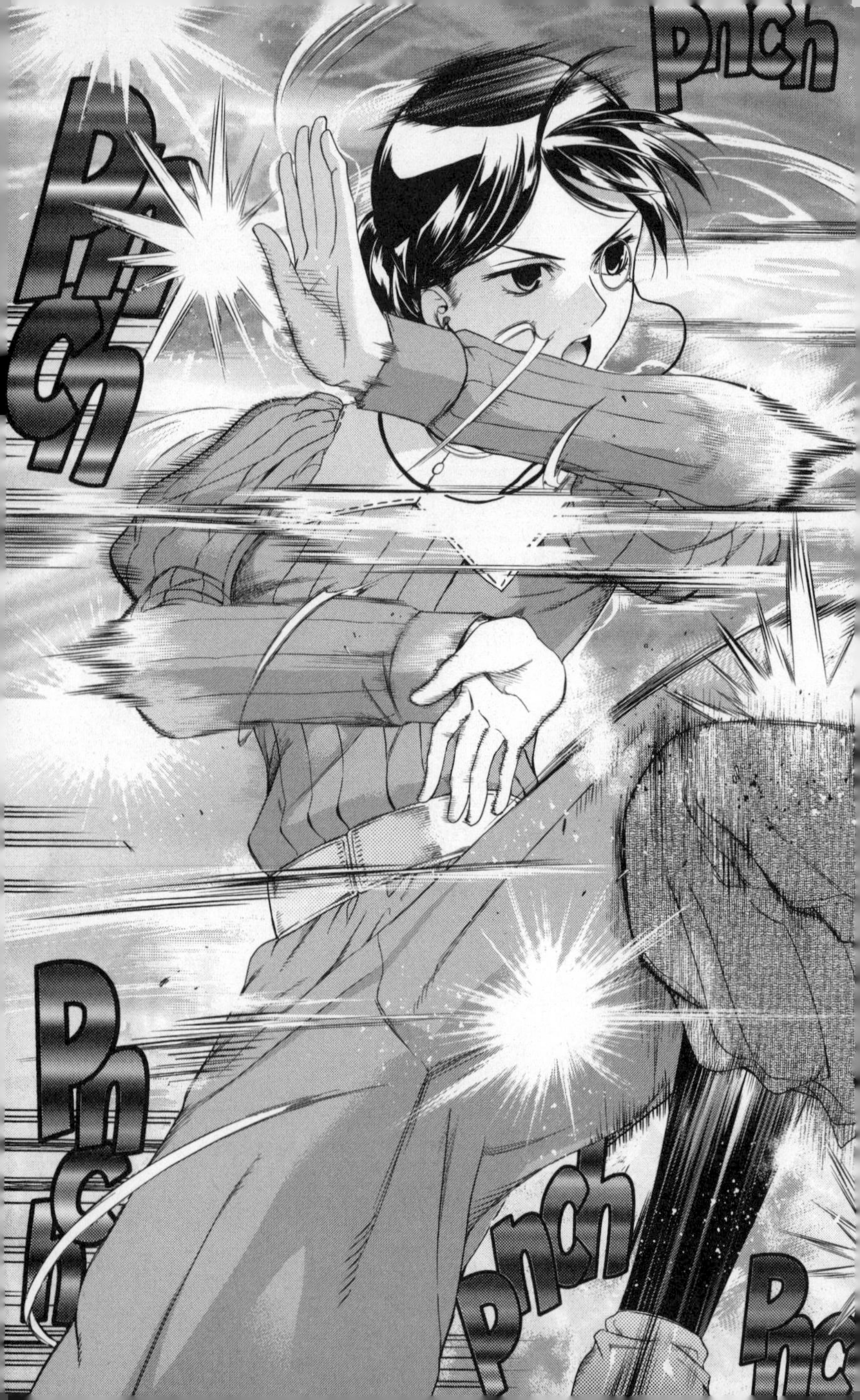
Pnch
Pnch
Pnch
Pnch

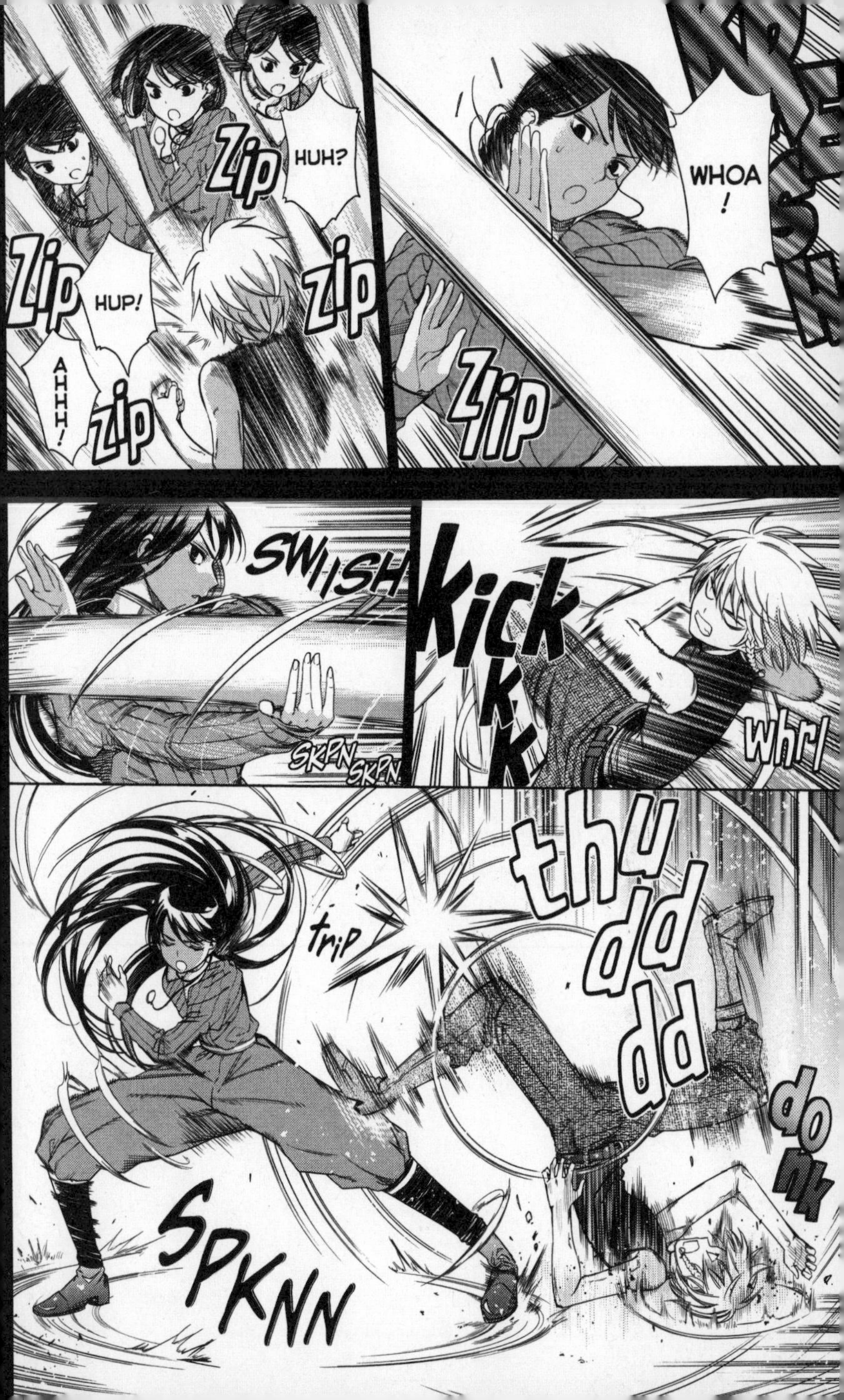

WHOA!
Zip
HUH?
Zip
zip
HUP!
Zip
AHHH!
zip
kick
k
k
whrl
SWISH
SKPN SKPN
thudd
dd
donk
trip
SPKNN

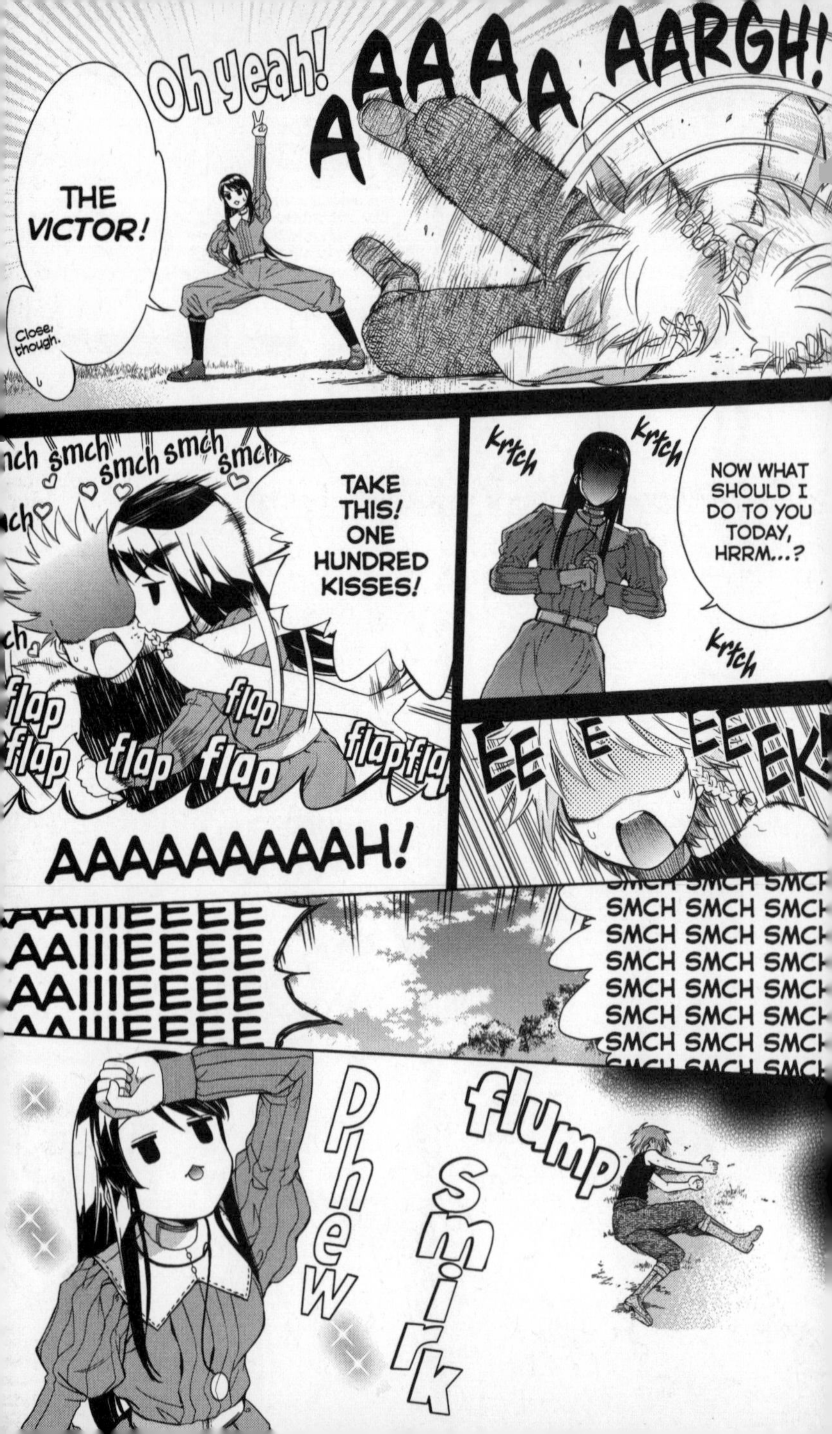
AAAAA AARGH!
Oh yeah!
THE VICTOR!
Close, though.
krtch
krtch
NOW WHAT SHOULD I DO TO YOU TODAY, HRRM...?
krtch
EEEEEEEK!
smch smch smch smch smch smch smch
TAKE THIS! ONE HUNDRED KISSES!
flap flap flap flap flap flap flap
AAAAAAAAAH!
SMCH SMCH SMCH
SMCH SMCH SMCH
SMCH SMCH SMCH
SMCH SMCH SMCH
SMCH SMCH SMCH
SMCH SMCH SMCH
SMCH SMCH SMCH
AAIIIEEEE
AAIIIEEEE
AAIIIEEEE
flump
smirk
Phew

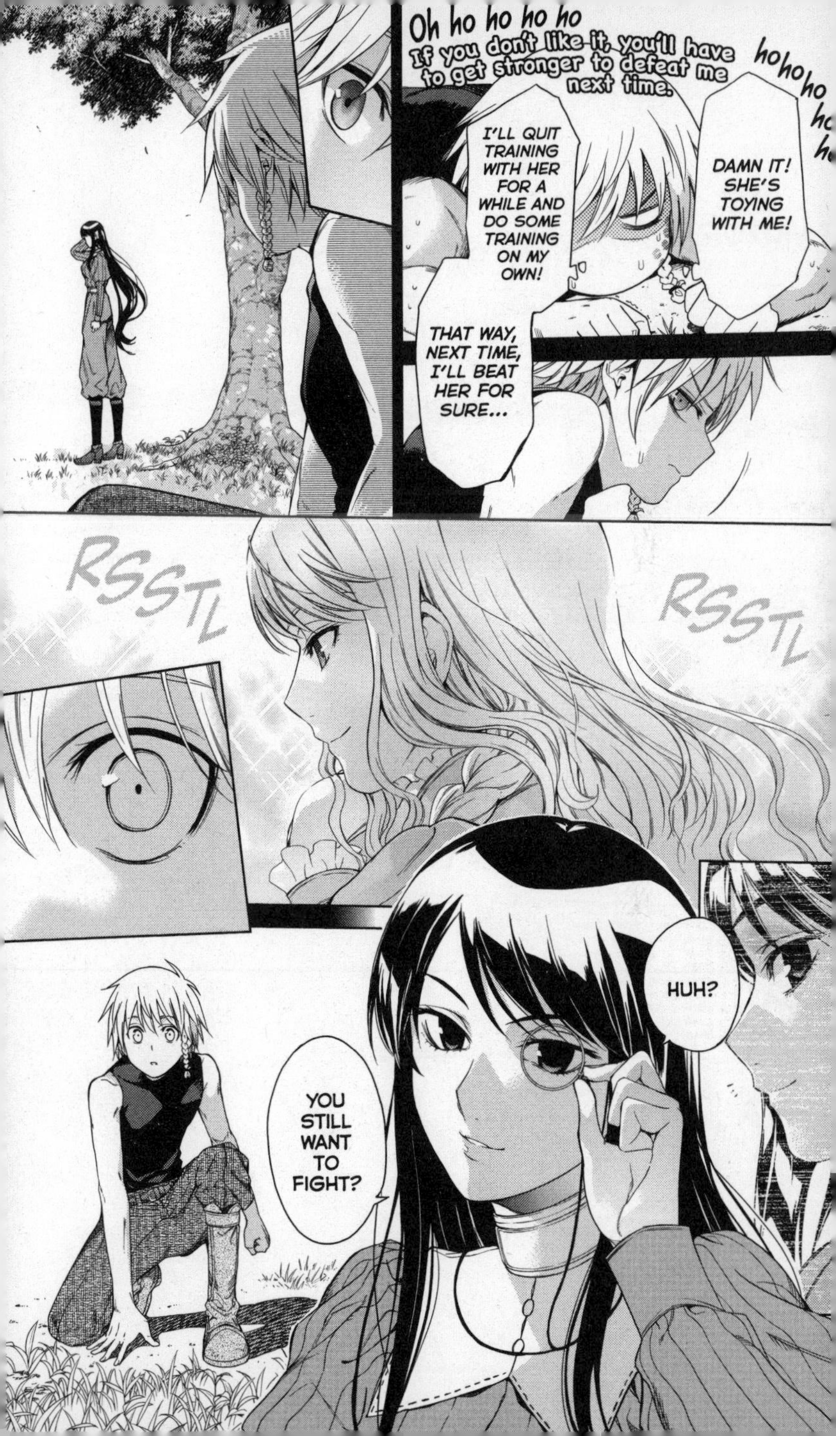
Oh ho ho ho ho
If you don't like it, you'll have to get stronger to defeat me next time.
hohoho
DAMN IT! SHE'S TOYING WITH ME!
I'LL QUIT TRAINING WITH HER FOR A WHILE AND DO SOME TRAINING ON MY OWN!
THAT WAY, NEXT TIME, I'LL BEAT HER FOR SURE...
RSSTL
RSSTL
HUH?
YOU STILL WANT TO FIGHT?

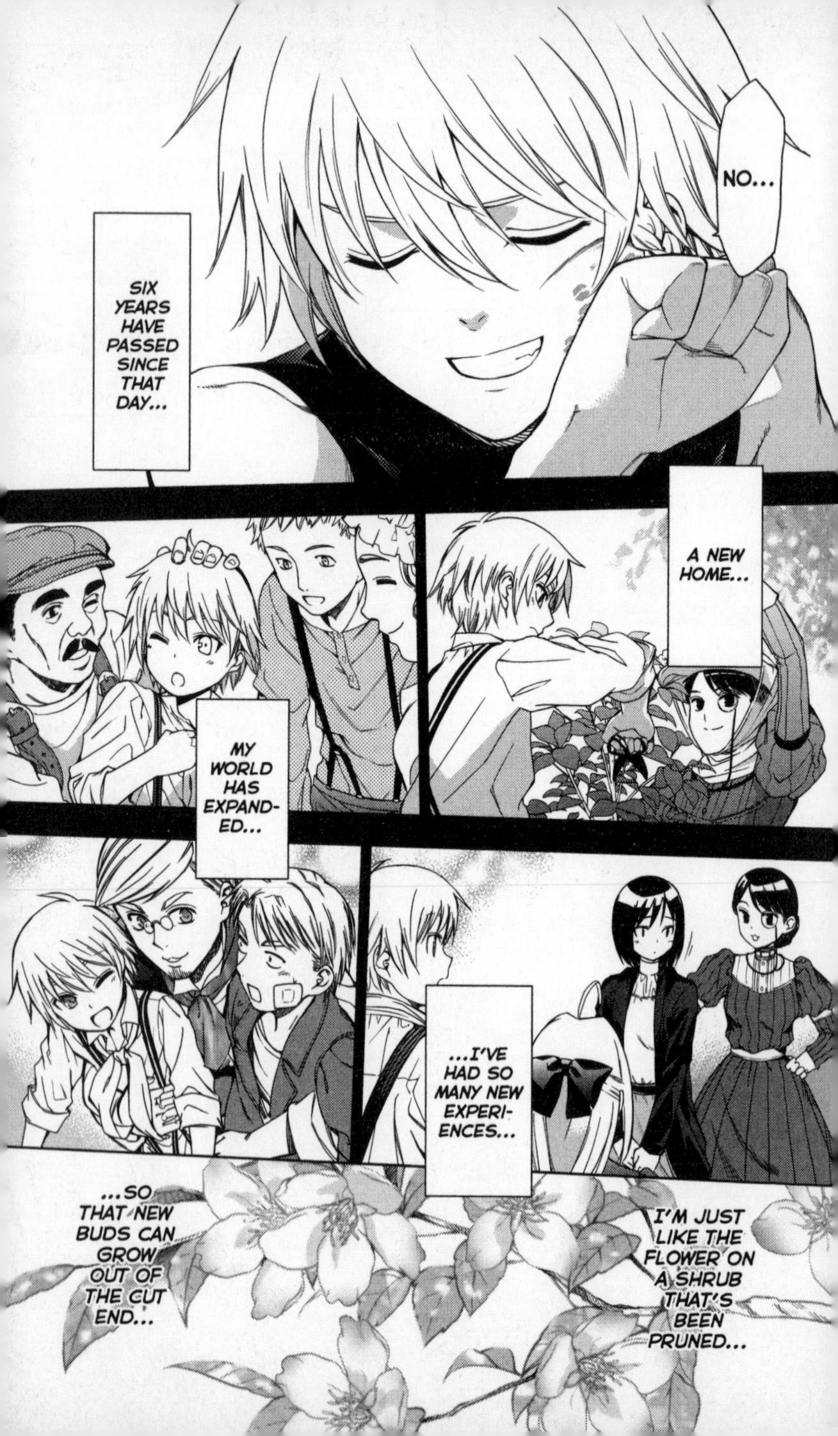
NO...
SIX YEARS HAVE PASSED SINCE THAT DAY...
A NEW HOME...
MY WORLD HAS EXPAND-ED...
...I'VE HAD SO MANY NEW EXPERI-ENCES...
I'M JUST LIKE THE FLOWER ON A SHRUB THAT'S BEEN PRUNED...
...SO THAT NEW BUDS CAN GROW OUT OF THE CUT END...

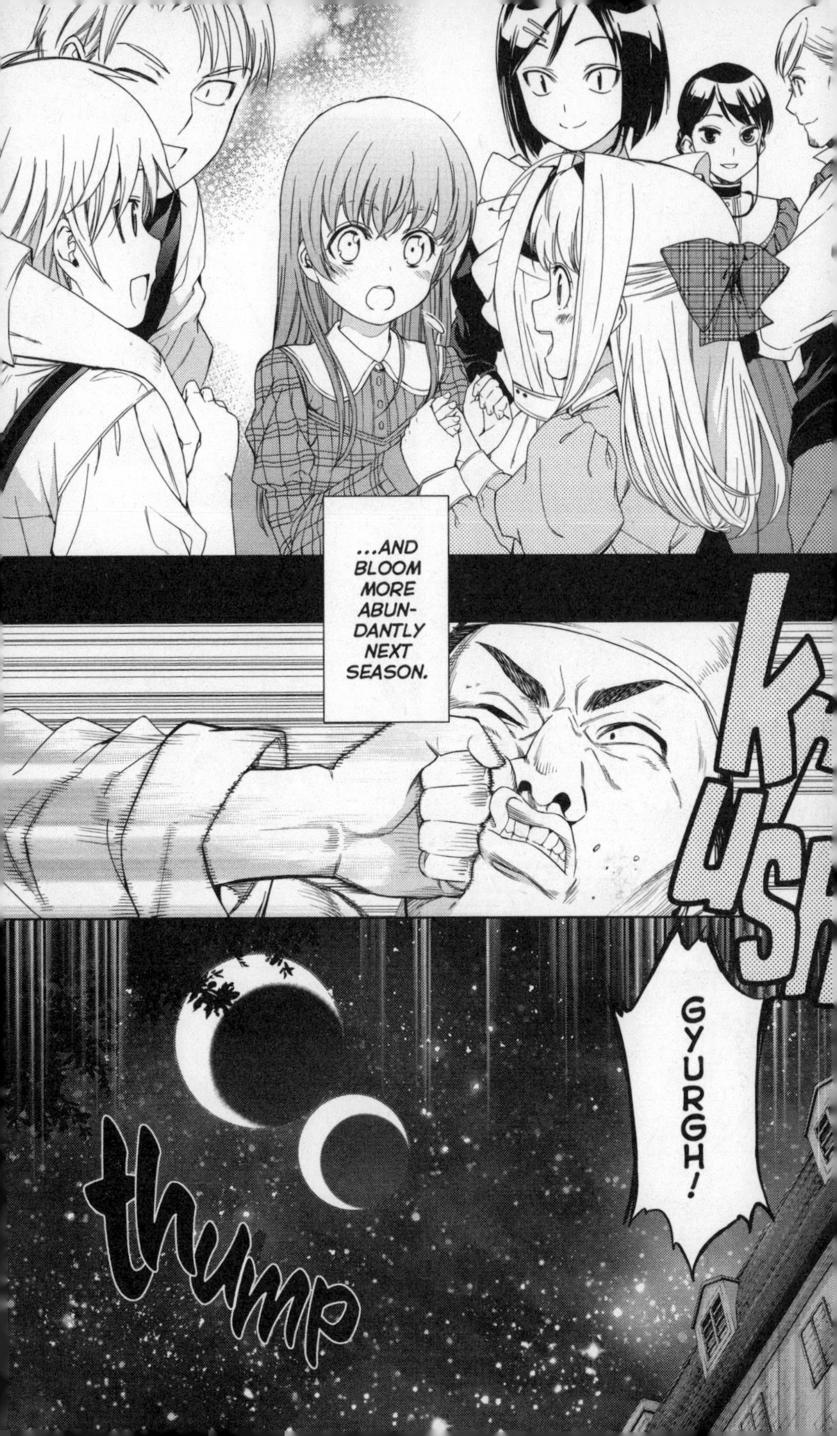
...AND BLOOM MORE ABUN-DANTLY NEXT SEASON.
GYURGH!
thump

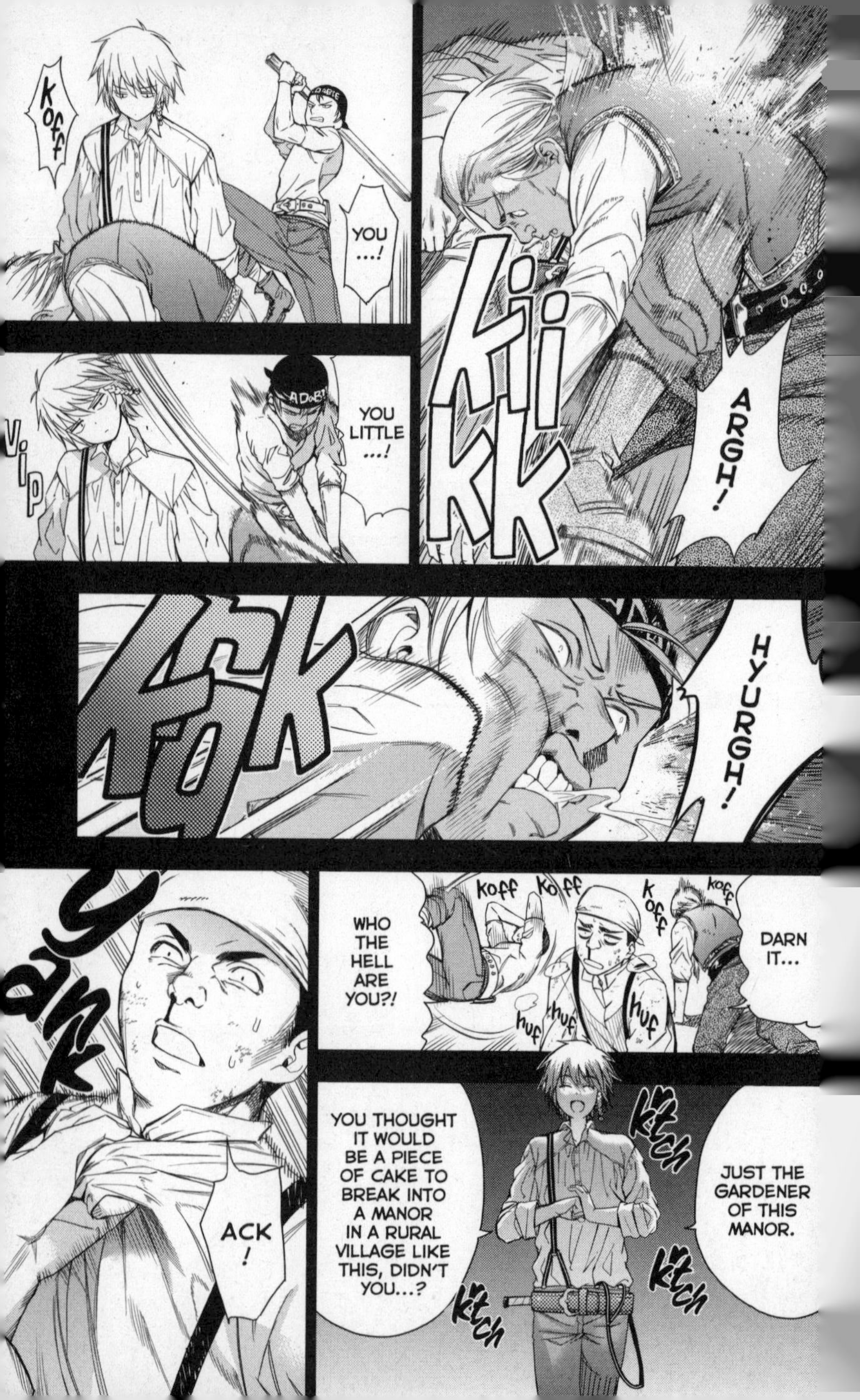
ARGH!
Liiikk
YOU ...!
Koff
YOU LITTLE ...!
Vip
HYURGH!
Kack
DARN IT...
koff
koff
koff
koff
huf
huf
huf
WHO THE HELL ARE YOU?!
JUST THE GARDENER OF THIS MANOR.
ktch
ktch
YOU THOUGHT IT WOULD BE A PIECE OF CAKE TO BREAK INTO A MANOR IN A RURAL VILLAGE LIKE THIS, DIDN'T YOU...?
ktch
Yank
ACK!

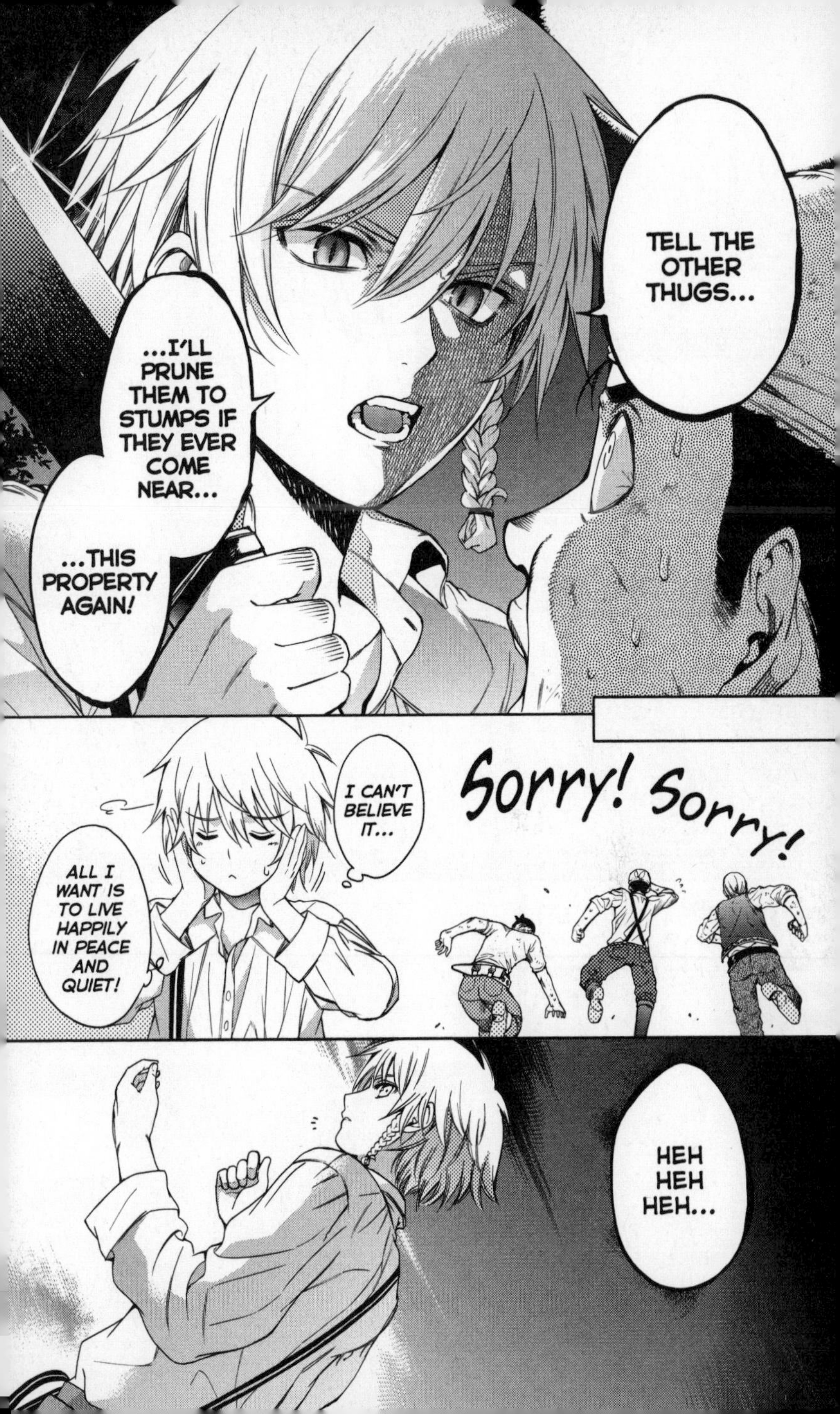
TELL THE OTHER THUGS...
...I'LL PRUNE THEM TO STUMPS IF THEY EVER COME NEAR...
...THIS PROPERTY AGAIN!
Sorry! Sorry!
I CAN'T BELIEVE IT...
ALL I WANT IS TO LIVE HAPPILY IN PEACE AND QUIET!
HEH HEH HEH...

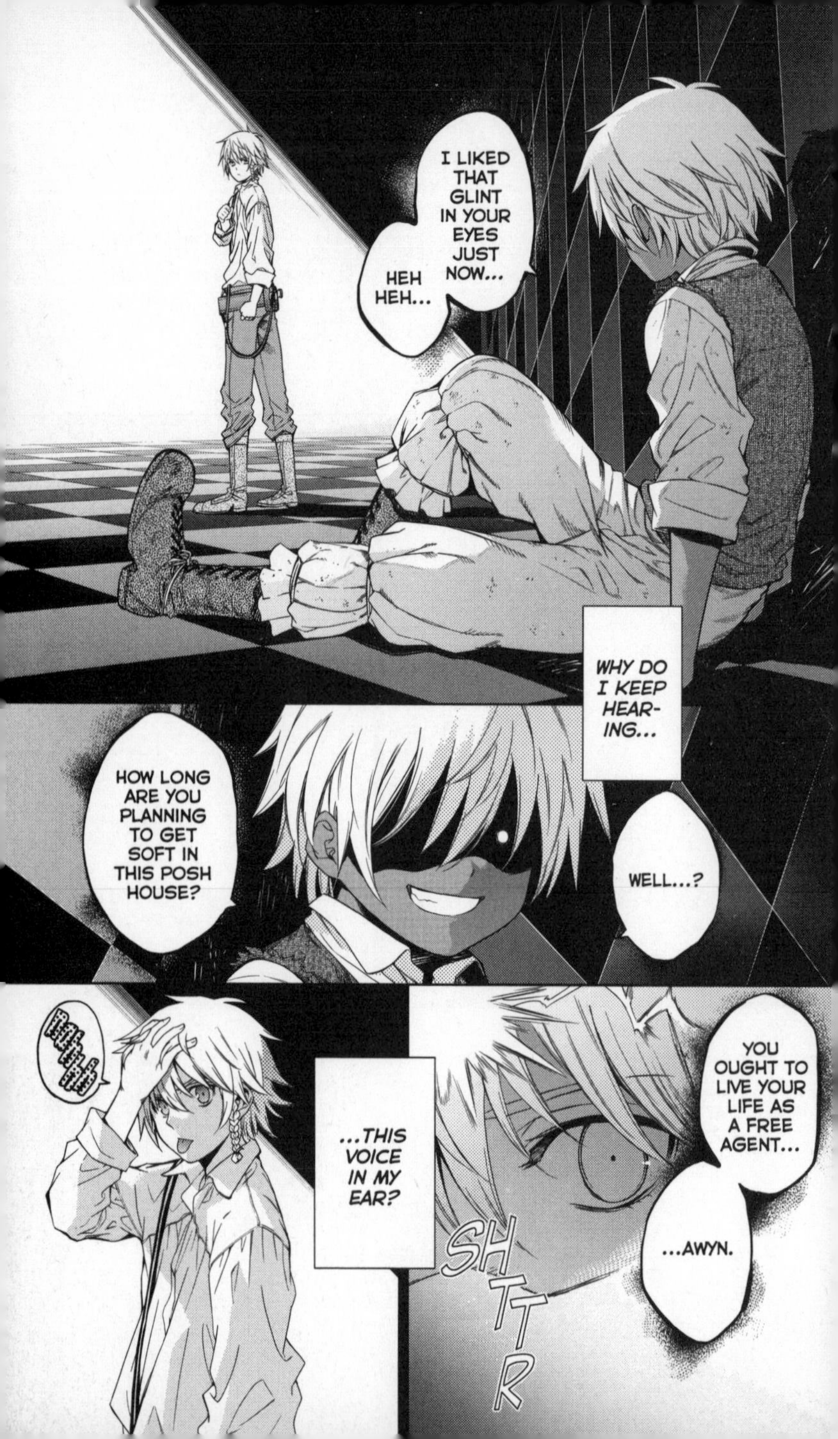
I LIKED THAT GLINT IN YOUR EYES JUST NOW...
HEH HEH...
WHY DO I KEEP HEAR-ING...
HOW LONG ARE YOU PLANNING TO GET SOFT IN THIS POSH HOUSE?
WELL...?
YOU OUGHT TO LIVE YOUR LIFE AS A FREE AGENT...
...AWYN.
SHTTR
...THIS VOICE IN MY EAR?

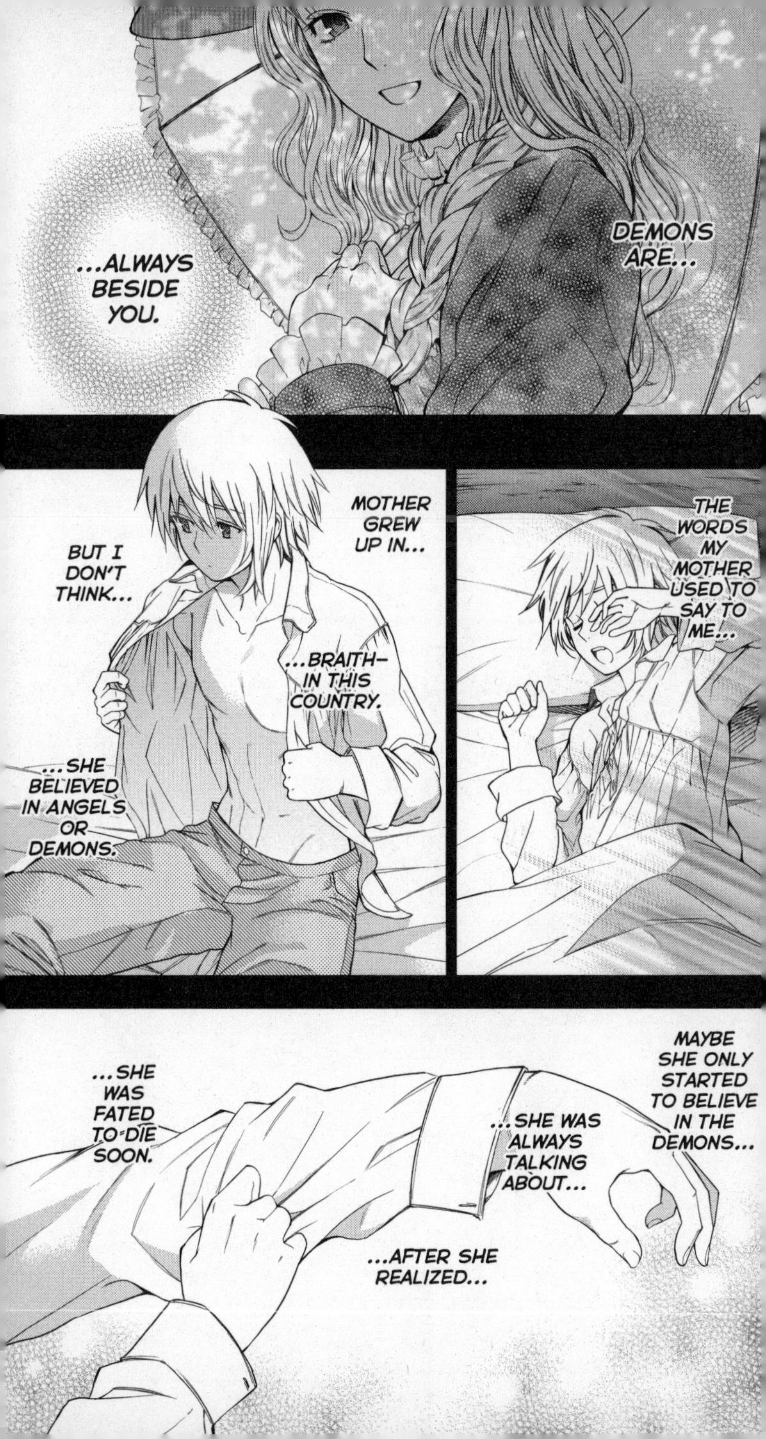
DEMONS ARE...
...ALWAYS BESIDE YOU.
THE WORDS MY MOTHER USED TO SAY TO ME...
MOTHER GREW UP IN...
...BRAITH— IN THIS COUNTRY.
BUT I DON'T THINK...
...SHE BELIEVED IN ANGELS OR DEMONS.
MAYBE SHE ONLY STARTED TO BELIEVE IN THE DEMONS...
...SHE WAS ALWAYS TALKING ABOUT...
...AFTER SHE REALIZED...
...SHE WAS FATED TO DIE SOON.

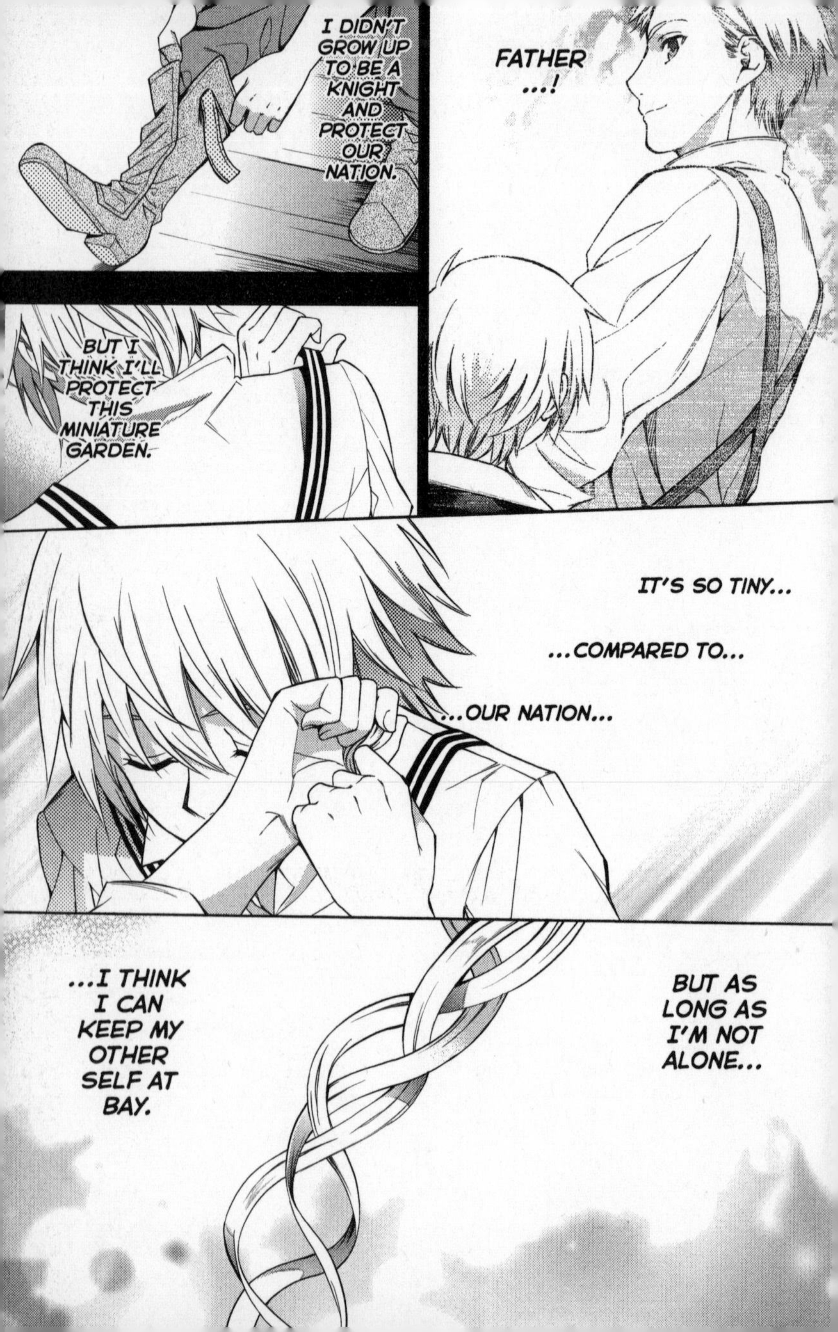
FATHER ...!
I DIDN'T GROW UP TO BE A KNIGHT AND PROTECT OUR NATION.
BUT I THINK I'LL PROTECT THIS MINIATURE GARDEN.
IT'S SO TINY...
...COMPARED TO...
...OUR NATION...
BUT AS LONG AS I'M NOT ALONE...
...I THINK I CAN KEEP MY OTHER SELF AT BAY.

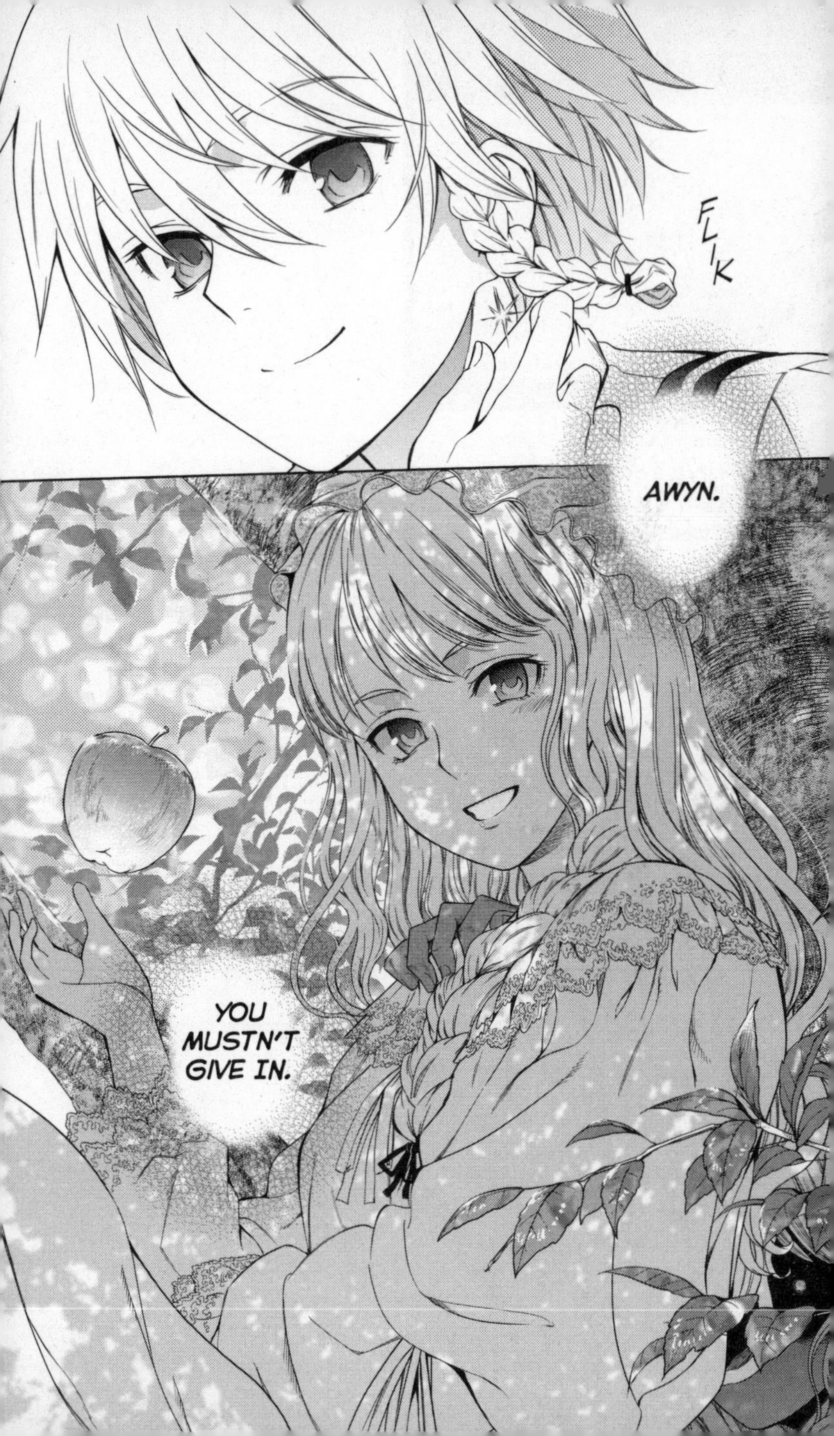
FLIK
AWYN.
YOU MUSTN'T GIVE IN.

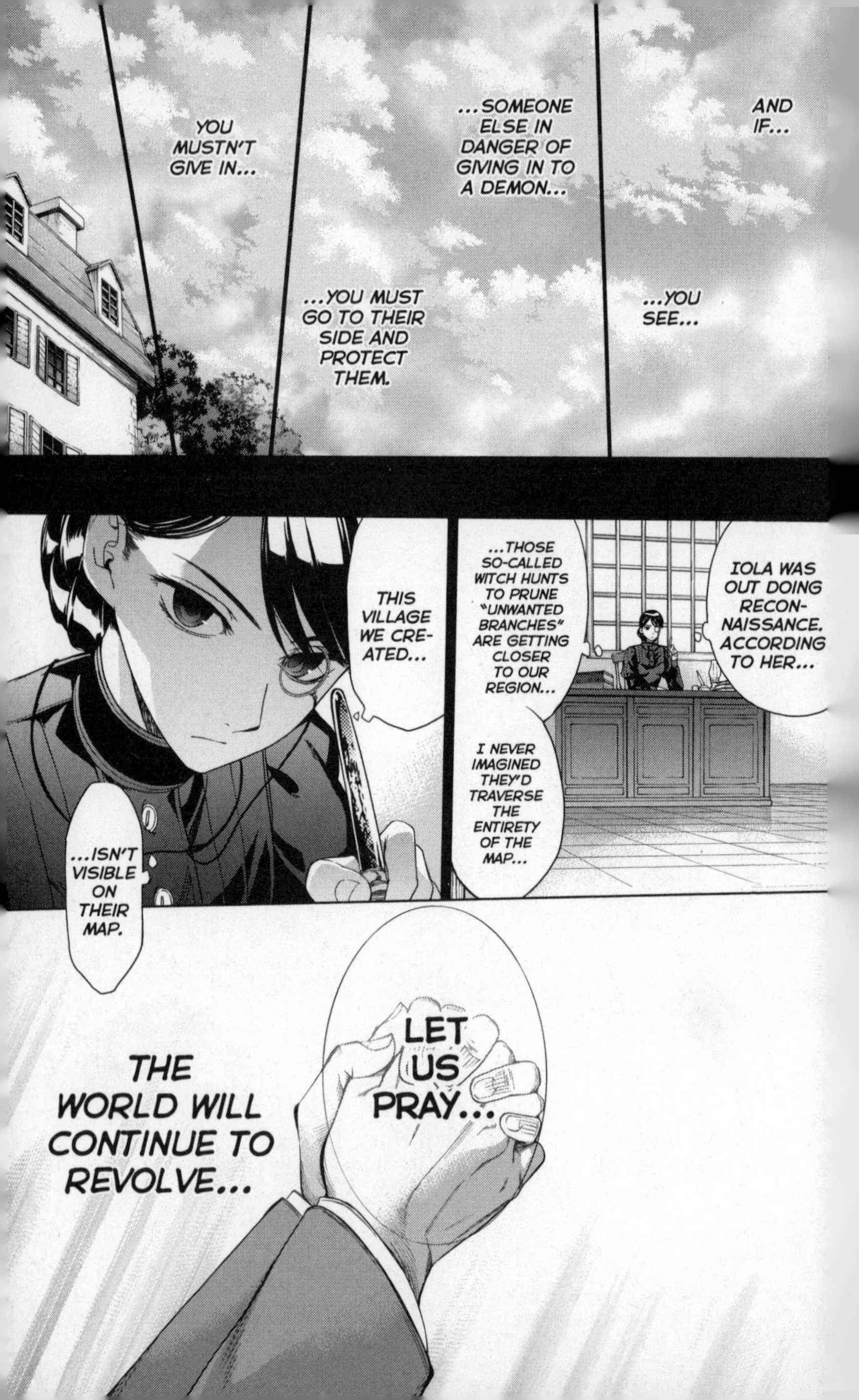
AND IF...
...YOU SEE...
...SOMEONE ELSE IN DANGER OF GIVING IN TO A DEMON...
...YOU MUST GO TO THEIR SIDE AND PROTECT THEM.
YOU MUSTN'T GIVE IN...
IOLA WAS OUT DOING RECONNAISSANCE. ACCORDING TO HER...
...THOSE SO-CALLED WITCH HUNTS TO PRUNE "UNWANTED BRANCHES" ARE GETTING CLOSER TO OUR REGION...
I NEVER IMAGINED THEY'D TRAVERSE THE ENTIRETY OF THE MAP...
THIS VILLAGE WE CREATED...
...ISN'T VISIBLE ON THEIR MAP.
LET US PRAY...
THE WORLD WILL CONTINUE TO REVOLVE...

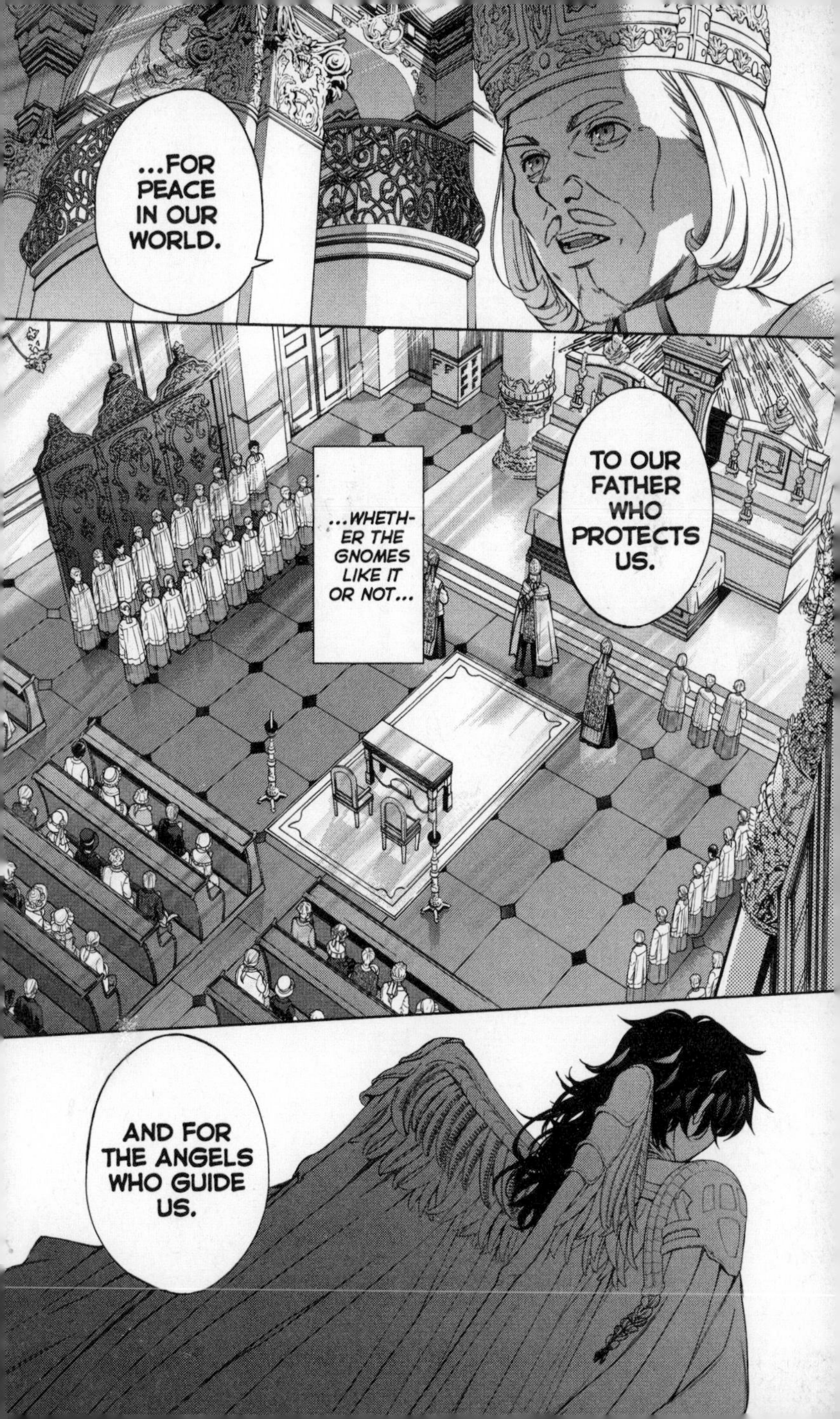
...FOR PEACE IN OUR WORLD.
TO OUR FATHER WHO PROTECTS US.
...WHETHER THE GNOMES LIKE IT OR NOT...
AND FOR THE ANGELS WHO GUIDE US.

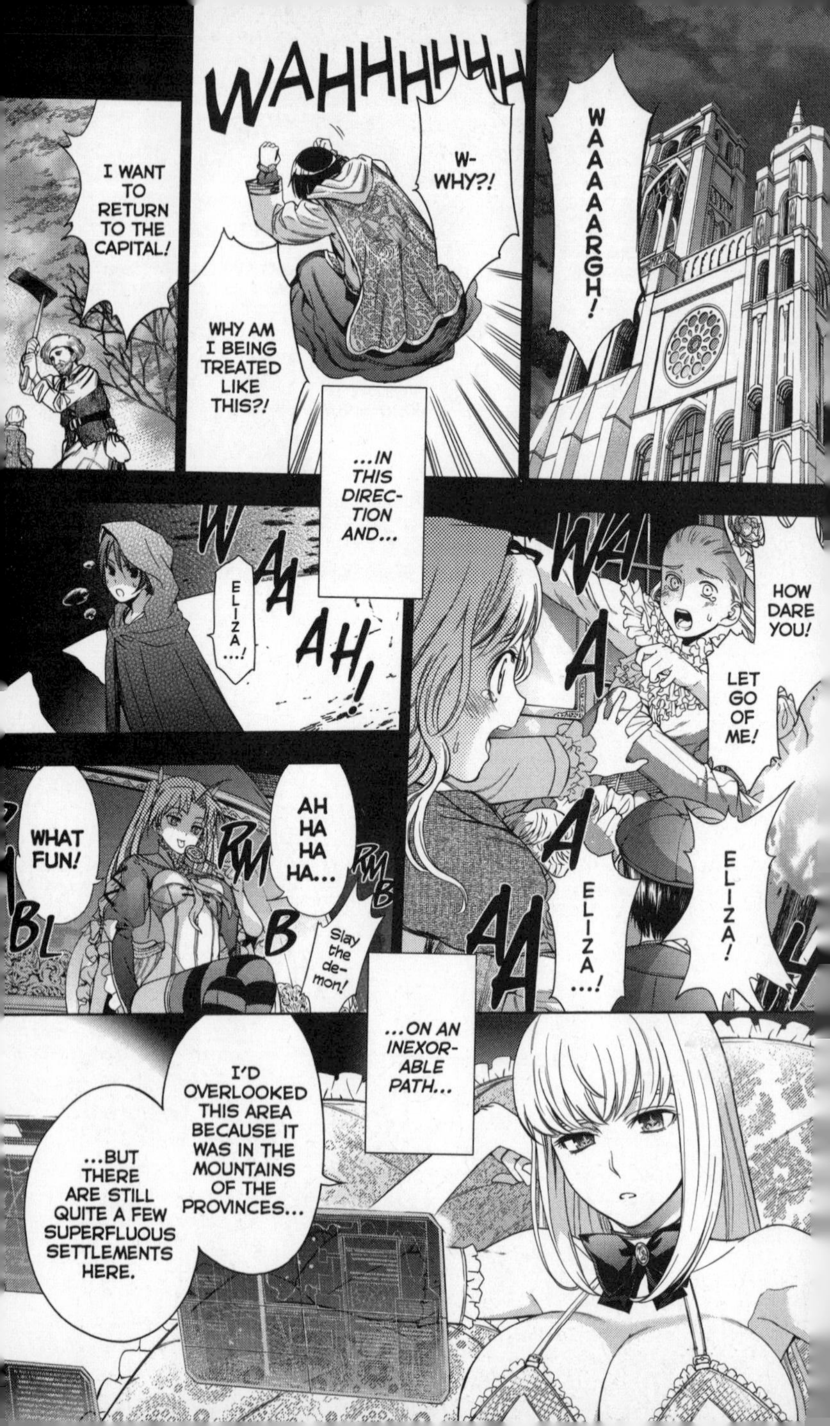
WAAAAAARGH!
WAHHHHHH
W-WHY?!
WHY AM I BEING TREATED LIKE THIS?!
I WANT TO RETURN TO THE CAPITAL!
...IN THIS DIRECTION AND...
WAAAAAA
HOW DARE YOU!
LET GO OF ME!
ELIZA!
ELIZA...!
WAAAH!
ELIZA...!
AH HA HA HA...
WHAT FUN!
RMB
RMB
BL
Slay the demon!
...ON AN INEXORABLE PATH...
I'D OVERLOOKED THIS AREA BECAUSE IT WAS IN THE MOUNTAINS OF THE PROVINCES...
...BUT THERE ARE STILL QUITE A FEW SUPERFLUOUS SETTLEMENTS HERE.

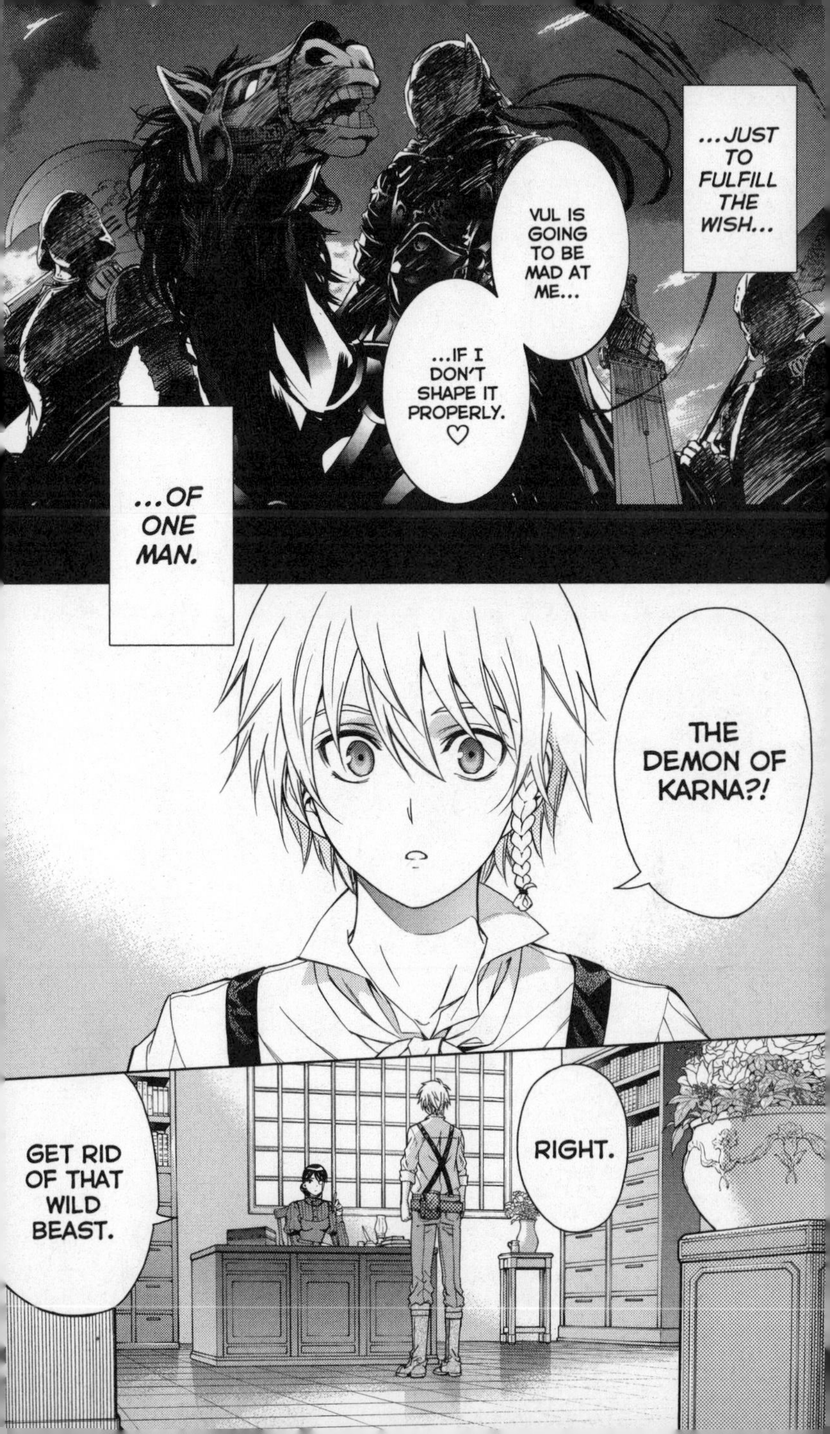
...JUST TO FULFILL THE WISH...
VUL IS GOING TO BE MAD AT ME...
...IF I DON'T SHAPE IT PROPERLY. ♡
...OF ONE MAN.
THE DEMON OF KARNA?!
RIGHT.
GET RID OF THAT WILD BEAST.

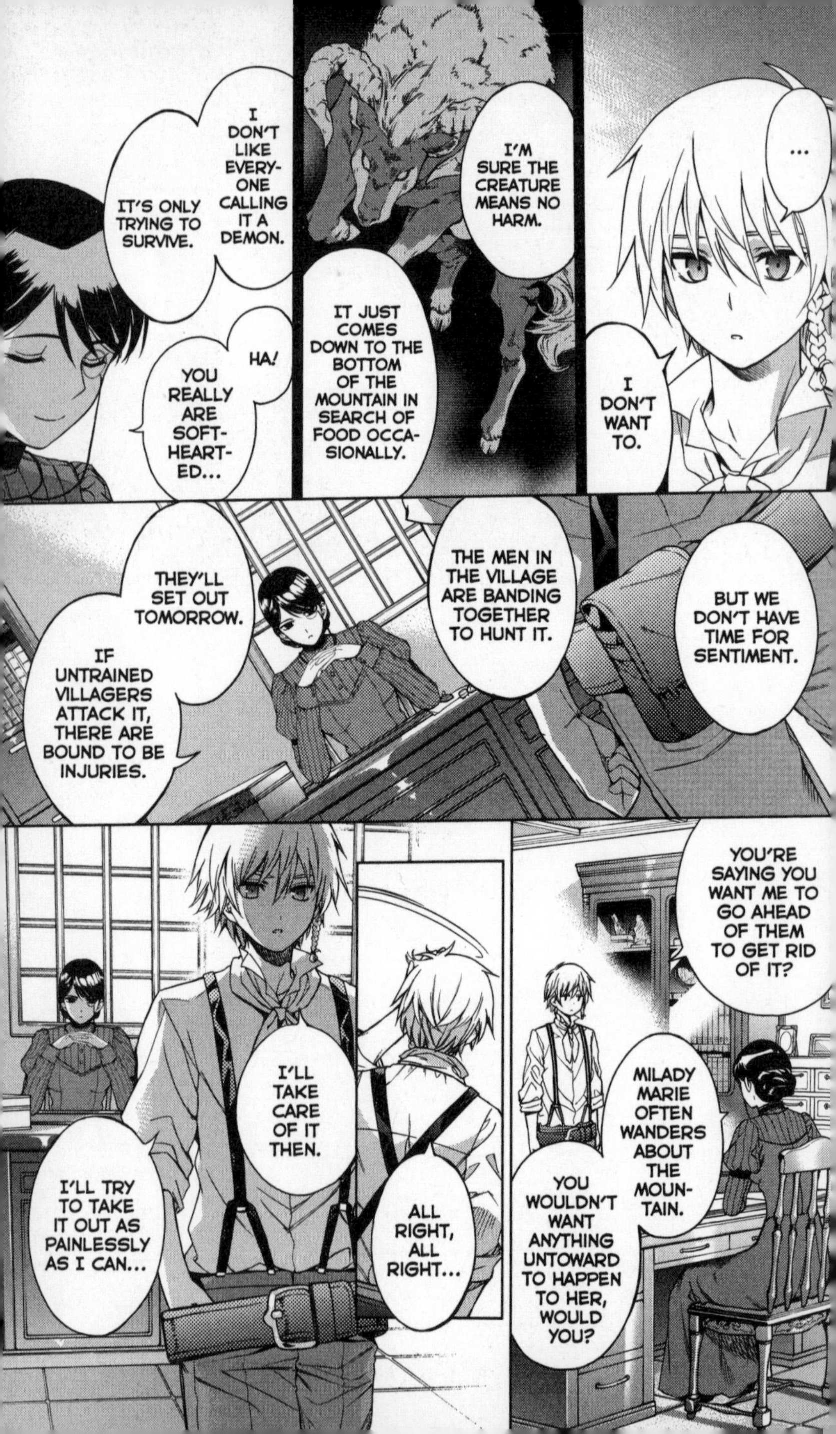
...
I DON'T WANT TO.
I'M SURE THE CREATURE MEANS NO HARM.
IT JUST COMES DOWN TO THE BOTTOM OF THE MOUNTAIN IN SEARCH OF FOOD OCCASIONALLY.
I DON'T LIKE EVERYONE CALLING IT A DEMON.
IT'S ONLY TRYING TO SURVIVE.
HA!
YOU REALLY ARE SOFT-HEARTED...
BUT WE DON'T HAVE TIME FOR SENTIMENT.
THE MEN IN THE VILLAGE ARE BANDING TOGETHER TO HUNT IT.
THEY'LL SET OUT TOMORROW.
IF UNTRAINED VILLAGERS ATTACK IT, THERE ARE BOUND TO BE INJURIES.
YOU'RE SAYING YOU WANT ME TO GO AHEAD OF THEM TO GET RID OF IT?
MILADY MARIE OFTEN WANDERS ABOUT THE MOUN-TAIN.
YOU WOULDN'T WANT ANYTHING UNTOWARD TO HAPPEN TO HER, WOULD YOU?
ALL RIGHT, ALL RIGHT...
I'LL TAKE CARE OF IT THEN.
I'LL TRY TO TAKE IT OUT AS PAINLESSLY AS I CAN...

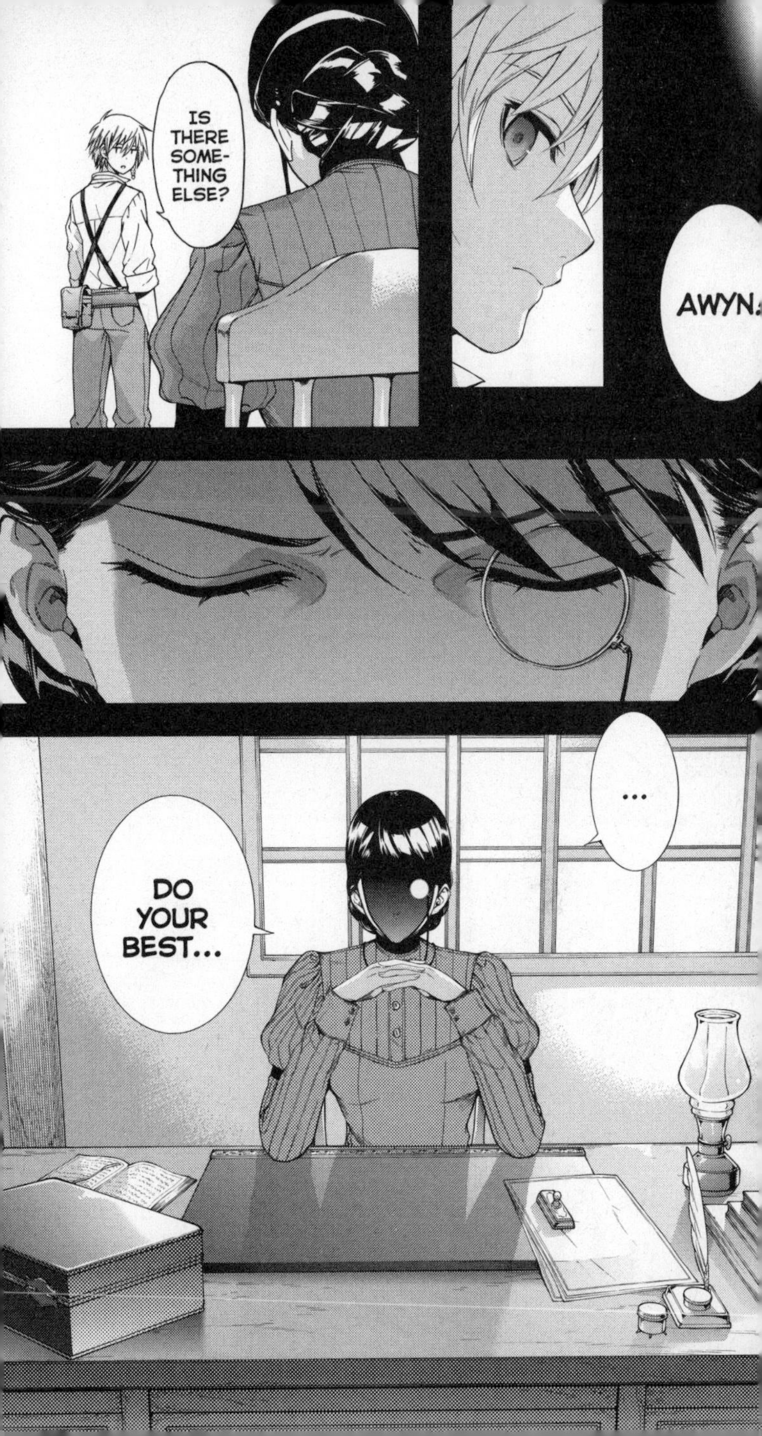
AWYN.
IS THERE SOMETHING ELSE?
...
DO YOUR BEST...

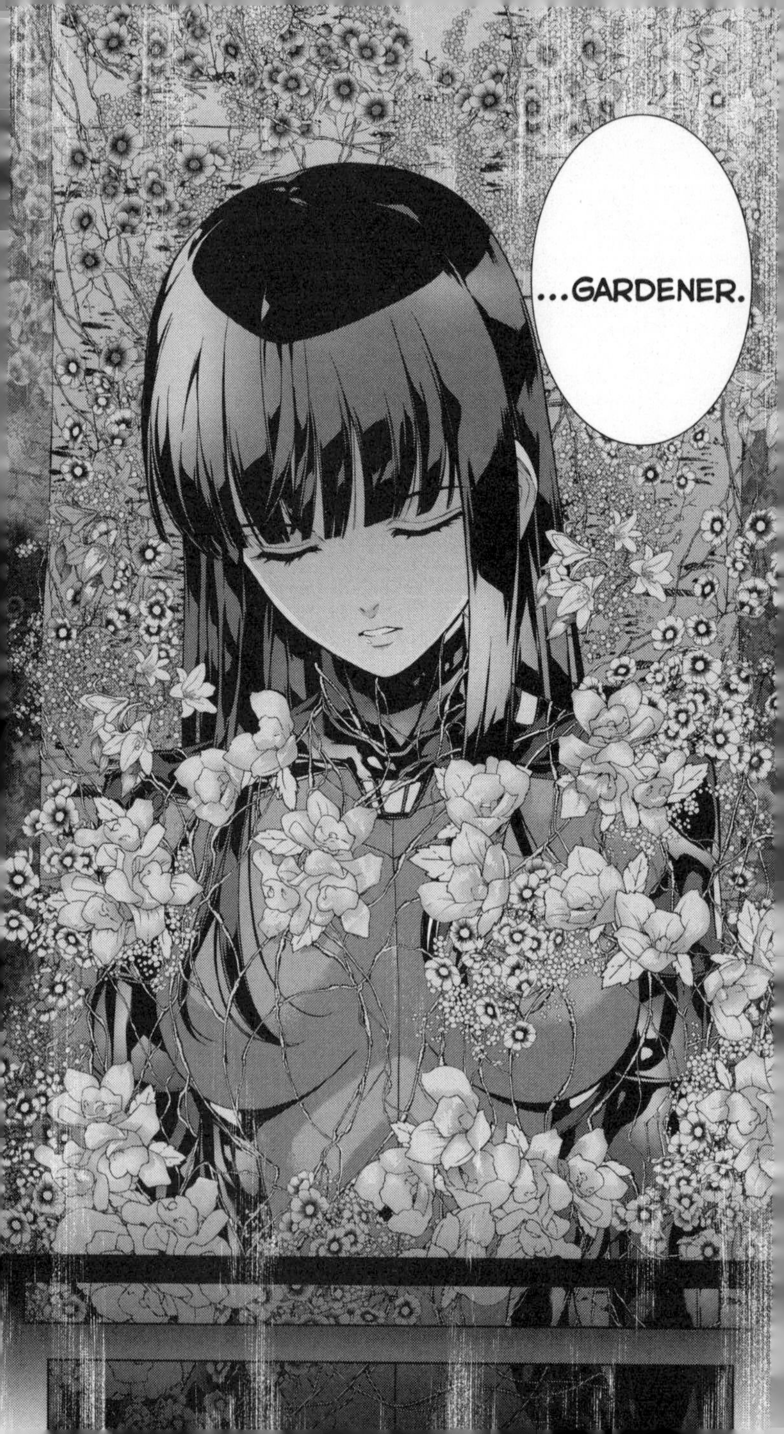
...GARDENER.

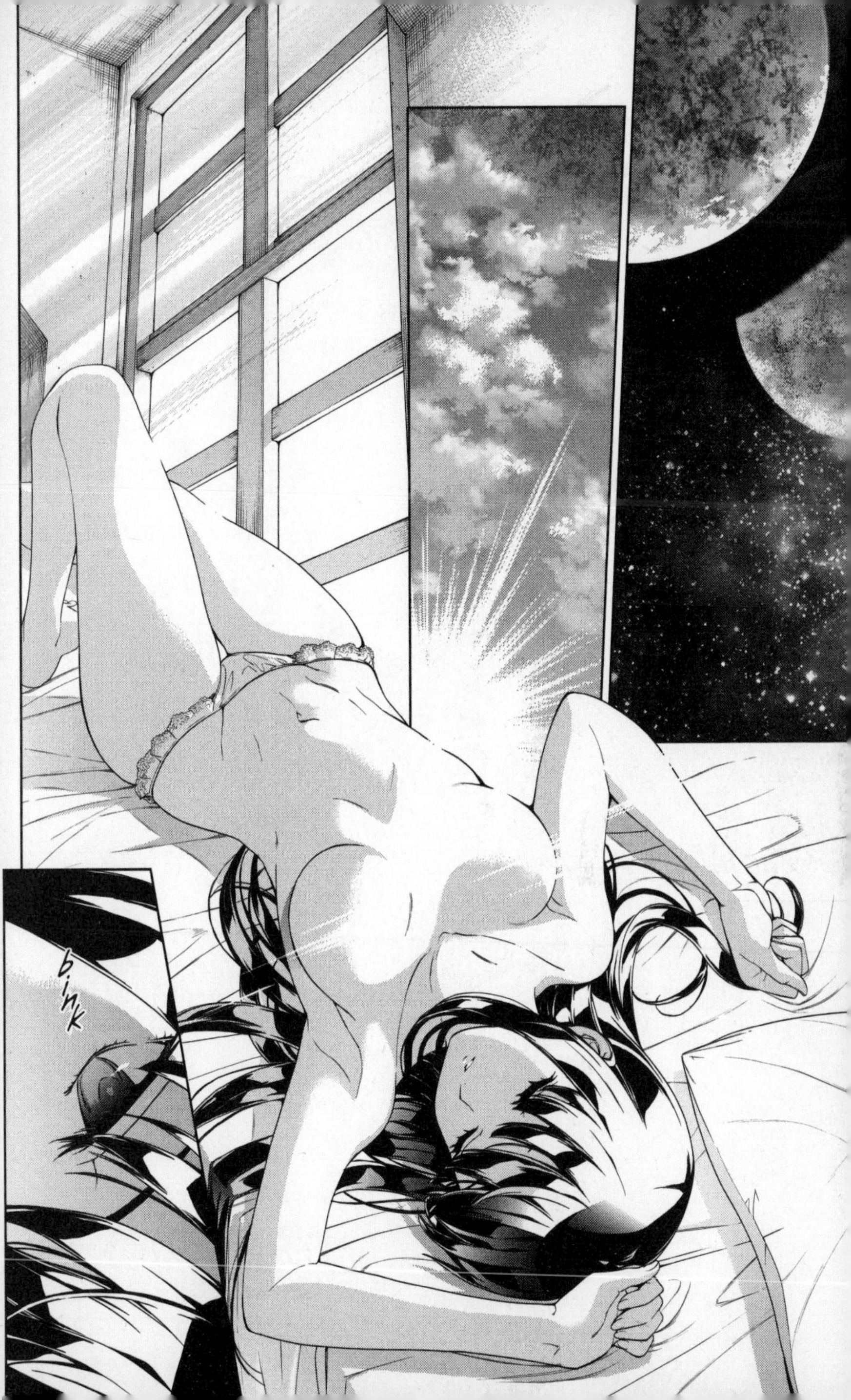
blink

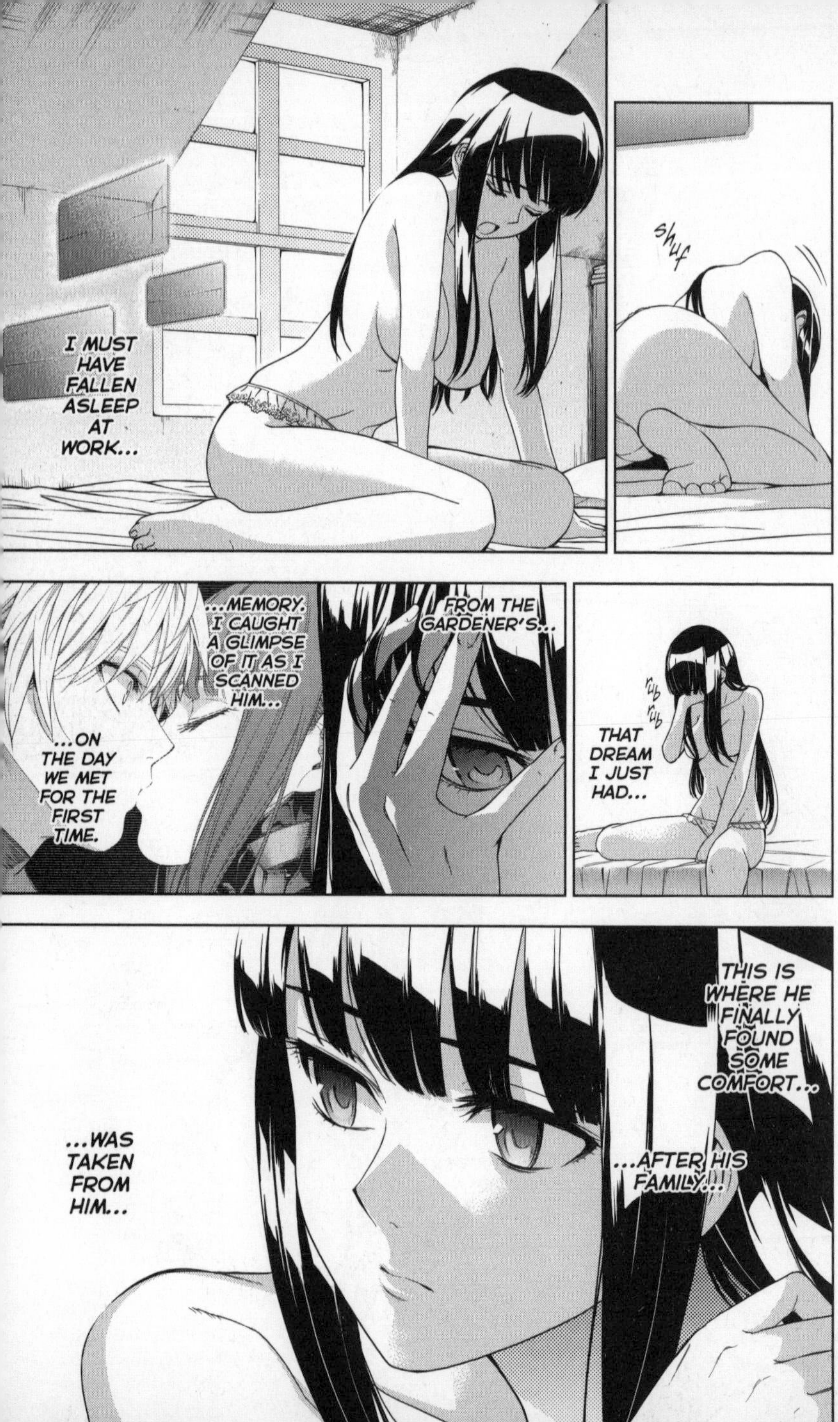
shuf
I MUST HAVE FALLEN ASLEEP AT WORK...
rub rub
THAT DREAM I JUST HAD...
FROM THE GARDENER'S...
...MEMORY. I CAUGHT A GLIMPSE OF IT AS I SCANNED HIM...
...ON THE DAY WE MET FOR THE FIRST TIME.
THIS IS WHERE HE FINALLY FOUND SOME COMFORT...
...AFTER HIS FAMILY...
...WAS TAKEN FROM HIM...

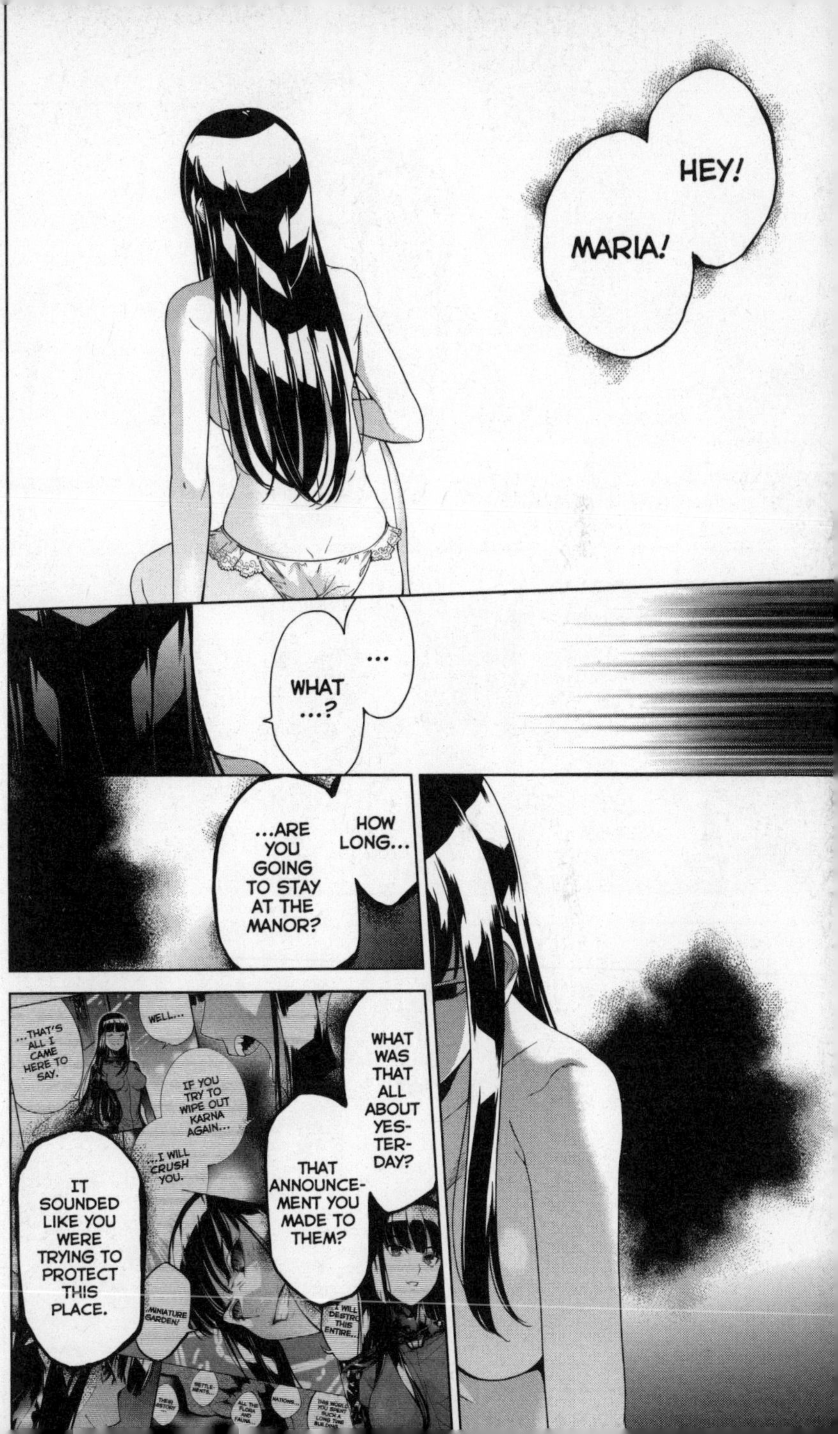
HEY! MARIA!
... WHAT ...?
HOW LONG...
...ARE YOU GOING TO STAY AT THE MANOR?
WHAT WAS THAT ALL ABOUT YESTERDAY?
THAT ANNOUNCEMENT YOU MADE TO THEM?
IT SOUNDED LIKE YOU WERE TRYING TO PROTECT THIS PLACE.
WELL...
...THAT'S ALL I CAME HERE TO SAY.
IF YOU TRY TO WIPE OUT KARNA AGAIN...
...I WILL CRUSH YOU.
...I WILL DESTRO THIS ENTIRE...
...MINIATURE GARDEN!
THIS WORLD YOU SPENT SUCH A LONG TIME
NATIONS...
ALL THE FLORA AND FAUNA...
SETTLEMENTS...
THEIR HISTORY...

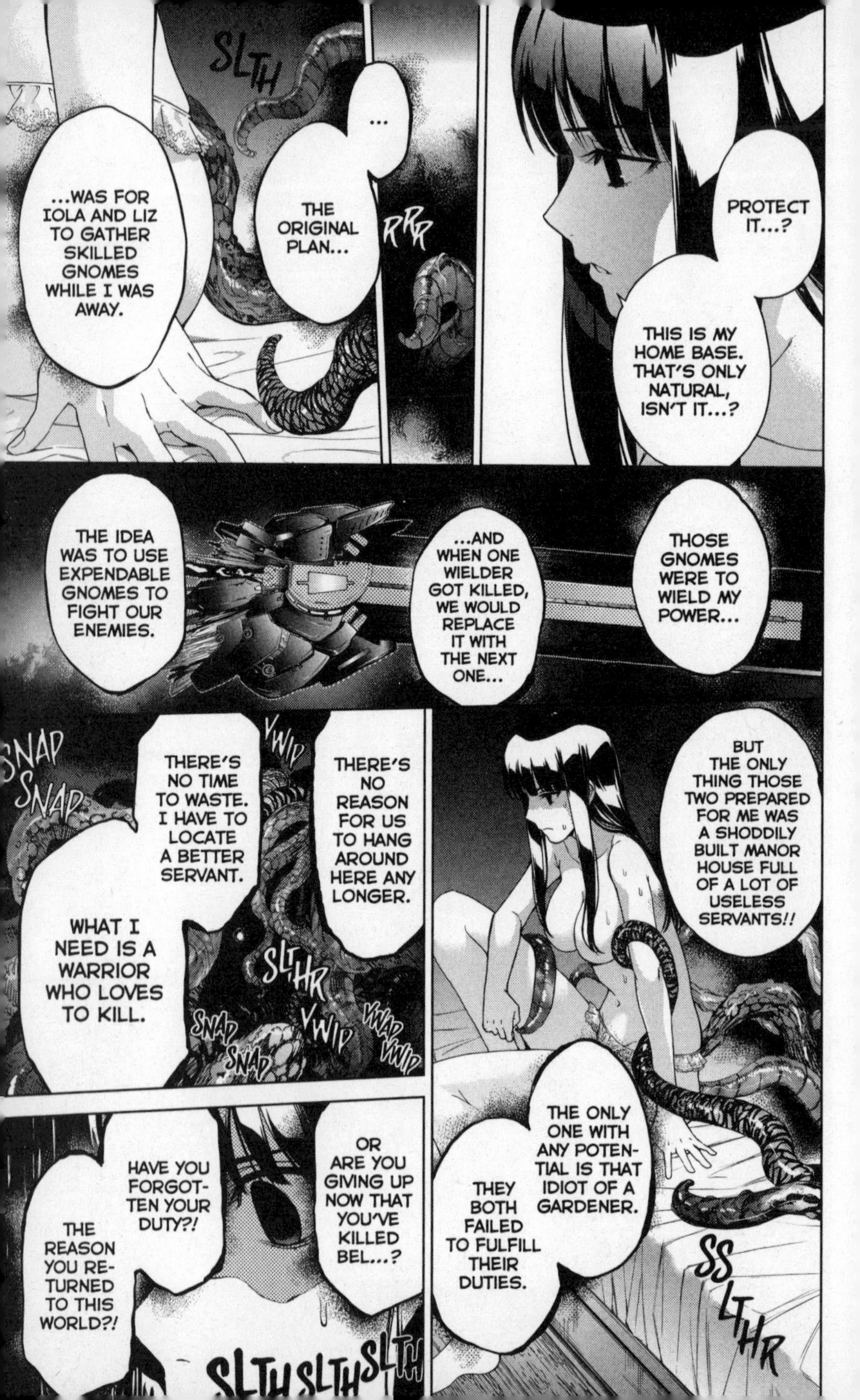
PROTECT IT...?
THIS IS MY HOME BASE. THAT'S ONLY NATURAL, ISN'T IT...?
...
THE ORIGINAL PLAN...
RRRR
SLTH
...WAS FOR IOLA AND LIZ TO GATHER SKILLED GNOMES WHILE I WAS AWAY.
THOSE GNOMES WERE TO WIELD MY POWER...
...AND WHEN ONE WIELDER GOT KILLED, WE WOULD REPLACE IT WITH THE NEXT ONE...
THE IDEA WAS TO USE EXPENDABLE GNOMES TO FIGHT OUR ENEMIES.
BUT THE ONLY THING THOSE TWO PREPARED FOR ME WAS A SHODDILY BUILT MANOR HOUSE FULL OF A LOT OF USELESS SERVANTS!!
THE ONLY ONE WITH ANY POTEN-TIAL IS THAT IDIOT OF A GARDENER.
THEY BOTH FAILED TO FULFILL THEIR DUTIES.
SSLTHR
VWIP
THERE'S NO REASON FOR US TO HANG AROUND HERE ANY LONGER.
THERE'S NO TIME TO WASTE. I HAVE TO LOCATE A BETTER SERVANT.
SNAP SNAP
WHAT I NEED IS A WARRIOR WHO LOVES TO KILL.
SLTHR
VWIP VWAP VWIP
SNAP SNAP
OR ARE YOU GIVING UP NOW THAT YOU'VE KILLED BEL...?
HAVE YOU FORGOT-TEN YOUR DUTY?!
THE REASON YOU RE-TURNED TO THIS WORLD?!
SLTH SLTH SLTH

REVENGE !!
TO BRING THE HAMMER OF JUSTICE...
...DOWN UPON THE SCUM WHO BETRAYED ME!!
RSSP RSSP RSSP
SKREEE
RSSP RSSP
SKWEE SKREECH
SKREEE

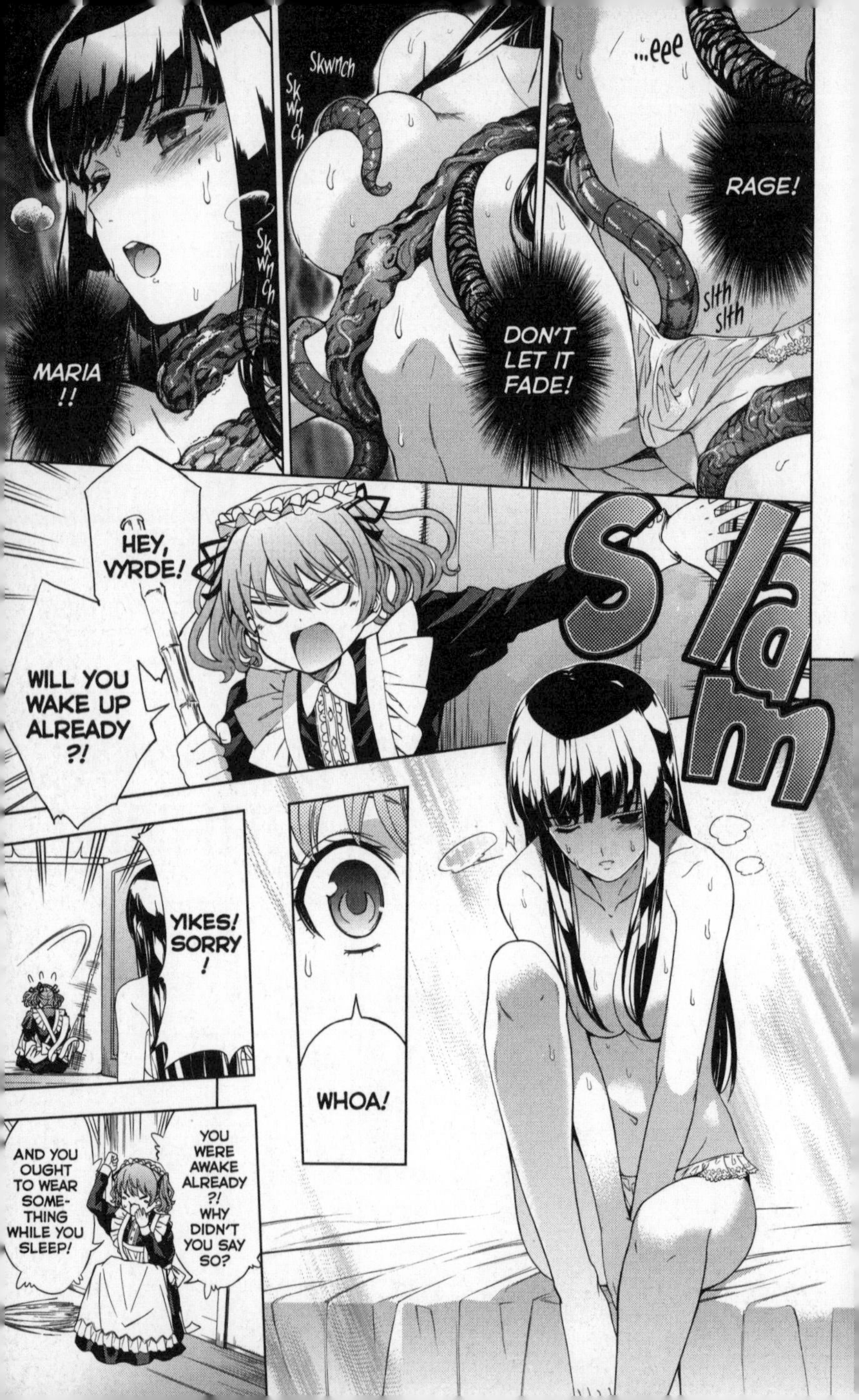
...eee
RAGE!
slth slth
Skwnch
Skwnch
DON'T LET IT FADE!
Skwnch
MARIA !!
Slam
HEY, VYRDE!
WILL YOU WAKE UP ALREADY ?!
WHOA!
YIKES! SORRY !
YOU WERE AWAKE ALREADY ?! WHY DIDN'T YOU SAY SO?
AND YOU OUGHT TO WEAR SOME-THING WHILE YOU SLEEP!

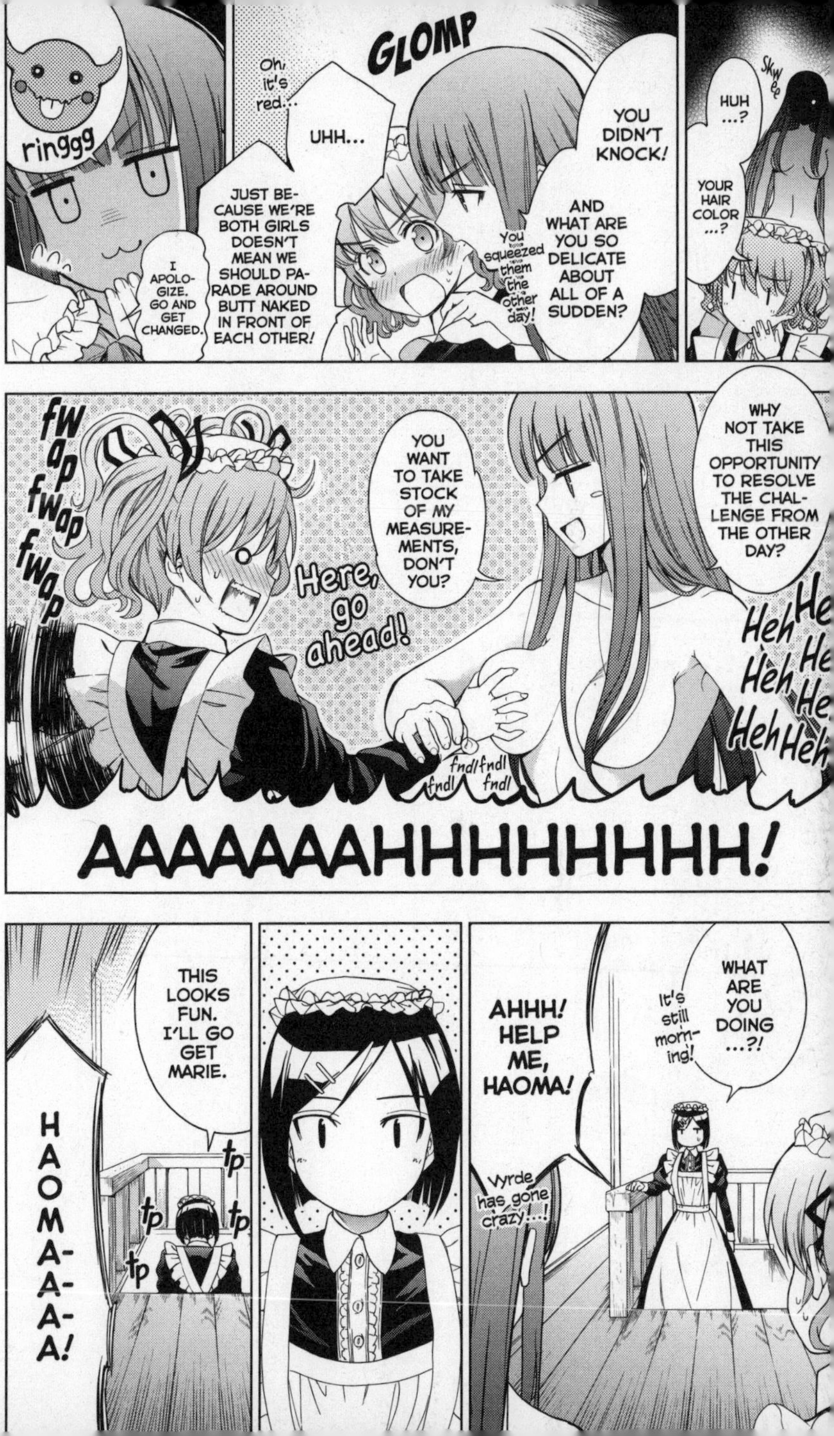
SKWEE
HUH ...?
YOUR HAIR COLOR ...?
GLOMP
YOU DIDN'T KNOCK!
AND WHAT ARE YOU SO DELICATE ABOUT ALL OF A SUDDEN?
You squeezed them the other day!
UHH...
Oh, it's red...
JUST BE-CAUSE WE'RE BOTH GIRLS DOESN'T MEAN WE SHOULD PA-RADE AROUND BUTT NAKED IN FRONT OF EACH OTHER!
ringgg
I APOLO-GIZE. GO AND GET CHANGED.
WHY NOT TAKE THIS OPPORTUNITY TO RESOLVE THE CHAL-LENGE FROM THE OTHER DAY?
Heh Heh Heh Heh He He He Heh
YOU WANT TO TAKE STOCK OF MY MEASURE-MENTS, DON'T YOU?
Here, go ahead!
fwap fwap fwap
fndl fndl fndl fndl
AAAAAAAHHHHHHHHH!
WHAT ARE YOU DOING ...?!
It's still morn-ing!
AHHH! HELP ME, HAOMA!
Vyrde has gone crazy...!
THIS LOOKS FUN. I'LL GO GET MARIE.
tp tp tp tp
HAOMAAAA-A-A!

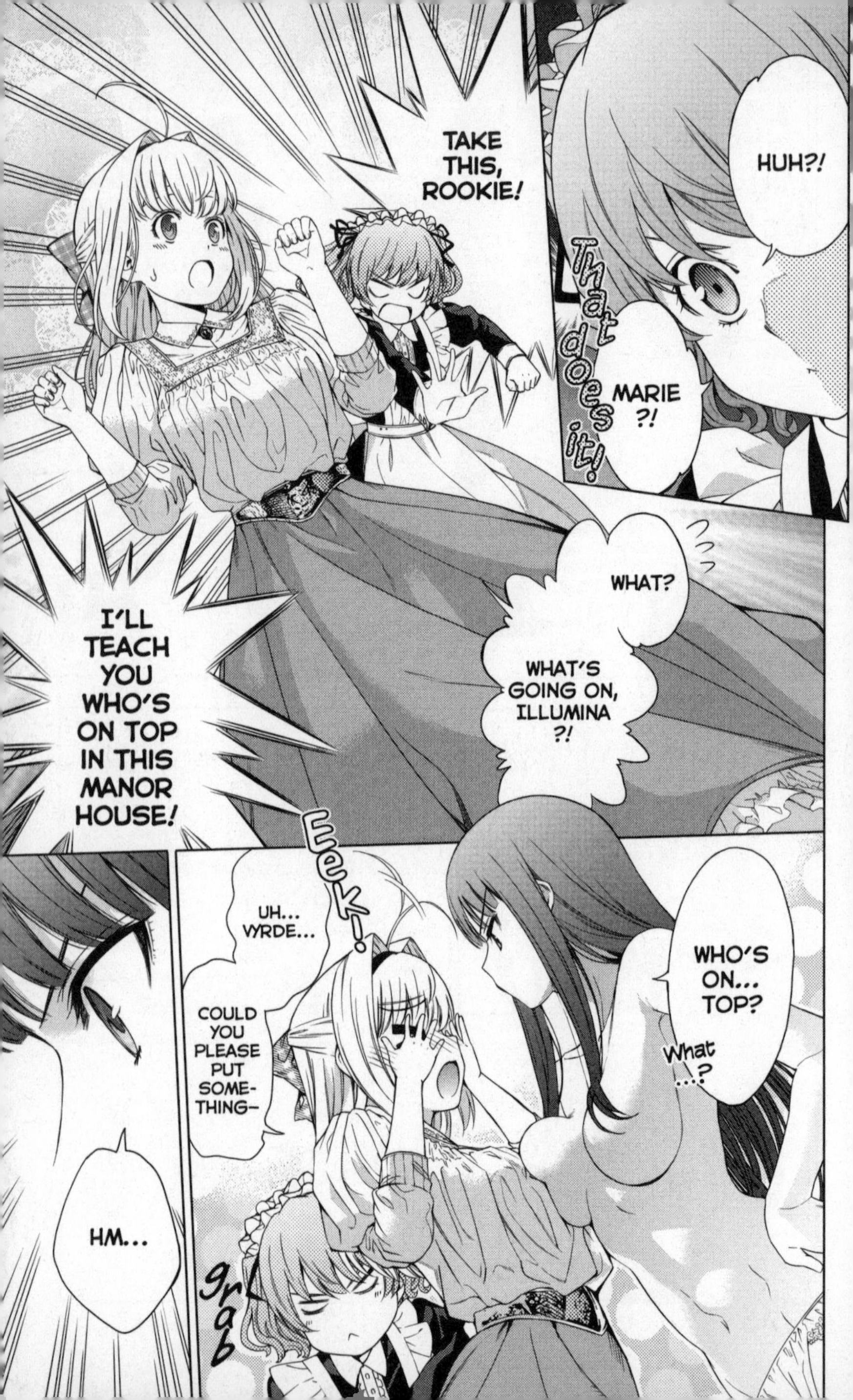
HUH?!
That does it!
MARIE ?!
WHAT?
WHAT'S GOING ON, ILLUMINA ?!
TAKE THIS, ROOKIE!
I'LL TEACH YOU WHO'S ON TOP IN THIS MANOR HOUSE!
WHO'S ON... TOP?
What ...?
Eek!
UH... VYRDE...
COULD YOU PLEASE PUT SOME-THING—
grab
HM...

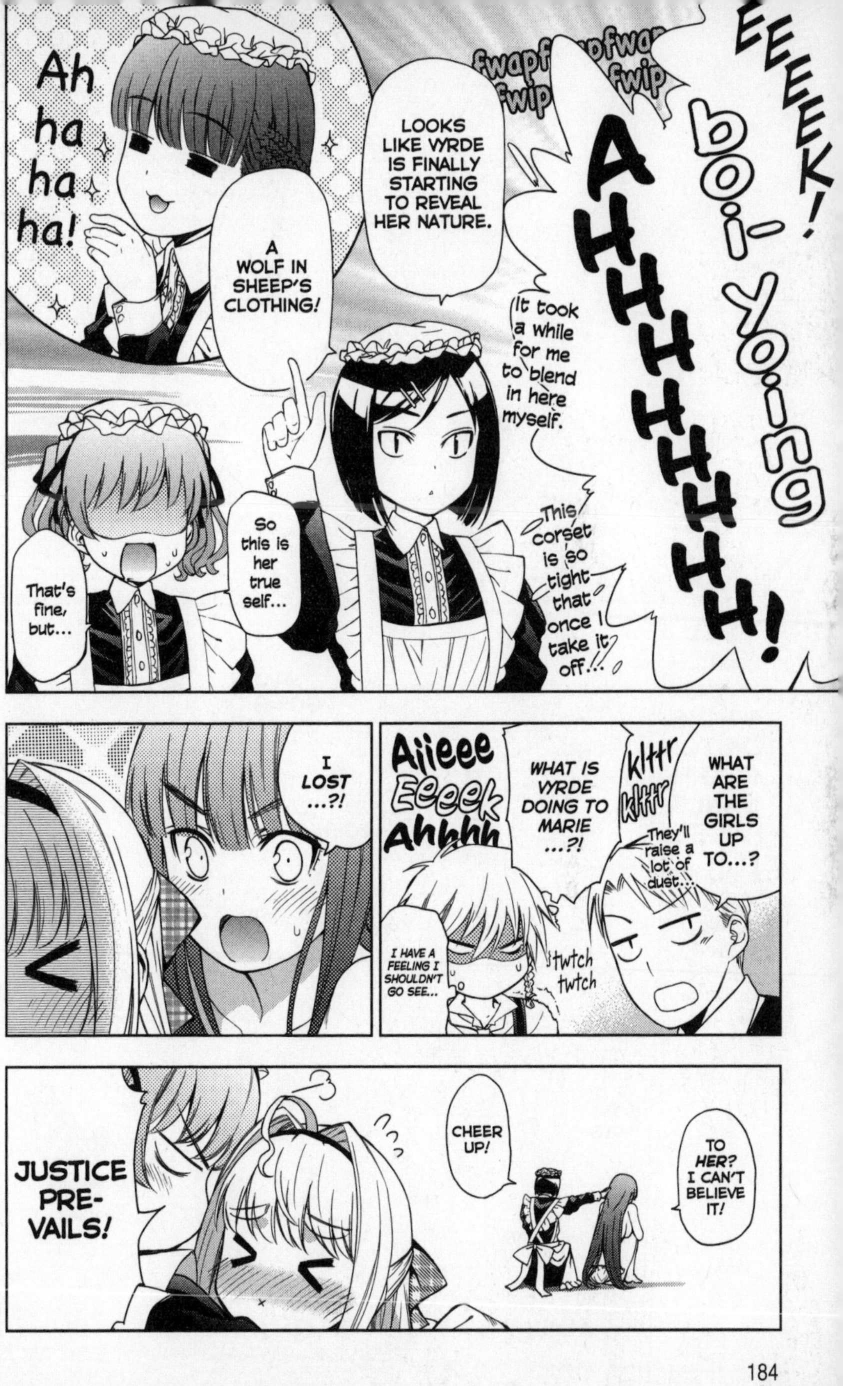
EEEEEK!
boi-yoing
AHHHHHHHHHH!
fwapf pfwap
fwip fwip
It took a while for me to blend in here myself.
This corset is so tight that once I take it off...!
LOOKS LIKE VYRDE IS FINALLY STARTING TO REVEAL HER NATURE.
A WOLF IN SHEEP'S CLOTHING!
Ah ha ha ha!
So this is her true self...
That's fine, but...
WHAT ARE THE GIRLS UP TO...?
klttr klttr
They'll raise a lot of dust...
WHAT IS VYRDE DOING TO MARIE ...?!
Aiieee Eeeek Ahhhh
twtch twtch
I HAVE A FEELING I SHOULDN'T GO SEE...
I LOST ...?!
TO HER? I CAN'T BELIEVE IT!
CHEER UP!
JUSTICE PRE-VAILS!

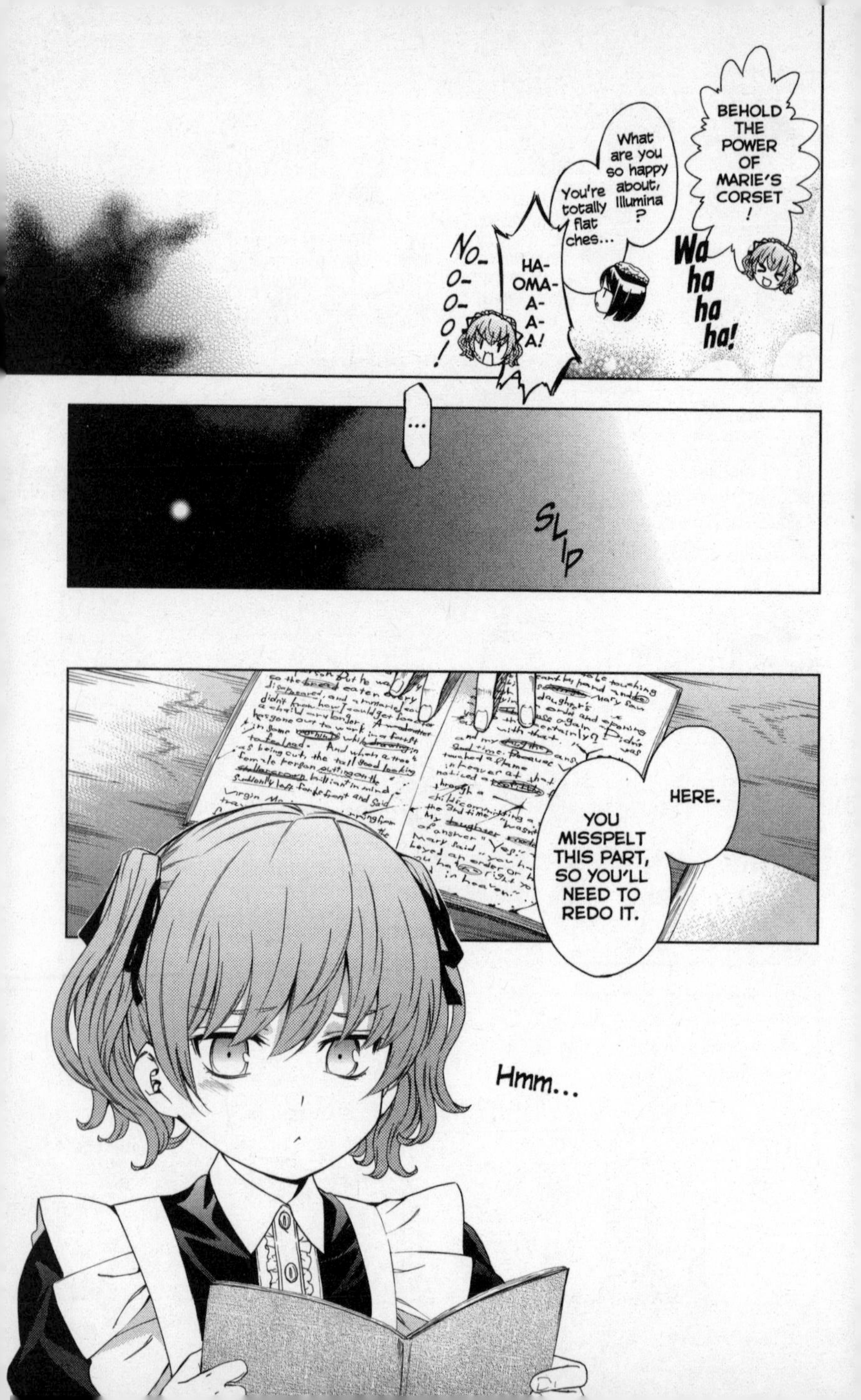
BEHOLD THE POWER OF MARIE'S CORSET!
Wahahaha!
What are you so happy about, Illumina?
You're totally flat ches...
HA-OMA-A-A-A!
NO-O-O-O-O!
...
SLIP
HERE.
YOU MISSPELT THIS PART, SO YOU'LL NEED TO REDO IT.
Hmm...

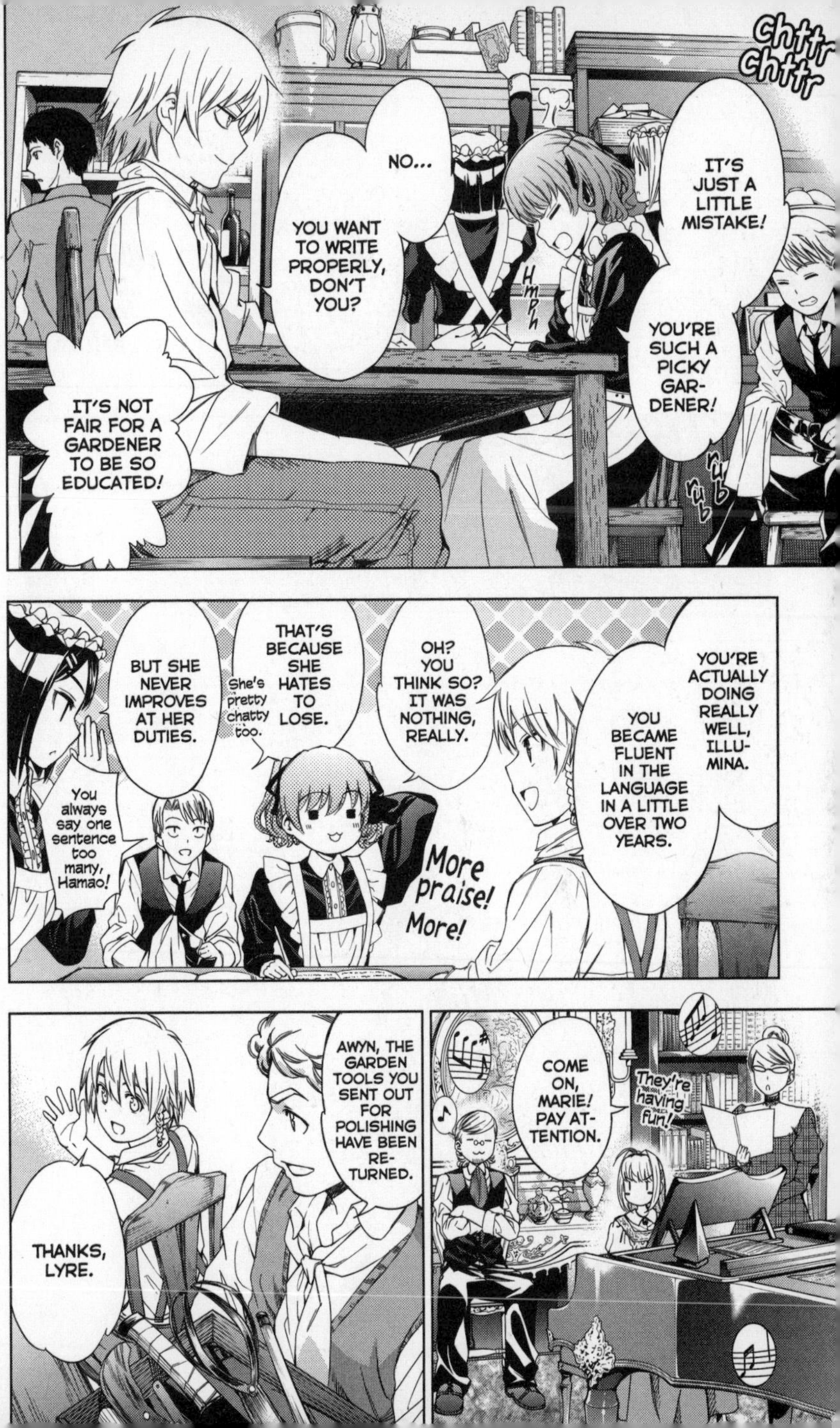
Chttr chttr
IT'S JUST A LITTLE MISTAKE!
NO...
YOU WANT TO WRITE PROPERLY, DON'T YOU?
YOU'RE SUCH A PICKY GARDENER!
Hmph
rub rub
IT'S NOT FAIR FOR A GARDENER TO BE SO EDUCATED!
YOU'RE ACTUALLY DOING REALLY WELL, ILLUMINA.
YOU BECAME FLUENT IN THE LANGUAGE IN A LITTLE OVER TWO YEARS.
OH? YOU THINK SO? IT WAS NOTHING, REALLY.
More praise! More!
THAT'S BECAUSE SHE HATES TO LOSE.
She's pretty chatty too.
BUT SHE NEVER IMPROVES AT HER DUTIES.
You always say one sentence too many, Hamao!
They're having fun!
COME ON, MARIE! PAY ATTENTION.
AWYN, THE GARDEN TOOLS YOU SENT OUT FOR POLISHING HAVE BEEN RETURNED.
THANKS, LYRE.

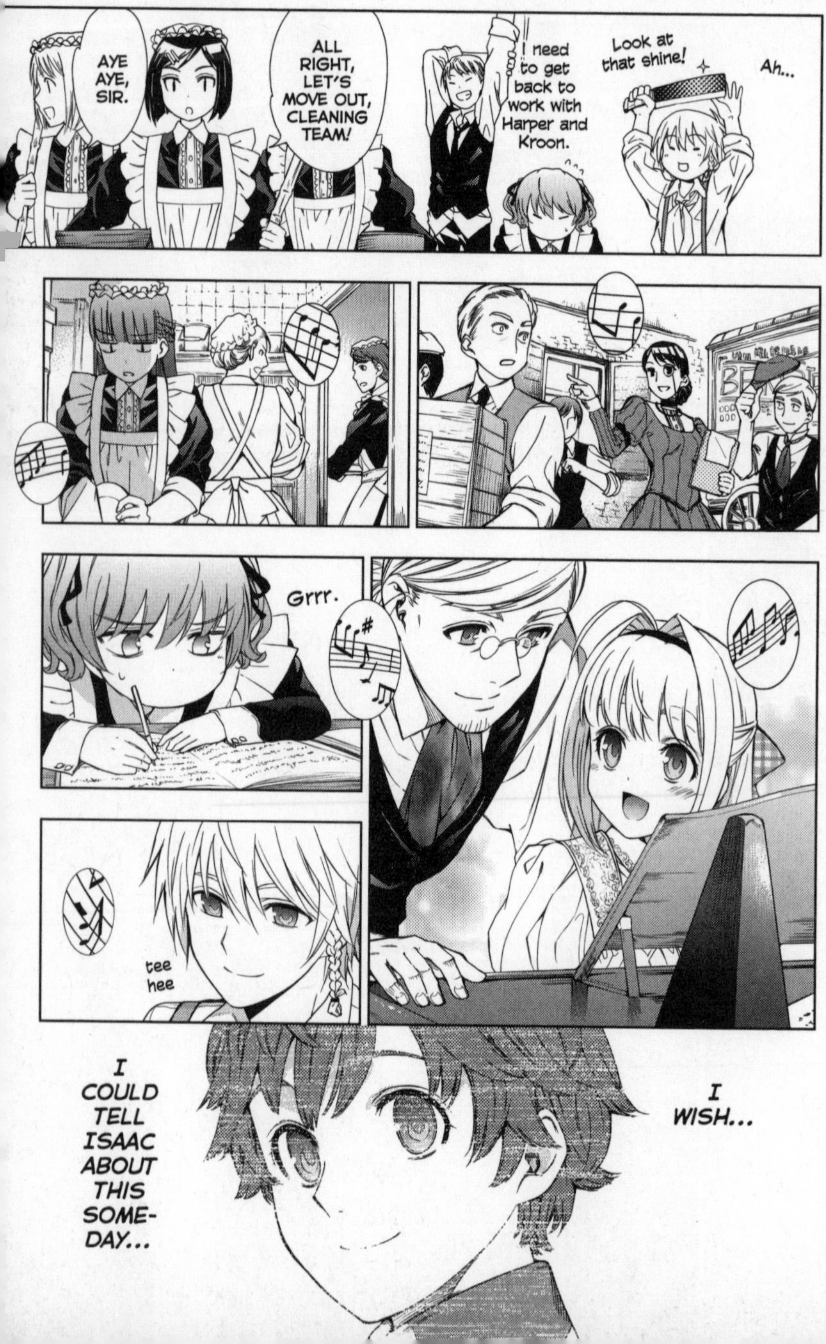
Ah...
Look at that shine!
I need to get back to work with Harper and Kroon.
ALL RIGHT, LET'S MOVE OUT, CLEANING TEAM!
AYE AYE, SIR.
Grrr.
tee hee
I WISH...
I COULD TELL ISAAC ABOUT THIS SOME-DAY...

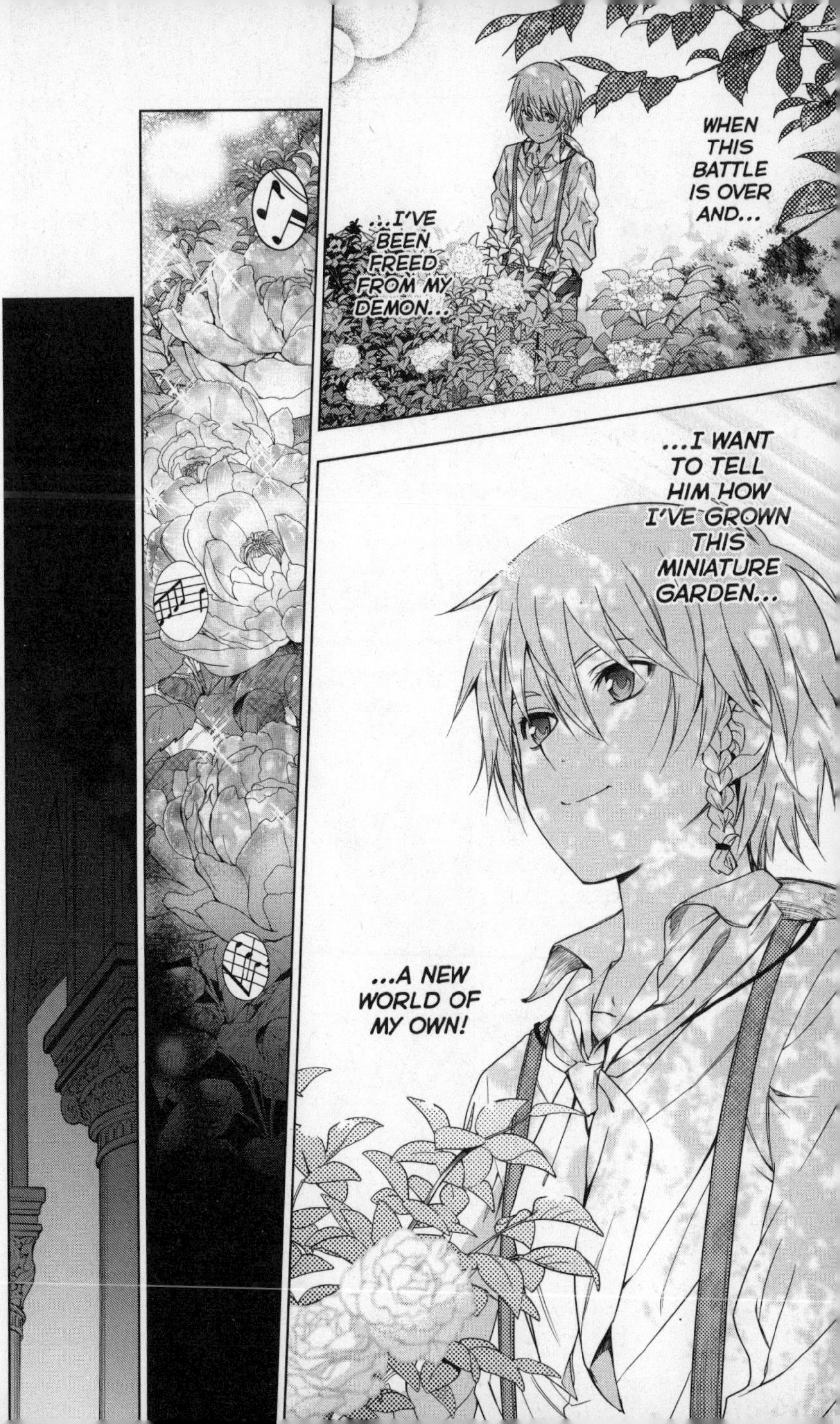
WHEN THIS BATTLE IS OVER AND...
...I'VE BEEN FREED FROM MY DEMON...
...I WANT TO TELL HIM HOW I'VE GROWN THIS MINIATURE GARDEN...
...A NEW WORLD OF MY OWN!

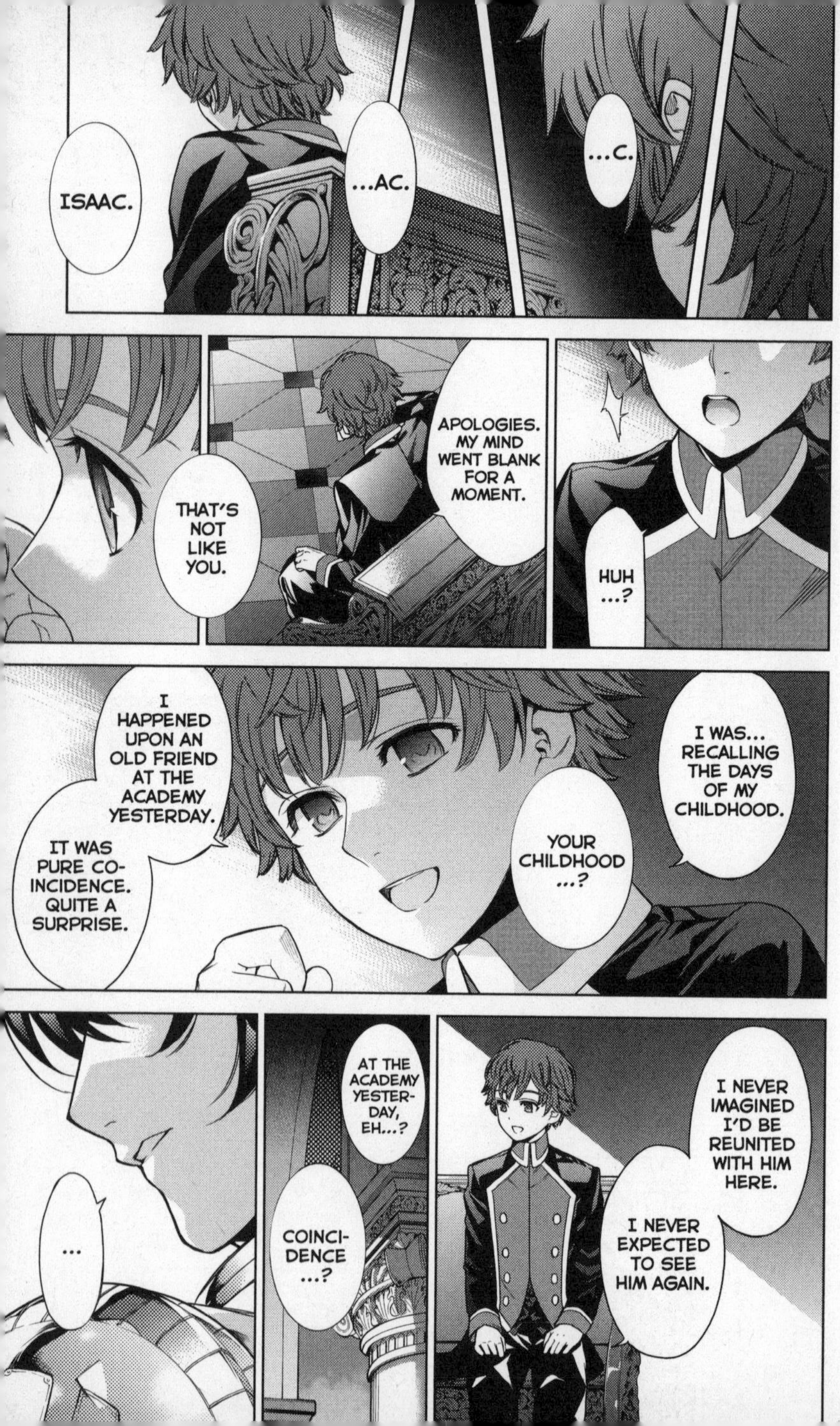
...C.
...AC.
ISAAC.
HUH ...?
APOLOGIES. MY MIND WENT BLANK FOR A MOMENT.
THAT'S NOT LIKE YOU.
I WAS... RECALLING THE DAYS OF MY CHILDHOOD.
YOUR CHILDHOOD ...?
I HAPPENED UPON AN OLD FRIEND AT THE ACADEMY YESTERDAY.
IT WAS PURE CO-INCIDENCE. QUITE A SURPRISE.
I NEVER IMAGINED I'D BE REUNITED WITH HIM HERE.
I NEVER EXPECTED TO SEE HIM AGAIN.
AT THE ACADEMY YESTER-DAY, EH...?
COINCI-DENCE ...?
...

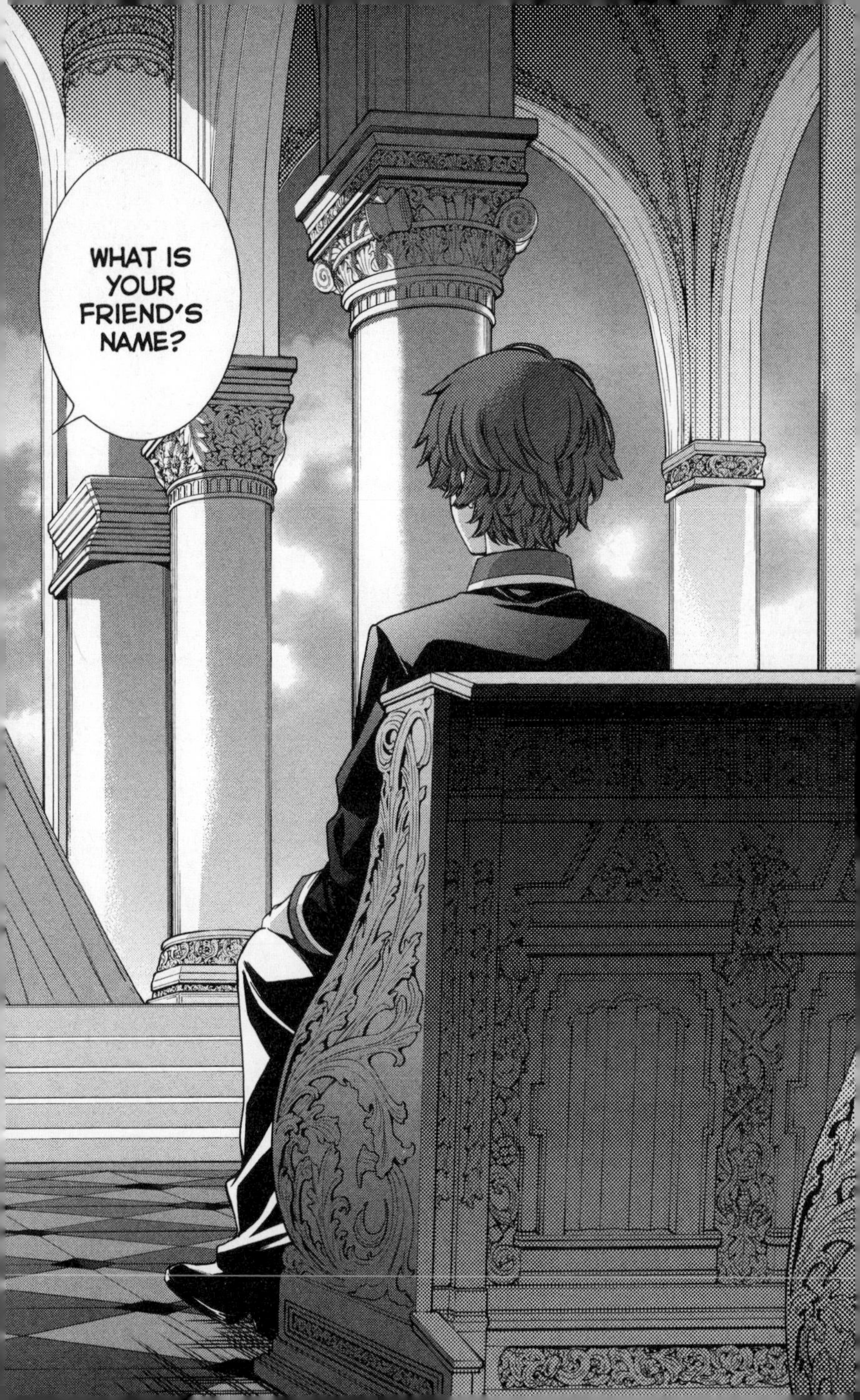
WHAT IS YOUR FRIEND'S NAME?

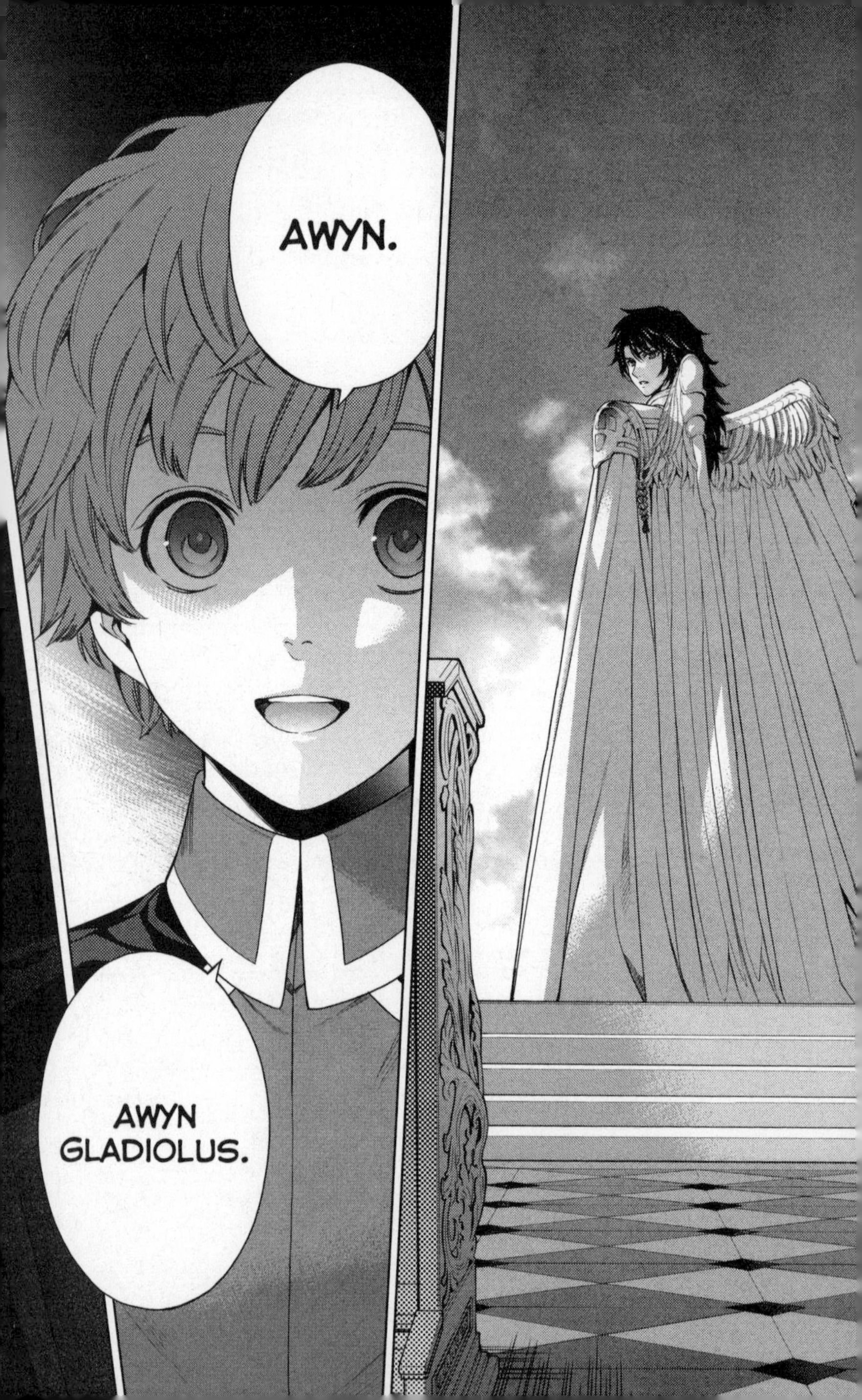
AWYN.
AWYN GLADIOLUS.

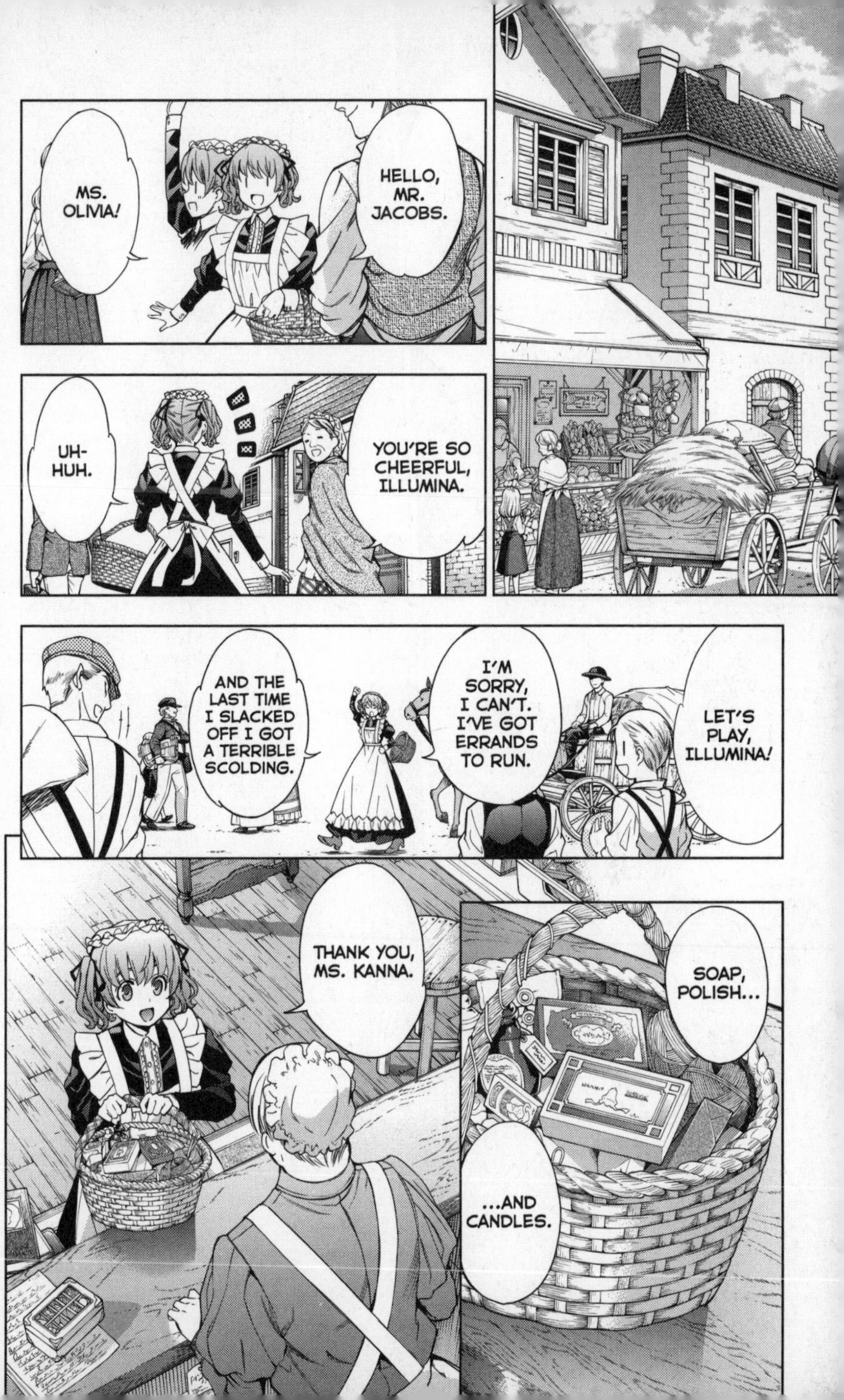
HELLO, MR. JACOBS.
MS. OLIVIA!
YOU'RE SO CHEERFUL, ILLUMINA.
UH-HUH.
LET'S PLAY, ILLUMINA!
I'M SORRY, I CAN'T. I'VE GOT ERRANDS TO RUN.
AND THE LAST TIME I SLACKED OFF I GOT A TERRIBLE SCOLDING.
SOAP, POLISH...
...AND CANDLES.
THANK YOU, MS. KANNA.

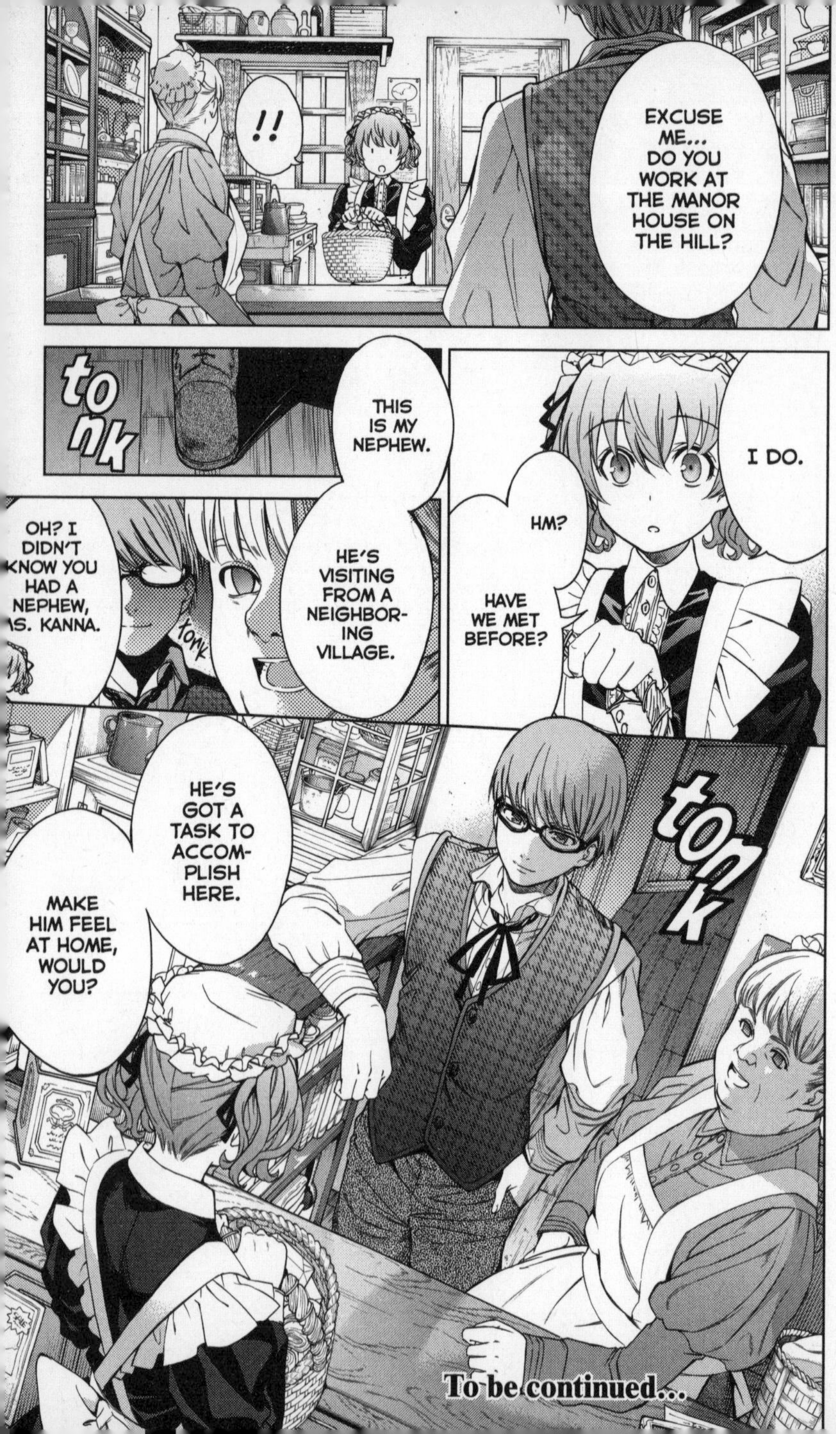

EXCUSE ME... DO YOU WORK AT THE MANOR HOUSE ON THE HILL?
!!
I DO.
HM?
HAVE WE MET BEFORE?
tonk
THIS IS MY NEPHEW.
HE'S VISITING FROM A NEIGHBOR-ING VILLAGE.
tonk
OH? I DIDN'T KNOW YOU HAD A NEPHEW, MS. KANNA.
tonk
HE'S GOT A TASK TO ACCOMPLISH HERE.
MAKE HIM FEEL AT HOME, WOULD YOU?
To be continued...

Mitsu Izumi

Mysterious manga creator Mitsu
Izumi was born on February 7
in Kanagawa Prefecture and is
the creator of the manga
adaptation of *Anohana:
The Flower We Saw That Day*,
originally serialized in *Jump SQ*.

NEVER LOSE.

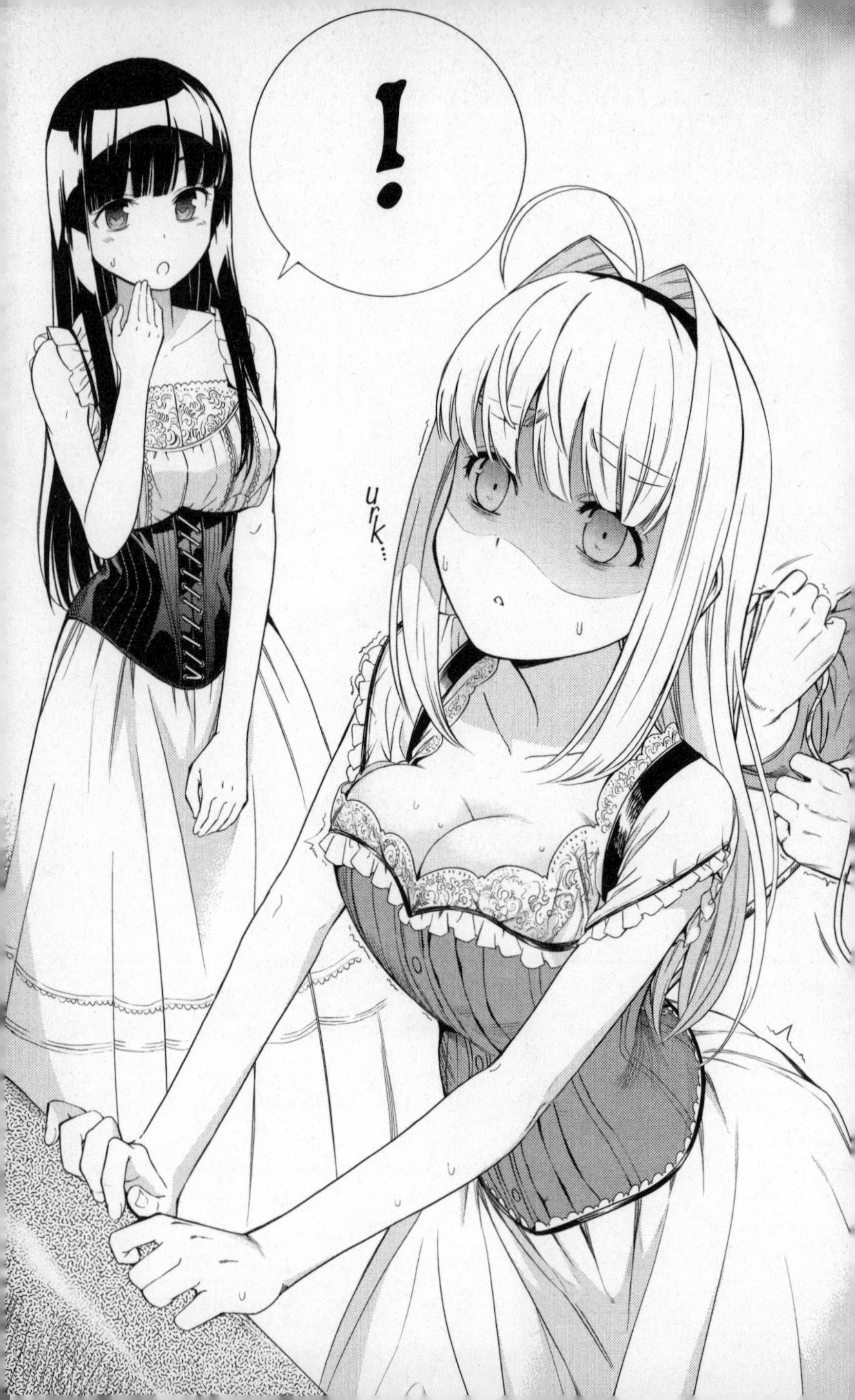
!
urk...

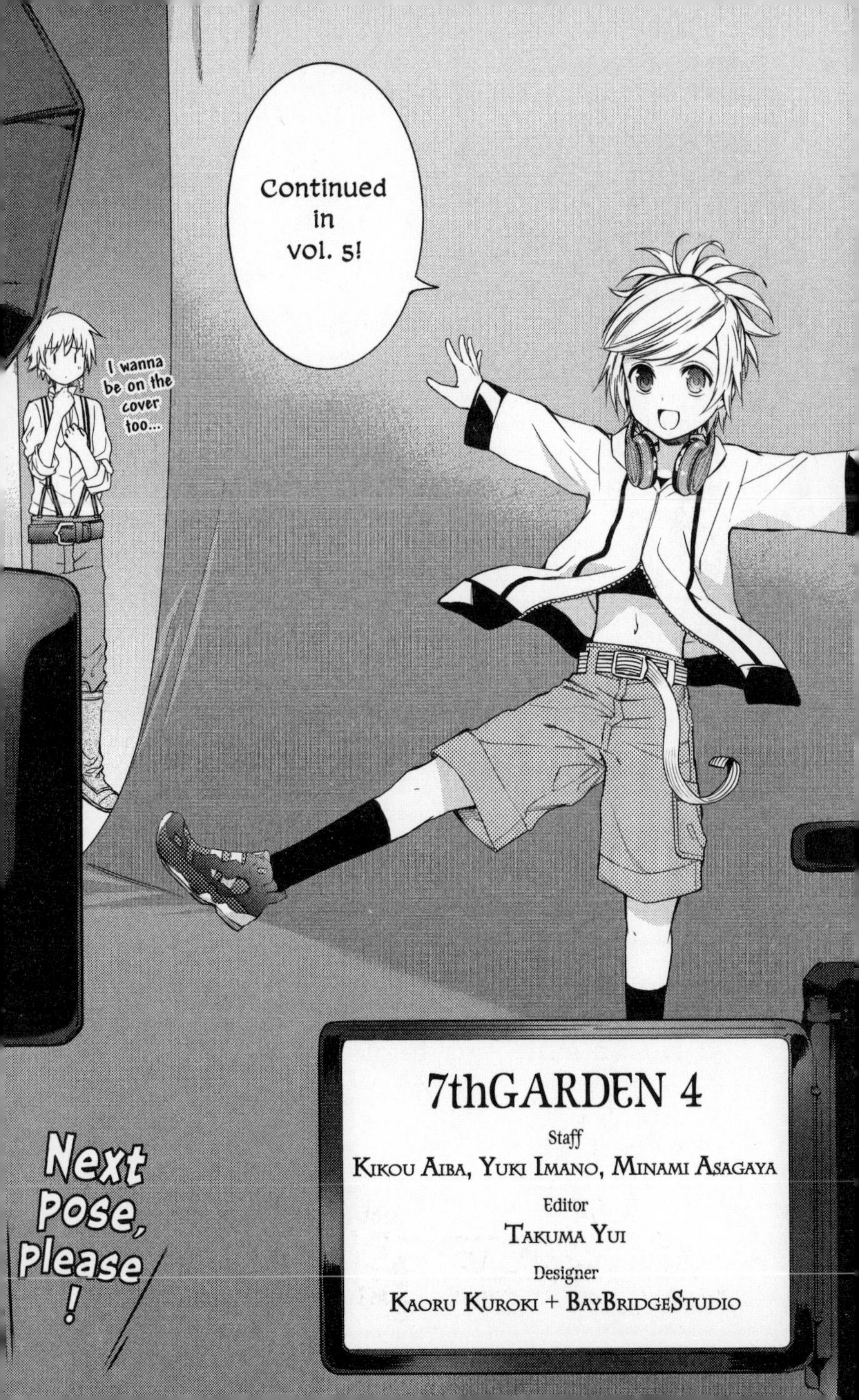
Continued in vol. 5!
I wanna be on the cover too...
7thGARDEN 4
Staff
Kikou Aiba, Yuki Imano, Minami Asagaya
Editor
Takuma Yui
Designer
Kaoru Kuroki + BayBridgeStudio
Next Pose, Please!

7thGARDEN
4

SHONEN JUMP Manga Edition

Story and Art by Mitsu Izumi

Translation/Tetsuichiro Miyaki
English Adaptation/Annette Roman
Touch-Up Art & Lettering/Susan Daigle-Leach
Cover & Interior Design/Izumi Evers
Editor/Annette Roman

Printed in the U.S.A.

Published by VIZ Media, LLC
P.O. Box 77010
San Francisco, CA 94107

10 9 8 7 6 5 4 3 2 1
First printing, April 2017

www.viz.com   www.shonenjump.com

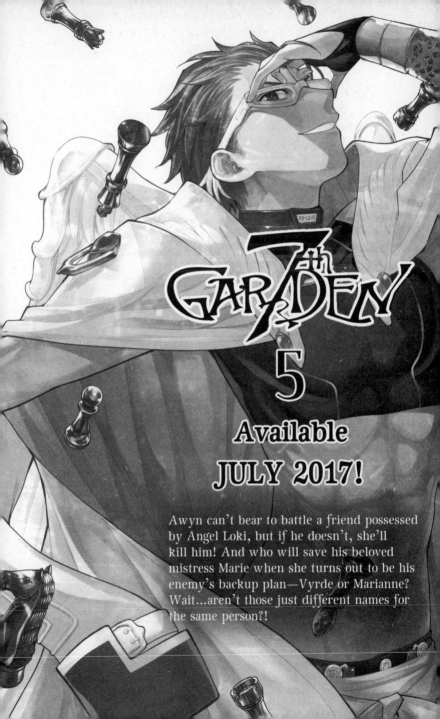

7th GARDEN

5

Available
JULY 2017!

Awyn can't bear to battle a friend possessed by Angel Loki, but if he doesn't, she'll kill him! And who will save his beloved mistress Marie when she turns out to be his enemy's backup plan—Vyrde or Marianne? Wait...aren't those just different names for the same person?!

Food Wars!
SHOKUGEKI NO SOMA

Saucy, action-packed food battles!

Story by **Yuto Tsukuda**
Art by **Shun Saeki**
Contributor **Yuki Morisaki**

Soma Yukihira's old man runs a small family restaurant in the less savory end of town. Aiming to one day surpass his father's culinary prowess, Soma hones his skills day in and day out until one day, out of the blue, his father decides to enroll Soma in a classy culinary school! Can Soma really cut it in a school that prides itself on a 10 percent graduation rate? And can he convince the beautiful, domineering heiress of the school that he belongs there at all?!

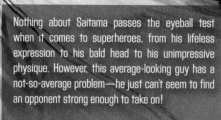

You're Reading in the Wrong Direction!!

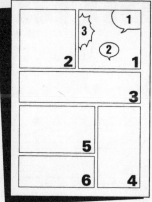

Whoops! Guess what? You're starting at the wrong end of the comic!

...It's true! In keeping with the original Japanese format, **7thGARDEN** is meant to be read from right to left, starting in the upper-right corner.

Unlike English, which is read from left to right, Japanese is read from right to left, meaning that action, sound effects and word-balloon order are completely reversed... something which can make readers unfamiliar with Japanese feel pretty backwards themselves. For this reason, manga or Japanese comics published in the U.S. in English have sometimes been published "flopped"—that is, printed in exact reverse order, as though seen from the other side of a mirror.

By flopping pages, U.S. publishers can avoid confusing readers, but the compromise is not without its downside. For one thing, a character in a flopped manga series who once wore in the original Japanese version a T-shirt emblazoned with "M A Y" (as in "the merry month of") now wears one which reads "Y A M"! Additionally, many manga creators in Japan are themselves unhappy with the process, as some feel the mirror-imaging of their art skews their original intentions.

We are proud to bring you Mitsu Izumi's **7thGARDEN** in the original unflopped format.

For now, though, turn to the other side of the book and let the adventure begin...!

—Editor